MURTY CLASSICAL
LIBRARY OF INDIA

*Sheldon Pollock, General Editor*

# BULLHE SHAH
# SUFI LYRICS

MCLI 1

BULLHE SHAH

ਬੁੱਲ੍ਹੇ ਸ਼ਾਹ

# SUFI LYRICS

Edited and translated by
**CHRISTOPHER SHACKLE**

MURTY CLASSICAL LIBRARY OF INDIA
HARVARD UNIVERSITY PRESS
Cambridge, Massachusetts
London, England
2015

SERIES DESIGN BY M9DESIGN

*Library of Congress Cataloging-in-Publication Data*

Bullhe Shah, 1680?–1758? author.
[Poems. Selections. English]
Sufi Lyrics / Bullhe Shah ; edited and translated by Christopher Shackle.
p.  cm. — (Murty Classical Library of India ; 1)
Includes bibliographical references and index.
ISBN 978-0-674-42784-6 (pbk.)
1. Sufi Poetry.  I. Shackle, C., editor, translator.  II. Title.
PK2659.B8A2  2014
891.4′213—dc23    2014015897

# CONTENTS

INTRODUCTION *vii*

NOTE ON THE TEXT AND TRANSLATION *xxxi*


LYRICS *1*


OTHER POEMS *269*

The Seven Days *270*

The Twelve Months *278*

The Forty Knots *292*

The Thirty Letters *320*

Verses *338*


ABBREVIATIONS *367*

NOTES TO THE TEXT *369*

NOTES TO THE TRANSLATION *375*

GLOSSARY *427*

BIBLIOGRAPHY *431*

CONCORDANCE *435*

INDEX *437*

# INTRODUCTION

*The Life*

Bullhe Shah (d. 1758) has long been rightly regarded as the greatest master of the mystical Sufi lyric in Panjabi. But in spite of his relatively recent date and his huge poetic reputation, remarkably few details of his life can be reliably established.

Neither the exact date nor the precise place of his birth is known for certain. His father, Shah Muhammad Darvesh, who came from a Sayyid family long established in Uch Gilaniyan in southwestern Panjab, migrated eastward, eventually to settle in the village of Pandoke near the town of Kasur, some thirty miles south of Lahore. The title "Bullhe Shah," by which the poet is commonly known, is the honorific form proper to a Sayyid descendant of the prophet Muhammad. His usual poetic signature, "Bullha," is the familiar form of his given name, Abdullah. These English spellings reflect the way his name is normally written in Panjabi, where a final "h" is not pronounced as such; the alternatives "Bulleh Shah" and "Bullah" are designed to reflect the etymology of his name.

Bullhe Shah's formal education took place in Kasur under the guidance of one Hafiz Ghulam Murtaza, a well-known scholar of the day. A popular tradition records that one of his fellow students was Varis Shah, the author of the classic poetic romance *Hīr*, completed in 1766, which has long been the most popular of all longer Panjabi poems. But the two poets can hardly have been such close contemporaries, and this association of the two greatest figures in the Panjabi poetic canon is certainly a later fabrication.

Bullhe Shah lived at a time of great social upheaval in Panjab,[1] as the central authority of the declining Mughal empire came under increasing challenge from armed rebellion by the Sikhs and from local notables establishing their own autonomy. Although these unsettled conditions are occasionally reflected in Bullhe Shah's poetry, its main focus is upon by far the most important figure in Bullhe Shah's adult life, his spiritual guide, Shah Inayat (d. 1728). By origin a member of the Arain caste of vegetable gardeners, Shah Inayat was a noted Sufi master who lived in Lahore, and was himself the author of a number of mystical treatises in Persian. The repeated references to Shah Inayat in Bullhe's poetry testify to the passionate quality of his devotion to his master, and most of the hagiographic stories associated with Bullhe Shah celebrate the fervor of his discipleship.[2]

Bullhe Shah remained unmarried and left no direct descendants. His later life was apparently spent in Kasur, which is the site of his tomb. This bears a Persian chronogram that gives the year of his death as AH 1171 according to the Muslim calendar, equivalent to 1757 or 1758 CE. Since AH 1171 runs from September 1757 to September 1758, the later year is somewhat more probable.

### The Context

Throughout the world, many older works of literature are admired as classics but may have become too remote in language and style for modern readers to take them readily to heart. In South Asia, a further profound disjunction between tradition and modernity resulted from the absorption of a whole set of new cultural values during the colonial period. In the continual search for literary works that may help give meaning to a culturally fractured present, the classics truly loved today therefore often belong to the literature of the more recent past, more accessible in language and sensibility.

The eighteenth-century poetry of Bullhe Shah, whose direct and simple style underpins its very strong appeal across formal religious and national boundaries, provides a notably clear instance of this broad tendency. Few regions of South Asia are more fractured than Panjab, where acute religious conflict resulted in its partition amid widespread communal violence in 1947. Almost uniquely in the modern world, Panjabi is a biscriptal language, being written from right to left in the Persian script in Pakistan and from left to right in the Gurmukhi script in India. And yet the Sufi lyrics of Bullhe Shah, whether through performances by well-known Sikh or Muslim singers or through the popular selections continually issued by Indian and Pakistani publishers in either of the two quite different scripts, continue to evoke a magical vision from the past of a timeless unity, transcending the modern divisions that trouble the present.

In a very broad sense, therefore, the poetry of Bullhe Shah lines up in the modern imagination with the living and accessible part of later premodern Indian literature that is valued for its universal message. This attractive universality, as typically expressed in the denial of true reality to any outward differences between Hindu and Muslim, is seen as more important than any differences in the underlying religious and cultural formation of the poets who created this great body of Indian literature. But fuller understandings depend upon proper attention being given to those differences, for while there are significant commonalities between *bhakti* and Sufi poetry, they are by no means identical in their fundamental presuppositions.

In the case of Panjabi, these two genres of religious poetry are represented by two distinct traditions,[3] which have been quite separately preserved and transmitted. On the one hand, the hymns of Guru Nanak (d. 1539) and his successors were carefully recorded in the Gurmukhi script and canonically assembled in the *Ādi Granth* or "Primal Book," the great scripture first compiled in 1604 that forms the center of Sikh devotion and ritual practice. The *Ādi Granth* also famously includes not only the compositions of earlier saint-poets in the *bhakti* tradition of devotion to a formless divinity but even the verses associated with the early Panjabi Sufi saint Shaikh Farid (d. 1265). On the other hand, the lyrics of Bullhe Shah and the other Sufi poets living at different times and in different areas of Panjab were never systematically preserved by an organized faith community, and they were for the most part recorded and assembled in printed collections only in the late nineteenth century.[4]

Parallels may certainly be drawn between strikingly shared features of these two traditions, including their common preference for popular poetic styles that draw upon folk-songs rather than the learned poetry of the courts.[5] But while the hymns of the Sikh Gurus may to a considerable extent be legitimately understood in their own terms, the character of Panjabi Sufi poetry is hardly to be properly understood without wider reference to the larger religious and literary traditions by which it is so intimately informed. This means understanding that Sufism in India is no exception to the general rule that Sufism is and always has been an integral part of Islam. Although so different, in their emphasis on the primacy of spiritual understanding, from the orthodox scholars with their legalistic constructions, the Sufis, like the scholars, found their core inspiration in the message of the Qur'an and the example of the prophet Muhammad.[6]

Islam is the defining case of a book religion, and the various traditions within it have generated their own extensive bodies of literature. By the ninth and tenth centuries, Sufis were already well established in Baghdad and other cities of the Middle East. These early Sufis, like the famous martyr Mansur al-Hallaj (d. 922), naturally used Arabic as the medium for their poetry and their prose treatises. Later, when various Muslim kingdoms won their independence in Iran and Afghanistan, Persian (written in the Arabic script and containing large numbers of Arabic loanwords) came to be cultivated as a literary language that supplanted Arabic, especially as a medium for poetry. Alongside the brilliant development of a courtly poetry, Persian was also used to spectacular spiritual as well as literary effect by many Sufi poets,[7] of whom the greatest was Jalal ud Din Rumi (d. 1273).

The Muslim conquest of northern India extended this Persianate cultural world to Panjab, where Persian remained the dominant literary language of the ruling elite down to the Mughal period and beyond. A strong Sufi presence was rapidly established with the arrival of charismatic figures associated with the main Sufi orders. These orders, within which spiritual authority and distinctive spiritual disciplines were transmitted from master to disciple, embraced interlocking sets of transregional lineages. Within the Chishti order, which occupied a leading place in the society of the Delhi Sultanate, for example, the life of the great Panjabi master Shaikh Farid is best known through the outstanding memoir compiled in Persian prose by a follower of Farid's leading disciple, Nizam ud Din Auliya, the most important Sufi saint of Delhi, whose circle also included Amir Khusrau (d. 1325), the premier Persian poet of medieval India.

Besides transmission within the circle of disciples formed around a master (called Shaikh or Pir), the Sufi message reached a wider audience through poetry. The prime genre for this poetry was the ghazal, a short love lyric with a strongly marked single rhyme whose characteristic blending of divine and human love was endlessly explored in the prolific output of such different poets as Rumi and Amir Khusrau.[8] Persian ghazals were sung in musical performances (called *samā*ʿ) that were a central part of Chishti ritual practice and usually took place at the shrines constructed around the tombs of former saints, which were themselves typically administered by a master's lineal descendants. They employed the specialist professional musicians known as qawwals. Their strongly rhythmic style of performance (called qawwali) has become a well-recognized form of world music while continuing to be practiced in its original setting.[9]

Music was generally regarded with disapproval in the clerical Islam upheld by the mullahs and the *qazis,* the religious judges qualified in Islamic law. But the singing of poetic lyrics in *samā'* continued to be widely practiced, not only among the Chishtis but also within the Qadiri order, which rose to prominence in India during the Mughal period. Most of the Panjabi Sufi poets of this era were affiliated with the Qadiri order, including Shah Husain (d. 1593) of Lahore and Sultan Bahu (d. 1691), besides Bullhe Shah himself, whose master, Shah Inayat, was a member of both the Qadiri and the Shattari orders.[10] Outside Panjab, another prominent poet of the time was Bullhe Shah's contemporary Shah Abdul Latif (d. 1752) of Bhit, universally regarded as the greatest Sufi poet in Sindhi. While these poets' use of the local languages has helped to ensure their continuing popularity across religious boundaries today, it should be remembered that their activity took place within a literary culture whose principal language was Persian.[11] A memorable life of Shah Husain was compiled in Persian verse by one of his followers, and the great bulk of Sultan Bahu's output consisted of Sufi treatises in Persian prose.

Only with the British conquest of Panjab in the 1840s did the literary culture of the Sufi tradition come to be overlaid by the new patterns of modernity. Persian was quite rapidly replaced as the language of education, administration, and elite literature by Urdu and English, and new styles and genres, often more or less directly influenced by English models, were disseminated by the newly established publishing industry. The publishers of Lahore were also responsible for bringing the older Sufi poetry, hitherto largely preserved by oral tradition, into the new print culture. Editions of works by Bullhe Shah and the other older poets were produced along with the work of contemporary authors, since Sufi poetry continued to be written in the local languages during the nineteenth century, notably by the narrative poet Mian Muhammad Bakhsh (d. 1907), yet another Qadiri affiliate, and by Khwaja Ghulam Farid (d. 1901), the head of a Chishti lineage and the last great master of the Sufi lyric as practiced by Bullhe Shah.[12]

As modernist interpretations of Islam came to supplant active affiliations to Sufism, twentieth-century understandings of Bullhe Shah and the other Sufi poets were increasingly influenced by the nationalist thinking prevalent among the new middle class of the colonial period. In Panjab the formulation of nationalist understandings was no simple process, given the complexities created by the simultaneous currency of three closely related languages, Urdu, Hindi, and Panjabi, whose differences were exploited to sharpen the rival cultural identities of Muslims, Hindus, and Sikhs respectively. As an important symbolic figure in the new constructions of Panjabi literary history that emerged, Bullhe Shah thus became subject to a variety of interpretations.[13] With so little known of his life, he came to be seen as, among other things, an exponent of universal spiritual truths owing as much to Vedanta as to Sufism; an authentic spokesman of the Panjabi folk tradition; a social revolutionary; or simply a Romantic poet *avant la lettre*.[14] Most of these interpretations may be shown to rely upon often highly selective readings of his poetry, which is thereby used to support already assumed ideological positions. The present volume, in which a complete translation of all the poems into English is presented for the first time, may help correct the biases that have too often continued to distort understandings of Bullhe Shah.

### The Poetry

The formal genres of Panjabi Sufi poetry fall into the same three broad categories as much premodern *bhakti* verse and the compositions of the Sikh Gurus. The main lyrical form is a strophic poem with refrain, called *kāfī* (Panjabi plural *kāfīāñ*), which is designed for singing in qawwali and also lends itself to solo singing by amateur devotees and professional performers. Less frequently attested are various longer strophic poems that may be either lyrical or didactic in character. And then there are the miscellaneous short verses typically used to express a single thought. Four lyrics and 112 short verses are attested for Farid, some 160 mostly very short lyrics for Shah Husain, about 200 short verses for Sultan Bahu, then 271 lyrics plus miscellaneous odd verses for the later Khwaja Ghulam Farid.[15]

Bullhe Shah is known primarily for his *kāfīs*. The present volume includes 157 of these lyrics, although the uncertain transmission of the text makes it difficult to be sure of the exact number of authentic items. The poetic form of the *kāfī* is similar to other major genres of premodern north Indian religious poetry, such as the Vaishnava *pad* of poets like Surdas or the *shabad* of the Sikh Gurus. Composed in simple syllabic meters with evenly distributed stresses, *kāfīs* consist of varying numbers of strongly rhymed verses;

those by Bullhe Shah range from examples comprising only one or two verses, which are possibly incomplete, to occasional much longer poems of twenty verses or more, which may contain later interpolations. All the verses have the same strongly marked final rhyme, usually consisting of two or more syllables. This rhyme is first introduced and then strongly reinforced throughout by a refrain that is typically shorter than the main verses of the *kāfī*. The verses themselves are made up of smaller units of half- and quarter-verses, each typically marked by different internal rhymes.

One of the commonest structures has verses consisting of four half-lines rhyming *BBBA, CCCA,* etc., as exemplified in the opening of one of Bullhe Shah's most famous lyrics:

> *bullhā kī jāṇāñ maiñ kauṇ*
> *nā maiñ moman vicc masītāñ, nā maiñ vic kufar dīāñ*
>     *rītāñ*
> *nā maiñ pākī vicc palītāñ, nā maiñ mūsā nā faraun*
> *bullhā kī jāṇāñ maiñ kauṇ*
> *nā maiñ andar bed kitābāñ, nā vic bhogāñ nā sharābāñ*
> *nā vic rindāñ mast k̲harābāñ, nā vic jāgaṇ nā vic sauṇ*
> *bullhā kī jāṇāñ maiñ kauṇ*

Bullha, what do I know about who I am?
I am not a believer in the mosques, nor do I follow the
      rites of unbelief. I am not among the pure or the
      polluted. I am not Moses or Pharaoh.
Bullha, what do I know about who I am?
I am not in the Vedas or in the scriptures; I am not in

> drugs or in liquor. I am not among the drunken
> reprobates. I am not in waking, nor am I in sleep.
> Bullha, what do I know about who I am?[16]

The final verse of the *kāfī* is regularly marked by the poet's signature. This often proclaims Bullhe Shah's powerful identification with his spiritual master, Shah Inayat, who is frequently alluded to as "the lord," as here:

> *avval ākhar āp nūñ jāṇāñ, nā koī dūjā hor pachāṇāñ*
> *maithoñ hor nā koī siāṇā, bullhā shahu khaṛā hai kauṇ*
> *bullhā kī jāṇāñ maiñ kauṇ*

> I know myself to be first and last, I do not recognize
> anyone else. No one is wiser than I am. Bullha,
> who is the lord standing here?
> Bullha, what do I know about who I am?[17]

Bullhe Shah also composed four longer poems in other genres consisting of stanzas arranged by chronological or other formal schemes. Two are lyrical in character and derive from the folk tradition. *Aṭhvārā* (The Seven Days) is a strophic poem whose stanzas describe the experiences of the poet-lover on successive days, ending with Friday, which has a special status in Islam as the day prescribed for congregational prayer. *Bārāñ Māh* (The Twelve Months), which belongs to a familiar genre very widely employed in most north Indian literatures, is similarly constructed, with each of its twelve stanzas devoted to a month in the Indian Vikrami calendar.

His other two longer poems are primarily didactic in character. *Gaṇḍhāñ* (The Forty Knots) appears to be a one-off form created by Bullhe Shah. The title derives from the traditional use of a knotted string to keep track of days before an important occasion, so each of the poem's forty verses begins with the undoing of another knot as the preparations of a bride for her wedding are used to symbolize the need to make ready for the inexorable approach of death. The other poem, *Sīharfī* (The Thirty Letters), follows the form most favored for longer didactic poems by Panjabi Muslim poets. It consists of thirty stanzas, each starting with a letter of the Arabic alphabet that determines the initial letter of the first word.[18]

There are also miscellaneous short *Dohṛe* (Verses) on a range of topics. These are written in a variety of meters, of which one of the commonest is the *dohā* meter historically preferred for verse of this type in north India. It consists of four half-lines with a strong rhyme at the end of each full line:

*bullhiā: mullāñ ate mashālcī, dohāñ ikko citt*
*lokāñ karde cānaṇā, āp hanere nitt*

Bullha, the mullah and the torch bearer both have the
    same intent. They spread light to people, but are
    always in the dark themselves.[19]

As in this example, the poet's signature is often added before the verse proper begins, so it is in itself no very reliable guarantee of the authenticity of any given item.

Absolute authenticity in the precise wording of any

poem generally agreed to be by Bullhe Shah is anyway hardly to be expected, given the well-known liberties taken by professional singers in South Asia and the uncertainties of the textual transmission. But while its boundaries cannot be defined with absolute precision,[20] the corpus of poetry that has come down to us provides ample evidence of a powerfully coherent poetical and mystical imagination.

Since it is its simplicity of expression that has helped to secure the wide appeal of Bullhe Shah's poetry, little needs to be said about the formal characteristics of its language, which is for the most part a straightforward register of Panjabi. In style too, Bullhe Shah's poetry shows little trace of the elaboration of conceits that is such a prominent characteristic of South Asian art-poetry in both the Sanskritic and Persianate traditions. The rhymes that are such a leading feature of the *kāfī* do, of course, generate their own creative associations, and some use is made of the simpler rhetorical devices like alliteration, assonance, and plays on words of similar sound, but such verbal effects are not exploited to the relentless degree that came to serve later Panjabi taste.

Although some of the *kāfīs* have a strong thematic unity, individual verses more commonly touch on seemingly quite different topics. Since the formal unity generated in the original language by the rhyme scheme announced in the refrain is hardly apparent in the English prose translations presented in this book, this internal thematic variety and the accompanying shifts of reference in the poet's voice can sometimes seem disconcerting. Most specific difficulties of understanding, which can seem greater when reading the poems as texts than when listening to them being sung, should be resolved in the explanatory endnotes. But for the proper general appreciation of Bullhe Shah's poetry, which is dedicated above all else to the evocation of a sense of the transcendent unity of all things, it is important to begin with a general idea of how its apparently varied thematic components actually form a closely interlocking imaginative structure.

Since that imaginative structure is also a hierarchical one, it can be useful to begin at the bottom by understanding that Bullhe Shah's critique of the social upheavals in early eighteenth-century Panjab, which is so interesting to many modern readers, represents only a very small, if vividly expressed part of his poetry. Like his occasional pungent attacks on the dishonesty of contemporary religious specialists, verses expressing social critique are quite subsidiary in quantity to the poems of admonition designed to arouse a very Islamic sense of the inevitability of death and the need to prepare for this rapidly approaching end by the performance of meritorious deeds. Several of Bullhe Shah's longest poems memorably develop this *memento mori* theme with metaphorical reference to the typical life cycle of a girl who grows up in the security of her parental home, but must dutifully spin the thread that will make up the clothes she will take with her as dowry after she has been married and goes to live with her husband's family. In these poems, the poet adopts a stern parental persona:

Get up, wake up, and do not snore. This sleeping is
    no good for you.

One day you must leave the world and go to be
　　interred in the grave. The worms will eat your
　　flesh. Be aware and do not forget death.
The day appointed for your wedding has drawn near;
　　have you had the clothes for your dowry dyed?
　　Why have you ruined yourself? Heedless one,
　　have you no awareness?
You have wasted your life in sleep; now your moment
　　has come. You have not even started spinning.
　　You have no dowry prepared, so what will you
　　do?[21]

Just as the observance of the requirements of Islamic law is regarded by most Sufis as a necessary, if insufficient prerequisite for the spiritual discipline that is their main object, so too is this didactic aspect of Bullhe Shah's poetry subsidiary to the mystical vision that is its principal theme. The core expression of this vision is again very Islamic, relying upon the repeated citation of a number of Qur'anic phrases and other sacred sayings in their original Arabic wording to convey an overwhelming sense of the absolute unity of the divine presence in all things, which for Sufis is confirmed by the evidence of scriptural revelation. For Bullhe Shah, as for so many Sufis, the primary reason for creation was God's desire to be loved, and the primal compact between God and man meant both man's recognition of God as the lord of his devotion and the special presence ofthe divine within man as the noblest of God's creatures. A particular role is accorded to the prophet Muhammad, whose other name, Ahmad, symbolizes his intimate connection with Ahad, or God the One. In the vivid apprehension of essential unity, the poet's voice moves with sometimes disconcerting speed from the role of a girl inviting her friends to listen to her profession of love to that of an expert able to provide copious citations of proof texts in Arabic, as in these verses:

> Oh girlfriends: Now I have found you, beloved. You are contained in each and every thing.
> You recited the song of *I am Ahad the One*. Then you decreed, *I am Ahmad*. Then you explained, *I am an Arab without the A*. Then you took the name of Apostle.
> Becoming manifest, you called yourself light. You made it present through Ahmad. From nonbeing you made being appear. You proclaimed, *And we breathed into him*.[22]

In continually repeated verses, Bullhe Shah proclaims the need to recognize this mystery of God being universally present, despite the apparently contrary evidence of superficial differences of appearance. He often speaks of this as the divine "peeping out" from the human. And his central perception of the meaninglessness of outward diversity inspired those memorable poems on the essential unity of "Turk" and "Hindu" that have acquired such a special significance in modern South Asia, with its long history of intensely pursued communal bigotry:

Behold, God is openly revealed, whatever the pandit
  may then proclaim from the Veda.
If you attend carefully, there are no unbelievers,
  whether they are called Hindu or Turk.
Whenever I look, only he, only he exists. Bullha, the
  lord is contained in every color.[23]

Bullhe Shah's mystical perception of the unity of all things in
the divine is not merely intellectual. It is a dynamic process
pursued through love, the source of both man's greatest
delights and his most acute emotional suffering. In keeping
with the Sufi doctrine of a disciple's self-obliteration in the
master,[24] the most important focus of Bullhe Shah's love is
his spiritual guide, Shah Inayat, who is so frequently named
in the concluding verses of his lyrics, now as the present
source of his joy, now as the absent cause of his pain, now as
the master who is mysteriously both different from and identical with his adoring disciple. More than once, Bullhe Shah
repudiates the criticism that it is inappropriate for him as a
Sayyid, the Muslim group with the highest religious status,
to be the disciple of Shah Inayat, a mere Arain:

Why ask what the lord's caste is? Bullha, be grateful
  for God's mercies. If you desire the joys of spring,
  remain the humble servant of the Arain.[25]

The poetry also bears out the gist of the most popular episode
in the hagiography of Bullhe Shah, which elaborates on how
he once fell out of favor with his guide, allegedly for being
too outspoken in his criticisms of formal Islam, and was

dismissed from his company. Since he knew of Shah Inayat's fondness for music and dancing, Bullhe Shah is then said to have gone away and taken lessons with a dancing girl, then reappeared in Lahore one day, himself dressed as a dancing girl. There he danced and sang in front of Shah Inayat, who was won over by his performance and readmitted him to his favor:

> Come to my assistance, doctor, I have lost my senses.
> Your love has set me dancing in rhythm.

> Bullha, let us go and sit at the gate of Shah Inayat, who
>     made me dress in green and red. When I started
>     dancing, I found my way to him.[26]

The extraordinary richness of the dynamic of love is conveyed by Bullhe Shah's remarkable range of poetic reference. This extends beyond the Islamic tradition to include occasional references to figures from the Hindu world,[27] but the sacred history of the past is mainly conceived as the story of a succession of martyrs to the divine power of love, starting with the scriptural figures regarded as prophets in Islam like Ibrahim, Sulaiman, Ayub, and Zakariya, all variously tested in their turn by God. Then there are the great Sufi saints, of whom by far the most frequently cited is the martyr Mansur, who was executed for daring to proclaim the mystery of identity with the divine in his famous saying *anā 'l-haq*, "I am God." To the prophets and the saints are added, both in incidental references and in long lists of those who have suffered in the name of love, the famous pairs of lovers of Islamic legend whose stories formed the core themes of the Persian romance, like Yusuf, who was loved by Zulaikha in Egypt,[28] and Laila, who was madly adored by Majnun in Arabia:

> They put Yusuf in the well, then sold him in the
> bazaar. He was paid for in full with a hank of yarn.
> You will be priced at a cowrie.
> Zulaikha fell in love and bought him. Lovers are
> writhing in agony over there. Majnun says, "Ah,
> ah, ah!" What will you bring back from over
> there?
> Over there some have their skins flayed, some are cut
> up with saws, others are seized and put on the
> gallows. You too will get your head cut off over
> there.[29]

This long story of the eternal power of love is simultaneously and immediately brought home through Bullhe Shah's frequent allusions to the local legends of the Indus valley.[30] The standard convention of Indian lyric poetry that makes the poet take on the persona of a female lover[31] is given added resonance by Bullhe Shah's assumption of the role of one of the local romantic heroines, like Sassi waking to find herself abandoned by her beloved Punnun or Sohni poised to make the dangerous crossing over the river Chenab to meet her Mahinval:

> On the other side of the Chenab there are jungles and
>     thickets, where cruel tigers and panthers roam.
>     May the lord bring me quickly to my beloved.
>     This anxiety is killing me.
> It is the middle of the night and the stars are waning.
>     Some have already waned; others are about to do
>     so. I have got up and come to the riverbank. Now
>     I am standing here waiting to cross.
> I cannot swim and do not have a clue what to do.
>     I have no pole or oar, and my raft is old. There are
>     whirlpools, and no crossing place is marked.
>     I weep and wring my hands.[32]

The greatest of these local romantic legends is the story of
Hir and Ranjha, which is set in the world of the Jat pastoral
tribes of western Panjab. The romance is best known through
the famous narrative treatment in the *Hīr* by Bullhe Shah's
younger contemporary Varis Shah, which tells the whole
story of how Dhido, known by his tribal name of Ranjha,
leaves his family home in Takht Hazara to come to Jhang, in
search of Hir, the daughter of the Sial chieftain Chuchak.
The latter is persuaded to hire Ranjha as a herdsman, allow-
ing Hir the chance to meet him in the river glades beside the
Chenab where the buffaloes are brought to graze. But when
their love is discovered, Hir's parents marry her off by force
to a man from the Khera tribe. In order to win her back,
Ranjha goes to the great yogi Gorakhnath for initiation. Thus
radically transformed in appearance from a herdsman into
a yogi,[33] Ranjha returns to win back Hir from her husband's
home:

I will go with the yogi, having put a mark on my
    forehead.
I will go, I will not be stopped from leaving. Who
    is going to turn me back as I go? It has become
    impossible for me to turn back, now that I have
    experienced reproaches for being in love.
He is not a yogi, but my heart's beloved. I have
    forgotten why I fell in love. I lost all control, once
    I gained a sight of him.
What did this yogi do to me? He put his hooks in my
    heart. He cast the net of love when he uttered his
    sweet talk.[34]

Although the story makes some appearances in the earlier
Sufi poetry of Shah Husain, it is Bullhe Shah who properly
exploits the rich potential for mystical allegory inherent in
the relationship between Hir and her beloved, which is taken
to symbolize the love between the human and the divine as
lived out in that between the poet and his lord, Shah Inayat.
Although Ranjha, the chieftain's son from Takht Hazara,
assumes different appearances, as a yogi or as a flute-playing
herdsman who recalls the divine figure of Krishna, the true
mystery lies in his being fundamentally identical with Hir.
Many of Bullhe Shah's most memorable lyrics express this
sweet yet painful contradiction:

Through repeating "Ranjha, Ranjha," I have myself
    now become Ranjha. Call me Dhido Ranjha, let no
    one call me Hir.

Ranjha is in me and I am in Ranjha, this is my only
    thought. There is no me, there is only him, and he
    is the one who shows tender care for himself.
Whoever dwells within us determines who we are.
    I have become just like the one I love.
With a staff in my hand I drive the buffaloes
    before me, wearing a rough blanket around my
    shoulders. Take me to Takht Hazara, Bullha,
    I can find no refuge with the Sials.[35]

With short and apparently simple Sufi lyrics like this, Bullhe
Shah shows the identity of the lover and the beloved, in that
world of true reality that lies behind the screen of apparent variety. Appealing at several levels to so many of the
deepest human aspirations, to a universal understanding of
the meaning of human existence in a divine world, Bullhe
Shah's assimilation of many diverse elements into his poetic
expression of the perennial philosophy of the unity of being
makes him an outstanding interpreter of the transcendent,
not just for Panjabis but for us all.

### *Acknowledgments*

I am most grateful to Leena Mitford and Marina Chellini for
helping me with access to materials from the British Library,
to Farjad Nabi for his invaluable gifts of books from Lahore,
and to Sheldon Pollock both for his original invitation to
contribute this volume to the Murty Classical Library of
India and for his subsequent steady provision of wise and
encouraging editorial guidance.

## NOTES

1   See further Nijjar 1972, Alam 1986.

2   See Rama Krishna 1938: 40–46 and Quraeshi 2009: 241–258, which is illustrated with photographs showing the radically modernized appearance of Bullhe Shah's shrine in Kasur today.

3   Shackle 1993 offers a comparative sketch of the earliest attested examples.

4   For details of the main printed editions, see the Note on the Text and Translation following this introduction.

5   Singh 2012 presents representative selections from both traditions in attractive translations.

6   For an informed introduction to Sufism, see Ernst 1997.

7   Schimmel 1982 remains the best introduction to Sufi poetry in Persian and other languages.

8   For recent books of translations that give an excellent idea of the character of this poetry, see Lewis 2008, and Losensky and Sharma 2011.

9   For qawwali, see Qureshi 1986; for the local context of Sufi music and its performers, see Pannke 1999.

10  For the Qadiri order in India, see Bilgrami 2005; for the Shattari order, see Ahmad 2012, in addition to the standard general account of the Sufi orders in India in Rizvi 1978–83.

11  See further Shackle 1999.

12  For an overall account of the tradition of Panjabi Sufi poetry, see further Shackle 2011.

13  There is no very satisfactory history of Panjabi literature in English, but compare Sekhon 1993–96. Studies of Bullhe Shah in English, none of which is at all comprehensive or very critical, include Usborne 1982 [first published c. 1905], Rama Krishna 1938: 40–71, and Kohli 1987.

14  Interesting explorations of this topic may be found in Rinehart 1996, 1999.

15  Complete English translations of all four poets are available, although these are of varying quality. See Talib 1974: 97–124 for Farid; Anwar 1966 for Shah Husain; Puri and Khak 1998 for Sultan Bahu, besides the attractive selections in Elias 1998; and Qaiser 2009 for Khwaja Ghulam Farid, in addition to the overambitious attempt at fully rhymed translations of selected poems in Shackle 1983.

16  *Kāfī* 106.1–3.

17  *Kāfī* 106.7.

18  The letters of the Arabic alphabet, several of which have an important symbolic function in Bullhe Shah's poetry, are illustrated at the beginning of each verse of the *Sīharfī*.

19  Verse V19.

20  Some attributions are doubtful on grounds of style, e.g., 35; of content, e.g., 108, V52, V53; or of authorship in the case of 29, 63, 130, and 145, which are also attributed to Shah Husain. The independent status of some poems is questionable, as in the case of the close pairs 49–50 and 130–131. Editorial amalgamations of other poems that have been reversed in this book include the separation of 76 from A7 and of V51 from 36.

21  *Kāfī* 2.1–4.

22  *Kāfī* 28.1–2, 5.

23  *Kāfī* 20.5–7.

24  This doctrine (Ar. *fanā fī 'l-shaikh*) was given particular importance within the Shattari order with which Shah Inayat was affiliated; compare Ahmad 2012: 151–154.

25  *Kāfī* 31.6.

26  *Kāfī* 105.1, 7. The image of Bullhe Shah dancing is a popular one in modern iconography; see Frembgen 2006: 106–107.

27  Matringe 1992 offers a helpful analysis of the Krishnaite and Nath elements in Bullhe Shah's poetry.

28  Shackle 1995 describes the influence of Jami's classic Persian poem *Yūsuf Zulaikhā* on narrative treatments of the story in Panjabi.

29  *Kāfī* 98.3–5.

30  Accessible popular versions of these legends are presented with lavish illustrations in Quraeshi 2005.

31  See further Petievich 2007, which uses Bullhe Shah as an illustrative example of this convention of "men speaking as women."

32  *Kāfī* 81.6–8.

33  Shackle 1992 discusses the Hir-Ranjha story with particular reference to the successive transformations of Ranjha.

34  *Kāfī* 137.1–4.

35  *Kāfī* 145.

# NOTE ON THE TEXT
# AND TRANSLATION

Given the disturbed conditions prevalent in Panjab during the eighteenth century and the lack of a line of direct descendants who might have safeguarded his poetic heritage, the transmission of the poetry of Bullhe Shah was entirely reliant on oral tradition for more than a century after his death. There appear to be no surviving manuscripts from the period preceding the first printed texts, which date from the later decades of the nineteenth century when Lahore became established as a major center of publishing. Produced in the cheapest format, these early Persian-script lithographs of individual poems include numerous quite uncritical editions of the *Bārāṅ Māh* from 1864, of the *Sīharfī* from 1873, and of selected *Kāfīāṅ* from 1882. The less well-attested early Gurmukhi lithographed editions from this period include a small selection of *Kāfīāṅ* by both Shah Husain and Bullhe Shah, published in 1878.

The earliest substantial edition, containing 116 *kāfīs*, is the *Qānūn-e 'ishq* edited by Anvar Ali Ruhtaki, which first appeared in 1889.[1] This incorporates an extensive Urdu commentary offering a detailed exposition of Sufi doctrine supported by numerous quotations from Persian Sufi poetry and determining the thematic order in which the *kāfīs* are arranged. The work continues to be valued for its commentary, and there have been several subsequent printings, including a Pakistani edition of 2006. The other significant early Persian-script edition is the *Kāfīhā-e Hazrat Bullhe Shāh,* published by Prem Singh of Kasur in 1896, which also includes the poems in other genres, including two additional *sīharfīs,* which have since generally been regarded as spurious. While its 131 *kāfīs* overlap with those in the *Qānūn-e 'ishq,* Prem Singh's selection tends to favor rather more distinctively Indian poems at the expense of those with a markedly Islamic focus, prominent in Ruhtaki's edition. These two early Persian-script editions, both compiled from contemporary oral tradition, together form the basis for all subsequent texts.

The first attempt at a critical edition was the small selection published in Gurmukhi as *50 Kāfīāñ* by Mohan Singh Ubirai in 1930. But the standard text on which all serious modern Pakistani and Indian editions are based is the comprehensive Persian-script *Kulliyāt* of 1960 edited by Faqir Muhammad Faqir, which contains 161 *kāfīs,* arranged by Persian alphabetical order of first lines, as well as all the other poems in Prem Singh's edition, and provides a summary critical apparatus citing the earliest editions. The highly selective edition by Nazir Ahmad, published in 1976 as *Kālam-e Bullhe Shāh,* offers some useful emendations, mostly on metrical grounds, as well as critical notes. A more radically revised complete Persian-script text, which sometimes makes very free use of editorial emendation to solve textual difficulties, is offered in the important *Mukammal Kāfīāñ* of 1991 edited by Muhammad Sharif Sabir, which includes 155 *kāfīs* and contains a full textual apparatus.

Quite a number of Gurmukhi editions have been published in India, but most of these appear to be based on the Faqir edition, whose Persian-script ordering of the *kāfīs* is often followed mechanically and whose text is often inaccurately transcribed. Two recent complete Gurmukhi editions do, however, have some independent value. The edition by Attarjit Singh and Gurcharan Singh, published in 2004 as *Bullheshāh [jīvan, Dohṛe, Sīharfīāñ te Kāfīāñ]*, includes 175 *kāfīs* and some suggestive variant texts, but without any critical apparatus or other indication of the sources used.[2] The only Indian edition to take explicit account of Sabir's indispensable, if radical text is Jagtar's *Bullhe Shāh: jīvan ate racnā*, published in 2008, which contains 161 *kāfīs*. The underlying text used in the present volume represents a compromise between the two best modern Persian-script editions by Faqir and Sabir and the recent Gurmukhi edition by Jagtar.

Panjabi spellings have yet to be fully standardized in either script, so quite numerous tacit adjustments have been made for consistency. Only the most significant textual variants are noted in the summary endnotes to the text, and the accompanying discussion of these textual matters is kept deliberately brief. The *kāfīs* are here mechanically arranged in strict Gurmukhi alphabetical order as determined by the first word of the refrain. In the interest of economy, the Gurmukhi text prints the refrains once only, at the beginning of each *kāfī* rather than after every verse. Single quotation marks have been used to mark the Arabic quotations from the Qur'an and other sources that can otherwise seem quite disconcerting to the reader in their Gurmukhi transcriptions.

Only a fine verse translation might hope to convey the

ecstatic tone of much of Bullhe Shah's poetry, although even
the most gifted English poet could hardly hope to reproduce
the many rhymes that are so defining a characteristic of the
*kāfī*. In reality, however, most attempts to make English
poetry out of Bullhe Shah's Panjabi seldom manage to do
proper justice to more than the odd verse here and there.
In keeping with the style of the Murty Library, the present
translation of the full corpus therefore tries only to convey
the sense of the poetry in a consistent style of plain English
prose that aims to steer a middle path between off-putting
formality and jarring colloquialism. So far as possible, the
underlying syntax of the verses has been maintained, with
a full stop marking the end of individual lines and a comma
indicating the half-line caesura. Italics are used to mark
Bullhe Shah's quite frequent citation of Qur'anic verses[3]
and other Arabic sayings.

Superscript Arabic numerals in the translation indicate
endnotes providing further explanations and comments.
Abbreviations used in the endnotes are explained in an introductory note. In order to keep the notes to the translation
down to a manageable size, points that regularly recur in
the text are generally explained in one note only, with parallel occurrences being listed as numerical cross-references
for comparison. The endnotes are followed by a glossary of
proper names, which are there printed with diacritics giving
a more precise indication of their pronunciation than is
always apparent from the simple roman-script spellings of
names used elsewhere in the book.

Diacritics are, however, used throughout for italicized
words and phrases transcribed from Panjabi and other

languages. These follow the usual academic conventions, in which long vowels are marked by macrons over *ā*, *ī*, and *ū*, and retroflex consonants by dots written under *ḍ*, *ṇ*, *ṛ*, and *ṭ*. Nasalized long vowels are transcribed with a following *ñ*, and dots are used to distinguish the fricative sounds *ḵh* and *ġh*. The Persian *izāfat* is transcribed phonetically as *-e*. Neither Gurmukhi nor the Persian script distinguishes the sibilants *ś* and *ṣ*, for which *sh* is regularly written instead. Graphic *'ain* and the distinction of *q* from *k* are both recorded where appropriate in the transcription of Perso-Arabic words, although neither feature is preserved in Panjabi pronunciation. The romanization of Qur'anic and other Arabic passages in the endnotes follows the standard rules for writing Arabic in the roman script.

The bibliography begins with listings in chronological order of publication of the texts and translations of Bullhe Shah consulted in the preparation of this book, before a general bibliography in alphabetical order of authors of other relevant titles. This is largely confined to works in English, and includes all works cited in the immediately following endnotes to this introduction and in the endnotes to the translations.

A numerical concordance of the *kāfīs* is provided for the convenience of readers who may be more familiar with the Persian script, and who may wish to check our translations of the Gurmukhi text against the standard Pakistani text of the Faqir edition (F).

## NOTES

1  See the bibliography at the end of this volume for full details of all editions cited.

2  While some of the additional poems included in this edition seem quite plausible stylistically, in the absence of verifiable textual support, I have excluded the following seven *kāfīs* here: *huṇ maiñ anhad nād vajāiā* (*kāfī* 4, p. 61); *belī jit ghar terā pher hoiā* (*kāfī* 17, pp. 70–71); *mainūñ kauṇ pachāṇe* (*kāfī* 21, p. 73); *birhoñ dā tāa nā lāiñ ve, sāiñ maiñḍiā* (*kāfī* 25, p. 74); *asiñ liv taiñḍe sang lāī ā* (*kāfī* 26, pp. 74–75); *je koī andar bole cāle* (*kāfī* 27, p. 75); *aisī man meñ āio re* (*kāfī* 49; p. 87).

3  The translations of Qur'anic verses are based on Yusuf Ali 1977.

# Lyrics

## ੧

ਉੱਠ ਗਏ ਗਵਾਂਢੋਂ ਯਾਰ, ਰੱਬਾ ਹੁਣ ਕੀ ਕਰੀਏ

ਉੱਠ ਗਏ ਹੁਣ ਰਹਿੰਦੇ ਨਾਹੀਂ, ਹੋਇਆ ਸਾਥ ਤਿਆਰ

ਡਾਢ ਕਲੇਜੇ ਬਲ ਬਲ ਉਠਦੀ, ਭੜਕੇ ਬਿਰਹੋਂ ਨਾਰ

ਬੁੱਲ੍ਹਾ ਸ਼ਹੁ ਪਿਆਰੇ ਬਾਝੋਂ, ਰਹੇ ਉਰਾਰ ਨਾ ਪਾਰ

## ੨

ਉਠ ਜਾਗ ਘੁਰਾੜੇ ਮਾਰ ਨਹੀਂ, ਇਹ ਸੌਣ ਤੇਰੇ ਦਰਕਾਰ ਨਹੀਂ

ਇਕ ਰੋਜ਼ ਜਹਾਨੋਂ ਜਾਣਾ ਏ, ਜਾ ਕਬਰੇ ਵਿਚ ਸਮਾਣਾ ਏ
ਤੇਰਾ ਗੋਸ਼ਤ ਕੀੜਿਆਂ ਖਾਣਾ ਏ, ਕਰ ਚੇਤਾ ਮਰਗ ਵਿਸਾਰ ਨਹੀਂ

ਤੇਰਾ ਸਾਹਾ ਨੇੜਾ ਆਇਆ ਏ, ਕੁਝ ਚੋਲੀ ਦਾਜ ਰੰਗਾਇਆ ਏ
ਕਿਉਂ ਅਪਣਾ ਆਪ ਵੰਞਾਇਆ ਏ, ਐ ਗ਼ਾਫ਼ਲ ਤੈਨੂੰ ਸਾਰ ਨਹੀਂ

ਤੂੰ ਸੁੱਤਿਆਂ ਉਮਰ ਵੰਞਾਈ ਏ, ਤੇਰੀ ਸਾਇਤ ਨੇੜੇ ਆਈ ਏ
ਤੂੰ ਚਰਖੇ ਤੰਦ ਨਾ ਪਾਈ ਏ, ਕੀ ਕਰਸੇਂ ਦਾਜ ਤਿਆਰ ਨਹੀਂ

੫ ਤੂੰ ਜਿਸ ਦਿਨ ਜੋਬਨ ਮੱਤੀ ਸੈਂ, ਤੂੰ ਨਾਲ ਸਈਆਂ ਦੇ ਰੱਤੀ ਸੈਂ
ਹੋ ਗ਼ਾਫ਼ਲ ਗੱਲੀਂ ਵੱਤੀ ਸੈਂ, ਇਹ ਬੇਰਾ ਤੈਨੂੰ ਸਾਰ ਨਹੀਂ

## 1

My beloved has left the neighborhood. Oh lord, what shall
    I do?[1]

Now he has gone, he does not stay. His company is ready
    to depart.

The fire in my heart blazes up. The flames of separation
    crackle.

Without the dear lord, Bullha is neither on this bank nor
    on the far side.[2]

## 2

Get[1] up, wake up, and do not snore. This sleeping is no
    good for you.

One day you must leave the world and go to be interred in
    the grave. The worms will eat your flesh. Be aware and
    do not forget death.

The day appointed[2] for your wedding has drawn near;
    have you had any of the clothes for your dowry dyed?
    Why have you ruined yourself? Heedless one, have
    you no awareness?

You have wasted your life in sleep; now your moment has
    come. You have not even started spinning thread on
    the wheel. You have no dowry prepared, so what will
    you do?

On the day you were intoxicated by your youth, you were    5
    completely taken up with your girlfriends. Carelessly
    you roamed the streets, without the least awareness.

ਤੂੰ ਮੁੱਢੋਂ ਬਹੁਤ ਕੁਚੱਜੀ ਸੈਂ, ਨਿਰਲੱਜਿਆਂ ਦੀ ਨਿਰਲੱਜੀ ਸੈਂ
ਤੂੰ ਖਾ ਖਾ ਖਾਣੇ ਰੱਜੀ ਸੈਂ, ਹੁਣ ਤਾਈਂ ਤੇਰਾ ਬਾਰ ਨਹੀਂ

ਅਜ ਕਲ ਤੇਰਾ ਮੁਕਲਾਵਾ ਏ, ਕਿਉਂ ਸੁੱਤੀ ਕਰ ਕਰ ਦਾਅਵਾ ਏ
ਅਟੱਡਿਠਿਆਂ ਨਾਲ ਮਿਲਾਵਾ ਏ, ਇਹ ਭਲਕੇ ਗਰਮ ਬਜ਼ਾਰ ਨਹੀਂ

ਤੂੰ ਏਸ ਜਹਾਨੋਂ ਜਾਏਂਗੀ, ਫਿਰ ਕਦਮ ਨਾ ਏਥੇ ਪਾਏਂਗੀ
ਇਹ ਜੋਬਨ ਰੂਪ ਵੰਞਾਏਂਗੀ, ਤੈਂ ਰਹਿਣਾ ਵਿਚ ਸੰਸਾਰ ਨਹੀਂ

ਮੰਜ਼ਲ ਤੇਰੀ ਦੂਰ ਦੁਰਾਡੀ, ਤੂੰ ਭੌਤੈਂ ਵਿਚ ਜੰਗਲ ਵਾਦੀ
ਔਖਾ ਪਹੁੰਚਣ ਪੈਰ ਪਿਆਦੀ, ਦਿਸਦੀ ਤੂੰ ਅਸਵਾਰ ਨਹੀਂ

੧੦ ਇੱਕ ਇਕੱਲੀ ਤਨਹਾ ਜੁਲਸੈਂ, ਜੰਗਲ ਬਰਬਰ ਦੇ ਵਿਚ ਰੁਲਸੈਂ
ਲੈ ਲੈ ਤੋਸ਼ਾ ਏਥੋਂ ਘੁਲਸੈਂ, ਉਥੇ ਲੈਣ ਉਧਾਰ ਨਹੀਂ

ਉਹ ਖ਼ਾਲੀ ਏ ਸੁੰਞ ਹਵੇਲੀ, ਤੂੰ ਵਿਚ ਰਹਿਸੈਂ ਇਕ ਇਕੇਲੀ
ਓਥੇ ਹੋਸੀ ਹੋਰ ਨਾ ਬੇਲੀ, ਸਾਥ ਕਿਸੇ ਦਾ ਬਾਰ ਨਹੀਂ

ਜਿਹੜੇ ਸਨ ਦੇਸਾਂ ਦੇ ਰਾਜੇ, ਨਾਲ ਜਿਨ੍ਹਾਂ ਦੇ ਵਜਦੇ ਵਾਜੇ
ਹੋ ਕੇ ਗਏ ਬੇ-ਤਖ਼ਤੇ ਤਾਜੇ, ਕੋਈ ਦੁਨੀਆਂ ਦਾ ਇਤਬਾਰ ਨਹੀਂ

ਕਿੱਥੇ ਹੈ ਸੁਲਤਾਨ ਸਿਕੰਦਰ, ਮੌਤ ਨਾ ਛੱਡੇ ਪੀਰ ਪੈਗ਼ੰਬਰ
ਸੱਭੇ ਛੱਡ ਛੱਡ ਗਏ ਅਡੰਬਰ, ਕੋਈ ਏਥੇ ਪਾਇਦਾਰ ਨਹੀਂ

ਕਿੱਥੇ ਯੂਸਫ਼ ਮਾਹੇ ਕਿਨਆਨੀ, ਲਈ ਜ਼ੁਲੈਖਾਂ ਫੇਰ ਜਵਾਨੀ
ਕੀਤੀ ਮੌਤ ਨੇ ਉੱਡਕ ਫ਼ਾਨੀ, ਫੇਰ ਉਹ ਹਾਰ ਸ਼ਿੰਗਾਰ ਨਹੀਂ

From the start you were completely undomesticated, you
were the most shameless of the shameless. You kept
eating and filling yourself with food, and still you have
no sense.[3]

Soon it will be time for you to be taken away.[4] Why are you
asleep and full of pretense? You must meet strangers
you have never seen. This bustling market will not be
here in the morning.

You will depart from this world, and will not set foot here
again. You will lose your youth and beauty. You are not
going to remain in the world.

Your destination lies far away. You must wander through
jungles and deserts. It will be difficult to get there on
foot, and you do not look like a rider.

You will be on your own, and will travel completely alone.  10
You will wander lost in jungles and deserts. You will
leave here with your own supplies. You will not be able
to borrow anything there.

That desolate mansion is empty, and you will live there
all by yourself. There will be no one to be your friend.
There will be no one to rely upon for company.

Those who were kings of countries, and who had bands
playing for them, have departed without their thrones
and crowns. There is no trusting in this world.

Where is the emperor Sikandar?[5] Death has not spared
saints or prophets. All have left their pomp and show
behind. No one is here permanently.

Where is Yusuf,[6] the moon of Canaan? Zulaikha[7] has taken
her youthful beauty away with her. In the end, death
made her perish. Her finery will not be restored.

੧੫ ਕਿੱਥੇ ਤਖ਼ਤ ਸੁਲੇਮਾਂ ਵਾਲਾ, ਵਿੱਚ ਹਵਾ ਉਡਦਾ ਸੀ ਬਾਲਾ
ਉਹ ਵੀ ਕਾਦਰ ਆਪ ਸੰਭਾਲਾ, ਕੋਈ ਜਿੰਦਗੀ ਦਾ ਇਤਬਾਰ ਨਹੀਂ

ਕਿੱਥੇ ਮੀਰ ਮਲਕ ਸੁਲਤਾਨਾਂ, ਸੱਭੇ ਫੜ ਫੜ ਗਏ ਠਿਕਾਣਾ
ਕੋਈ ਮਾਰ ਨਾ ਬੈਠੇ ਠਾਣਾ, ਲਸ਼ਕਰ ਦਾ ਜਿਨ੍ਹਾਂ ਸ਼ੁਮਾਰ ਨਹੀਂ

ਫੁੱਲਾਂ ਫੁੱਲ ਚੰਬੇਲੀ ਲਾਲਾ, ਸੋਸਨ ਸੁੰਬਲ ਸਰੂ ਨਿਰਾਲਾ
ਬਾਦਿ-ਖ਼ਜ਼ਾਂ ਕੀਤਾ ਬੁਰ ਹਾਲਾ, ਨਰਗਸ ਨਿਤ ਖ਼ੁਮਾਰ ਨਹੀਂ

ਜੋ ਕੁਝ ਕਰਸੇਂ ਸੋ ਕੁਝ ਪਾਸੇਂ, ਨਹੀਂ ਤੇ ਉੜਕ ਪਛੋਤਾਸੇਂ
ਸੁੰਜੀ ਕੂੰਜ ਵਾਂਗੂੰ ਕੁਰਲਾਸੇਂ, ਖੰਭਾਂ ਬਾਝ ਉਡਾਰ ਨਹੀਂ

ਡੇਰਾ ਕਰਸੇਂ ਉਹਨੀਂ ਥਾਈਂ, ਜਿਥੇ ਸ਼ੇਰ ਪਲੰਗ ਬਲਾਈਂ
ਖ਼ਾਲੀ ਰਹਿਸਣ ਮਹਿਲ ਸਰਾਈਂ, ਫਿਰ ਤੂੰ ਵਿਰਸੇਦਾਰ ਨਹੀਂ

੨੦ ਅਸੀਂ ਆਜਜ਼ ਕੋਟ ਇਲਮ ਦੇ, ਓਸੇ ਆਂਦੇ ਵਿਚ ਕਲਮ ਦੇ
ਬਿਨ ਕਲਮੇ ਦੇ ਨਹੀਂ ਕੰਮ ਦੇ, ਬਾਝੋਂ ਕਲਮੇ ਪਾਰ ਨਹੀਂ

ਬੁੱਲ੍ਹਾ ਸ਼ਹੁ ਬਿਨ ਕੋਈ ਨਹੀਂ, ਏਥੇ ਉਥੇ ਦੋਹੀਂ ਸਰਾਈਂ
ਸੰਭਲ ਸੰਭਲ ਕਦਮ ਟਿਕਾਈਂ, ਫੇਰ ਆਵਣ ਦੂਜੀ ਵਾਰ ਨਹੀਂ

Where is the throne of Sulaiman,[8] which used to fly          15
    high in the air? It too has been taken care of by the
    almighty. There is no trusting in life.

Where are those princes, kings, and emperors? All have
    quit their royal residences. Those whose armies were
    uncountable cannot capture a mere police station
    now.

All the flowers, like the jasmine, the tulip, the lily, the iris,
    the hyacinth, and the wonderful cypress, have been
    reduced to a sorry state by the autumn wind.[9] The
    intoxication of the narcissus[10] does not last forever.

As you perform, so you will receive. Otherwise you will
    be sorry. You will lament like the desolate crane.[11]
    Without wings there is no flying.[12]

You will make your camp in places where lions, leopards,
    and terrors dwell. Your palaces and caravanserais will
    remain empty. You will have no hereditary claim on
    them.

In the citadel of knowledge[13] we are helpless. It is he who          20
    brought us under his authority. Without the word I
    am no use, without the word there is no deliverance.

Bullha, there is no one besides the lord, here or there, in
    either world. So tread with great care, for there is no
    coming back a second time.

### ੩

ਉਲਟੀ ਗੰਗ ਬਹਾਇਓ ਰੇ ਸਾਧੋ, ਤਬ ਹਰਿ ਦਰਸਨ ਪਾਏ

ਪ੍ਰੇਮ ਕੀ ਪੂਟੀ ਹਾਥ ਮੇਂ ਲੀਜੋ, ਗੁੜ ਮਰੋੜੀ ਪੜਨੇ ਨਾ ਦੀਜੋ

ਗਿਆਨ ਕਾ ਤਕਲਾ ਧਿਆਨ ਕਾ ਚਰਖਾ, ਉਲਟਾ ਫੇਰ ਭੁਵਾਏ

ਉਲਟੇ ਪਾਓਂ ਪਰ ਕੁੰਭਕਰਨ ਜਾਏ, ਤਬ ਲੰਕਾ ਕਾ ਭੇਦ ਉਪਾਏ

੫ ਦਹਿਸਰ ਲੁੱਟਿਆ ਹੁਣ ਲਛਮਣ ਬਾਕੀ, ਤਬ ਅਨਹਦ ਨਾਦ ਬਜਾਏ

ਇਹ ਗਤ ਗੁਰ ਕੇ ਪਰਿਉਂ ਪਾਵੇ, ਗੁਰ ਕਾ ਸੇਵਕ ਤਭੀ ਸਦਾਏ

ਅੰਮ੍ਰਿਤ ਮੰਡਲ ਮੋਂ ਟੁੱਭ ਐਸੀ ਦੇ ਕੇ, ਹਰੀ ਹਰਿ ਹੋ ਜਾਏ

### ੪

ਉਲਟੇ ਹੋਰ ਜ਼ਮਾਨੇ ਆਏ, ਤਾਂ ਮੈਂ ਭੇਦ ਸਜਨ ਦੇ ਪਾਏ

ਕਾਂ ਲਗੜ ਨੂੰ ਮਾਰਨ ਲੱਗੇ, ਚਿੜੀਆਂ ਜੁੱਰੇ ਢਾਏ

ਘੋੜੇ ਚੁਗਾਟ ਅਰੂੜੀਆਂ ਉੱਤੇ, ੧ ਗੱਦੋਂ ਖੁਦ ਪਵਾਏ

ਆਪਣਿਆਂ ਵਿਚ ਉਲਫਤ ਨਾਹੀਂ, ਕਿਆ ਚਾਚੇ ਕਿਆ ਤਾਏ

੫ ਪਿਉ ਪੁਤਰਾਂ ਇਤਫ਼ਾਕ ਨਾ ਕਾਈ, ਧੀਆਂ ਨਾਲ ਨਾ ਮਾਏ

ਸੱਚਿਆਂ ਨੂੰ ਪਏ ਮਿਲਦੇ ਧੱਕੇ, ਝੂਠੇ ਕੋਲ ਬਹਾਏ

### 3

Make[1] the Ganges flow backward,[2] yogis, and you will gain
    a vision of God.

Take the cotton roll of love in your hand. Twist the axle,
    do not let it fall.

With the spindle of knowledge and the spinning wheel of
    meditation, make things spin backward.[3]

When Kumbhakaran goes back the way he came, the
    mystery of Lanka is created.[4]

Now that Ravan the ten-headed is destroyed and        5
    Lachhman remains, the unstruck music[5] sounds.

It is when this ecstatic state is attained through association
    with the guru that one is called theguru's servant.

Plunge into the circle of nectar[6] so as to become God.

### 4

Different,[1] topsy-turvy times have come, so I have
    discovered the beloved's secrets.[2]

Crows have started killing hawks, sparrows have brought
    down falcons.

Horses graze on rubbish heaps, donkeys are fed fine meal.

There is no affection among kinsfolk, or among senior and
    junior uncles.[3]

There is no harmony at all between fathers and sons, or    5
    mothers and daughters.[4]

The true get shoved aside, while the false are given seats
    of honor.

ਅਗਲੇ ਹੋ ਕੰਗਾਲੇ ਬੈਠੇ, ਪਿਛਲਿਆਂ ਫ਼ਰਸ਼ ਵਿਛਾਏ

ਭੁਰਿਆਂ ਵਾਲੇ ਰਾਜੇ ਕੀਤੇ, ਰਾਜਿਆਂ ਭੀਖ ਮੰਗਾਏ

ਬੁੱਲ੍ਹਿਆ ਹੁਕਮ ਹਜ਼ੂਰੋਂ ਆਇਆ, ਤਿਸ ਨੂੰ ਕੌਣ ਹਟਾਏ

੫

ਅੱਖਾਂ ਵਿਚ ਦਿਲਜਾਨੀ ਪਿਆਰਿਆ, ਕੇਹਾ ਚੇਟਕ ਲਾਇਆ ਈ

ਤੇਰੇ ਵਿਚ ਨਾ ਜ਼ਰਾ ਜੁਦਾਈ, ਸਾਥੋਂ ਆਪ ਛੁਪਾਇਆ ਈ

ਮਝੀਂ ਆਈਆਂ ਯਾਰ੍ਹਾ ਨਾ ਆਇਆ, ਚੂਕ ਬਿਰੋਂ ਡੁਲਾਇਆ ਈ

ਮੈਂ ਨੇੜੇ ਮੈਨੂੰ ਦੂਰ ਕਿਉਂ ਦਿਸਨੈਂ, ਸਾਥੋਂ ਆਪ ਛੁਪਾਇਆ ਈ

੫ ਵਿਚ ਮਿਸਰ ਦੇ ਵਾਂਗ ਜ਼ੁਲੈਖਾ, ਘੁੰਘਟ ਖੋਲ੍ਹ ਰੁਲਾਇਆ ਈ

ਸ਼ਹੁ ਬੁੱਲ੍ਹੇ ਦੇ ਸਿਰ ਪਰ ਬੁਰਕਾ, ਤੇਰੇ ਇਸ਼ਕ ਨਚਾਇਆ ਈ

Former leaders sit in destitution, while carpets are spread
    for those who were at the back.
Those who wore rough blankets have been made kings,
    while former kings beg for alms.
Bullha, the order came from the divine presence. Who can
    turn it aside?


5

My dearest beloved, what is this attraction that you have
    made my eyes feel?
There is not the slightest distance between you and me.
    You have hidden yourself from me.
The buffaloes have come, but my beloved has not come.
    Separation has consumed me and shaken me.
I am near, so why do you seem far away? You have hidden
    yourself from me.
You have raised your veil and made me wander, like     5
    Zulaikha in Egypt.[1]
With a burqa on his head, lord, Bullha has been made to
    dance[2] by your love.

੬

ਅਪਣੇ ਸੰਗ ਰਲਾਈਂ ਪਿਆਰੇ, ਅਪਣੇ ਸੰਗ ਰਲਾਈਂ

ਪਹਿਲੋਂ ਨੇਹੁੰ ਲਗਾਇਆ ਸੀ ਤੈਂ, ਆਪੇ ਚਾਈਂ ਚਾਈਂ

ਮੈਂ ਲਾਇਆ ਕਿ ਤੁੱਧ ਲਾਇਆ, ਅਪਣੀ ਓਰ ਨਿਭਾਈਂ

ਰਾਹ ਪਵਾਂ ਤਾਂ ਧਾੜੇ ਬੇਲੇ, ਜੰਗਲ ਲੱਖ ਬਲਾਈਂ

੫    ਬੁਕਟ ਚੀਤੇ ਚਿੱਤ ਮੁਚਿੱਤੇ, ਭੋਗਟ ਕਰਨ ਅਦਾਈਂ

ਤੇਰੇ ਪਾਰ ਜਗਾਤਰ ਚੜ੍ਹਿਆ, ਕੰਢੇ ਲੱਖ ਬਲਾਈਂ

ਹੌਲ ਦਿਲੇ ਦਾ ਥਰ ਥਰ ਕੰਬਦਾ, ਬੇੜਾ ਪਾਰ ਲੰਘਾਈਂ

ਕਰ ਲਈ ਬੰਦਗੀ ਰਬ ਸੱਚੇ ਦੀ, ਪਵਣ ਕਬੂਲ ਦੁਆਈਂ

ਬੁੱਲੇ ਸ਼ਾਹ ਨੂੰ ਸ਼ਹੁ ਦਾ ਮੁੱਖੜਾ, ਘੁੰਗਟ ਖੋਲ੍ਹ ਵਿਖਾਈਂ

੭

ਅਬ ਹਮ ਗੁੰਮ ਹੁਏ, ਪਰੇਮ ਨਗਰ ਕੇ ਸ਼ਹਿਰ

ਆਪਣੇ ਆਪ ਨੂੰ ਸੋਧ ਰਿਹਾ ਹੁੰ, ਨਾ ਸਿਰ ਹਾਥ ਨਾ ਪੈਰ

ਖੁਦੀ ਖੋਈ ਅਪਨਾ ਪਦ ਚੀਤਾ, ਤਬ ਹੋਈ ਗੱਲ ਖ਼ੈਰ

ਲੱਭੇ ਪਗੜੇ ਪਹਿਲੇ ਘਰ ਥੀਂ, ਕੌਣ ਕਰੇ ਨਿਰਵੈਰ

੫    ਬੁੱਲਾ ਸ਼ਹੁ ਹੈ ਦੋਹੀਂ ਜਹਾਨੀਂ, ਕੋਈ ਨਾ ਦਿਸਦਾ ਗ਼ੈਰ

12

## 6

Bring me close to you, my dearest, bring me close to you.

It was you who first fell in love and were full of delight.

Whether it was me or you who started it, keep faith with
me to the end.

When I set out on the road, there are robbers and thickets,
jungles and countless terrors.

The spotted leopards roar, as they delight in graceful            5
movements.[1]

On your side a flood[2] has arisen; there are many terrors on
the bank.

My heart is filled with fear and trembling. Please get my
boat across.

I have performed obeisance to God the true master; may
my prayers be accepted.

Remove your veil, and show Bullhe Shah the face of his
lord.

## 7

Now I am lost in the city of love.

I am setting myself in order, not just my head or arms
or legs.

When selfhood is lost and I bear my true rank in mind,
then all is well.

I was disgraced from the first; who can sort this out?[1]

It is the lord who exists in both worlds, Bullha; no other       5
is to be seen.

۸

ਅਬ ਕਿਉਂ ਸਾਜਨ ਚਿਰ ਲਾਇਓ ਰੇ

ਐਸੀ ਆਈ ਮਨ ਮੇਂ ਕਾ, ਦੁਖ ਸੁਖ ਸਭ ਵੰਜਾਇਓ ਰੇ
ਹਾਰ ਸ਼ਿੰਗਾਰ ਕੋ ਆਗ ਲਗਾਊਂ, ਘਟ ਉਪਰ ਢਾਂਡ ਮਚਾਇਓ ਰੇ

ਸੁਣਕੇ ਗਿਆਨ ਕੀ ਐਸੀ ਬਾਤਾਂ, ਨਾਮ ਨਿਸ਼ਾਨ ਸਭੀ ਅਣਘਾਤਾਂ
ਕੋਇਲ ਵਾਂਗੂੰ ਕੂਕਾਂ ਰਾਤਾਂ, ਤੈਂ ਅਜੇ ਵੀ ਤਰਸ ਨਾ ਆਇਓ ਰੇ

ਗਲ ਮਿਰਗਾਨੀ ਸੀਸ ਖਪਰੀਆ, ਦਰਸ਼ਨ ਕੀ ਭਿਖ ਮੰਗਣ ਚੜ੍ਹਿਆ
ਜੋਗਨ ਨਾਮ ਭਇਓ ਲਿਟ ਧਰਿਆ, ਅੰਗ ਬਿਭੂਤ ਰਮਾਇਓ ਰੇ

੫   ਇਸ਼ਕ ਮੁਅੱਜ਼ਨ ਬਾਂਗ ਸੁਣਾਈ, ਉੱਠ ਦੋੜਨ ਗੱਲ ਵਾਜਬ ਆਈ
ਕਰ ਕਰ ਸਜਦੇ ਘਰ ਵਲ ਧਾਈ, ਮੱਥੇ ਮਹਿਰਾਬ ਟਿਕਾਇਓ ਰੇ

ਪ੍ਰੇਮ ਨਗਰ ਦੇ ਉਲਟੇ ਚਾਲੇ, ਖ਼ੂਨੀ ਨੈਨ ਹੋਏ ਖ਼ੁਸ਼ਹਾਲੇ
ਆਪੇ ਆਣ ਫਸੇ ਵਿਚ ਜਾਲੇ, ਹਸ ਹਸ ਆਪ ਕੁਹਾਇਓ ਰੇ

ਦੁੱਖ ਬਿਰਹੋਂ ਨਾ ਹੋਣ ਪੁਰਾਣੇ, ਜਿਸ ਤਨ ਪੀੜਾਂ ਸੋ ਤਨ ਜਾਣੇ
ਅੰਦਰ ਝਿੜਕਾਂ ਬਾਹਰ ਤਾਅਨੇ, ਨੇਹੁੰ ਲੱਗਿਆਂ ਦੁੱਖ ਪਾਇਓ ਰੇ

ਮੈਨਾ ਮਾਲਣ ਰੋਂਦੀ ਪਕੜੀ, ਬਿਰਹੋਂ ਪਕੜੀ ਕਰਕੇ ਤਕੜੀ
ਇਕ ਮਰਨਾ ਦੂਜੀ ਜਗ ਦੀ ਫਕੜੀ, ਹੁਣ ਕੋਟ ਬੰਨਾ ਬਣ ਆਇਓ ਰੇ

ਬੁੱਲ੍ਹੂ ਸ਼ਹੁ ਸੰਗ ਪ੍ਰੀਤ ਲਗਾਈ, ਸੋਹਣੀ ਬਣ ਤਣ ਸਭ ਕੋਈ ਆਈ
ਵੇਖ ਕੇ ਸ਼ਾਹ ਇਨਾਇਤ ਸਾਈਂ, ਜੀ ਮੇਰਾ ਭਰ ਆਇਓ ਰੇ

14

## 8

Now why, beloved, have you taken so long?

What came into my mind to banish all ideas of sorrow and joy? I set my finery on fire. You have lit a blaze in my heart.

After hearing such words of wisdom, all names and forms are mysterious.[1] I cry out through the nights like a *koil* bird,[2] but you still have not felt pity.

Wearing a deerskin[3] and carrying a skull, I went to beg for a sight of you. Calling myself a yogini, I wore my hair long and rubbed ashes on my body.

Love acted as muezzin and gave the call to prayer. They       5
get up and run there, since it is their religious duty. They perform their prostrations, then race home, where you have made your forehead their *mihrab*.[4]

Things are the other way round in the city of love. Blood-filled eyes become happy. It is you who trap yourself in the net, then laugh as you have yourself slaughtered.

The pains of separation do not get old. It is the body that has the pain that knows about it. Scolding at home and taunts outside are the sorrows I have found through falling in love.

Caught by the gardener's wife, the mynah weeps. Caught by separation, she is tormented. First there is death, and there is also disgrace in the world. What sort of bridegroom have you come as now?

Bullha, I have fallen in love with the lord. Everyone has come beautifully adorned. After seeing my lord Shah Inayat, my heart is filled with joy.

੯

ਅਬ ਲਗਨ ਲਗੀ ਕੀ ਕਰੀਏ, ਨਾ ਜੀ ਸਕੀਏ ਤੇ ਨਾ ਮਰੀਏ

ਤੁਮ ਸੁਣੋ ਹਮਾਰੀ ਬੈਨਾ, ਮੋਹੇ ਰਾਤ ਦਿਨੇ ਨਹੀਂ ਚੈਨਾ
ਹੁਣ ਪੀ ਬਿਨ ਪਲਕ ਨਾ ਸਰੀਏ

ਇਹ ਅਗਨ ਬਿਰਹੋਂ ਦੀ ਜਰੇ, ਕੋਈ ਹਮਰੀ ਪੀਤ ਨਿਵਾਰੇ
ਬਿਨ ਦਰਸ਼ਨ ਕੈਸੇ ਤਰੀਏ

ਬੁੱਲਾ ਪਈ ਮੁਸੀਬਤ ਭਾਰੀ, ਕੋਈ ਕਰੇ ਹਮਾਰੀ ਕਾਰੀ
ਇਹ ਅਜਰ ਦੁੱਖ ਕਿਵੇਂ ਜਰੀਏ

੧੦

ਅੰਮਾਂ ਬਾਬੇ ਦੀ ਭਲਿਆਈ, ਉਹ ਹੁਣ ਕੰਮ ਅਸਾਡੇ ਆਈ

ਅੰਮਾਂ ਬਾਬਾ ਚੋਰ ਘੁਰੋਂ ਦੇ, ਪੁੱਤਰ ਦੀ ਵਡਿਆਈ

ਦਾਟੇ ਉੱਤੋਂ ਗੁੱਤ ਬਿਗੁੱਤੀ, ਘਰ ਘਰ ਪਈ ਲੜਾਈ

ਅਸਾਂ ਕਜ਼ੀਏ ਤਦ ਹੀ ਜਾਲੇ, ਜਦਾਂ ਕਟਕ ਉਨ੍ਹਾਂ ਟਰਕਾਈ

੫ ਖਾਏ ਖ਼ੈਰਾ ਤੇ ਫਾਟੀਏ ਜ਼ੁੰਮਾ, ਉਲਟੀ ਦਸਤਕ ਲਾਈ

ਬੁੱਲੂ ਤੋਤੇ ਮਾਰ ਬਾਗ਼ਾਂ ਥੀਂ ਕੱਢੇ, ਉੱਲੂ ਰਹਿਣ ਉਸ ਜਾਈ

## 9

Now I have fallen in love. What can I do? I cannot live,
and cannot die.

Listen to my lament. I have no peace by night or day. Now
I cannot endure for an instant without my beloved.

The fire of separation consumes me. Preserve me,
someone, from my love! How can I be saved without
seeing him?

Bullha, I am in great trouble. May someone come to my
aid. How can I endure this insupportable pain?

## 10

Mother's and Father's[1] good deeds now benefit us.

Mother and Father were the original thieves. Now the son
is great.

The squabbling started over a grain.[2] Every house was
filled with strife.

We suffered this quarreling from the very moment they
stole the wheat.

Khaira profits and Jumma[3] gets beaten; the wrong person    5
gets the summons.

The parrots are driven with blows from the gardens, while
the owls stay where they were.

## ੧੧

ਅਲੜ ਅੱਲੂ ਰੱਤਾ ਦਿਲ ਮੇਰਾ, ਮੈਨੂੰ ਬੇ ਦੀ ਖ਼ਬਰ ਨਾ ਕਾਈ

ਬੇ ਪੜ੍ਹਿਆਂ ਮੈਨੂੰ ਸਮਝ ਨਾ ਆਵੇ, ਲੱਜ਼ਤ ਅਲੜ ਦੀ ਆਈ

ਫ਼ਰਕ ਐਨ ਤੇ ਗ਼ੈਨ ਨਾ ਜਾਣਾਂ, ਇਹ ਗੱਲ ਅਲੜ ਸੁਝਾਈ

ਬੁੱਲ੍ਹਿਆ ਕੋਲ ਅਲੜ ਦੇ ਪੂਰੇ, ਜਿਹੜੇ ਦਿਲ ਦੀ ਕਰਨ ਸਫ਼ਾਈ

## ੧੨

ਆ ਸੱਜਣ ਗਲ ਲੱਗ ਅਸਾਡੇ, ਕੇਹਾ ਝੇੜਾ ਲਾਇਓ ਈ
ਸੁੱਤਿਆਂ ਬੈਠਿਆਂ ਕੁਝ ਨਹੀਂ ਡਿੱਠਾ, ਜਾਗਦਿਆਂ ਸ਼ਹੁ ਪਾਇਓ ਈ

'ਕੁੰਮ ਬਿਇਜ਼ਨੀ' ਸ਼ਮਸ ਬੋਲੇ, ਉਲਟਾ ਕਰ ਲਟਕਾਇਓ ਈ
ਇਸ਼ਕਨ ਇਸ਼ਕਨ ਜੱਗ ਵਿੱਚ ਹੋਈਆਂ, ਦੇ ਦਿਲਾਸ ਬਿਠਾਇਓ ਈ

ਮੈਂ ਤੈਂ ਕਾਈ ਨਹੀਂ ਜੁਦਾਈ, ਫਿਰ ਕਿਉਂ ਆਪ ਛੁਪਾਇਓ ਈ
ਮਝੀਆਂ ਆਈਆਂ ਮਾਹੀ ਨਹੀਂ ਆਇਆ, ਰੁਕ ਬਿਰਹੋਂ ਡੁਲਾਇਓ ਈ

ਏਸ ਇਸ਼ਕ ਦੇ ਵੇਖੇ ਕਾਰੇ, ਯੂਸਫ਼ ਖੂਹ ਪਵਾਇਓ ਈ
ਵਾਂਗ ਜ਼ੁਲੈਖ਼ਾ ਵਿਚ ਮਿਸਰ ਦੇ, ਘੁੰਗਟ ਖੋਲ੍ਹ ਰੁਲਾਇਓ ਈ

18

## 11

*Alif*[1] is for Allah, in whom my heart is steeped. About *be*
    I know nothing at all.

I understand nothing from studying *be*. My delight has
    been in *alif*.

I know no difference between *'ain* and *ġhain*.[2] This is what
    *alif* has made clear.

Bullha, those who cleanse their hearts are perfect in their
    profession of *alif*.

## 12

Come, beloved, and embrace me. What is this quarrel you
    have started? When sleeping or sitting I saw nothing,
    but when awake I found the lord.

When Shams said, *Arise by my permission,*[1] it was you who
    had him hanged upside down. There have been many
    women disgraced for love in the world. It was you who
    encouraged and stationed me here.

There is no separation between me and you, so why have
    you hidden yourself? The buffaloes[2] have come; the
    beloved has not come. It is you who have fanned the
    flames of separation and driven me to distraction.

I have seen what this love has done, and how you had
    Yusuf[3] put into the well. You have lifted your veil
    and ruined me, like Zulaikha in Egypt.

੫  'ਰੱਬਿ ਅਰਿਨੀ' ਮੂਸਾ ਬੋਲੇ, ਤਦ ਕੋਹ-ਤੂਰ ਡੁਲਾਇਓ ਈ
'ਲਨ ਤਰਾਨੀ' ਝਿੜਕਾਂ ਵਾਲਾ, ਆਪੇ ਹੁਕਮ ਸੁਣਾਇਓ ਈ

ਇਸ਼ਕ ਦਿਵਾਨੇ ਕੀਤਾ ਫ਼ਾਨੀ, ਦਿਲ ਯਤੀਮ ਬਣਾਇਓ ਈ
ਬੁੱਲ੍ਹਾ ਸ਼ਹੁ ਘਰ ਵਸਿਆ ਆ ਕੇ, ਸ਼ਾਹ ਇਨਾਇਤ ਪਾਇਓ ਈ

## ੧੩

ਆ ਮਿਲ ਯਾਰ ਸਾਰ ਲੈ ਮੇਰੀ, ਮੇਰੀ ਜਾਨ ਦੁਖਾਂ ਨੇ ਘੇਰੀ

ਅੰਦਰ ਖ਼ਾਬ ਵਿਛੋੜਾ ਹੋਇਆ, ਖ਼ਬਰ ਨਾ ਪੈਂਦੀ ਤੇਰੀ

ਸੁੰਜੀ ਬਣ ਵਿਚ ਲੁੱਟੀ ਸਾਈਆਂ, ਸੁਰ ਪਲੰਗ ਨੇ ਘੇਰੀ

ਮੁੱਲਾਂ ਕਾਜ਼ੀ ਰਾਹ ਬਤਾਵਟ, ਦੇਣ ਭਰਮ ਦੇ ਫੇਰੇ

੫  ਇਹ ਤਾਂ ਠੱਗ ਜਗਤ ਦੇ ਸ਼ੀਵਰ, ਲਾਵਟ ਜਾਲ ਚੁਫੇਰੇ

ਕਰਮ ਸ਼ਰ੍ਹਾ ਦੇ ਧਰਮ ਬਤਾਵਟ, ਸੰਗਲ ਪਾਵਟ ਪੈਰੀ

ਜ਼ਾਤ ਮਜ਼ਹਬ ਇਹ ਇਸ਼ਕ ਨਾ ਪੁਛਦਾ, ਇਸ਼ਕ ਸ਼ਰ੍ਹਾ ਦਾ ਵੈਰੀ

ਨਦੀਓਂ ਪਾਰ ਮੁਲਕ ਸਜਨ ਦਾ, ਲਹਿਵ ਲਾਅਬ ਨੇ ਘੇਰੀ

ਸਤਿਗੁਰ ਬੇੜੀ ਫੜੀ ਖਲੋਤੇ, ਤੈਂ ਕਿਉਂ ਲਾਈਆ ਦੇਰੀ

੧੦  ਬੁੱਲ੍ਹਾ ਸ਼ਾਹ ਸ਼ਹੁ ਤੈਨੂੰ ਮਿਲਸੀ, ਦਿਲ ਨੂੰ ਦੇਹ ਦਲੇਰੀ

When Moses said, *Show me, lord*, you made Mount Sinai    5
    tremble. With the reprimand *You shall not see me*,[4]
    you uttered your command.
My mad love has destroyed me, you have orphaned my
    heart. Bullha, the lord came to live in your house, once
    you found Shah Inayat.

## 13

Come, my love, and notice me. My soul is beset by
    suffering.
I dream that we have become separated. I get no news
    of you.
I am desolate and destroyed in the jungle, lord. I am
    surrounded by wild boars and leopards.
The mullah and the *qazi* show me the road, setting me in
    a circuit of confusion.
But these robbers are the world's fowlers, who spread    5
    their nets everywhere.
They preach the duties and actions required by the law,
    and shackle my feet in chains.
Love does not ask about caste or religion, love is the
    enemy of the law.
The land of my beloved lies across the river, but I am
    caught in worldly pleasures.[1]
The boat is held still by the true guru, so why do you
    delay?
Bullha Shah, the lord will come to you, so your heart    10
    should be encouraged.

ਪ੍ਰੀਤਮ ਪਾਸ ਤੇ ਟੇਲੇਂ ਕਿਸ ਨੂੰ, ਭੁੱਲ ਗਿਓਂ ਸਿਖ਼ਰ ਦੁਪਿਹਰੀ

## ੧੪

ਆਓ ਸਈਓ ਰਲ ਦਿਓ ਨੀ ਵਧਾਈ, ਮੈਂ ਬਰ ਪਾਇਆ ਰਾਂਝਾ ਮਾਹੀ

ਅੱਜ ਤਾਂ ਰੋਜ਼ ਮੁਬਾਰਕ ਚੜ੍ਹਿਆ, ਰਾਂਝਾ ਸਾਡੇ ਵਿਹੜੇ ਵੜਿਆ
ਹਥ ਖੁੰਡੀ ਮੋਢੇ ਕੰਬਲ ਧਰਿਆ, ਚਾਕਾਂ ਵਾਲੀ ਸ਼ਕਲ ਬਟਾਈ

ਮੁਕਟ ਪਿਆ ਗਊਆਂ ਵਿਚ ਰੁਲਦਾ, ਜੰਗਲ ਜੂਹਾਂ ਵਿਚ ਕਿਸ ਮੁਲ ਦਾ
ਹੈ ਕੋਈ ਅੱਲ੍ਹੂ ਦੇ ਵਲ ਭੁਲਦਾ, ਅਸਲ ਹਕੀਕਤ ਖ਼ਬਰ ਨਾ ਕਾਈ

ਬੁੱਲ੍ਹੇ ਸ਼ਾਹ ਇਕ ਸੌਦਾ ਕੀਤਾ, ਪੀਤਾ ਜ਼ਹਿਰ ਪਿਆਲਾ ਪੀਤਾ
ਨਾ ਕੁਝ ਲਾਹਾ ਟੋਟਾ ਲੀਤਾ, ਦਰਦ ਦੁੱਖਾਂ ਦੀ ਗਠੜੀ ਚਾਈ

## ੧੫

ਆਓ ਫ਼ਕੀਰੋ ਮੇਲੇ ਚਲੀਏ, ਆਰਫ਼ ਕਾ ਸੁਣ ਵਾਜਾ ਰੇ

ਅਨਹਦ ਸ਼ਬਦ ਸੁਣੈ ਬਹੁਰੰਗੀ, ਤਜੀਏ ਭੇਖ ਬਿਆਜਾ ਰੇ

ਅਨਹਦ ਵਾਜਾ ਸਰਬ ਮਿਲਾਪੀ, ਨਿਰਵੈਰੀ ਸਰਨਾਜਾ ਰੇ

The beloved is beside you, so who are you looking for? It is
high noon, but you have lost your way.

14

Gather together, girls, and congratulate me. I have found
my bridegroom, my dear Ranjha.

Today a blessed day has dawned: Ranjha has entered my
courtyard. With a staff in his hand and a blanket
around his shoulders, he has taken the form of a
herdsman.

The diadem has fallen among cattle and is tossed about.
What value does it have in the jungle and pastures?
Are people so confused about God that they have no
awareness of true reality?[1]

Bullha Shah made a deal and drank the cup of love's
poison. He had no profit or loss, but took up a bundle
of pain and grief.

15

Come, fakirs, let us go to the fair, and listen to the music
of the adept.[1]

Listen to the many-hued unstruck music[2] and abandon
your robe of falseness.

The unstruck instrument is friendly to all, the pipe has no
hostility.

ਮੇਲੇ ਬਾਝੋਂ ਮੇਲਾ ਐਤਰ, ਰੁੜੁ ਗਿਆ ਮੂਲ ਵਿਹਾਜਾ ਰੇ

੫  ਕਠਨ ਫਕੀਰੀ ਰਸਤਾ ਆਸ਼ਕ, ਕਾਇਮ ਕਰੋ ਮਨ ਭਾਜਾ ਰੇ

ਬੰਦਾ ਰਬ ਥਿਓ ਇਕ ਬੁੱਲੂ, ਪੜਾ ਜਹਾਨ ਬਿਰਾਜਾ ਰੇ


## ੧੬
ਐਸਾ ਜਗਿਆ ਗਿਆਨ ਪਲੀਤਾ

ਨਾਹਿਮ ਹਿੰਦੂ ਨਾ ਤੁਰਕ ਜ਼ਰੂਰੀ, ਨਾਮ ਇਸ਼ਕ ਦੀ ਹੈ ਮਨਜ਼ੂਰੀ
ਆਸ਼ਕ ਨੇ ਹਰ ਜੀਤਾ, ਐਸਾ ਜਗਿਆ ਗਿਆਨ ਪਲੀਤਾ

ਵੇਖੋ ਠੱਗਾਂ ਸ਼ੋਰ ਮਚਾਇਆ, ਜੰਮਣਾ ਮਰਨਾ ਚਾ ਬਣਾਇਆ
ਮੂਰਖ ਭੁੱਲੇ ਰੌਲਾ ਪਾਇਆ, ਜਿਸ ਨੂੰ ਆਸ਼ਕ ਜ਼ਾਹਰ ਕੀਤਾ

ਬੁੱਲਿਆ ਇਸ਼ਕ ਦੀ ਬਾਤ ਨਿਆਰੀ, ਪ੍ਰੇਮ ਵਾਲਿਆਂ ਬੜੀ ਕਰਾਰੀ
ਮੂਰਖ ਦੀ ਮੱਤ ਐਵੇਂ ਮਾਰੀ, ਵਾਕ ਸੁਖਨ ਚੁੱਪ ਕੀਤਾ


## ੧੭
ਇਸ਼ਕ ਅਸਾਂ ਨਾਲ ਕੇਹੀ ਕੀਤੀ, ਲੋਕ ਮਰੇਂਦੇ ਤਾਮਨੇ

ਦਿਲ ਦੀ ਵੇਦਨ ਕੋਈ ਨਾ ਜਾਣੇ, ਅੰਦਰ ਦੇਸ ਬੇਗਾਨੇ
ਜਿਸ ਨੂੰ ਚਾਟ ਅਮਰ ਦੀ ਹੋਵੇ, ਸੋਈ ਅਮਰ ਪਛਾਣੇ
ਏਸ ਇਸ਼ਕ ਦੀ ਔਖੀ ਘਾਟੀ, ਜੋ ਚੜ੍ਹਿਆ ਸੋ ਜਾਣੇ

Without union the fair is no good; both capital and
　　interest are squandered.

Fakirhood is difficult, but it is the path of the lover, so　　　5
　　make your restless mind settle.

The creature and the lord become one, Bullha, while the
　　world is ungoverned.

## 16

The wick of true knowledge is lit like this.

For sure I am no Hindu or Turk,[1] it is the name of love
　　to which I adhere. The lover is conquered by God.
　　The wick of true knowledge is lit like this.

See what a clamor the robbers[2] have raised, how they have
　　created birth and death. The fool makes a loud fuss
　　when lost in confusion, which the lover exposes.

Bullha, love is something unique; the followers of love
　　are very steadfast. The fool loses his wits for nothing.
　　True communication lies in silence.

## 17

What has love done to me? People utter reproaches.

No one knows the pain in my heart; I am a stranger in
　　my own land. Only someone who has tasted the divine
　　command knows what it means. The mountain of love
　　is hard to ascend; only someone who has climbed it
　　knows about it.

ਆਤਸ਼ ਇਸ਼ਕ ਫ਼ਰਾਕ ਤੇਰੇ ਦੀ, ਪਲ ਵਿਚ ਸਾੜ ਵਿਖਾਈਆਂ
ਏਸ ਇਸ਼ਕ ਦੇ ਸਾੜੇ ਕੋਲੋਂ, ਜਗ ਵਿਚ ਦਿਆਂ ਦੁਹਾਈਆਂ
ਜਿਸ ਤਨ ਲੱਗੇ ਸੋ ਤਨ ਜਾਣੇ, ਦੂਜਾ ਕੋਈ ਨਾ ਜਾਣੇ

ਇਸ਼ਕ ਕਸਾਈ ਜੇਹੀ ਕੀਤੀ, ਰਹਿ ਗਈ ਖ਼ਬਰ ਨਾ ਕਾਈ
ਇਸ਼ਕ ਚੁਆਤੀ ਲਾਈ ਛਾਤੀ, ਫੇਰ ਨਾ ਝਾਤੀ ਪਾਈ
ਮਾਪਿਆਂ ਕੋਲੋਂ ਛੁਪ ਛੁਪ ਰੋਵਾਂ, ਕਰ ਕਰ ਲੱਖ ਬਹਾਨੇ

੫ ਹਿਜਰ ਤੇਰੇ ਨੇ ਝੱਲੀ ਕਰਕੇ, ਕਮਲੀ ਨਾਮ ਧਰਾਇਆ
'ਸ਼ੁੰਮਨ ਬੁਕਮਨੁ ਉਮਯੁਨ' ਹੋ ਕੇ, ਅਪਣਾ ਵਕਤ ਲੰਘਾਇਆ
ਕਰ ਹੁਣ ਨਜ਼ਰ ਕਰਮ ਦੀ ਸਾਈਆਂ, ਨਾ ਕਰ ਜ਼ੋਰ ਧਿੰਗਾਣੇ

ਹੱਸ ਬੁਲਾਵਾ ਤੇਰਾ ਜਾਨੀ, ਯਾਦ ਕਰਾਂ ਹਰ ਵੇਲੇ
ਪਲ ਪਲ ਦੇ ਵਿਚ ਦਰਦ ਜੁਦਾਈ, ਇਸ਼ਕ ਮਰੋੜੈ ਸੇਲੇ
ਰੋ ਰੋ ਯਾਦ ਕਰਾਂ ਦਿਨ ਰਾਤੀਂ, ਪਿਛਲੇ ਵਕਤ ਵਿਹਾਣੇ

ਇਸ਼ਕ ਤੇਰਾ ਦਰਕਾਰ ਅਸਾਂ ਨੂੰ, ਹਰ ਵੇਲੇ ਹਰ ਹੀਲੇ
ਪਾਕ ਰਸੂਲ ਮੁਹੰਮਦ ਸਾਹਿਬ, ਮੇਰੇ ਖ਼ਾਸ ਵਸੀਲੇ
ਬੁੱਲ੍ਹੇ ਸ਼ਾਹ ਜੇ ਮਿਲੇ ਪਿਆਰਾ, ਲੱਖ ਕਰਾਂ ਸ਼ੁਕਰਾਨੇ

੧੮
ਇਸ਼ਕ ਹਕੀਕੀ ਨੇ ਮੁੱਠੀ ਕੁੜੇ, ਮੈਨੂੰ ਦੱਸੋ ਪੀਆ ਦਾ ਦੇਸ

ਮਾਪਿਆਂ ਦੇ ਘਰ ਬਾਲ ਅਵਾਣੀ, ਪੀਤ ਲਗਾ ਕੇ ਲੁੱਟੀ ਕੁੜੇ

Love is a fire that in my separation from you has consumed
me in an instant. Because of the burning pain of this
love, I utter appeals for help in the world. It is the
body that has experienced the pain that knows about
it; no one else does.

Love has treated me like a butcher, and I have lost all
awareness. Love applied its brand to my breast, then
did not glance at me. I hide my tears from my parents,
making up endless false explanations.

Separation from you has made me mad, and has labeled          5
me "crazy girl." I spend my time as one who is *deaf,
dumb, and blind*.[1] Look with favor on me now, lord,
do not be violent and forceful.

Your summons made me happy, beloved. I remember
you all the time. At every moment I suffer the pain of
separation, and love spears me. Day and night I weep
and remember you; those former times are over.

Your love is what we need, at every time and in every
way. The holy apostle Muhammad is my special
intercessor.[2] Bullhe Shah, if the beloved comes to me,
I will offer a hundred thousand thanks.

## 18

Real love[1] has destroyed me, my girl. Show me the land of
my beloved.

In my parents' house I was an innocent girl, but when I fell
in love I was ruined, my girl.

ਮੱਤਕ ਮਾਅਨੇ ਕਨਜ਼ ਕਦੂਰੀ, ਮੈਂ ਪੜ੍ਹ ਪੜ੍ਹ ਇਲਮ ਵਗੁੱਚੀ ਕੁੜੇ

ਨਮਾਜ਼ ਰੋਜ਼ਾ ਓਹਨਾਂ ਕੀ ਕਰਨਾ, ਜਿਨ੍ਹਾਂ ਪ੍ਰੇਮ ਸੁਰਾਹੀ ਲੁੱਟੀ ਕੁੜੇ

੫    ਬੁੱਲ੍ਹੂ ਸ਼ਹੁ ਦੀ ਮਜਲਸ ਬਹਿ ਕੇ, ਸਭ ਕਰਨੀ ਮੇਰੀ ਛੁੱਟੀ ਕੁੜੇ

੧੯

ਇਸ਼ਕ ਦੀ ਨਵੀਓਂ ਨਵੀਂ ਬਹਾਰ

ਜਾਂ ਮੈਂ ਸਬਕ ਇਸ਼ਕ ਦਾ ਪੜ੍ਹਿਆ, ਮਸਜਦ ਕੋਲੋਂ ਜੀਉੜਾ ਡਰਿਆ
ਦੈਰੇ ਜਾ ਠਾਕਰ ਦੇ ਵੜਿਆ, ਜਿੱਥੇ ਵੱਜਦਾ ਨਾਦ ਹਜ਼ਾਰ

ਜਾਂ ਮੈਂ ਰਮਜ਼ ਇਸ਼ਕ ਦੀ ਪਾਈ, ਮੈਨਾ ਤੋਤਾ ਮਾਰ ਗਵਾਈ
ਅੰਦਰ ਬਾਹਰ ਹੋਈ ਸਫ਼ਾਈ, ਜਿਤ ਵਲ ਵੇਖਾਂ ਯਾਰੋ ਯਾਰ

ਹੀਰ ਰਾਂਝੇ ਦੇ ਹੋ ਗਏ ਮੇਲੇ, ਭੁੱਲੀ ਹੀਰ ਢੁੰਡੇਂਦੀ ਬੇਲੇ
ਰਾਂਝਾ ਯਾਰ ਬੁੱਕਲ ਵਿਚ ਖੇਲੇ, ਮੈਨੂੰ ਸੁਧ ਰਹੀ ਨਾ ਸਾਰ

੫    ਬੇਦ ਕੁਰਆਨਾਂ ਪੜ੍ਹ ਪੜ੍ਹ ਥੱਕੇ, ਸਜਦੇ ਕਰਦਿਆਂ ਘਸ ਗਏ ਮੱਥੇ
ਨਾ ਰਬ ਤੀਰਥ ਨਾ ਰਬ ਮੱਕੇ, ਜਿਸ ਪਾਇਆ ਤਿਸ ਨੂਰ ਅਨਵਾਰ

I have studied logic and semantics, the *Kanz* and the
    *Qudūrī,*[2] but all this learning has destroyed me, my
    girl.
What use are prayer and fasting to those who have drained
    the flask of love, my girl?
Bullha, when I sat in the circle of the lord, I became free     5
    of all observances, my girl.

## 19

The spring of love is ever new.
When I studied the lesson of love, my heart became afraid
    of the mosque. I went to enter the temple of the lord,
    where a thousand conches are blown.
When I discovered the mystery of love, I destroyed the
    mynah and the parrot.[1] I became purified inside and
    out; no matter where I look, only the beloved is there.
Meetings have taken place between Hir and Ranjha. Hir
    is lost, searching in the river glade. My lover Ranjha
    plays inside the folds of my scarf;[2] I have lost all
    conscious awareness.
People become exhausted reciting Vedas and Qur'ans.     5
    From prostrating themselves, their foreheads have
    become worn. The lord is not in the sacred bathing
    places, nor is the lord in Mecca. Whoever finds him is
    filled with brilliant light.

ਚੁਕ ਮੁਸੱਲਾ ਭੰਨ ਸੁੱਟ ਲੋਟਾ, ਨਾ ਫੜ ਤਸਬੀ ਆਸਾ ਸੋਟਾ
ਆਸ਼ਕ ਕਹਿੰਦੇ ਦੇ ਦੇ ਹੋਕਾ, ਤਰਕ ਹਲਾਲੋਂ ਖਾਹ ਮੁਰਦਾਰ

ਉਮਰ ਗਵਾਈ ਵਿਚ ਮਸੀਤੀ, ਅੰਦਰ ਭਰਿਆ ਨਾਲ ਪਲੀਤੀ
ਕਦੇ ਨਮਾਜ਼ ਤੌਹੀਦ ਨਾ ਕੀਤੀ, ਹੁਣ ਕੀ ਕਰਨਾ ਏਂ ਸ਼ੋਰ ਪੁਕਾਰ

ਇਸ਼ਕ ਭੁਲਾਇਆ ਸਜਦਾ ਤੇਰਾ, ਹੁਣ ਕਿਉਂ ਐਵੇਂ ਪਾਵੇਂ ਝੇੜਾ
ਬੁੱਲ੍ਹਾ ਹੁੰਦਾ ਚੁੱਪ ਬਥੇਰਾ, ਇਸ਼ਕ ਕਰੇਂਦਾ ਮਾਰੋ ਮਾਰ


### ੨੦

ਇਹ ਅਚਰਜ ਸਾਧੂ ਕੌਟ ਕਹਾਵੇ, ਛਿਨ ਛਿਨ ਰੂਪ ਕਿੰਤੇ ਬਟ ਆਵੇ

ਮੱਕਾ ਲੰਕਾ ਸਹਿਦੇਵ ਕੇ ਭੇਦ, ਦੋਊ ਕੋ ਏਕ ਬਤਾਵੇ

ਜਬ ਜੋਗੀ ਤੁਮ ਵਸਲ ਕਰੋਗੇ, ਬਾਂਗਾ ਕਹੇ ਭਾਵੇਂ ਨਾਦ ਬਜਾਵੇ

ਭਗਤੀ ਭਗਤ ਨਤਾਰੋ ਨਾਹੀਂ, ਭਗਤ ਸੋਈ ਜਿਹੜਾ ਮਨ ਭਾਵੇ

੫    ਹਰ ਪਰਗਟ ਪਰਗਟ ਹੀ ਦੇਖੇ, ਕਿਆ ਪੰਡਤ ਫਿਰ ਭੇਦ ਸੁਨਾਵੇ

ਧਿਆਨ ਧਰੋ ਇਹ ਕਾਫ਼ਰ ਨਾਹੀਂ, ਕਿਆ ਹਿੰਦੂ ਕਿਆ ਤੁਰਕ ਕਹਾਵੇ

ਜਬ ਦੇਖੂੰ ਤਬ ਓਹੀ ਓਹੀ, ਬੁੱਲ੍ਹਾ ਸ਼ਾਹੁ ਹਰ ਰੰਗ ਸਮਾਵੇ

Burn your prayer rug and break up your ablutions pot;
    do not pick up your rosary, your staff, or your stick.
    Lovers loudly proclaim, "Give up halal food and eat
    dead meat."[3]
Your life has been wasted in mosques, while inside you
    are full of pollution. You have never performed with
    proper intent a prayer to God's unity, so why create
    this loud clamor now?
Love has made me forget to prostrate myself to you. Why
    do you start this quarrel now? However long Bullha's
    silence lasts, love drives me on with constant blows.

## 20

What[1] is this wonderful holy man called? At each moment
    he comes in many forms.
Lanka and Mecca are mysteries of Sahadev,[2] who
    demonstrates that the two are one.
Oh yogi, when you are united with God, you give the call
    to prayer though you sound the conch.
Do not distinguish devotees by their different devotions.
    The true devotee is the one who pleases you.
Behold, God is openly revealed, whatever the pandit may    5
    then proclaim from the Veda.
If you attend carefully, there are no unbelievers, whether
    they are called Hindu or Turk.[3]
Whenever I look, only he, only he exists. Bullha, the lord
    is contained in every color.

२१

ਇਹ ਦੁੱਖ ਜਾ ਕਹੂੰ ਕਿਸ ਆਗੇ, ਰੁਮ ਰੁਮ ਘਾਉ ਪਰੇਮ ਕੇ ਲਾਗੇ

ਸਿਕਤ ਸਿਕਤ ਹੋ ਰੈਟ ਵਿਹਾਟੀ, ਹਮਰੇ ਪੀਆ ਨੇ ਪੀੜ ਨਾ ਜਾਟੀ
ਕਿਆ ਜਾਟੂੰ ਕਿਆ ਪੀ ਮਨ ਭਾਟੀ

ਬਿਲਕਤ ਬਿਲਕਤ ਰੈਟ ਵਿਹਾਸੀ, ਹਾਸੇ ਦੀ ਗੱਲ ਪੈ ਗਈ ਫਾਸੀ
ਇਕ ਮਰਨਾ ਦੂਜਾ ਜਗ ਦੀ ਹਾਸੀ

ਕਰਤ ਫਿਰਤ ਮੋਹੀ ਰੇ ਮੋਹੀ, ਕੋਂਟ ਕਰੇ ਮੋਹੀ ਸੇ ਦਿਲਜੋਈ
ਸ਼ਾਮ ਪੀਆ ਮੈਂ ਦੇਤੀ ਹੁੰ ਧਰੋਈ

५  ਦੁਖ ਜਗ ਕੇ ਮੋਹੇ ਪੂਛਟ ਆਏ, ਨਾ ਪੀਆ ਆਏ ਨਾ ਪੀਆ ਜਾਏ
ਇਹ ਦੁਖ ਜਾ ਕਹੂੰ ਕਿਸ ਜਾਏ

ਬੁੱਲ੍ਹਾ ਸ਼ਾਹ ਘਰ ਆ ਪਿਆਰਿਆ, ਇੱਕ ਘੜੀ ਕੋ ਕਰਨ ਗੁਜ਼ਾਰਿਆ
ਤਨ ਮਨ ਧਨ ਜੀਅ ਤੋਂ ਪਰ ਵਾਰਿਆ


२२

ਇਕ ਅਲਫ਼ ਪੜ੍ਹੋ ਛੁਟਕਾਰਾ ਏ

ਇਕ ਅਲਫ਼ੋਂ ਦੋ ਤਿਨ ਚਾਰ ਹੋਏ, ਫਿਰ ਲੱਖ ਕਰੋੜ ਹਜ਼ਾਰ ਹੋਏ
ਫਿਰ ਉਥੋਂ ਬਾਝ ਸ਼ੁਮਾਰ ਹੋਏ, ਹਿਕ ਅਲਫ਼ ਦਾ ਨੁਕਤਾ ਨਿਆਰਾ ਏ

ਕਿਉਂ ਪੜ੍ਹਨਾ ਐਂ ਗੱਡ ਕਿਤਾਬਾਂ ਦੀ, ਸਿਰ ਚਾਨੈਂ ਪੰਡ ਅਜ਼ਾਬਾਂ ਦੀ
ਹੁਣ ਹੋਇਓ ਸ਼ਕਲ ਜਲਾਦਾਂ ਦੀ, ਅੱਗੇ ਪੈਂਡਾ ਮੁਸ਼ਕਲ ਭਾਰਾ ਏ

## 21

To whom shall I go and tell of this pain? Every pore of my
body is marked by the wounds of love.

The night has passed in yearning. My beloved does not
know my pain. How should I know if I please him?

My night will be spent sobbing. Laughter is like a noose
around my neck. Besides death, there is also the
laughter of the world.

I roam about, saying, "I am lost, oh, I am lost." Who will
console this lost creature? I appeal for help to my
dark-skinned beloved.

The pains of the world came to question me. My love does     5
not come, my love does not go. To whom shall I go and
tell of this pain?

Bullha Shah says: Come home, beloved. Each moment
that you come this way is a century for me. I sacrifice
my body and soul, my possessions, and my life to you.

## 22

Study only the one letter *alif* [1] to gain deliverance.

From the one *alif* come two, three, and four; then come
thousands, lakhs, and crores. The numbers then
become infinite. How strange the point of a single
*alif* is!

Why study loads of books and put bundles of troubles
on your head? Now your appearance is as grim as
an executioner, and the way that lies before you is
dreadfully difficult.

ਬਣ ਹਾਫ਼ਜ਼ ਹਿਫ਼ਜ਼ ਕੁਰਾਨ ਕਰੋ, ਪੜ੍ਹ ਪੜ੍ਹ ਕੇ ਸਾਫ਼ ਜ਼ਬਾਨ ਕਰੋ
ਫਿਰ ਨਿਅਮਤ ਵਿੱਚ ਧਿਆਨ ਕਰੋ, ਮਨ ਫਿਰਦਾ ਜਿਉਂ ਹਲਕਾਰਾ ਏ

੫    ਬੁੱਲ੍ਹਾ ਬੀ ਬੋਤੂ ਦਾ ਬੋਇਆ ਸੀ, ਉਹ ਬਿਰਛ ਵੱਡਾ ਜਾਂ ਹੋਇਆ ਸੀ
ਜਦ ਬਿਰਛ ਉਹ ਫ਼ਾਨੀ ਹੋਇਆ ਸੀ, ਫਿਰ ਰਹਿ ਗਿਆ ਬੀ ਇਕਾਹਰਾ ਏ

## ੨੩

ਇਕ ਰਾਂਝਾ ਮੈਨੂੰ ਲੋੜੀਦਾ

'ਕੁਨ ਫ਼ਯਕੂਨ' ਅੱਗੇ ਦੀਆਂ ਲਗੀਆਂ, ਨੇਹੁੰ ਨਾ ਲਗੜਾ ਚੋਰੀ ਦਾ

ਆਪ ਛਿੜ ਜਾਂਦਾ ਨਾਲ ਮਝੀਂ ਦੇ, ਕਿਉਂ ਸਾਨੂੰ ਬੇਲਿਓ ਹੇੜੀਦਾ

ਰਾਂਝੇ ਜਿਹਾ ਮੈਨੂੰ ਹੋਰ ਨਾ ਕੋਈ, ਮਿੰਨਤਾਂ ਕਰ ਕਰ ਮੋੜੀਦਾ

੫    ਸਾਂਵਲਿਆਂ ਦੇ ਨੈਣ ਸਲੋਨੇ, ਸੂਹ ਦੁਪੱਟਾ ਗੋਰੀ ਦਾ

ਅਹਦ ਅਹਿਮਦ ਵਿਚ ਫ਼ਰਕ ਨਾ ਬੁੱਲ੍ਹਿਆ, ਰੱਤੀ ਇਕ ਭੇਤ ਮਰੋੜੀ ਦਾ

## ੨੪

ਇਕ ਨੁਕਤਾ ਯਾਰ ਪੜ੍ਹਾਇਆ ਏ

ਐਨ ਗ਼ੈਨ ਦੀ ਹਿਕ ਸੂਰਤ, ਹਿਕ ਨੁਕਤੇ ਸ਼ੋਰ ਮਚਾਇਆ ਏ

You may remember the Qur'an by heart and become
    a Hafiz,[2] and purify your tongue with continual
    recitation. Then you think of the good things in life,
    and your mind wanders all over the place like
    a courier.
Bullha, the banyan seed was sown and grew into a great     5
    tree. Then the tree perished, and only the simple
    seed[3] was left.

## 23

All I need is Ranjha.
We were betrothed before the time of *Let it be, and it was.*[1]
    Ours is no stolen love.
He goes with the buffaloes to pasture. Why am I kept back
    from the river glade?[2]
There is no one else like Ranjha for me. I keep pleading to
    make him return.
The dark-skinned lovers' eyes are lustrous. The fair girl's     5
    shawl is bright red.[3]
Bullha, there is no difference between Ahad and Ahmad,[4]
    only the little mystery of a squiggle.

## 24

My beloved has taught me a single dot.[1]
The letters *'ain* and *ġhain*[2] have the same shape. A single
    dot has created the havoc.

ਸੱਸੀ ਦਾ ਦਿਲ ਲੁੱਟਣ ਕਾਰਨ, ਹੋਤ ਪੁੰਨੂ ਬਣ ਆਇਆ ਏ

ਬੁੱਲ੍ਹੂ ਸ਼ਹੁ ਦੀ ਜ਼ਾਤ ਨਾ ਕਾਈ, ਮੈਂ ਸ਼ਹੁ ਇਨਾਇਤ ਪਾਇਆ ਏ

## ੨੫

ਇਕ ਨੁਕਤੇ ਵਿਚ ਗਲ ਮੁਕਦੀ ਏ

ਫੜ੍ਹ ਨੁਕਤਾ ਛੋੜ ਹਿਸਾਬਾਂ ਨੂੰ, ਕਰ ਦੂਰ ਕੁਫਰ ਦਿਆਂ ਬਾਬਾਂ ਨੂੰ
ਲਾਹ ਦੋਜ਼ਖ਼ ਗੋਰ ਅਜ਼ਾਬਾਂ ਨੂੰ, ਕਰ ਸਾਫ਼ ਦਿਲੇ ਦਿਆਂ ਖ਼ਾਬਾਂ ਨੂੰ
ਗੱਲ ਏਸੇ ਘਰ ਵਿਚ ਚੁਕਦੀ ਏ

ਐਵੇਂ ਮੱਥਾ ਜ਼ਿਮੀਂ ਘਸਾਈਦਾ, ਲੰਮਾ ਪਾ ਮਹਿਰਾਬ ਦਿਖਾਈਦਾ
ਪੜ੍ਹ ਕਲਮਾ ਲੋਕ ਮੁਸਾਈਦਾ, ਦਿਲ ਅੰਦਰ ਸਮਝ ਨਾ ਲਿਆਈਦਾ
ਕਦੀ ਬਾਤ ਸੱਚੀ ਵੀ ਲੁਕਦੀ ਏ

ਕਈ ਹਾਜੀ ਬਣ ਬਣ ਆਏ ਜੀ, ਗਲ ਨੀਲੇ ਜਾਮੇ ਪਾਏ ਜੀ
ਹਜ ਵੇਚ ਟਕੇ ਲੈ ਖਾਏ ਜੀ, ਭਲਾ ਇਹ ਗੱਲ ਕਿਹਨੂੰ ਭਾਏ ਜੀ
ਕਦੀ ਬਾਤ ਸੱਚੀ ਵੀ ਲੁਕਦੀ ਏ

੫  ਇਕ ਜੰਗਲ ਬਹਿਰੀਂ ਜਾਂਦੇ ਨੇ, ਇਕ ਦਾਣਾ ਰੋਜ਼ੀ ਖਾਂਦੇ ਨੇ
ਬੇਸਮਝ ਵਜੂਦ ਥਕਾਂਦੇ ਨੇ, ਘਰ ਹੋਵਟ ਹੋ ਕੇ ਮਾਂਦੇ ਨੇ
ਐਵੇਂ ਚਿੱਲਿਆਂ ਵਿਚ ਜਿੰਦ ਮੁਕਦੀ ਏ

ਫੜ ਮੁਰਸ਼ਦ ਅਬਦ ਖੁਦਾਈ ਹੋ, ਵਿੱਚ ਮਸਤੀ ਬੇਪਰਵਾਹੀ ਹੋ
ਬੇਖ਼ਾਹਸ਼ ਬੇਨਵਾਈ ਹੋ, ਵਿੱਚ ਦਿਲ ਦੇ ਖੁਬ ਸਫ਼ਾਈ ਹੋ
ਬੁੱਲ੍ਹੂ ਬਾਤ ਸੱਚੀ ਕਦ ਰੁਕਦੀ ਏ

To steal the heart of Sassi,[3] he came as Punnun the Hot.
Bullha, the lord has no caste.[4] I have found Shah Inayat.

## 25

The whole thing[1] ends in a dot.[2]

Grasp the dot and quit counting, put aside the chapters of
    unbelief. Get rid of the torments of hell and the grave,
    cleanse the visions of your heart. It is in this house
    that the matter is found.

It is for nothing that the forehead is rubbed upon the
    ground, and that through prostration the mihrab[3]
    is displayed. The profession of faith[4] is recited and
    people are robbed, but it is not brought into the heart
    and understood. Can the matter that is true ever
    be hidden?

Many become Hajjis and come wearing blue garments.[5]
    They sell the Haj[6] and live on the coins they collect,
    but who can possibly be pleased by this? Can the
    matter that is true ever be hidden?

Some go into the jungle or out on the rivers, some eat     5
    a single grain as their daily diet. Senselessly they
    exhaust their bodies and stay at home in a weak state.
    In performing austerities, their life ends for nothing.

Take hold of the guide and become the creature of the
    divine; in ecstasy there is freedom from care. In lack
    of desire and lack of provisions, there is perfect purity
    in the heart. Bullha, can the matter that is true ever
    be blocked?

## ੨੬

ਇਲਮੋਂ ਬੱਸ ਕਰੀਂ ਓ ਯਾਰ

ਇਲਮ ਨਾ ਆਵੇ ਵਿਚ ਸ਼ੁਮਾਰ, ਇੱਕੋ ਅਲਫ਼ ਤੇਰੇ ਦਰਕਾਰ
ਜਾਂਦੀ ਉਮਰ ਨਹੀਂ ਇਤਬਾਰ, ਇਲਮੋਂ ਬੱਸ ਕਰੀਂ ਓ ਯਾਰ

ਪੜ੍ਹ ਪੜ੍ਹ ਇਲਮ ਲਗਾਵੇਂ ਢੇਰ, ਕੁਰਆਨ ਕਿਤਾਬਾਂ ਚਾਰ ਚੁਫ਼ੇਰ
ਗਿਰਦੇ ਚਾਨਣ ਵਿਚ ਅਨ੍ਹੇਰ, ਬਾਝੋਂ ਰਹਿਬਰ ਖ਼ਬਰ ਨਾ ਸਾਰ

ਪੜ੍ਹ ਪੜ੍ਹ ਸ਼ੇਖ਼ ਮਸ਼ਾਇਖ਼ ਹੋਇਆ, ਭਰ ਭਰ ਪੇਟ ਨੀਂਦਰ ਭਰ ਸੋਇਆ
ਜਾਂਦੀ ਵਾਰ ਨੈਣ ਭਰ ਰੋਇਆ, ਡੁੱਬਾ ਵਿਚ ਉਰਾਰ ਨਾ ਪਾਰ

੫    ਪੜ੍ਹ ਪੜ੍ਹ ਸ਼ੇਖ਼ ਮਸ਼ਾਇਖ਼ ਕਹਾਵੇਂ, ਉਲਟੇ ਮਸਲੇ ਘਰੋਂ ਬਟਾਵੇਂ
ਬੇਅਕਲਾਂ ਨੂੰ ਲੁਟ ਲੁਟ ਖਾਵੇਂ, ਉਲਟੇ ਸਿੱਧੇ ਕਰੋ ਕਰਾਰ

ਪੜ੍ਹ ਪੜ੍ਹ ਨਫ਼ਲ ਨਮਾਜ਼ ਗੁਜ਼ਾਰੇਂ, ਉੱਚੀਆਂ ਬਾਂਗਾਂ ਚਾਂਘਾਂ ਮਾਰੇਂ
ਮੰਬਰ ਤੇ ਚੜ੍ਹ ਵਾਅਜ਼ ਪੁਕਾਰੇਂ, ਕੀਤਾ ਤੈਨੂੰ ਹਿਰਸ ਖ਼ੁਆਰ

ਪੜ੍ਹ ਪੜ੍ਹ ਮੁੱਲਾਂ ਹੋਏ ਕਾਜ਼ੀ, ਅੱਲ੍ਹਾ ਇਲਮਾਂ ਬਾਝੋਂ ਰਾਜ਼ੀ
ਹੋਏ ਹਿਰਸ ਦਿਨੋ ਦਿਨ ਤਾਜ਼ੀ, ਨਫ਼ਾ ਨੀਅਤ ਵਿੱਚ ਗੁਜ਼ਾਰ

ਪੜ੍ਹ ਪੜ੍ਹ ਮਸਲੇ ਰੋਜ਼ ਸੁਣਾਵੇਂ, ਖਾਟਾ ਸ਼ਕ ਸ਼ੁਬ੍ਹੇ ਦਾ ਖਾਵੇਂ
ਦੱਸੇਂ ਹੋਰ ਤੇ ਹੋਰ ਕਮਾਵੇਂ, ਅੰਦਰ ਖੋਟ ਬਾਹਰ ਸਚਿਆਰ

## 26

That is enough of learning, friend.

Your learning may be beyond reckoning, but all you need
is *alif*.[1] There is no trusting in life, which departs from
us. That is enough of learning, friend.

Reading and reading, you amass heaps of learning, with
the Qur'an and the scriptures all around you. You are
surrounded by light, but there is darkness[2] within you.
Without the guide, you have no awareness or clue.

Reading and reading, you became a Shaikh of Shaikhs,
who filled his belly and slept his fill. When it was
time to go, you wept floods of tears. You drowned in
midstream, neither on this bank nor on the far side.

Reading and reading, you call yourself a Shaikh of                    5
Shaikhs, and from your house you devise tricky
questions of the law. You eat by plundering the
foolish, and make your obscure pronouncements.

Reading and reading, you perform prescribed and
supererogatory prayers, and shout out loud calls to
prayer. You go up into the pulpit and deliver sermons,
but your greed has dishonored you.

Reading and reading, you become a mullah, then a *qazi*,[3]
but God is content without all this learning. Your
greed increases day by day, and your pious intent is set
on profit.

Reading and reading, you discuss legal questions every
day, and you feed on doubts and queries. You preach
one thing and practice another, being false within
while seeming true on the outside.

ਪੜ੍ਹ ਪੜ੍ਹ ਇਲਮ ਨਜੂਮ ਵਿਚਾਰੇ, ਗਿਣਦਾ ਰਾਸਾਂ ਬੁਰਜ ਸਤਾਰੇ
ਪੜ੍ਹੇ ਅਜ਼ੀਮਤਾਂ ਮੰਤਰ ਝਾੜੇ, ਅਬਜਦ ਗਿਣਟੇ ਤਅਵੀਜ਼ ਸ਼ੁਮਾਰ

੧੦ ਇਲਮੋਂ ਪਏ ਨੇ ਕਜ਼ੀਏ ਹੋਰ, ਅੱਖੀਂ ਵਾਲੇ ਅੰਨ੍ਹੇ ਕੋਰ
ਫੜ ਲਏ ਸਾਧ ਤੇ ਛੱਡੇ ਚੋਰ, ਦੋਹੀਂ ਜਹਾਨੀਂ ਹੋਇਆ ਖੁਆਰ

ਇਲਮੋਂ ਪਏ ਹਜ਼ਾਰਾਂ ਫਸਤੇ, ਰਾਹੀ ਅਟਕ ਰਹੇ ਵਿਚ ਰਸਤੇ
ਮਾਰਿਆ ਹਿਜਰ ਹੋਏ ਦਿਲ ਖਸਤੇ, ਪਿਆ ਵਿਛੋੜੇ ਦਾ ਸਿਰ ਭਾਰ

ਇਲਮੋਂ ਮੀਆਂ ਜੀ ਕਹਾਵੇਂ, ਤੰਬਾ ਚੁੱਕ ਚੁੱਕ ਮੰਡੀ ਜਾਵੇਂ
ਧੇਲਾ ਲੈ ਕੇ ਛੁਰੀ ਚਲਾਵੇਂ, ਨਾਲ ਕਸਾਈਆਂ ਬਹੁਤ ਪਿਆਰ

ਬਹੁਤਾ ਇਲਮ ਅਜ਼ਾਜ਼ੀਲ ਨੇ ਪੜ੍ਹਿਆ, ਝੱਗਾ ਝਾਹ ਉਸੇ ਦਾ ਸੜਿਆ
ਗਲ ਵਿਚ ਤੌਕ ਲਾਹਨਤ ਦਾ ਪੜਿਆ, ਉੜਕ ਗਿਆ ਉਹ ਬਾਜ਼ੀ ਹਾਰ

ਜਦ ਮੈਂ ਸਬਕ ਇਸ਼ਕ ਦਾ ਪੜ੍ਹਿਆ, ਦਰਿਆ ਵੇਖ ਵਹਦਤ ਦਾ ਵੜਿਆ
ਘੁੰਮਣ ਘੇਰਾਂ ਦੇ ਵਿਚ ਅੜਿਆ, ਸ਼ਾਹ ਇਨਾਇਤ ਲਾਇਆ ਪਾਰ

੧੫ ਬੁੱਲ੍ਹਾ ਨਾ ਰਾਫ਼ਜ਼ੀ ਨਾ ਸੁੰਨੀ, ਆਲਮ ਫ਼ਾਜ਼ਲ ਨਾ ਆਮਲ ਜੁੰਨੀ
ਇੱਕੋ ਪੜ੍ਹਿਆ ਇਲਮ ਲਦੁੰਨੀ, ਵਾਹਦ ਅਲਫ਼ ਮੀਮ ਦਰਕਾਰ

Reading and reading, you think about the science of
 astrology, and calculate zodiacal signs, houses, and
 planets. You study incantations, spells, and exorcisms;
 you calculate the *abjad*[4] and devise amulets.[5]

From learning, other confusions arise, and the sighted    10
 become quite blind. Holy men are arrested and thieves
 are released, and you are disgraced in both worlds.

From learning, thousands of obstacles arise, and travelers
 are stuck on their journey. Struck by separation, they
 become sick at heart, and the load of parting falls on
 their heads.

From learning, you get to be called "Reverend," and
 hitching up your loose pants, you go to the market.
 You take your penny and wield the knife, so you are
 very fond of the butchers.[6]

Azazil[7] studied greatly, but he was the one whose hut was
 burned. He studied the collar of curses around his
 neck, and in the end he lost the game.

When I studied the lesson of love, I beheld the ocean of
 unity and entered it. I got caught in its whirlpools, but
 Shah Inayat delivered me to the other side.

Bullha is not a Shia or a Sunni, neither a learned scholar    15
 nor a magician or philosopher.[8] He has studied only
 that inspirational knowledge[9] in which *alif* and *mīm*[10]
 alone are needed.

੨੧

ਏਸ ਨੇਹੁੰ ਦੀ ਉਲਟੀ ਚਾਲ

ਸਾਬਰ ਨੇ ਜਦ ਨੇਹੁੰ ਲਗਾਇਆ, ਦੇਖ ਪੀਆ ਨੇ ਕੀ ਦਿਖਲਾਇਆ
ਰਗ ਰਗ ਅੰਦਰ ਕਿਰਮ ਚਲਾਇਆ, ਜ਼ੋਰਾਵਰ ਦੀ ਗੱਲ ਮੁਹਾਲ

ਜ਼ਕਰੀਆ ਨੇ ਜਦ ਪਾਇਆ ਖਾਰਾ,੧ ਜਿਸ ਦਮ ਵਜਿਆ ਇਸ਼ਕ ਨਕਾਰਾ
ਧਰਿਆ ਸਿਰ ਤੇ ਤਿੱਖਾ ਆਰਾ, ਕੀਤਾ ਐਡ ਜਵਾਲ

ਜਦੋਂ ਜ਼ਹੀਯੇ ਨੇ ਪਾਈ ਝਾਤੀ, ਰਮਜ਼ ਇਸ਼ਕ ਦੀ ਲਾਈ ਕਾਤੀ
ਜਲਵਾ ਦਿੱਤਾ ਆਪਣਾ ਜ਼ਾਤੀ, ਤਨ ਖ਼ੰਜਰ ਕੀਤਾ ਲਾਲ

੫ ਆਪ ਇਸ਼ਾਰਾ ਅਖ ਦਾ ਕੀਤਾ, ਤਾਂ ਮਧੂਆ ਮਨਸੂਰ ਨੇ ਪੀਤਾ
ਸੂਲੀ ਚੜੂ ਕੇ ਦਰਸ਼ਨ ਲੀਤਾ, ਹੋਇਆ ਇਸ਼ਕ ਕਮਾਲ

ਸੁਲੇਮਾਂ ਨੂੰ ਇਸ਼ਕ ਜੋ ਆਇਆ, ਮੁੰਦਰਾ ਹੱਥੋਂ ਚਾ ਗਵਾਇਆ
ਤਖ਼ਤ ਨਾ ਪਰੀਆਂ ਦਾ ਫਿਰ ਆਇਆ, ਭੱਠ ਝੋਕੇ ਪਿਆ ਬੇਹਾਲ

ਬੁੱਲ੍ਹੇ ਸ਼ਾਹ ਹੁਣ ਚੁੱਪ ਚੰਗੇਰੀ, ਨਾ ਕਰ ਏਥੇ ਐਡ ਦਲੇਰੀ
ਗੱਲ ਨਾ ਬਣਦੀ ਤੇਰੀ ਮੇਰੀ, ਛੱਡ ਦੇ ਸਾਰੇ ਵਹਿਮ ਖ਼ਿਆਲ

## 27

The behavior of this love is perverse.

When Ayub the patient[1] was affected by love, see what
the beloved showed him. God filled all his veins with
worms. It is impossible to describe the mighty one.

Zakariya[2] was set on high, then at the moment when love
sounded its drum, God put a sharp saw to his head and
reduced him to such misery.

When Yahya[3] stole a look, the mystery of love laid its knife
upon him. God displayed the glory of his essence, and
the dagger was reddened by his body.

When God signaled with his eye, Mansur[4] drank the wine.    5
He mounted the gallows and obtained a vision of God.
His love was made perfect.

When love came to Sulaiman,[5] it made his ring vanish
suddenly. His throne borne by the fairies did not
return. He was in a sorry state as he fueled the
furnace.

Bullhe Shah, now it is better to be silent; do not be so bold
here. It is no good speaking of "yours" and "mine."
Give up all these idle thoughts and fantasies.

## ੨੮

ਸਈਓ ਹੁਣ ਮੈਂ ਸਾਜਨ ਪਾਇਓ ਈ, ਹਰ ਹਰ ਦੇ ਵਿੱਚ ਸਮਾਇਓ ਈ

'ਅਨਾ ਅਹਦ' ਦਾ ਗੀਤ ਸੁਣਾਇਓ, 'ਅਨਾ ਅਹਿਮਦ' ਫਿਰ ਫਰਮਾਇਓ
'ਅਨਾ ਅਰਬ' ਬੇ ਐਨ ਬਤਾਇਓ, ਫਿਰ ਨਾਮ ਰਸੂਲ ਧਰਾਇਓ ਈ

'ਫਸੁੱਮ ਵਜਹੁੱਲੂ' ਨੂਰ ਤੇਰਾ, ਹਰ ਹਰ ਕੇ ਬੀਚ ਜ਼ਹੂਰ ਤੇਰਾ
ਹੈ 'ਅਲਇਨਸਾਨ' ਮਜ਼ਕੂਰ ਤੇਰਾ, ਏਥੇ ਆਪਣਾ ਸਿਰ ਲੁਕਾਇਓ ਈ

ਤੂੰ ਆਇਓ ਤੇ ਮੈਂ ਨਾ ਆਈ, ਗੰਜ ਮਖ਼ਫ਼ੀ ਦੀ ਤੈਂ ਮੁਰਲੀ ਬਜਾਈ
ਆਖ 'ਅਲਸਤ' ਗਵਾਹੀ ਚਾਹੀ, ਓਥੇ 'ਕਾਲੂ ਬਲਾ' ਸੁਣਾਇਓ ਈ

੫  ਪਰਗਟ ਹੋ ਕਰ ਨੂਰ ਸਦਾਇਓ, ਅਹਿਮਦ ਤੋਂ ਮੌਜੂਦ ਕਰਾਇਓ
ਨਾਬੂਦੋਂ ਕਰ ਬੁਦ ਦਿਖਲਾਇਓ, 'ਫਨਫ਼ਖ਼ਤੁ ਫ਼ੀਹਿ' ਸੁਣਾਇਓ ਈ

'ਨਹਨੁ ਅਕਰਬ' ਲਿਖ ਦਿਤੋਈ, 'ਹੁਵ ਮਅਕੁਮ' ਸਬਕ ਦਿਤੋਈ
'ਵਫ਼ੀ ਅਨਫ਼ੁਸਿਕੁਮ' ਹੁਕਮ ਕੀਤੋਈ, ਫਿਰ ਕੇਹਾ ਘੁੰਗਟ ਪਾਇਓ ਈ

ਭਰ ਕੇ ਵਹਦਤ ਜਾਮ ਪਿਲਾਇਓ, ਮਨਸੂਰੇ ਨੂੰ ਮਸਤ ਕਰਾਇਓ
ਉਸ ਤੋਂ 'ਅਨਲਹੱਕ' ਆਪ ਕਹਾਇਓ, ਫਿਰ ਸੂਲੀ ਪਕੜ ਚੜ੍ਹਾਇਓ ਈ

ਘੁੰਘਟ ਖੋਲ ਜਮਾਲ ਵਿਖਾਇਆ, ਸ਼ੈਖ ਜੁਨੈਦ ਕਮਾਲ ਸਦਾਇਆ
'ਲੈਸ ਫ਼ੀ ਜੁੱਬਤੀ' ਹਾਲ ਬਣਾਇਆ, ਅਸ਼ਰਫ ਇਨਸਾਨ ਬਣਾਇਓ ਈ

## 28

Oh[1] girlfriends:[2] Now I have found you, beloved. You
    are contained in each and every thing.[3]

You recited the song of *I am Ahad*[4] *the One.* Then you
    decreed, *I am Ahmad.* Then you explained, *I am
    an Arab without the A.*[5] Then you took the name of
    Apostle.

*Then there is the face of God*[6] reveals your light. You are
    manifest in each and every thing. The word *Man*[7]
    refers to you. Here you have hidden your face.

You came, and I did not come. You played the flute of a
    hidden treasure.[8] You said, *Am I not?*[9] and desired
    testimony. There you announced, *They said, "Yes."*

Becoming manifest, you called yourself light. You made    5
    it present through Ahmad. From nonbeing you made
    being appear. You proclaimed, *And I breathed into
    him.*[10]

You wrote *We are nearer.*[11] You taught the lesson of *He is
    with you.*[12] You gave the command *And in your own
    selves.*[13] So what is this veil that you have put on?

You filled the cup of oneness and gave it him to drink. You
    made Mansur drunk. You were the one who made him
    say, *I am God.*[14] Then you seized him and set him on
    the gallows.

You removed your veil and displayed your beauty. You
    called Shaikh Junaid perfect. You created the ecstasy
    of *There is nothing in my robe.*[15] You made man the
    noblest of creatures.[16]

'ਵਲਕਦ ਕੱਰਮਨਾ' ਯਾਦ ਕਰਾਇਓ, 'ਲਾ ਇਲਾਹ' ਦਾ ਪਰਦਾ ਲਾਹਿਓ
'ਇੱਲੱਲ੍ਹੁ' ਕਹੋ ਝਾਤੀ ਪਾਇਓ, ਫਿਰ ਬੁੱਲ੍ਹੁ ਨਾਮ ਧਰਾਇਓ ਈ

## ੨੯

ਸਜਟਾਂ ਦੇ ਵਿਛੋੜੇ ਕੋਲੋਂ, ਤਨ ਦਾ ਲੇਹੁ ਛਾਟੀਦਾ

ਦੁੱਖਾਂ ਸੂਲਾਂ ਕੀਤਾ ਏਕਾ, ਨਾ ਕੋਈ ਸਹੁਰਾ ਨਾ ਕੋਈ ਪੇਕਾ
ਦਰਦ ਵਿਹੁਟੀ ਪਈ ਦਰ ਤੇਰੇ, ਤੂੰ ਹੈਂ ਦਰਦ ਰੰਜਾਟੀ ਦਾ

ਕੱਢ ਕਲੇਜਾ ਕਰਨੀ ਆਂ ਬੇਰੇ, ਇਹ ਭੀ ਨਹੀਂ ਹੈ ਲਾਇਕ ਤੇਰੇ
ਹੋਰ ਤੱਫ਼ੀਕ ਨਹੀਂ ਵਿਚ ਮੇਰੇ, ਪੀਓ ਕਟੋਰਾ ਪਾਟੀ ਦਾ

ਹੁਣ ਕਿਉਂ ਰੋਦੇ ਨੈਟ ਨਿਰਾਸੇ, ਆਪੇ ਉੜਕ ਫਾਹੀ ਫਾਸੇ
ਹੁਣ ਤਾਂ ਛੁੱਟਣ ਔਖਾ ਹੋਇਆ, ਚਾਰਾ ਨਹੀਂ ਨਿਮਾਟੀ ਦਾ

੫  ਬੁੱਲ੍ਹੂ ਸ਼ਾਹੁ ਪਿਆ ਹੁਣ ਗੱਜੇ, ਇਸ਼ਕ ਦਮਾਮੇ ਸਿਰ ਤੇ ਵੱਜੇ
ਚਾਰ ਦਿਹਾੜੇ ਗੋਇਲ ਵਾਸਾ, ਉੜਕ ਕੂਚ ਨਕਾਰੇ ਦਾ

You made him remember *And we have honored them.*[17]
    You removed the veil of *There is no God.* You said *but
    God,*[18] and peeped out. Then you assumed the name
    of Bullha.

## 29

Because[1] of separation from my beloved, my body's blood
    is filtered.

Pains and sorrows have united. I have no in-laws or
    parental home. Bereft of sympathy, I lie at your door.
    You are the comfort of this suffering creature.

I take out my heart and chop it to pieces, but even this is
    not worthy of you. I have nothing else to offer, so just
    drink a cup of water.

Why do these despairing eyes now weep? In the end, you
    were the one who put the noose around your neck.
    Now it has become difficult to escape, and this poor
    wretch has no recourse.

Bullha, the lord is now thundering, and love is beating     5
    its drum by my head. After a few days' stay in this
    herdsman's hut, the drum is finally sounded for
    departure.

३०

ਸਦਾ ਮੈਂ ਸਾਹਵਿਰਆਂ ਘਰ ਜਾਣਾ, ਨੀ ਮਿਲ ਲਓ ਸਹੇਲੜੀਓ
ਤੁਸਾਂ ਵੀ ਹੋਸੀ ਅੱਲ੍ਹਾ ਭਾਣਾ, ਨੀ ਮਿਲ ਲਓ ਸਹੇਲੜੀਓ

ਰੰਗ ਬਰੰਗੀ ਸੂਲ ਉਪੱਠੇ, ਚੰਬੜ ਜਾਵਣ ਮੈਨੂੰ
ਦੁਖ ਅਗਲੇ ਮੈਂ ਨਾਲ ਲੈ ਜਾਵਾਂ, ਪਿਛਲੇ ਸੌਂਪਾਂ ਕੈਨੂੰ

ਇਕ ਵਿਛੋੜਾ ਸਈਆਂ ਦਾ, ਜਿਉਂ ਡਾਰੋਂ ਕੂੰਜ ਵਿਛੁੰਨੀ
ਮਾਪਿਆਂ ਮੈਨੂੰ ਇਹ ਕੁਝ ਦਿੱਤਾ, ਇਕ ਚੋਲੀ ਇਕ ਚੁੰਨੀ

ਦਾਜ ਇਨ੍ਹਾਂ ਦਾ ਵੇਖ ਕੇ ਹੂਟ, ਮੈਂ ਹੰਝੂ ਭਰ ਭਰ ਰੁੰਨੀ
ਸੱਸ ਨਨਾਂ ਦੇਵਣ ਤਾਹਨੇ, ਮੁਸ਼ਕਿਲ ਭਾਰੀ ਪੁੰਨੀ

੫    ਬੁੱਲ੍ਹਾ ਸ਼ਹੁ ਸੱਤਾਰ ਸੁਟੀਂਦਾ, ਇਹ ਵੇਲਾ ਟਲ ਜਾਵੇ
ਅਦਲ ਕਰੇ ਤਾਂ ਜਾਹ ਨਾ ਕਾਈ, ਫਜ਼ਲੋਂ ਬਖਰਾ ਪਾਵੇ


३१

ਸਭ ਇਕੋ ਰੰਗ ਕਪਾਹੀਂ ਦਾ

ਤਾਣੀ ਤਾਣਾ ਪੇਟਾ ਨਲੀਆਂ, ਪੀਠ ਨੜਾ ਤੇ ਛਿੱਬਾਂ ਛਲੀਆਂ
ਆਪੇ ਆਪਟੇ ਨਾਮ ਜਿਤਾਵਣ, ਵੱਖੋ ਵੱਖੀ ਜਾਹੀਂ ਦਾ

ਚੌਂਸੀ ਪੈਂਸੀ ਖੱਦਰ ਧੋਤਰ, ਮਲਮਲ ਖਾਸਾ ਇੱਕਾ ਸੂਤਰ
ਪੂਟੀ ਵਿੱਚੋਂ ਬਾਹਰ ਆਵੇਂ, ਭਗਵਾਂ ਭੇਸ ਗੋਸਾਈਂ ਦਾ

### 30

I must go to my in-laws forever. Oh, gather round me,
    girls.[1] You too will have to experience God's will. Oh,
    gather round me, girls.
I am stuck in all kinds of awkward sufferings. My future
    woes I take with me; to whom shall I give the old ones?
One thing I suffer is the separation from my girlfriends,
    like a crane[2] parted from the flock. All my parents
    gave me was a single blouse and a single scarf.
When I saw the dowry they had given me, I wept floods of
    tears. My husband's mother and his sisters mock me,
    and a grievous fate has overtaken me.
Bullha, the lord is reported to be the veiler of sins.[3] Just let    5
    this time be put off. If he acts with strict justice, I have
    no place. May he grant me a portion of his grace.

### 31

Bolls of cotton are all the same color.
Warp, woof, bobbins, texture, shuttle, spools, and hanks—
    each one announces its own name, and has its separate
    place.
All the different kinds of cloth—*cauñsī,* [1] *paiñsī, khaddar,*
    *dhotar, malmal,* and *khāsā*—are made of the same
    yarn. They come out of the cotton roll dyed in the
    ochre[2] color of the lord.

ਕੁੜੀਆਂ ਹੱਥੀਂ ਫ਼ਾਪਾਂ ਫ਼ੱਲੇ, ਆਪੇ ਅਪਟੇ ਨਾਮ ਸਵੱਲੇ
ਸੱਭੇ ਹਿੱਕਾ ਚਾਂਦੀ ਆਖੇ, ਕੰਗਟ ਚੂੜਾ ਬਾਹੀਂ ਦਾ

੫   ਭੇਡ ਬਕਰੀਆਂ ਚਾਰਨਵਾਲਾ, ਉਠ ਮੱਝੀਆਂ ਦਾ ਕਰੇ ਸੰਭਾਲਾ
ਰੁੜੀ ਉੱਤੇ ਗੱਯੋ ਚਾਰੇ, ਉਹ ਭੀ ਵਾਗੀ ਗਾਈਂ ਦਾ

ਬੁੱਲ੍ਹੂ ਸ਼ਹੁ ਦੀ ਜ਼ਾਤ ਕੀ ਪੁੱਛਨੈਂ, ਸ਼ਾਕਰ ਹੋ ਰਜ਼ਾਈਂ ਜਾ
ਜੇ ਤੂੰ ਲੋੜੇਂ ਬਾਗ਼ ਬਹਾਰਾਂ, ਚਾਕਰ ਰਹੁ ਅਰਾਈਂ ਦਾ

## ੩੨
ਸਾਈਂ ਫ਼ੁਪ ਤਮਾਸ਼ੇ ਨੂੰ ਆਇਆ, ਤੁਸੀਂ ਰਲ ਮਿਲ ਨਾਮ ਧਿਆਓ

ਲਟਕ ਸਜਨ ਦੀ ਨਾਹੀਂ ਫ਼ੁਪਦੀ, ਸਾਰੀ ਖ਼ਲਕਤ ਸਿਕਦੀ ਤਪਦੀ
ਤੁਸੀਂ ਦੂਰ ਨਾ ਭੁੰਡਟ ਜਾਓ

ਰਲ ਮਿਲ ਸਈਓ ਅੱਟਟ ਪਾਓ, ਇਕ ਬਈ ਦੇ ਵਿੱਚ ਸਮਾਓ
ਨਾਲੇ ਗੀਤ ਸਜਟ ਦਾ ਗਾਓ

ਬੁੱਲ੍ਹੂ ਬਾਤ ਅਨੋਖੀ ਏਹਾ, ਨੱਚਟ ਲੱਗੀ ਤਾਂ ਘੁੰਗਟ ਕੇਹਾ
ਤੁਸੀਂ ਪਰਦਾ ਅੱਖੀਂ ਥੀਂ ਲਾਹੋ

Girls wear rings and signets on their fingers, each with
their distinctive names. You can say that they are all
the same silver,[3] like the bangles and bracelets on their
arms.

The herdsman looks after sheep and goats, camels and    5
buffaloes. He grazes donkeys on the rubbish heap. He
is also a herdsman of cows.[4]

Why ask what the lord's caste is? Bullha, be grateful for
God's mercies. If you desire the joys of spring, remain
the humble servant of the Arain.[5]

## 32

The lord has come to the show in disguise. Gather
together and meditate on the name.

The beloved's charms cannot be concealed; the whole of
creation is on fire with longing. Do not go far to look
for him.

Get together, girls, set up the spinning party,[1] and mingle
with one another. Join together and sing a song to the
beloved.

Bullha, it is indeed a strange thing for a woman to start
dancing with her veil on.[2] Remove the veil from in
front of your eyes.

### ੩੩

ਸਾਡੇ ਵਲ ਮੁਖੜਾ ਮੋੜ ਵੇ ਪਿਆਰਿਆ, ਸਾਡੇ ਵਲ ਮੁਖੜਾ ਮੋੜ

ਆਪੇ ਹੀ ਤੂੰ ਲਾਈਆਂ ਕੁੰਡੀਆਂ, ਤੇ ਆਪੇ ਖਿਚਦੈਂ ਡੋਰ

ਅਰਸ਼ ਕੁਰਸੀ ਤੋਂ ਬਾਂਗਾਂ ਮਿਲੀਆਂ, ਮੱਕੇ ਪੈ ਗਿਆ ਸ਼ੋਰ

ਡੋਲੀ ਪਾ ਲੈ ਚੱਲੇ ਖੇੜੇ, ਨਾ ਕੁਝ ਉਜ਼ਰ ਨਾ ਜ਼ੋਰ

੫  ਜੇ ਮਾਏਂ ਤੈਨੂੰ ਖੇੜੇ ਪਿਆਰੇ, ਡੋਲੀ ਪਾ ਦਈਂ ਹੋਰ

ਬੁੱਲੇ ਸ਼ਾਹ ਅਸਾਂ ਮਰਨਾ ਨਾਹੀਂ, ਵੇ ਮਰ ਗਿਆ ਕੋਈ ਹੋਰ

### ੩੪

ਸਾਨੂੰ ਆ ਮਿਲ ਯਾਰ ਪਿਆਰਿਆ, ਤੇਰੇ ਦੁਖਾਂ ਨੇ ਸਾਨੂੰ ਮਾਰਿਆ

ਦੂਰ ਦੂਰ ਅਸਾਥੋਂ ਤੂਹਿ ਰਹਿਓਂ,੧ ਆਸਲ ਤੇ੨ ਆ ਕੇ ਬਹਿ ਰਹਿਓਂ
ਕੀ ਕਸਰ ਕਸੂਰ ਵਿਸਾਰਿਆ

ਮੇਰਾ ਇਕ ਅਨੋਖਾ ਯਾਰ ਹੈ, ਮੇਰਾ ਉਸੇ ਨਾਲ ਪਿਆਰ ਹੈ
ਕਦੇ ਸਮਝੀਂ ਵੱਡ ਪਰਵਾਰਿਆ

ਜਦੋਂ ਅਪਟੀ ਅਪਟੀ ਪੈ ਗਈ, ਧੀ ਮਾਂ ਨੂੰ ਲੁਟ ਕੇ ਲੈ ਗਈ
ਮੂੰਹ ਬਾਹਰਵੀਂ ਸਦੀ ਪਸਾਰਿਆ

੫  ਦਰ ਖੁੱਲ੍ਹਾ ਹਸ਼ਰ ਅਜ਼ਾਬ ਦਾ, ਬੁਰਾ ਹਾਲ ਹੋਇਆ ਪੰਜਾਬ ਦਾ
ਡਰ ਹਾਵੀਏ ਦੋਜ਼ਖ ਮਾਰਿਆ

## 33

Turn your face toward us, darling. Turn your face toward
 us.

You are the one who has cast your hooks, it is you who tugs
 the line.[1]

Calls were received from the heavenly throne, and uproar
 broke out in Mecca.[2]

The Kheras[3] have taken me away in the palanquin. No
 pleading or force is of any use.

Mother, if you are so fond of the Kheras, put someone else 5
 in the palanquin.

Bullhe Shah, we are not going to die. Oh, someone else is
 dead.[4]

## 34

Come[1] to me, my dear beloved. The sufferings you have
 caused have killed me.

You have retreated far, far away from us, and have come to
 stay at Asal.[2] What fault[3] has made you forget Kasur?

My beloved is strange, but he is the one I love. Will you,
 who possess so great a following,[4] please understand?

With everyone after their own thing, the daughter has
 robbed her mother and taken whatever she owns. The
 twelfth century[5] has come with gaping mouth.

The door of doom and torment has opened, and Panjab 5
 is in a bad state. It has been struck by fear of the pit
 of hell.

ਬੁੱਲ੍ਹਾ ਸ਼ਹੁ ਮੇਰੇ ਘਰ ਆਵਸੀ, ਮੇਰੀ ਬਲਦੀ ਭਾਹ ਬੁਝਾਵਸੀ
ਇਨਾਇਤ ਦਮਦਮ ਨਾਲ ਚਿਤਾਰਿਆ

### ੩੫

ਸੁਨੋ ਤੁਮ ਇਸ਼ਕ ਕੀ ਬਾਜ਼ੀ, ਮੁਲਾਇਕ ਹੋ ਕਹਾਂ ਰਾਜ਼ੀ
ਜਹਾਂ ਬਿਰਹੋਂ ਪਰ੍ਹੇ ਗਾਜੀ, ਵੇਖਾਂ ਫਿਰ ਕੌਣ ਹਾਰੇਗਾ

ਸਜਨ ਕੀ ਭਾਲ ਹੁਣ ਹੋਈ, ਮੈਂ ਲੋਹੁ ਨੈਣ ਭਰ ਰੋਈ
ਨਚੇ ਹਮ ਲਾਹ ਕਰ ਲੋਈ, ਹੈਰਤ ਕੇ ਪੱਥਰ ਮਾਰੇਗਾ

ਮਹੂਰਤ ਪੁੱਛ ਕਰ ਜਾਊਂ, ਸਜਨ ਕੌ ਦੇਖਨੇ ਪਾਊਂ
ਉਸੇ ਮੈਂ ਲੈ ਗਲੇ ਲਾਊਂ, ਨਹੀਂ ਫਿਰ ਖ਼ੁਦ ਗੁਜ਼ਾਰੇਗਾ

ਇਸ਼ਕ ਕੀ ਤੇਗ਼ ਸੇ ਮੂਈ, ਨਹੀਂ ਵੇਹ ਜ਼ਾਤ ਕੀ ਦੂਈ
ਮੈਂ ਪੀਆ ਪੀਆ ਕਰ ਮੂਈ, ਮੂਇਆਂ ਫਿਰ ਰੂਹ ਚਿਤਾਰੇਗਾ

੫    ਸਜਨ ਕੀ ਭਾਲ ਸਰ ਦੀਆ, ਲਹੁ ਮਧ ਆਪਨਾ ਪੀਆ
ਕਢਨ ਬਾਹੋਂ ਸੇ ਸੀ ਲੀਆ, ਲਹਦ ਮੇਂ ਪਾ ਉਤਾਰੇਗਾ

ਬੁੱਲ੍ਹਾ ਸ਼ਹੁ ਇਸ਼ਕ ਹੈ ਤੇਰਾ, ਉਸੀ ਨੇ ਜੀ ਲੀਆ ਮੇਰਾ
ਮੇਰੇ ਘਰ ਬਾਰ ਕਰ ਫੇਰਾ, ਵੇਖਾਂ ਸਿਰ ਕੌਣ ਵਾਰੇਗਾ

Bullha, the lord will come to my house. He will extinguish
    the fire which blazes inside me. With every breath
    I have remembered Inayat.

### 35

Listen[1] to the game of love. How could angels be content?
    Here in the assembly the pain of love proclaims its
    challenge. Let us see who will lose.
Now, as I search for the beloved, my eyes have filled with
    blood. I have stripped off my blanket and dance,
    making him hurl astonished looks at me.
I ask about an auspicious moment and go, hoping that
    I may get to see the beloved and embrace him.
    Otherwise he himself will make me pass from this life.
I have died from the sword of love; there is no essential
    duality. I have died crying, "Beloved, beloved," and as
    I die he will remember my spirit.
I have sacrificed my head in my search for the beloved,    5
    and have drunk the wine of my blood. I have used my
    arms to sew my shroud, and he will lay me down in the
    grave.
Bullha Shah, it is my love for you that has captured my
    heart. Come and visit my house, and let us see who
    will sacrifice his head.

੩੬

ਸੇ ਵਟਜਾਰੇ ਆਏ ਨੀ ਮਾਏ, ਸੇ ਵਟਜਾਰੇ ਆਏ
ਲਾਲਾਂ ਦਾ ਉਹ ਵਟਜ ਕਰੋਂਦੇ, ਹੋਕਾ ਆਖ ਸੁਣਾਏ

ਲਾਲ ਨੇ ਗਹਿਟੇ ਸੋਹਟੇ ਸਾਥੀ, ਮਾਏ ਨਾਲ ਲੈ ਜਾਵਾਂ
ਸੁਟਿਆ ਹੋਕਾ ਮੈਂ ਦਿਲ ਗੁੱਝਰੀ, ਮੈਂ ਭੀ ਲਾਲ ਲਿਆਵਾਂ
ਇਕ ਨਾ ਇਕ ਕੰਨਾਂ ਵਿਚ ਪਾ ਕੇ, ਲੋਕਾਂ ਨੂੰ ਦਿਖਲਾਵਾਂ
ਲੋਕ ਜਾਟਨ ਇਹ ਲਾਲਾਂ ਵਾਲੀ, ਲਈਆਂ ਮੈਂ ਭਰਮਾਏ

ਉੱਝਕ ਜਾ ਖਲੋਤੀ ਉਨ੍ਹਾਂ ਥੇ, ਮੈਂ ਮਨੋਂ ਸਧਰਾਈਆਂ
ਭਾਈ ਵੇ ਲਾਲਾਂ ਵਾਲਿਓ ਮੈਂ ਵੀ, ਲਾਲ ਲੈਵਟ ਨੂੰ ਆਈਆਂ
ਉਨ੍ਹਾਂ ਭਰੇ ਸੰਦੂਕ ਦਿਖਾਏ, ਮੈਨੂੰ ਰੀਝਾਂ ਆਈਆਂ
ਵੇਖੇ ਲਾਲ ਸੁਹਾਨੇ ਸਾਰੇ, ਇਕ ਤੋਂ ਇਕ ਸਵਾਏ

ਭਾਈ ਵੇ ਲਾਲਾਂ ਵਾਲਿਆ ਵੀਰਾਂ, ਇਨ੍ਹਾਂ ਦਾ ਮੁੱਲ ਦਸਾਈਂ
ਜੇ ਤੂੰ ਆਈ ਹੈਂ ਲਾਲ ਖਰੀਦਟ, ਧੜ ਤੋਂ ਸੀਸ ਲੁਹਾਈਂ
ਡਮੂ ਕਦੀ ਸੁਈ ਦਾ ਨਾ ਸਹਿਆ, ਸਿਰ ਕਿਥੋਂ ਦਿੱਤਾ ਜਾਈਂ
ਲਾਜ਼ਮ ਹੋ ਕੇ ਮੁੜ ਘਰ ਆਈ, ਪੁੱਫਟ ਗਵਾਂਢੀ ਆਏ

੫ ਤੂੰ ਜੁ ਗਈ ਸੈਂ ਲਾਲ ਖਰੀਦਟ, ਉੱਚੀ ਅੱਡੀ ਚਾਈ
ਕਿਹੜਾ ਮੁਹਰਾ ਓਥੋਂ ਰੰਨੇ, ਤੂੰ ਲੈ ਕੇ ਘਰ ਆਈ
ਲਾਲ ਸੀ ਭਾਰੇ ਮੈਂ ਸਾਂ ਹਲਕੀ, ਖਾਲੀ ਕੰਨੀ ਸਾਈ
ਭਾਰਾ ਲਾਲ ਅਟਾਮੁੱਲਾ ਓਥੋਂ, ਮੈਥੇ ਚੁੱਕਿਆ ਨਾ ਜਾਏ

56

## 36

Those traders[1] have come, Mother, those traders have
   come. They deal in rubies, and call out their wares.
Rubies and ornaments make fair companions, Mother;
   I will take them with me. When I heard their cries,
   I thought that I too would get some rubies. Wearing
   one or two in my ears, I will show them off to people.
   Then they will know that this is a girl who has rubies,
   and they will be attracted to her.
Finally I went and stood beside them, telling them what
   I desired. "Oh brother ruby men, I too have come to
   buy rubies." They display caskets full, and I am filled
   with desire. She sees how lovely all the rubies look,
   each better than the other.
"Oh brother ruby man, tell me what the price is." "If you
   have come to buy rubies, let your head be removed
   from your body." "I have never suffered the prick of
   a needle, so how can I give you my head?" Helplessly
   she returns home, where her neighbors come to
   question her.
"When you went to buy rubies, you strode out so                5
   confidently. What bead did you bring back home from
   there, girl?" "The rubies were heavy and I was light,
   and had only a token payment in my hem.[2] Heavy
   rubies are priceless; I did not manage to pick any up
   from there."

ਕੱਚੀ ਕੱਚ ਵਿਹਾਜ ਨਾ ਜਾਣਾਂ, ਲਾਲ ਵਿਹਾਜਟ ਚੱਲੀ
ਪੱਲੇ ਖਰਚ ਨਾ ਸਾਖ ਨਾ ਕਾਈ, ਹੱਥੋਂ ਹਾਰਨ ਚੱਲੀ
ਮੈਂ ਮੋਟੀ ਮੁਸ਼ਟੰਡੀ ਦਿੱਸਾਂ, ਲਾਲ ਨੂੰ ਚਾਵਟ ਚੱਲੀ
ਜਿਸ ਸ਼ਾਹ ਨੇ ਮੁੱਲ ਲੈ ਕੇ ਦੇਣਾ, ਸੋ ਸ਼ਾਹ ਮੂੰਹ ਨਾ ਲਾਏ

ਲਾਲ ਚੁਗੇਂਦੀ ਨਾਜ਼ਕ ਹੋਈ, ਇਹ ਗੱਲ ਕੌਟ ਨਿਤਾਰੇ
ਜਾਂ ਮੈਂ ਮੁੱਲ ਉਨ੍ਹਾਂ ਨੂੰ ਪੁੱਛਿਆ, ਮੁੱਲ ਕਰਨ ਉਹ ਭਾਰੇ
ਡਮੂ ਸੂਈ ਦਾ ਕਦੇ ਨਾ ਖਾਧਾ, ਉਹ ਆਖਣ ਸਿਰ ਵਾਰੇ
ਜਿਹੜੀਆਂ ਗਾਈਆਂ ਲਾਲ ਵਿਹਾਜਟ, ਉਹਨਾਂ ਸੀਸ ਲੁਹਾਏ

### ੩੫

ਹੱਥੀ ਢਿਲਕ ਪਈ ਮੇਰੇ ਚਰਖੇ ਦੀ, ਹੁਣ ਮੈਥੋਂ ਕੱਤਿਆ ਨਾ ਜਾਵੇ

ਹੁਣ ਦਿਨ ਚੜ੍ਹਿਆ ਕਦ ਹੋਵੇ ਮੈਨੂੰ, ਪਿਆਰਾ ਮੂੰਹ ਦਿਖਲਾਵੇ
ਤਕਲੇ ਨੂੰ ਵਲ ਪੈ ਪੈ ਜਾਂਦੇ, ਕੌਟ ਲੁਹਾਰ ਲਿਆਵੇ

ਤਕਲਿਓਂ ਵਲ ਕੱਢ ਲੁਹਾਰਾ, ਤੰਦ ਚਲੇਂਦੀ ਨਾਹੀਂ
ਘੜੀ ਘੜੀ ਇਹ ਝੋਲੇ ਖਾਂਦਾ, ਛੱਲੀ ਕਿਤ ਬਿਧ ਲਾਹਵੇ

ਪਲੀਤਾ ਨਹੀਂ ਜੋ ਬੀੜੀ ਬੰਨ੍ਹਾਂ, ਬਾਇੜ ਹੱਥ ਨਾ ਆਵੇ
ਚਮੜਿਆਂ ਨੂੰ ਚੋਪੜ ਨਾਹੀਂ, ਮਾਲੂ ਪਈ ਭਰੜਾਵੇ

੫   ਤ੍ਰਿੰਜਣ ਕੱਤਣ ਸੱਦਣ ਸਈਆਂ, ਬਿਰਹੋਂ ਢੋਲ ਬਜਾਵੇ
    ਤੀਲੀ ਨਹੀਂ ਜੋ ਪੂਣੀਆਂ ਵੱਟਾਂ, ਵੱਢਾ ਗੋਹੜੇ ਖਾਵੇ

I do not know how to buy cheap glass, but went to buy
rubies. I had no cash in my hem, nor any credit, and
I went set to make a loss. I looked like a fine strapping
girl when I went to pick up the rubies. The lord who
was supposed to buy them and give them to me
disregarded me.

Picking up rubies, you have become thin. Who can decide
what this means? When I asked them the price, they
named a heavy one. I have never suffered the prick of
a needle, but they told me to sacrifice my head. The
girls who went to buy rubies had their heads removed.

### 37

The[1] handle of my spinning wheel has got loose, so now
I cannot spin.

Now the day is well advanced, when will my beloved show
his face to me? The wheel shaft keeps getting twisted.
Who will fetch me the blacksmith?

Oh blacksmith, get the kink out of the spindle, it does not
let the thread run properly. It sways about all the time,
so how can it produce balls of yarn?

I have no waxed thread to fasten the washer, and I cannot
find the connecting string. There is no grease on the
leather straps, and the driving band keeps squeaking.

My friends call me to spin in the spinning party, but the    5
pain of love beats its drum. I do not have a stick to
twist the cotton rolls, and the calf eats the bunches
of carded cotton.

ਮਾਹੀ ਛਿੜ ਗਿਆ ਨਾਲ ਮਹੀਂ ਦੇ, ਹੁਣ ਕੱਤਣ ਕਿਸ ਨੂੰ ਭਾਵੇ
ਜਿਤ ਵਲ ਯਾਰ ਉਤੇ ਵੱਲ ਅਖੀਆਂ, ਮੇਰਾ ਦਿਲ ਬੇਲੇ ਵਲ ਧਾਵੇ

ਅਰਜ਼ ਏਹੋ ਮੈਨੂੰ ਆਣ ਮਿਲੇ ਹੁਣ, ਕੌਣ ਵਸੀਲਾ ਜਾਵੇ
ਸੈ ਮਣਾਂ ਦਾ ਕਤ ਲਿਆ ਬੁੱਲ੍ਹਾ, ਜੇ ਸ਼ਹੁ ਮੈਨੂੰ ਗਾਲ ਲਾਵੇ


## ੩੮

ਹਾਜੀ ਲੋਕ ਮੱਕੇ ਨੂੰ ਜਾਂਦੇ, ਮੇਰਾ ਰਾਂਝਾ ਮਾਹੀ ਮੱਕਾ
ਨੀ ਮੈਂ ਕਮਲੀ ਹਾਂ

ਮੈਂ ਤੇ ਮੰਗ ਰਾਂਝੇ ਦੀ ਹੋਈਆਂ, ਮੇਰਾ ਬਾਬਲ ਕਰਦਾ ਧੱਕਾ

ਹਾਜੀ ਲੋਕ ਮੱਕੇ ਨੂੰ ਜਾਂਦੇ, ਮੇਰੇ ਘਰ ਵਿਚ ਨੌਂਸ਼ਹੁ ਮੱਕਾ

ਵਿੱਚੇ ਹਾਜੀ ਵਿੱਚੇ ਗ਼ਾਜ਼ੀ, ਵਿੱਚੇ ਚੋਰ ਉਚੱਕਾ

The beloved has taken the buffaloes out to pasture, so now
who cares to spin? My eyes are drawn to wherever my
beloved is; my heart races to the river glade.

Now my only plea is that he may come and meet me. Who
will go as my intermediary? I will have spun a hundred
maunds[2] of thread, Bullha, if the lord embraces me.

### 38

Hajjis go to Mecca.[1] My Mecca is my beloved Ranjha. Oh,
I am crazy.

My betrothal is to Ranjha. My father pressures me harshly.

Hajjis go to Mecca. My Mecca is having my bridegroom in
my house.

The hajji is within, the ghazi[2] is within. The burglar and
the thief are within.

## ੩੯

ਹਿਜਾਬ ਕਰੋਂ ਦਰਵੇਸ਼ੀ ਕੋਲੋਂ, ਕਦ ਤਕ ਹੁਕਮ ਚਲਾਵੇਂਗਾ
ਗਲ ਅਲਫ਼ੀ ਸਿਰ ਪਾ ਬਰਹਨਾ, ਭਲਕੇ ਰੂਪ ਵਟਾਵੇਂਗਾ

ਇਸ ਲਾਲਚ ਨਫ਼ਸਾਨੀ ਮੁੱਠੋਂ, ਉੜਕ ਮੂਨ ਮਨਾਵੇਂਗਾ
ਘਾਟ ਜ਼ੁਕਾਤ ਮੰਗਣਗੇ ਪਿਆਦੇ, ਕਹੁ ਕੀ ਅਮਲ ਵਿਖਾਵੇਂਗਾ
ਆਣ ਬਣੀ ਜਦ ਸਿਰ ਪਰ ਭਾਰੀ, ਅੱਗੋਂ ਕੀ ਬਤਲਾਵੇਂਗਾ

ਹਕ ਪਰਾਇਆ ਜਾਤੇ ਨਾਹੀਂ, ਖਾ ਕਰ ਭਾਰ ਉਠਾਵੇਂਗਾ
ਫੇਰ ਨਾ ਆ ਕਰ ਬਦਲਾ ਦੇਸੇਂ, ਲਾਖੀ ਖੇਤ ਲੁਟਾਵੇਂਗਾ
ਦਾਅ ਲਾ ਕੇ ਵਿਚ ਜਗ ਦੇ ਜੂਏ, ਜਿੱਤੇ ਦਾਮ ਹਰਾਵੇਂਗਾ

ਜੈਸੀ ਕਰਨੀ ਵੈਸੀ ਭਰਨੀ, ਪਰੇਮ ਨਗਰ ਵਰਤਾਰਾ ਏ
ਏਥੇ ਦੋਜ਼ਖ ਕੱਟ ਤੂੰ ਦਿਲਬਰ, ਅੱਗੇ ਖੁੱਲ੍ਹ ਬਹਾਰਾ ਏ
ਕੇਸਰ ਬੀਜ ਜੂ ਕੇਸਰ ਜੰਮੇ, ਲੱਸਣ ਬੀਜ ਠਗਾਵੇਂਗਾ

੫　ਕਰੋ ਕਮਾਈ ਮੇਰੇ ਭਾਈ, ਏਹੋ ਵਕਤ ਕਮਾਵਣ ਦਾ
ਪੌਂ ਸਤਾਰਾਂ ਪੈਂਦੇ ਨੇ, ਹੁਣ ਦਾਅ ਨਾ ਬਾਜ਼ੀ ਹਾਰਣ ਦਾ
ਉਜੜੀ ਖੇਡ ਛਪਟਗੀਆਂ ਨਰਦਾਂ, ਝਾੜ ਦੁਕਾਨ ਉਠਾਵੇਂਗਾ

ਖਾਵੇਂ ਰਾਸ ਚਬਾਵੇਂ ਬੀੜੇ, ਅੰਗ ਪੁਸ਼ਾਕ ਲਗਾਇਆ ਈ
ਟੇਢੀ ਪਗੜੀ ਆਕੜ ਚੱਲੇਂ, ਜੁੱਤੀ ਪੈਰ ਅੜਾਇਆ ਈ
ਪਲਦਾ ਹੈਂ ਤੂੰ ਜਮ ਦਾ ਬਕਰਾ, ਅਪਣਾ ਆਪ ਕੁਹਾਵੇਂਗਾ

## 39

You turn your face from a fakir's life, but how long will
    your authority run? Wearing a shroud[1] and with bare
    head and feet, you will look quite different tomorrow.

You have been led astray by your carnal appetites, but
    in the end you will have your head shaven. At the
    crossing place the constables will demand the toll,
    so say: what good deeds will you have to show? When
    things become very difficult for you, what account will
    you give then?

You did not recognize other people's rights, so you will
    suffer the burden of what you have enjoyed. You will
    not return to pay recompense, and you will let your
    precious field be stripped. By gambling on the world,
    you will lose the coins you had won.

The rule of the city of love is that actions bring their own
    rewards. If you suffer hell here, my dear, then ahead
    the joys of spring lie open. Sow saffron to produce
    saffron. If you sow garlic, you will be deceived.

Practice earning, brother, for this is the time to earn.      5
    When you throw a seventeen,[2] it is no time to bet on
    losing the game. When the game is lost, the pieces are
    put away, and you will shut up shop with no winnings.

You live off your capital and chew betel, dressing your
    body in fine clothes. You tilt your turban[3] to one side
    and strut about with your slippers stuck on the front
    of your feet. Reared for death like a goat, you will get
    yourself slaughtered.

ਗੋਇਲ ਵਾਸਾ ਵੱਸਣ ਐਥੇ, ਰਹਿਣ ਨੂੰ ਅੱਗੇ ਡੇਰਾ ਏ
ਲੈ ਲੈ ਤੁਹਾਡੇ ਘਰ ਨੂੰ ਘੱਲੀਂ, ਐਹੋ ਵੇਲਾ ਤੇਰਾ ਏ
ਉਥੇ ਹੱਥ ਨਾ ਲਗਦਾ ਕੁਝ ਵੀ, ਐਥੋਂ ਹੀ ਲੈ ਜਾਵੇਂਗਾ

ਸਬਕ ਮੁਹੱਬਤ ਪੜੂ ਉਸੇ ਦਾ, ਬੇਮੁਜਬ ਕਿਉਂ ਡੁਬਨਾ ਏਂ
ਪੜੂ ਪੜੂ ਕਿੱਸੇ ਮਗ਼ਜ਼ ਖਪਾਵੇਂ, ਕਿਉਂ ਖੂੱਡਣ ਵਿਚ ਖੁਭਨਾ ਏਂ
ਹਰਫ਼ ਇਸ਼ਕ ਦਾ ਇਕੋ ਨੁਕਤਾ, ਕਾਹ ਕੋ ਉੱਠ ਲਦਾਵੇਂਗਾ

ਭੁੱਖ ਮਰੇਂਦਿਆਂ ਨਾਮ ਸਾਈਂ ਦਾ, ਐਹੋ ਬਾਤ ਚੰਗੇਰੀ ਏ
ਦੇਵੇਂ ਥੋਕ ਪਥਰ ਥੀਂ ਭਾਰੇ, ਔਖੀ ਜਿਹੀ ਇਹ ਫੇਰੀ ਏ
ਆਣ ਬਣੀ ਜਦ ਸਿਰ ਪਰ ਭਾਰੀ, ਅੱਗੋਂ ਕਿਆ ਬਤਲਾਵੇਂਗਾ

੧੦ ਅੰਮਾ ਬਾਬਾ ਬੇਟੀ ਬੇਟਾ, ਪੁਛ ਵੇਖਾਂ ਕਿਉਂ ਰੋਂਦੇ ਨੀ
ਰੰਨਾਂ ਕੰਜਕਾਂ ਭੈਣਾਂ ਭਾਈ, ਵਾਰਸ ਆਣ ਖਲੋਂਦੇ ਨੀ
ਇਹ ਜੋ ਲੁੱਟਦੇ ਤੂੰ ਨਹੀਂ ਲੁੱਟਦਾ, ਮਰਕੇ ਆਪ ਲੁਟਾਵੇਂਗਾ

ਇਕ ਇੱਕਲਿਆਂ ਜਾਣਾ ਈ ਤੈਂ, ਨਾਲ ਨਾ ਕੋਈ ਜਾਵੇਗਾ
ਖੇਸ਼ ਕਬੀਲਾ ਰੋਂਦਾ ਪਿੱਟਦਾ, ਰਾਹੋਂ ਹੀ ਮੁੜ ਆਵੇਗਾ
ਸ਼ਹਿਰੋਂ ਬਾਹਰ ਜੰਗਲ ਵਿਚ ਵਾਸਾ, ਓਥੇ ਡੇਰਾ ਪਾਵੇਂਗਾ

ਕਰਾਂ ਨਸੀਹਤ ਵੱਡੀ ਜੇ ਕੋਈ, ਸੁਣ ਕਰ ਦਿਲ ਤੇ ਲਾਵੇਗਾ
ਮੋਏ ਤਾਂ ਰੋਜ਼ ਹਸ਼ਰ ਨੂੰ ਉਠਸਣ, ਆਸ਼ਕ ਨਾ ਮਰ ਜਾਵੇਂਗਾ
ਜੇ ਤੂੰ ਮਰੇਂ ਮਰਨ ਤੋਂ ਅੱਗੇ, ਮਰਨੇ ਦਾ ਮੁੱਲ ਪਾਵੇਂਗਾ

Dwelling here is like a stay in a herdsman's hut—the place
to live in lies ahead. Collect your gifts and send them
to that home; now is your opportunity. You will not
find anything there, you will have to take everything
from here.

Study the lesson of loving only him. Why do you drown
yourself for no reason? You keep reading stories and
troubling your brain, but why get stuck in the mire?
The letter of love has a single dot,[4] so why load up
trains of camels with your books?

When dying of hunger, the name of the lord is the one
thing that is of benefit. Both heaps[5] are full of stones,
making this a difficult trip. When things get really
difficult for you, what will you tell them then?

Mother, father, daughter, son—ask them why they are 10
crying. Women, girls, sisters, brothers—all come and
stand as your heirs. It is they who rob, not you; after
death it is you who will let yourself be robbed.

You must go quite alone, no one will go with you. Your
family and kinsfolk weep and beat themselves, asking
if you will return by the way you went. You will find
your permanent abode dwelling in the wilderness
outside the city.

Let me offer some weighty advice for anyone listening
to take to heart. The dead will arise on the day of
resurrection, but a lover will not die. You will discover
the value of dying, if you die before you die.[6]

ਜਾਂ ਰਾਹ ਸ਼ਰ੍ਹਾ ਦਾ ਪਕੜੇਂਗਾ, ਤਾ ਓਟ ਮੁਹੰਮਦੀ ਹੋਵੇਗੀ
ਕਹਿੰਦੀ ਏ ਪਰ ਕਰਦੀ ਨਾਹੀਂ, ਏਹੋ ਖ਼ਲਕਤ ਰੋਵੇਗੀ
ਹੁਣ ਸੁੱਤਿਆਂ ਤੈਨੂੰ ਕੌਣ ਜਗਾਵੇ, ਜਾਗਦਿਆਂ ਪੱਛੋਤਾਵੇਂਗਾ

ਜੇ ਤੂੰ ਸਾਡੇ ਆਖੇ ਲੱਗੇਂ, ਤੈਨੂੰ ਤਖ਼ਤ ਬਹਾਵਾਂਗੇ
ਜਿਸਨੂੰ ਸਾਰਾ ਆਲਮ ਢੂੰਡੇ, ਤੈਨੂੰ ਆਣ ਮਿਲਾਵਾਂਗੇ
ਜੁਹਦੀ ਹੋ ਕੇ ਜੁਹਦ ਕਮਾਵੇਂ, ਲੈ ਪੀਆ ਗਲ ਲਾਵੇਂਗਾ

੧੫   ਐਵੇਂ ਉਮਰ ਗਵਾਈਆ ਔਗਤ, ਅਕਬਤ ਚਾ ਰੁਜ਼ੂਈ ਏ
ਲਾਲਚ ਕਰ ਕਰ ਦੁਨੀਆਂ ਉੱਤੇ, ਮੁੱਖ ਸਫ਼ੈਦੀ ਆਈ ਏ
ਅਜੇ ਵੀ ਸੁਣ ਜੇ ਤਾਇਬ ਹੋਵੇਂ, ਤਾਂ ਅਸ਼ਨਾ ਸਦਾਵੇਂਗਾ

ਬੁੱਲ੍ਹਾ ਸ਼ਹੁ ਦੇ ਚਲਵੈਂ ਤਾਂ ਚੱਲ, ਕਿਹਾ ਚਿਰ ਲਾਇਆ ਈ
ਜੱਕੋ ਧੱਕੀ ਕੀ ਕਰਨੀ, ਜਾਂ ਵਤਨੋਂ ਦਫ਼ਤਰ ਆਇਆ ਈ
ਵਾਚਦਿਆਂ ਖ਼ਤ ਅਕਲ ਗਈਓਈ, ਰੋ ਰੋ ਹਾਲ ਵੰਜਾਵੇਂਗਾ

If you take the path of righteousness, you will find the
protection of Muhammad.[7] It is people who talk but
do not act who will weep. Now who will wake you as
you sleep? You will be sorry when you do wake up.

If you do as we say, we will seat you on a throne. We will
unite you with the one the whole world is looking for.
If you become abstinent and practice abstinence, you
will embrace the beloved.

You have uselessly wasted your life for nothing, and you     15
have destroyed your existence in the world to come.
With your unceasing greed for the world, your face
has grown pale. Even now, though, listen. If you
repent, you will be called a lover.

Bullha, if you mean to go the lord, then go, what are you
delaying for? Why dither when the summons has
come from the land where you belong? Reading the
letter[8] has made you go out of your mind, but all this
weeping will destroy you.

## ੪੦

ਹਿੰਦੂ ਨਾ ਨਹੀਂ ਮੁਸਲਮਾਨ
ਭਏ ਨਿਰੰਜਨ੧ ਤਜ ਅਭਿਮਾਨ

ਸੁੰਨੀ ਨਾ ਨਹੀਂ ਹਮ ਸ਼ੀਆ
ਸੁਲਾ ਕੁੱਲ ਕਾ ਮਾਰਗ ਲੀਆ

ਭੁੱਖੇ ਨਾ ਨਹੀਂ ਹਮ ਰੱਜੇ
ਨੰਗੇ ਨਾ ਨਹੀਂ ਹਮ ਕੱਜੇ

ਰੋਂਦੇ ਨਾ ਨਹੀਂ ਹਮ ਹਸਦੇ
ਉਜੜੇ ਨਾ ਨਹੀਂ ਹਮ ਵਸਦੇ

੫    ਪਾਪੀ ਨਾ ਸੁਧਰਮੀ ਨਾ
ਪਾਪ ਪੁੰਨ ਕੀ ਰਾਹ ਨਾ ਜਾਣਾਂ

ਬੁੱਲ੍ਹਾ ਸ਼ਾਹੁ ਜੋ ਹਰਿ ਚਿਤ ਲਾਗੇ
ਹਿੰਦੂ ਤੁਰਕ ਦੂਜਨ ਤਿਆਗੇ

## ੪੧

ਹੁਣ ਇਸ਼ਕ ਅਸਾਂ ਵਲ ਆਇਆ ਹੈ,੧ ਤੂੰ ਆਇਆ ਹੈਂ ਮਨ ਭਾਇਆ ਹੈਂ੨

ਇਬਰਾਹੀਮ ਚਾ ਚਿਖ਼ਾ ਸੁਟਾਇਓ, ਜ਼ਕਰੀਏ ਸਿਰ ਕਲਵੱਤੂ ਧਰਾਇਓ
ਯੂਸਫ਼ ਹੱਟੇ ਹੱਟ ਵਿਕਾਇਓ, ਕਹੁ ਸਾਨੂੰ ਕੀ ਲਿਆਇਆ ਹੈਂ

## 40

I[1] am not a Hindu, nor a Muslim. I have forsaken pride
and become unsullied.

I am not a Sunni, nor a Shia. I have adopted the path of
peace toward all.[2]

I am not hungry, nor am I full. I am not naked, nor am
I covered.

I do not weep, nor do I laugh. I am not ruined, nor do
I flourish.

I am not a sinner, nor am I virtuous. I do not know about     5
the path of sin and merit.

Bullhe Shah, the mind that is fixed on God leaves behind
the duality of Hindu and Turk.[3]

## 41

Now, love, you have come to us. You have come and we
are happy to see you.

You had Ibrahim thrown onto the pyre.[1] You had
Zakariya's head sawn.[2] You had Yusuf hawked from
stall to stall.[3] Tell us what you have brought for us.

ਸ਼ੈਖ ਸੁਨਆਨੋਂ ਖੂਕ ਚਰਾਇਓ, ਸ਼ਮਸ ਦੀ ਖੱਲ ਉਲਟ ਲੁਹਾਇਓ
ਸੂਲੀ ਤੇ ਮਨਸੂਰ ਚੜ੍ਹਾਇਓ, ਕਰ ਹੱਠ ਹੁਣ ਮੈਂ ਵੱਲ ਧਾਇਆ ਹੈਂ

ਜਿਸ ਘਰ ਤੇਰਾ ਫੇਰ ਹੋਇਆ, ਸੋ ਜਲ ਬਲ ਕੋਇਲਾ ਢੇਰ ਹੋਇਆ
ਜਦ ਰਾਖ ਉੱਡੀ ਤਦ ਸੇਰ ਹੋਇਆ, ਕਹੁ ਕਿਸ ਗੱਲ ਦਾ ਸਯਰਾਇਆ ਹੈਂ

੫    ਬੁੱਲ੍ਹੂ ਸ਼ਹੁ ਦੇ ਕਾਰਨ ਕਰੀਏ, ਤਨ ਭੱਠੀ ਮਨ ਆਹਰਣ ਕਰੀਏ
ਪਰੇਮ ਹਥੋੜਾ ਮਾਰਨ ਕਰੀਏ, ਦਿਲ ਲੋਹਾ ਅੱਗ ਪੰਘਾਇਆ ਹੈਂ


## ੪੨

ਹੁਣ ਕਿਸ ਥੀਂ ਆਪ ਛੁਪਾਈਦਾ

ਕਿਤੇ ਮੁੱਲਾਂ ਹੋ ਬੁਲੇਂਦੇ ਹੋ, ਕਿਤੇ ਸੁੰਨਤ ਫ਼ਰਜ਼ ਦਸੇਂਦੇ ਹੋ
ਕਿਤੇ ਰਾਮ ਦੁਹਾਈ ਦੇਂਦੇ ਹੋ, ਕਿਤੇ ਮੱਥੇ ਤਿਲਕ ਲਗਾਈਦਾ

ਮੈਂ ਮੇਰੀ ਹੈ ਕਿ ਤੇਰੀ ਹੈ, ਇਹ ਅੰਤ ਭਸਮ ਦੀ ਢੇਰੀ ਹੈ
ਇਹ ਢੇਰੀ ਪੀਆ ਨੇ ਘੇਰੀ ਹੈ, ਢੇਰੀ ਨੂੰ ਨਾਚ ਨਚਾਈਦਾ

ਕਿਤੇ ਬੇਸਰ ਚੁੜਾ ਪਾਓਗੇ, ਕਿਤੇ ਜੋੜਾ ਪਾ ਹੰਢਾਓਗੇ
ਕਿਤੇ ਆਦਮ ਹਵਾ ਬਣ ਆਓਗੇ, ਕਦੀ ਮੈਥੋਂ ਵੀ ਭੁੱਲ ਜਾਈਦਾ

You had the pigs grazed by Shaikh Sanaan.[4] You had
Shams[5] hanged upside down and flayed. You had
Mansur[6] put up on the gallows. Now you have
determinedly attacked me.

The house that you have visited has been on fire and
turned into a heap of ashes. Only when the ash flies
away are you satisfied. Tell us what you have set your
heart on.

Bullha, for the sake of the lord, let us make the body the      5
furnace, the mind the anvil, and love the hammer to
beat the iron of the heart that is melted in the fire.

## 42

Who are you hiding yourself from now?

Sometimes as a mullah you give the call to prayer,
sometimes you tell of religious practice and duty.
Sometimes you utter appeals to Ram, sometimes you
put the *tilak*[1] on your forehead.

This "I" may be mine or yours, but in the end it is a heap
of ashes. This heap has been surrounded by the
beloved, and it is set to dance.

Sometimes you will put on a nose ring and topknot,
sometimes you will put on a costume and dress up.
Sometimes you will come as Adam and Eve. Can you
ever be mistaken, even by me?

੫ ਬਾਹਰ ਜ਼ਾਹਰ ਡੇਰਾ ਪਾਇਓ, ਆਪੇ ਢੋਂ ਢੋਂ ਢੋਲ ਬਜਾਇਓ
ਜਗ ਤੇ ਆਪਣਾ ਆਪ ਜਤਾਇਓ, ਫਿਰ ਅਬਦੁੱਲੂ ਦੇ ਘਰ ਧਾਈਦਾ

ਜੋ ਭਾਲ ਤੁਸਾਡੀ ਕਰਦਾ ਹੈ, ਮੋਇਆਂ ਤੋਂ ਅੱਗੇ ਮਰਦਾ ਹੈ
ਮੋਇਆਂ ਵੀ ਤੈਥੋਂ ਡਰਦਾ ਹੈ, ਮਤ ਮੋਇਆਂ ਨੂੰ ਮਾਰ ਕੁਹਾਈਦਾ

ਬਿੰਦਰਾਬਨ ਮੇਂ ਗਊਆਂ ਚਰਾਵੇਂ, ਲੰਕਾ ਚੜ੍ਹ ਕੇ ਨਾਦ ਵਜਾਵੇਂ
ਮੱਕੇ ਦਾ ਬਣ ਹਾਜੀ ਆਵੇਂ, ਵਾਹ ਵਾਹ ਰੰਗ ਵਟਾਈਦਾ

ਮਨਸੂਰ ਤੁਸਾਂ ਥੇ ਆਇਆ ਏ, ਤੁਸਾਂ ਸੂਲੀ ਪਕੜ ਚੜ੍ਹਾਇਆ ਏ
ਮੇਰਾ ਬੀਰਨ ਬਾਬਲ ਜਾਇਆ ਏ, ਦਿਓ ਖ਼ੂਨ ਬਹਾ ਮੇਰੇ ਭਾਈ ਦਾ

ਤੁਸੀਂ ਸਭਨੀਂ ਭੇਖੀਂ ਥੀਂਦੇ ਹੋ, ਮੈਨੂੰ ਹਰ ਜਾ ਤੁਸੀਂ ਦਸੀਂਦੇ ਹੋ
ਮਧ ਆਪੇ ਆਪੇ ਪੀਂਦੇ ਹੋ, ਆਪੇ ਆਪ ਕੋ ਆਪ ਛਕਾਈਦਾ

੧੦ ਹੁਣ ਪਾਸ ਤੁਸਾਡੇ ਵੱਸਾਂਗੀ, ਨਾ ਬੇਦਿਲ ਹੋ ਕੇ ਨੱਸਾਂਗੀ
ਸਭ ਭੇਤ ਤੁਹਾਡੇ ਦੱਸਾਂਗੀ, ਕਿਉਂ ਮੈਨੂੰ ਅੰਗ ਨਾ ਲਾਈਦਾ

ਵਾਹ ਜਿਸ ਪਰ ਕਰਮ ਅਵੇਹਾ ਹੈ, ਤਹਿਕੀਕ ਉਹ ਵੀ ਤੈਂ ਜੇਹਾ ਹੈ
ਸੱਚ ਸਹੀ ਰਵਾਇਤ ਏਹਾ ਹੈ, ਤੇਰੀ ਨਜ਼ਰ ਮਿਹਰ ਤਰ ਜਾਈਦਾ

ਵਿਚ ਭਾਂਬੜ ਬਾਗ਼ ਲਵਾਈਦਾ, ਚਰੂ ਵਿੱਚੋਂ ਆਪ ਵਖਾਈਦਾ
ਜਾਂ ਅਲਫ਼ੋਂ ਅਹਦ ਬਣਾਈਦਾ, ਤਾਂ ਬਾਤਨ ਕਿਆ ਬਤਲਾਈਦਾ

You set up your camp outside in plain view, and it is 5
    you who beat the drum with a loud beat. You made
    yourself known to the world; then you raced to the
    house of Abdullah.[2]

Whoever searches for you dies before he is dead.[3] Even
    after death he fears you, in case the dead are killed and
    slaughtered.

In Bindraban[4] you take the cows to pasture. You sound
    the conch when attacking Lanka.[5] You come as a hajji
    from Mecca. How amazingly your appearance
    is varied.

Mansur[6] came to you; it is you who seized him and made
    him mount the gallows. He is my dear brother, born
    of the same father. Blood money for my brother
    should be paid.

You are in all guises, you appear to me everywhere. It is
    you who are the wine and you who drink it. You are
    the one who makes you taste yourself.

Now I will remain with you. I will not lose heart and run 10
    away. I will tell all your mysteries. Why am I not to be
    embraced?

How wonderful, the one so favored is indeed just like you.
    It is a reliable tradition that salvation is to be attained
    through your look of kindness.

If the garden is planted in the flames, you display yourself
    from the fire pit. When Ahad is made from *alif*,[7] how
    is the hidden revealed?

ਬੇਲੀ ਅੱਲ੍ਹਾ ਵਾਲੀ ਮਾਲਿਕ ਹੋ, ਤੁਸੀਂ ਆਪੇ ਅਪਣੇ ਸਾਲਿਕ ਹੋ
ਆਪੇ ਖ਼ਲਕਤ ਆਪੇ ਖ਼ਾਲਿਕ ਹੋ, ਆਪੇ ਅਮਰ ਮਰੂਫ਼ ਕਰਾਈਦਾ

ਕਿਤੇ ਚੋਰ ਹੋ ਕਿਧਰੇ ਕਾਜ਼ੀ ਹੋ, ਕਿਤੇ ਮੰਬਰ ਤੇ ਬਹਿ ਵਾਅਜ਼ੀ ਹੋ
ਕਿਤੇ ਤੇਗ ਬਹਾਦਰ ਗ਼ਾਜ਼ੀ ਹੋ, ਆਪੇ ਅਪਣਾ ਕਟਕ ਚੜ੍ਹਾਈਦਾ

੧੫  ਆਪੇ ਯੂਸਫ਼ ਕੈਦ ਕਰਾਇਓ, ਯੂਨਸ ਮੱਛੀ ਤੋਂ ਨਿਗਲਾਇਓ
ਸਾਬਰ ਕੀੜੇ ਘਤ ਬਹਾਇਓ, ਫਿਰ ਉਹਨੂੰ ਤਖ਼ਤ ਚੜ੍ਹਾਈਦਾ

ਜੇ 'ਅਲਿਨਸਾਨ' ਪੜ੍ਹਾਇਆ ਈ, ਤਾਂ ਆਪ ਨੂੰ ਭਲਾ ਛੁਪਾਇਆ ਈ
ਦਿਲ ਚੌਂਦਾਂ ਤਬਕ ਬਟਾਇਆ ਈ, ਕਿਤੇ ਲੰਮਾ ਝੇੜਾ ਪਾਈਦਾ

ਬੁੱਲ੍ਹਾ ਸ਼ਹੁ ਹੁਣ ਸਹੀ ਸੰਞਾਤੇ ਹੋ, ਹਰ ਸੂਰਤ ਨਾਲ ਪਛਾਤੇ ਹੋ
ਕਿਤੇ ਆਤੇ ਕਿਤੇ ਜਾਤੇ ਹੋ, ਹੁਣ ਮੈਥੋਂ ਭੁੱਲ ਨਾ ਜਾਈਦਾ

## ੪੩

ਹੁਣ ਮੈਂ ਲਖਿਆ ਸੋਹਣਾ ਯਾਰ, ਜਿਸ ਦੇ ਹੁਸਨ ਦਾ ਗਰਮ ਬਜ਼ਾਰ

ਜਦ ਅਹਦ ਇਕ ਇਕੱਲਾ ਸੀ, ਨਾ ਜ਼ਾਹਰ ਕੋਈ ਤਜੱਲਾ ਸੀ
ਨਾ ਰੱਬ ਰਸੂਲ ਨਾ ਅੱਲ੍ਹਾ ਸੀ, ਨਾ ਜੱਬਾਰ ਤੇ ਨਾ ਕੱਹਾਰ

You are friend, God, lord, and master. It is you who are
your own devoted follower. It is you who are the
creation and the creator. It is you who causes good
deeds to be performed.

Sometimes you are a thief, sometimes a *qazi,* sometimes a
preacher who climbs into the pulpit, sometimes Tegh
Bahadur,[8] the warrior for faith. You are the one who
causes your army to attack.

It is you who had Yusuf [9] imprisoned, you who had Yunus[10]   15
swallowed by the fish, you who put the worms into
Ayub the patient,[11] then caused him to ascend the
throne.

If you taught the lesson of the word *man,*[12] then you
hid yourself well. You made the heart embrace the
fourteen spheres.[13] Thus this lengthy debate is
created.

Bullha, you are clearly recognized; lord, you are
apprehended through every form. Here you come,
here you go. Now you cannot be mistaken by me.


### 43

Now I have seen the fair beloved, whose beauty is always
in such demand.

When Ahad alone existed, no divine glory was manifest.
There was no Lord or Prophet or Allah, no Almighty,
no all-powerful God.

ਬੇਚੂਨੋ ਬੇਚਗੂਨਾ ਸੀ, ਬੇਸ਼ਿਬ੍ਹਾ ਬੇਨਮੂਨਾ ਸੀ
ਨਾ ਕੋਈ ਰੰਗ ਨਮੂਨਾ੧ ਸੀ, ਹੁਣ ਗੁਨਾਂ ਗੁਨ ਹਜ਼ਾਰ

ਪਿਆਰਾ ਪਹਿਨ ਪੋਸ਼ਾਕਾਂ ਆਇਆ, ਆਦਮ ਆਪਣਾ ਨਾਮ ਧਰਾਇਆ
ਅਹਦ ਤੇ ਬਣ ਅਹਿਮਦ ਆਇਆ, ਬਣਿਆਂ ਨਬੀਆਂ ਦਾ ਸਰਦਾਰ

੫ 'ਕੁਨ' ਕਿਹਾ 'ਫ਼ਯਕੂਨ' ਕਹਾਇਆ, ਬੇਚੂਨੀ ਸੇ ਚੁਨ ਬਣਾਇਆ
ਅਹਦ ਦੇ ਵਿਚ ਮੀਮ ਰਲਾਇਆ, ਤਾਂ ਕੀਤਾ ਐਡ ਪਸਾਰ

ਤਜੂੰ ਮਸੀਤ ਤਜੂੰ ਬੁਤਖ਼ਾਨਾ, ਬਰਤੀ ਰਹਾਂ ਨਾ ਰੋਜ਼ਾ ਜਾਨਾ
ਭੁੱਲ ਗਿਆ ਵਜ਼ੂ ਨਮਾਜ਼ ਦੁਗਾਨਾ, ਤੈਂ ਪਰ ਜਾਨ ਕਰਾਂ ਬਲਿਹਾਰ

ਪੀਰ ਪੈਗ਼ੰਬਰ ਇਸ ਦੇ ਬਰਦੇ, ਇਨਸ ਮਲਾਇਕ ਸਜਦੇ ਕਰਦੇ
ਸਿਰ ਕਦਮਾਂ ਦੇ ਉੱਤੇ ਧਰਦੇ, ਸਭ ਤੋਂ ਵੱਡੀ ਉਹ ਸਰਕਾਰ

ਜੋ ਕੋਈ ਉਸ ਨੂੰ ਲਖਿਆ ਚਾਹੇ, ਬਾਝ ਵਸੀਲੇ ਲਖਿਆ ਨ ਜਾਏ
ਸ਼ਾਹ ਇਨਾਇਤ ਭੇਤ ਬਤਾਏ, ਤਾਂ ਖੁੱਲ੍ਹੇ ਸਭ ਇਸਰਾਰ

੪੪
ਹੁਣ ਮੈਨੂੰ ਕੌਣ ਪਛਾਣੇ, ਹੁਣ ਮੈਂ ਹੋ ਗਈ ਨੀ ਕੁਝ ਹੋਰ

ਹਾਦੀ ਮੈਨੂੰ ਸਬਕ ਪੜ੍ਹਾਇਆ, ਓਥੇ ਗ਼ੈਰ ਨਾ ਆਇਆ ਜਾਇਆ
ਮੁਤਲਕ ਜ਼ਾਤ ਜਮਾਲ ਵਿਖਾਇਆ, ਵਹਦਤ ਪਾਇਆ ਨੀ ਸ਼ੋਰ

He was without parallel or analogy, without likeness or
comparison. There was no spectacle or model; now
there are thousands of things of all kinds.

The beloved came to put on various clothes; he called
himself Adam. From Ahad he turned himself into
Ahmad[1] and came as the leader of the prophets.

He said *Let it be* and caused *and it was*[2] to be said, making 5
form from formlessness. He mingled the *mīm* into
Ahad, and created this vast expanse.

I abandon the mosque, I abandon the idol temple. I do
not keep Hindu fasts, nor do I observe Ramadan.
I have forgotten ablutions and prayers with two
prostrations.[3] I sacrifice my life to you.

Saints and prophets are his slaves. Men and angels
prostrate themselves to him, laying their heads at his
feet. He is the greatest overlord of all.

No one who wishes to see him can do so without an
intermediary. If Shah Inayat reveals the secret, then
all mysteries are solved.


## 44

Now who can recognize me? Now I have become
something else.[1]

The guide taught me this lesson. There is no coming or
going of the other there. The absolute being displays
his beauty. Divine unity has created confusion.

ਅੱਵਲ ਹੋ ਕੇ ਲਾਮਕਾਨੀ, ਜ਼ਾਹਰ ਬਾਤਨ ਦਿਸਦਾ ਜਾਨੀ
ਰਿਹਾ ਨਾ ਮੇਰਾ ਨਾਮ ਨਿਸ਼ਾਨੀ, ਮਿਟ ਗਿਆ ਝਗੜਾ ਸ਼ੋਰ

ਪਿਆਰਾ ਆਪ ਜਮਾਲ ਵਿਖਾਲੇ, ਮਸਤ ਕਲੰਦਰ ਹੋ ਮਤਵਾਲੇ
ਹੰਸਾਂ ਦੇ ਹੁਣ ਵੇਖ ਕੇ ਚਾਲੇ, ਬੁੱਲ੍ਹਾ ਕਾਗਾਂ ਦੀ ਭੁੱਲ ਗਈ ਟੋਰ

## ੪੫

ਹੋਰੀ ਖੇਲੁੰਗੀ ਕਹਿ 'ਬਿਸਮਿੱਲ੍ਹਾ'

ਨਾਮ ਨਬੀ ਕੀ ਰਤਨ ਚੜ੍ਹੀ, ਬੁੰਦ ਪੜੀ 'ਇਲੱਲ੍ਹਾ'
ਰੰਗ ਰੰਗੀਲੀ ਓਹੀ ਖਿਲਾਵੇ, ਜੋ ਸਿੱਖੀ ਹੋਵੇ 'ਫਨਾ ਫ਼ਿੱਲ੍ਹਾ'

'ਅਲਸਤੁ ਬਿਰੱਬਿਕੁਮ' ਪ੍ਰੀਤਮ ਬੋਲੇ, ਸਭ ਸਖੀਆਂ ਨੇ ਘੁੰਘਟ ਖੋਲੇ
'ਕਾਲੂ ਬਲਾ' ਹੀ ਜੁੰਕਰ ਬੋਲੇ, 'ਲਾ ਇਲਾਹ ਇਲੱਲ੍ਹਾ'

'ਨਹਨੁ ਅਕਰਬ' ਕੀ ਬੰਸੀ ਬਜਾਈ, 'ਮਨ ਅਰਫ਼ ਨਫ਼ਸਹੁ' ਕੀ ਕੂਕ
          ਸੁਣਾਈ
'ਫ਼ਸੰਮ ਵਜਹੁੱਲ੍ਹਾ' ਕੀ ਧੂਮ ਮਚਾਈ, ਵਿਚ ਦਰਬਾਰ ਰਸੂਲ ਅੱਲ੍ਹਾ

੫  ਹਾਥ ਜੋੜ ਕਰ ਪਾਓਂ ਪੜੁੰਗੀ, ਆਜਿਜ਼ ਹੋ ਕਰ ਬੇਨਤੀ ਕਰੁੰਗੀ
   ਫਗਵਾ ਝਗੜਾ¹ ਭਰ ਝੋਲੀ ਲੁੰਗੀ, ਨੂਰ ਮੁਹੰਮਦ ' ਸੱਲ੍ਹਾ '

'ਫ਼ਜ਼ਕੁਰੂਨੀ' ਕੀ ਹੋਰੀ ਬਨਾਉਂ, 'ਵਸ਼ਕੁਰੂਨੀ' ਪੀਆ ਕੋ ਰਿਝਾਉਂ
ਐਸੇ ਪੀਆ ਕੇ ਮੈਂ ਬਲ ਬਲ ਜਾਉਂ, ਕੈਸਾ ਪੀਆ 'ਸੁਬਹਾਨੱਲ੍ਹਾ'

Infinite at first, the beloved appears as manifest and
    hidden. I have no name or mark anymore; all dispute
    and confusion are ended.
When the beloved displays his beauty, drunken fakirs
    become intoxicated. Now that I have observed the
    graceful movement of the wild geese,[2] Bullha, I have
    forgotten the motion of the crows.


### 45

I will play Holi, after saying *bismillāh*.[1]
I wear the name of the Prophet as my jewel, and the
    words *but God*[2] as my pendant. He is the one who
    operates this colorful show, from which the lesson of
    *annihilation in God*[3] is learned.
When the beloved said, *Am I not your lord?*[4] the girls all
    removed their veils. With the words *They said, "Yes,"*
    they said, *There is no god but God*.[5]
He played the flute of *We are nearer*,[6] and called out
    *Whoever has known himself*.[7] *Then there is the face
    of God*[8] was loudly proclaimed in the court of God's
    Apostle.
I will humbly fold my hands and fall at his feet, and in my        5
    helplessness I will entreat him. As my Holi offering,
    I will fill my lap with the light of Muhammad, *may
    God's blessing be upon him*.[9]
I will make *Then remember me* my Holi, and I will delight
    my beloved with *And be thankful to me*.[10] Such is the
    beloved to whom I am sacrificed, *glory be to God*.[11]

'ਸਿਬਗ਼ਤੁੱਲੂ' ਕੀ ਭਰ ਪਿਚਕਾਰੀ, 'ਅੱਲਾਹੁੱਸਮਦ' ਪਿਆ ਮੂੰਹ ਪਰ ਮਾਰੀ

ਨੂਰ ਨਬੀ ਦਾ ਹੱਕ ਸੇ ਜਾਰੀ, ਨੂਰ ਮੁਹੰਮਦ 'ਸੱਲੱਲੂ'

ਬੁੱਲ੍ਹੂ ਸ਼ਹੁ ਦੀ ਧੂਮ ਮਚੀ ਹੈ, 'ਲਾ ਇਲਾਹ ਇੱਲੱਲੂ'


## ੪੬

ਕੱਤ ਕੁੜੇ ਨਾ ਵੱਤ ਕੁੜੇ, ਛੱਲੀ ਲਾਹ ਭਰੋਟੇ ਘੱਤ ਕੁੜੇ


ਜੇ ਪੁਟੀ ਪੁਟੀ ਕੱਤੇਂਗੀ, ਤਾਂ ਨੰਗੀ ਮੂਲ ਨਾ ਵੱਤੇਂਗੀ

ਸੈ ਵਰ੍ਹਿਆਂ ਵੀ ਜੇ ਨਾ ਕੱਤੇਂਗੀ, ਤਾਂ ਕਾਗਾ ਮਾਰੇਗਾ ਝੁਟ ਕੁੜੇ


ਵਿਚ ਗ਼ਫ਼ਲਤ ਜੇ ਤੂੰ ਦਿਨ ਜਾਲੇ, ਕੱਤ ਤੇ ਕੁਝ ਨਾ ਲਿਉ ਸੰਭਾਲੇ

ਬਾਝੋਂ ਗੁਣ ਸ਼ਹੁ ਅਪਣੇ ਨਾਲੇ, ਤੇਰੀ ਕਿਉਂ ਕਰ ਹੋਸੀ ਗੱਤ ਕੁੜੇ


ਮਾਂ ਪਿਉ ਤੇਰੇ ਗੰਢੀਂ ਪਾਈਆਂ, ਅਜੇ ਨਾ ਤੈਨੂੰ ਸੁਰਤਾਂ ਆਈਆਂ

ਦਿਨ ਥੋੜੇ ਤੇ ਚਾਅ ਮੁਕਾਈਆਂ, ਨਾ ਆਸੇਂ ਪੇਕੇ ਵੱਤ ਕੁੜੇ


੫ ਜੇ ਦਾਜ ਵਿਹੂਟੀ ਜਾਵੇਂਗੀ, ਤਾਂ ਕਿਸੇ ਭਲੀ ਨਾ ਭਾਵੇਂਗੀ

ਓਥੇ ਸ਼ਹੁ ਨੂੰ ਕਿਵੇਂ ਰੀਝਾਵੇਂਗੀ, ਕੁਝ ਲੈ ਫ਼ਕਰਾਂ ਦੀ ਮੱਤ ਕੁੜੇ


ਤੇਰੇ ਨਾਲ ਦੀਆਂ ਦਾਜ ਰੰਗਾਏ ਨੀ, ਓਹਨਾਂ ਸੂਹੇ ਸਾਲੂ ਪਾਏ ਨੀ

ਤੂੰ ਉਲਟੇ ਪੈਰ ਕਿਉਂ ਚਾਏ ਨੀ, ਜਾ ਓਥੇ ਲਖਸੇਂ ਤੱਤ ਕੁੜੇ

The syringe[12] was filled with *the dye of God*[13] and was
    squirted on the face of *God the eternal*.[14] The light
    of the Prophet proceeded from God, the light of
    Muhammad, *may God's blessing be upon him*. Bullha,
    the fame of the lord is loudly proclaimed: *There is no*
    *god but God*.

## 46

Spin, my girl, do not idle. Take off your ball of yarn and
    place it in the basket.

If you spin rolls and rolls of yarn, you will never wander
    naked. If for a hundred years you do not spin, the crow
    will swoop and attack you, my girl.

If you spend your days in obliviousness, if you do not spin
    and accumulate something, then without any virtues
    when your lord is beside you, how will you be saved,
    my girl?

Your parents have tied your knots,[1] but you have still
    not become aware. The days are few, but you have
    wasted them in enjoyment. You will not return to your
    parents' home, my girl.

If you go without a dowry, you will not please anyone.     5
    How will you delight your lord when you get there?
    Take some guidance from the fakirs, my girl.

Your companions have had their dowry clothes dyed and
    are wearing their red outfits. Why have you gone the
    wrong way? When you get there, you will realize the
    true state of things, my girl.

ਬੁੱਲ੍ਹਾ ਸ਼ਹੁ ਘਰ ਅਪਣੇ ਆਵੇ, ਚੂੜਾ ਬੇੜਾ ਸਭ ਸੁਹਾਵੇ
ਗੁਣ ਹੋਸੀ ਤਾਂ ਗਲੇ ਲਗਾਵੇ, ਨਹੀਂ ਰੋਸੇਂ ਨੈਟੀਂ ਰੱਤ ਕੁੜੇ

## ੪੧

ਕਦੀ ਅਪਣੀ ਆਖ ਬੁਲਾਓਗੇ

ਮੈਂ ਬੇਗੁਣ ਕਿਆ ਗੁਣ ਕੀਆ ਹੈ, ਤਨ ਪੀਆ ਹੈ ਮਨ ਪੀਆ ਹੈ
ਉਹ ਪੀਆ ਸੁ ਮੇਰਾ ਜੀਆ ਹੈ, ਪੀਆ ਪੀਆ ਸੇ ਰਲ ਮਿਲ ਜਾਓਗੇ

ਮੈਂ ਫ਼ਾਨੀ ਆਪ ਕੋ ਦੂਰ ਕਰਾਂ, ਤੈਂ ਬਾਕੀ ਆਪ ਹਜ਼ੂਰ ਕਰਾਂ
ਜੇ ਅਜ਼ਹਰ ਵਾਂਗ ਮਨਸੂਰ ਕਰਾਂ, ਖੜ ਸੂਲੀ ਪਕੜ ਚੜ੍ਹਾਓਗੇ

ਮੈਂ ਜਾਗੀ ਸਭ ਜਗ ਸੋਇਆ ਹੈ, ਖੁਲ੍ਹੀ ਪਲਕ ਤਾਂ ਉਠ ਕੇ ਰੋਇਆ ਹੈ
ਜੁੱਝ ਮਸਤੀ ਕਾਮ ਨਾ ਹੋਇਆ ਹੈ, ਕਦੀ ਮਸਤ 'ਅਲਸਤ' ਬਣਾਓਗੇ

ਪ   ਜਦੋਂ ਅਨਹਦ ਬਣ ਦੇ ਨੈਟ ਧਰੇ, ਅਗੇ ਸਿਰ ਬਿਨ ਧੜ ਕੇ ਲਾਖ ਪੜੇ
ਉਛਲ ਰੰਗਟ ਦੇ ਦਰਿਆ ਚੜੇ, ਮੇਰੇ ਲਹੁ ਦੀ ਨਦੀ ਵਗਾਓਗੇ

ਕਿਸੇ ਆਸ਼ਕ ਦਾ ਸੁਖ ਸੋਟਾ ਹੈ, ਅਸਾਂ ਰੋ ਰੋ ਕੇ ਮੁਖ ਧੋਤਾ ਹੈ
ਇਹ ਜਾਦੂ ਹੈ ਕਿ ਟੂਟਾ ਹੈ, ਇਸ ਰੋਗ ਦਾ ਭੋਗ ਬਣਾਓਗੇ

Bullha, if the lord comes home, your bangles and anklets
all look fine. If you possess good qualities, he will
embrace you. Otherwise you will weep tears of blood,
my girl.

### 47

Will[1] you ever call me your own?

I am without merit; what virtuous action have I
performed? My body is the beloved, my heart is the
beloved. It is the beloved who is my life. Will you
come to me as beloved to beloved?

As the transitory, I make myself distant. As the enduring,
I make myself ever-present. If like Mansur[2] I make
things very clear, will you seize me and make me
mount the gallows?

I am awake, but the whole world is asleep. When it opens
its eyes, it gets up and weeps. Intoxication is the only
thing that works. Will you ever make me drunk on
*Am I not?*[3]

When you became unstruck,[4] you set your two eyes at     5
them. Hundreds of thousands laid down their severed
heads before you, and the ocean billowed with waves
of delight. Will you make the river of my blood flow?

Does any lover sleep peacefully? We have wept copiously
and bathed our face in tears. Is it magic or a spell that
you will use to turn this suffering into pleasure?

ਕਹੋ ਕਿਆ ਸਿਰ ਇਸ਼ਕ ਬਿਚਾਰੇਗਾ, ਫਿਰ ਕਿਆ ਬੀਸੀ ਨਿਰਵਾਰੇਗਾ
ਜਬ ਦਾਰ ਉਪਰ ਸਿਰ ਵਾਰੇਗਾ, ਤਬ ਪਾਛੇ ਢੋਲ ਬਜਾਓਗੇ

ਮੈਂ ਅਪਣਾ ਮਨ ਕਬਾਬ ਕੀਆ, ਅੱਖੋਂ ਕਾ ਅਰਕ ਸ਼ਰਾਬ ਕੀਆ
ਰਗ ਤਾਰਾਂ ਹੱਡ ਰਬਾਬ ਕੀਆ, ਕਿਆ ਮਤ ਕਾ ਨਾਮ ਬੁਲਾਓਗੇ੧

ਸ਼ਕੰਜੇ੨ ਕੋ ਕਿਆ ਕੀਜੇਗਾ, ਮਨ ਭਾਣਾ ਸੌਦਾ ਲੀਜੇਗਾ
ਇਹ ਦੀਨ ਦੁਨੀ ਕਿਸ ਦੀਜੇਗਾ, ਮੁਝੇ ਆਪਣਾ ਦਰਸ ਬਤਾਓਗੇ

੧੦ ਮੈਨੂੰ ਆਣ ਨਜ਼ਾਰੇ ਤਾਇਆ ਹੈ, ਦੋ ਨੈਣਾਂ ਬਰਖਾ ਲਾਇਆ ਹੈ
ਜੀਵੇਂ ਰੋਜ਼ ਇਨਇਤ ਆਇਆ ਹੈ, ਐਵੇਂ ਅਪਣਾ ਆਪ ਜਤਾਓਗੇ

ਬੁੱਲ੍ਹਾ ਸ਼ਹੁ ਨੂੰ ਵੇਖਣ ਜਾਓਗੇ, ਇਨ੍ਹਾਂ ਅੱਖੀਆਂ ਨੂੰ ਸਮਝਾਓਗੇ
ਦੀਦਾਰ ਤਦਾਹੀਂ ਪਾਓਗੇ, ਬਣ ਸ਼ਾਹ ਇਨਇਤ ਘਰ ਆਓਗੇ

੪੮
ਕਦੀ ਆ ਮਿਲ ਬਿਰਹੋਂ ਸਤਾਈ ਨੂੰ

ਇਸ਼ਕ ਲੱਗੇ ਤਾਂ ਹੈ ਹੈ ਕੂਕੇਂ, ਤੂੰ ਕੀ ਜਾਣੇ ਪੀੜ ਪਰਾਈ ਨੂੰ

ਜੇ ਕੋਈ ਇਸ਼ਕ ਵਿਹਾਜਿਆ ਲੋੜੇ, ਸਿਰ ਦੇਵੇ ਪਹਿਲੇ ਸਾਈ ਨੂੰ

ਅਮਲਾਂ ਵਾਲੀਆਂ ਲੰਘ ਲੰਘ ਗਈਆਂ, ਸਾਡੀਆਂ ਲੱਜਾਂ ਮਾਹੀ ਨੂੰ

Say, what secret will love ponder? Then what will happen
    when it decides? When the head has been sacrificed
    on the gallows, will you later bang the drum?
I have made my heart a kebab. I have turned the liquor of
    my eyes into wine, my veins into strings, and my bones
    into a rebeck. What will you call this religion?
What is the point of torment? Deal in what pleases the
    heart. Who is going to be given this world and the
    next? Will you show me a vision of yourself?
Your vision has come and set me on fire. My two eyes have    10
    created a downpour. Daily you have come as Inayat.
    Is this how you will make yourself known?
Bullha, when you go to look at the lord, you will make
    these eyes see properly. It is then that you will obtain
    a true vision of him. Will you return home as Shah
    Inayat?

## 48

Do come someday and meet this wretch who is oppressed
    by separation.
If you fell in love, you would shriek, "Ah, ah!" What do
    you know of another's pain?
If anyone wants to purchase love, he should first give his
    head as a down payment.
The girls who have acted well have all passed over in turn.
    It is for the beloved to protect our honor.

੫ ਗ਼ਮ ਦੇ ਵਹਿਣ ਸਿਤਮ ਦੀਆਂ ਕਾਂਗਾਂ, ਕਿਸੇ ਕਾਅਰ ਕਪੜ ਵਿਚ
ਪਾਈ ਨੂੰ

ਮਾਂ ਪਿਓ ਛੱਡ ਸਈਆਂ ਮੈਂ ਭੁਲੀਆਂ, ਬਲਿਹਾਰੀ ਰਾਮ ਦੁਹਾਈ ਨੂੰ

ਬੁੱਲ੍ਹੂ ਸ਼ਹੁ ਦੇ ਇਸ਼ਕ ਖਪਾਈ ਆਂ, ਘੇਰ ਘੁਮਟ ਵਿਚ ਪਾਈ ਨੂੰ

੪੯

ਕਦੀ ਆ ਮਿਲ ਯਾਰ ਪਿਆਰਿਆ, ਤੇਰੀਆਂ ਵਾਟਾਂ ਤੋਂ ਸਿਰ ਵਾਰਿਆ

ਚੜ੍ਹ ਬਾਗ਼ੀਂ ਕੋਇਲ ਕੂਕਦੀ, ਨਿਤ ਸੋਜ਼ੇ ਅਲਮ ਦੇ ਢੁਕਦੀ
ਮੈਨੂੰ ਤਤੜੀ ਕੋ ਸ਼ਾਮ ਵਿਸਾਰਿਆ

ਬੁੱਲ੍ਹੂ ਸ਼ਹੁ ਕਦੀ ਘਰ ਆਸੀ, ਮੇਰੀ ਬਲਦੀ ਭਾਹ ਬੁਝਾਸੀ
ਉਹਦੀ ਵਾਟਾਂ ਤੋਂ ਸਿਰ ਵਾਰਿਆ

੫੦

ਕਦੀ ਸੇਝ ਮੁਹਾਰਾਂ ਢੋਲਿਆ, ਤੇਰੀਆਂ ਵਾਟਾਂ ਤੋਂ ਸਿਰ ਘੋਲਿਆ

ਮੈਂ ਨ੍ਹਾਤੀ ਧੋਤੀ ਰਹਿ ਗਈ, ਕੋਈ ਗੰਢ ਸਜਨ ਦਿਲ ਬਹਿ ਗਈ
ਕੋਈ ਸੁਖਨ ਅਵੱਲਾ ਬੋਲਿਆ

Currents of pain and waves of cruelty surround this      5
    wretch, who has been sucked into the bottom of
    a whirlpool.[1]
I have left my parents and forgotten my girlfriends. I am
    sacrificed to the lord, to whom I appeal for justice.
Bullha, I am exhausted by my love for the lord, who has
    cast me into the whirlpool.

## 49

Do[1] come someday and meet me,[2] my beloved friend.
    My head is sacrificed to the roads on which you travel.
The *koil*[3] flies up in the gardens and cries out, exhaling
    her burning pain. I am wretched, my dark beloved has
    forgotten me.
Bullha, one day the lord will come home, and he will
    extinguish the fire that blazes within me. My head is
    sacrificed to the roads on which he travels.[4]

## 50

Sometime[1] do turn back your reins, my love. My head
    is offered to the roads on which you travel.
Freshly washed and bathed, I have been left here. Some
    knot has settled in my lover's heart. Did I say
    something inappropriate?

ਬੁੱਲ੍ਹਾ ਸ਼ਾਹੁ ਕਦੀ ਘਰ ਆਵਸੀ, ਮੇਰੀ ਬਲਦੀ ਭਾਹ ਬੁਝਾਵਸੀ
ਜਿਹਦੇ ਦੁੱਖਾਂ ਨੇ ਮੂੰਹ ਖੋਲ੍ਹਿਆ

## ੫੧

ਕਪੂਰੀ ਰੇਵੜੀ ਕਿਉਂ ਕਰ ਲੜੇ ਪਤਾਸੇ ਨਾਲ

ਤੇਲ ਤਿਲਾਂ ਦੇ ਲੱਡੂ ਨੇ, ਜਲੇਬੀ ਪਕੜ ਮੰਗਾਈ
ਡਰਦੀ ਨੱਠੀ ਕੰਦ ਸ਼ਕਰ ਤੋਂ, ਮਿਸਰੀ ਨਾਲ ਲੜਾਈ
ਕਾਂ ਲਗੜ ਨੂੰ ਮਾਰਨ ਲੱਗੇ, ਗਦੋਂ ਦੀ ਗਲੂ ਲਾਲ

ਹੋ ਫਰਿਆਦੀ ਲਖਪਤੀਆਂ ਨੇ, ਲੂਟ ਤੇ ਦਸਤਕ ਲਾਈ
ਗੁਲਗੁਲਿਆਂ ਮਨਸੂਬਾ ਬੱਧਾ, ਪਾਪੜ ਚੋਟ ਚਲਾਈ
ਭੇਡਾਂ ਮਾਰ ਪਲੰਗ ਖਪਾਏ, ਗੁਰਗਾਂ ਬੁਰਾ ਅਹਿਵਾਲ

ਗੁੜ ਦੇ ਲੱਡੂ ਗੁੱਸੇ ਹੋ ਕੇ, ਪੇੜਿਆਂ ਤੇ ਫਰਿਆਦੀ
ਬਰਫ਼ੀ ਨੂੰ ਕਹੇ ਦਾਲ ਚਨੇ ਦੀ, ਤੂੰ ਹੈਂ ਮੇਰੀ ਬਾਂਦੀ
ਚੜੂ ਸਹੇ ਸ਼ੀਹਾਂ ਤੇ ਨੱਚਟ, ਵੱਡੀ ਪਈ ਧਮਾਲ

੫ ਸ਼ਕਰ ਖੰਡ ਕਹੇ ਮਿਸਰੀ ਨੂੰ, ਮੇਰੀ ਵੇਖ ਸਢਾਈ
ਚਿੜਵੇ ਚਨੇ ਇਹ ਕਰਨ ਲੱਗੇ, ਬਦਾਨੇ ਨਾਲ ਲੜਾਈ
ਚੂਹਿਆਂ ਕੰਨ ਬਿੱਲੀ ਦੇ ਕੁਤਰੇ, ਹੋ ਹੋ ਕੇ ਖ਼ੁਸ਼ਹਾਲ

ਬੁੱਲ੍ਹਾ ਸ਼ਾਹੁ ਹੁਣ ਕਿਆ ਬਤਾਵੇ, ਜੋ ਦਿੱਸੇ ਸੋ ਲੜਦਾ
ਲੱਤ ਬਲੱਤੀ ਗੁੱਤ ਬਗੁੱਤੀ, ਕੋਈ ਨਹੀਂ ਹਥ ਫੜਦਾ
ਵੇਖੇ ਕੇਹੀ ਕਿਆਮਤ ਆਈ, ਆਇਆ ਖਰ ਦੱਜਾਲ

Bullha, one day the lord will come home. He will
    extinguish the fire that blazes within me, whose pains
    are ready to devour me.

51

Why[1] does the yellow *revaṛī* fight with the *patāsā*?
The *laḍḍū* made with sesame seeds has arrested the *jalebī*.
    The *kand* has run in fear from the sugar and fought
    with the *misrī*. The crow has started killing the hawk,
    and the donkey's cheek is red.
The millionaires[2] seek justice, and issue a summons on
    the salt. The *gulgalās* have made a plan and wounded
    the *pāpaṛ*. The sheep have attacked the leopards and
    destroyed them, and the wolves are in a sorry state.
The *guṛ* and the *laḍḍū* have got angry and complained
    against the *peṛās*. The *canā dāl* said to the *barfī*, "You
    are my slave girl." The rabbits attack and dance upon
    the lions, and have a merry time.
The *shakar khand* says to the *misrī*, "Look how clean I    5
    am." The *ciṛvās* and *canās* have started fighting with
    the *badānās*. The rats nibble the cat's ears in great
    delight.
Now what can Bullhe Shah say? Everyone you can see is
    fighting. Kicking and pulling each other's hair, no one
    holds another back. Behold the arrival of the day of
    doom, with Dajjal[3] on his donkey.

## ੫੨

ਕਰ ਕੱਤਣ ਵੱਲ ਧਿਆਨ ਕੁੜੇ

ਨਿਤ ਮੱਤੀਂ ਦੇਂਦੀ ਮਾਂ ਧੀਆ, ਕਿਉਂ ਫਿਰਨੀਂ ਐਵੇਂ ਅਹਿਦੀਆ
ਨਾ ਸ਼ਰਮ ਹਜਾ ਗਵਾ ਧੀਆ, ਤੂੰ ਕਦੀ ਤਾਂ ਸਮਝ ਨਦਾਨ ਕੁੜੇ

ਚਰਖਾ ਮੁਫ਼ਤ ਤੇਰੇ ਹੱਥ ਆਇਆ, ਪਲਿਓ ਨਹੀਂ ਕੁਝ ਖੋਲੂ ਗਵਾਇਆ
ਨਹੀਓਂ ਕਦਰ ਮਿਹਨਤ ਦਾ ਪਾਇਆ, ਜਦ ਹੋਇਆ ਕੰਮ ਅਸਾਨ ਕੁੜੇ

ਚਰਖਾ ਬਣਿਆ ਖ਼ਾਤਰ ਤੇਰੀ, ਖੇਡਣ ਦੀ ਕਰ ਹਿਰਸ ਬੁਰੇੜੀ
ਹੋਣਾ ਨਹੀਓਂ ਹੋਰ ਵਡੇਰੀ, ਮਤ ਕਰ ਕੋਈ ਅਗਿਆਨ ਕੁੜੇ

੫ ਚਰਖਾ ਤੇਰਾ ਰੰਗ ਰੰਗੀਲਾ, ਰੀਸ ਕਰੇਂਦਾ ਸਭ ਕਬੀਲਾ
ਚਲਦੇ ਚਾਰੇ ਕਰ ਲੈ ਹੀਲਾ, ਹੋ ਘਰ ਦੇ ਵਿਚ ਅਵਾਦਾਨ ਕੁੜੇ

ਇਸ ਚਰਖੇ ਦੀ ਕੀਮਤ ਭਾਰੀ, ਤੂੰ ਕੀ ਜਾਣੇਂ ਕਦਰ ਗਵਾਰੀ
ਉੱਚੀ ਨਜ਼ਰ ਫਿਰੇ ਹੰਕਾਰੀ, ਵਿਚ ਅਪਣੇ ਸ਼ਾਨ ਗੁਮਾਨ ਕੁੜੇ

ਮੈਂ ਕੂਕਾਂ ਕਰ ਖਲੀਆਂ ਬਾਹੀਂ, ਗ਼ਾਫ਼ਲ ਸਮਝ ਕਦਾਹੀਂ
ਐਸਾ ਚਰਖਾ ਘੜਨਾ ਨਾਹੀਂ, ਫੇਰ ਕਿਸੇ ਤਰਖ਼ਾਣ ਕੁੜੇ

ਇਹ ਚਰਖਾ ਤੂੰ ਕਿਉਂ ਗਵਾਇਆ, ਕਿਉਂ ਤੂੰ ਖੇਹ ਦੇ ਵਿਚ ਰੁਲਾਇਆ
ਜਦ ਦਾ ਹੱਥ ਤੇਰੇ ਇਹ ਆਇਆ, ਤੂੰ ਕਦੇ ਨਾ ਡਾਹਿਆ ਆਣ ਕੁੜੇ

## 52

Pay[1] attention to your spinning, my girl.

Your mother is always admonishing you: Daughter, why
are you idly wandering about, you lazy thing? Do not
destroy your honor and reputation, daughter. Do have
some sense, you ignorant girl.

You got your spinning wheel for nothing. You did not have
to use any of your own money on it. You have not
realized the value of hard work, when the work has
proved easy, my girl.

The spinning wheel was made for you. Do not be so keen
to play. You are not going to be growing up anymore,
so come to your senses, you ignorant girl.

Your spinning wheel is brightly colored; the whole clan is      5
envious of it. Work as hard as you can and do well in
the house, my girl.

This spinning wheel has a high price, but what do you
know of its value, you peasant? You look down at
everyone as you strut about filled with arrogance,
being proud of your status, my girl.

I stand with arms outstretched and cry: Will you ever
come to your senses, you heedless one? No carpenter
is ever going to make you another spinning wheel like
this one, my girl.

Why have you spoiled this spinning wheel? Why have you
let it lie in the dust? Ever since you have had it, you
have never come to set it up, my girl.

ਨਿਤ ਮੱਤੀਂ ਦਿਆਂ ਵਲੱਲੀ ਨੂੰ, ਇਸ ਭੋਲੀ ਕਮਲੀ ਝੱਲੀ ਨੂੰ
ਜਦ ਪਾਵੇਗਾ ਵਖ਼ਤ ਇਕੱਲੀ ਨੂੰ, ਤਦ ਹਾਏ ਹਾਏ ਕਰਸੀ ਜਾਨ ਕੁੜੇ

੧੦ ਮੁਦੋਂ ਦੀ ਤੂੰ ਰਿਜ਼ਕ ਵਿਹੂਟੀ, ਗੋਹੜਿਓਂ ਨਾ ਤੂੰ ਕੱਤੀ ਪੂਟੀ
ਹੁਣ ਕਿਉਂ ਫਿਰਨੀ ਏਂ ਨਿੰਮੋਝੂਟੀ, ਕਿਸ ਦਾ ਕਰੇਂ ਗੁਮਾਨ ਕੁੜੇ

ਨਾ ਤਕਲਾ ਰਾਸ ਕਰਾਵੇਂ ਤੂੰ, ਨਾ ਬਾਇੜ ਮਾਲੂ ਪਵਾਵੇਂ ਤੂੰ
ਕਿਉਂ ਘੜੀ ਮੁੜੀ ਚਰਖ਼ਾ ਚਾਵੇਂ ਤੂੰ, ਤੂੰ ਕਰਨੀ ਏਂ ਅਪਣਾ ਜ਼ਿਆਨ ਕੁੜੇ

ਡਿੰਗਾ ਤਕਲਾ ਰਾਸ ਕਰਾ ਲੈ, ਨਾਲ ਸ਼ਤਾਬੀ ਬਾਇੜ ਪਵਾ ਲੈ
ਜਿਉਂਕਰ ਵੱਗੇ ਤਿਵੇਂ ਵਗਾ ਲੈ, ਮਤ ਕਰ ਕੋਈ ਅਗਿਆਨ ਕੁੜੇ

ਅੱਜ ਘਰ ਵਿਚ ਨਵੀਂ ਕਪਾਹ ਕੁੜੇ, ਤੂੰ ਝਬ ਝਬ ਵੇਲਣ ਢਾਹ ਕੁੜੇ
ਤੂੰ ਵੇਲ ਪਿੰਜਾਵਟ ਜਾਹ ਕੁੜੇ, ਮੁੜ ਕੱਲੂ ਨਾ ਤੇਰਾ ਜਾਣ ਕੁੜੇ

ਜਦ ਤੂੰ ਪਿੰਜਾ ਲਿਆਵੇਂਗੀ, ਸਈਆਂ ਵਿਚ ਪੂਟੀਆਂ ਪਾਵੇਂਗੀ
ਮੁੜ ਆਪੇ ਹੀ ਪਈ ਭਾਵੇਂਗੀ, ਵਿਚ ਸਾਰੇ ਜਗ ਜਹਾਨ ਕੁੜੇ

੧੫ ਤੇਰੇ ਨਾਲ ਦੀਆਂ ਸਭ ਸਈਆਂ ਨੀ, ਕਤ ਪੂਟੀਆਂ ਸਭਨਾਂ ਲਈਆਂ ਨੀ
ਤੈਨੂੰ ਬੈਠੀ ਨੂੰ ਪਿੱਛੇ ਪਈਆਂ ਨੀ, ਕਿਉਂ ਬੈਠੀ ਏਂ ਤੂੰ ਹੈਰਾਨ ਕੁੜੇ

ਦੀਵਾ ਆਪਣੇ ਪਾਸ ਜਗਾਵੀਂ, ਕਤ ਕਤ ਸੂਤ ਭਰੋਟੇ ਪਾਵੀਂ
ਅੱਖੀ ਵਿਚੋਂ ਰਾਤ ਲੰਘਾਵੀਂ, ਔਖੀ ਕਰਕੇ ਜਾਨ ਕੁੜੇ

I am always telling this half-witted, simple, mad, and
    crazy girl: When you are all alone and bad times come,
    your soul will cry "Alas, alas," my girl.

From the outset you have been without anything to live     10
    by. You have not spun cotton rolls from the bunches
    of yarn. Why do you go around now looking sad, and
    what are you so proud of, my girl?

You do not set the spindle straight, nor do you set up the
    connecting string and the driving band. Why do you
    keep packing the spinning wheel away all the time?
    You are bringing about your own ruin, my girl.

Set the twisted spindle straight, and quickly set up the
    connecting string. Keep it moving naturally; do not
    do anything stupid, my girl.

Today there is a fresh lot of raw cotton in the house, my
    girl. Quickly start to roll it, my girl. Once it is rolled,
    go to get it carded, my girl. You will not get to return
    to it tomorrow, my girl.

When you bring the carded cotton, you will put the cotton
    rolls on the wheel with your friends. Then you will be
    the one who is popular throughout the whole world,
    my girl.

All the girls who are your companions have spun their     15
    cotton rolls.[2] As you sit there, they come for you,
    asking: Why are you sitting in such a daze, my girl?

Light a lamp beside you. Keep spinning and putting the
    hanks in the basket. Let night pass before your eyes,
    and do not take things easy, my girl.

ਇਹ ਪੇਕਾ ਰਾਜ ਦਿਨ ਚਾਰ ਕੁੜੇ, ਨਾ ਖੇੜੇ ਖੇਡ ਗੁਜ਼ਾਰ ਕੁੜੇ
ਨਾ ਰਹੁ ਵਿਹਲੀ ਕਰ ਕਾਰ ਕੁੜੇ, ਘਰ ਬਾਰ ਨਾ ਕਰ ਵੀਰਾਨ ਕੁੜੇ

ਤੂੰ ਸੁੱਤਿਆਂ ਰੈਣ ਗੁਜ਼ਾਰ ਨਹੀਂ, ਮੁੜ ਆਉਣਾ ਦੂਜੀ ਵਾਰ ਨਹੀਂ
ਫਿਰ ਬਹਿਣਾ ਏਸ ਭੰਡਾਰ ਨਹੀਂ, ਵਿਚ ਇਕੋ ਜੋੜੇ ਹਾਣ ਕੁੜੇ

ਤੂੰ ਸਦਾ ਨਾ ਪੇਕੇ ਰਹਿਣਾ ਏ, ਨਾ ਪਾਸ ਅੰਬੜੀ ਦੇ ਬਹਿਣਾ ਏ
ਭਾ ਅੰਤ ਵਿਛੋੜਾ ਸਹਿਣਾ ਏ, ਵੱਸ ਪਏਂਗੀ ਸੱਸ ਨਨਾਨ ਕੁੜੇ

੨੦ ਕੱਤ ਲੈ ਨੀ ਕੁਝ ਕਤਾ ਲੈ ਨੀ, ਹੁਣ ਤਾਣੀ ਤੰਦ ਉਣਾ ਲੈ ਨੀ
ਤੂੰ ਅਪਣਾ ਦਾਜ ਰੰਗਾ ਲੈ ਨੀ, ਤੂੰ ਤਦ ਹੋਵੇਂ ਪਰਧਾਨ ਕੁੜੇ

ਜਦ ਘਰ ਬੇਗਾਨੇ ਜਾਵੇਂਗੀ, ਮੁੜ ਵੱਤ ਨਾ ਉਥੋਂ ਆਵੇਂਗੀ
ਉਥੇ ਜਾ ਕੇ ਪੱਛੋਤਾਵੇਂਗੀ, ਕੁਝ ਅਗਦੋਂ ਕਰ ਸਮਿਆਨ ਕੁੜੇ

ਅੱਜ ਐਡਾ ਤੇਰਾ ਕੰਮ ਕੁੜੇ, ਕਿਉਂ ਹੋਈਂ ਏਂ ਬੇਗ਼ਮ ਕੁੜੇ
ਕੀ ਕਰ ਲੈਤਾ ਇਸ ਦਮ ਕੁੜੇ, ਜਦ ਘਰ ਆਏ ਮਹਿਮਾਨ ਕੁੜੇ

ਜਦ ਸਭ ਸਈਆਂ ਤੁਰ ਜਾਉਣਗੀਆਂ, ਫਿਰ ਉਥੇ ਮੂਲ ਨਾ ਆਉਣਗੀਆਂ
ਆ ਚਰਖੇ ਮੂਲ ਨਾ ਡਾਹੁਣਗੀਆਂ, ਤੇਰਾ ਤ੍ਰਿੰਜਣ ਪਿਆ ਵੀਰਾਨ ਕੁੜੇ

ਕਰ ਮਾਣ ਨਾ ਹੁਸਨ ਜਵਾਨੀ ਦਾ, ਪਰਦੇਸ ਨਾ ਰਹਿਣ ਸੈਲਾਨੀ ਦਾ
ਕੋਈ ਦੁਨੀਆਂ ਝੂਠੀ ਫ਼ਾਨੀ ਦਾ, ਨਾ ਰਹਿਸੀ ਨਾਮ ਨਿਸ਼ਾਨ ਕੁੜੇ

You get just a few days to lord it in your father's house,
my girl. Do not spend your time playing about, my
girl. Do not remain idle but do something, my girl.
Do not ruin your family, my girl.

Do not spend the night asleep. You are not going to come
back a second time. You are not going to sit in this
company again among your age-mates, my girl.

You are not going to remain in your father's house forever.
You are not going to sit beside your dear mother. In
the end you must endure separation from them, and
you will come under the authority of your husband's
mother and sisters, my girl.

Spin, and have it spun. Have the thread woven in the 20
warp. Have your dowry clothes dyed; then you will be
respected, my girl.

When you go to that house of strangers, you will never
return from there again. When you arrive there, you
will be sorry. Get your things ready in advance, my
girl.

Today you have so much work to do, my girl. Why have
you become so unconcerned, my girl? What will you
do at that moment, when the guests come to the
house, my girl?

When all your girlfriends leave, they will certainly not
come there again. They will never come to set up their
spinning wheels. Your spinning party will be deserted,
my girl.

Do not be proud of your beauty and youth. Travelers do
not remain in a foreign country. No name or mark of
this false and transitory world will remain, my girl.

੨੫ ਇਕ ਔਖਾ ਵੇਲਾ ਆਵੇਗਾ, ਸਭ ਸਾਕ ਸੈਨ ਭਜ ਜਾਵੇਗਾ
ਕਰ ਮੱਦਦ ਪਾਰ ਲੰਘਾਵੇਗਾ, ਉਹ ਬੁੱਲ੍ਹੇ ਦਾ ਸੁਲਤਾਨ ਕੁੜੇ

## ੫੩

ਕਿਉਂ ਓਹਲੇ ਬਹਿ ਬਹਿ ਝਾਕੀਦਾ, ਇਹ ਪਰਦਾ ਕਿਸ ਤੋਂ ਰਾਖੀਦਾ

ਕਾਰਨ ਪੀਤ ਮੀਤ ਬਣ ਆਇਆ, ਮੀਮ ਦਾ ਘੁੰਘਟ ਮੁੱਖ ਪਰ ਪਾਇਆ
ਅਹਦ ਤੇ ਅਹਿਮਦ ਨਾਮ ਧਰਾਇਆ, ਸਿਰ ਛਤਰ ਝੁੱਲੇ 'ਲੌਲਾਕੀ' ਦਾ

ਤੁਸੀਂ ਆਪੇ ਆਪ ਹੀ ਸਾਰੇ ਹੋ, ਕਿਉਂ ਕਹਿੰਦੇ ਅਸੀਂ ਨਿਆਰੇ ਹੋ
ਆਏ ਅਪਣੇ ਆਪ ਨਜ਼ਾਰੇ ਹੋ, ਵਿਚ ਬਰਜ਼ਖ਼ ਰਖਿਆ ਖ਼ਾਕੀ ਦਾ

ਤੁਧ ਬਾਝੋਂ ਦੂਜਾ ਕਿਹੜਾ ਹੈ, ਕਿਉਂ ਪਾਇਆ ਉਲਟਾ ਝੇੜਾ ਹੈ
ਇਹ ਡਿਠਾ ਬੜਾ ਅੰਧੇਰਾ ਹੈ, ਹੁਣ ਆਪ ਨੂੰ ਆਪੇ ਆਖੀਦਾ

੫ ਕਿਤੇ ਰੂਮੀ ਹੋ ਕਿਤੇ ਸ਼ਾਮੀ ਹੋ, ਕਿਤੇ ਸਾਹਿਬ ਕਿਤੇ ਗ਼ੁਲਾਮੀ ਹੋ
ਤੁਸੀਂ ਆਪੇ ਆਪ ਤਮਾਮੀ ਹੋ, ਕਹੂੰ ਖੋਟਾ ਖਰਾ ਸੁਲਾਖੀਦਾ

ਜਿਸ ਤਨ ਵਿਚ ਇਸ਼ਕ ਦਾ ਜੋਸ਼ ਹੋਇਆ, ਉਹ ਬੇਖ਼ੁਦ ਹੋ ਬੇਹੋਸ਼ ਹੋਇਆ
ਉਹ ਕਿਉਂ ਕਰ ਰਹੇ ਖ਼ਮੋਸ਼ ਹੋਇਆ, ਜਿਸ ਪਿਆਲਾ ਪੀਤਾ ਸਾਕੀ ਦਾ

ਤੁਸੀਂ ਆਪ ਅਸਾਂ ਵਲ ਧਾਏ ਜੀ, ਕਦ ਰਹਿੰਦੇ ਡੁਪੇ ਛੁਪਾਏ ਜੀ
ਤੁਸੀਂ ਸ਼ਾਹ ਇਨਾਇਤ ਬਣ ਆਏ ਜੀ, ਹੁਣ ਲਾ ਲਾ ਨੈਣ ਝੁਮਾਕੀਦਾ

96

A difficult time will come. All your family and kin will flee.    25
    The one who will come to your aid and get you across
    is Bullha's sovereign,[3] my girl.

53

Why do you sit in concealment and peep out? Who are you
    veiling yourself from?

You came for the sake of love, turning yourself into
    someone to love. You placed the veil of *mīm* over your
    face, and from Ahad you made your name Ahmad.[1]
    The royal umbrella of *If it were not for you*[2] sways over
    your head.

You yourself are all things, so why do you say you are
    separate? You have come as your own spectacle,
    interposing the dividing line of earthliness.[3]

Apart from you, who else is there? Why have you created
    this futile dispute? You saw a great darkness; now you
    call yourself yourself.

Sometimes you are a Turk, sometimes a Syrian,[4]    5
    sometimes the master, sometimes the slave. You
    yourself embrace entirety, irrespective of the
    appearance of things being false or true.

The body that is filled with the passion of love loses self
    and consciousness. How can someone who has drunk
    from the cupbearer's[5] goblet remain silent?

You were the one who rushed at us; when did you ever
    remain hidden? You have come as Shah Inayat. Now
    keep your eyes fixed on us.

ਬੁੱਲ੍ਹੇ ਸ਼ਾਹ ਤਨ ਭਾਠੀ ਕਰ, ਅਗ ਬਾਲ ਹਡਾਂ ਤਨ ਮਾਟੀ ਕਰ
ਇਹ ਸ਼ੌਕ ਮੁਹੱਬਤ ਬਾਟੀ ਕਰ, ਇਹ ਮਧਵਾ ਇਸ ਬਿਧ ਛਾਕੀਦਾ

੫੪

ਕਿਉਂ ਲੜਨਾ ਹੈਂ ਕਿਉਂ ਲੜਨਾ ਹੈਂ ਗ਼ੈਰ ਗੁਨਾਹੇ

'ਲਾ ਤਤਹੱਰਕੁ' ਖ਼ੁਦ ਲਿਖਿਓ ਈ, ਕਿਸ ਨੂੰ ਦੇਨਾ ਏਂ ਫਾਹੇ

ਸ਼ਰ੍ਹਾ ਤੇ ਅਹਿਲ ਕੁਰਆਨ ਭੀ ਆਹੇ, ਅਸੀਂ ਅੱਗੇ ਸੱਦੇ ਆਏ

'ਅਲਸਤੁ ਬਿਰੱਬਿਕੁਮ' ਵਾਰਦ ਹੋਇਆ, 'ਕਾਲੂ ਬਲਾ' ਧੂਮ ਪਾਏ

੫    'ਕੁਨ ਫ਼ਯਕੂਨ' ਆਵਾਜ਼ਾ ਹੋਇਆ, ਤਦਾਂ ਅਸੀਂ ਭੀ ਕੋਲੇ ਆਹੇ

ਲੱਜ਼ਤ ਮਾਰ ਦਿਵਾਨੇ ਕੀਤੇ, ਨਹੀਂ ਜ਼ਾਤੇ ਅਸਲੀ ਆਹੇ

੫੫

ਕਿਹਨੂੰ ਲਾਮਕਾਨੀ ਦਸਦੇ ਹੋ, ਤੁਸੀਂ ਹਰ ਰੰਗ ਦੇ ਵਿਚ ਵਸਦੇ ਹੋ

'ਕੁਨ' ਕਹਿਓ 'ਫ਼ਯਕੂਨ' ਕਹਾਇਓ, ਤੈਂ ਬਾਝੋਂ ਹੋਰ ਕਿਹੜਾ ਆਇਓ
ਇਸ਼ਕੋਂ ਸਭ ਜ਼ਹੂਰ ਬਣਾਇਓ, ਆਸ਼ਕ ਹੋ ਕੇ ਵਸਦੇ ਹੋ

98

Bullhe Shah, make your body a furnace, burn your bones
  in the fire, and turn your body into dust. Make this
  love and desire your food for the journey; this is how
  to taste this wine.

## 54

Why do you dispute, why do you dispute with us over
  another's sin?[1]
You were the one who wrote *You do not move*.[2] So who are
  you causing to be hanged?
There was the law and the followers of the Qur'an, but we
  were called before they were.
*Am I not your lord?*[3] was revealed, and up went the loud
  cry *They said, "Yes."*
When *Let it be, and it was*[4] was proclaimed, we too were          5
  there.
Inflicting ecstasy, he has driven us mad; otherwise we
  should have retained our original nature.

## 55

Whom do you describe as infinite? You dwell in every
  color.
You are the one who said *Let it be,* and caused *as it was* to be
  said.[1] Who came but you? From love you created the
  manifest world, where you dwell as your lover.[2]

ਪੁੱਛੇ ਆਦਮ ਕਿਸ ਨੇ ਆਂਦਾ ਏ, ਕਿਥੋਂ ਆਇਆ ਕਿਥੇ ਜਾਂਦਾ ਏ
ਉਥੇ ਕਿਸ ਦਾ ਤੈਨੂੰ ਲਾਂਝਾ ਏ, ਉਥੇ ਖਾ ਦਾਣਾ ਉੱਠ ਨਸਦੇ ਹੋ

ਆਪੇ ਸੁਣੇਂ ਤੇ ਆਪ ਸੁਣਾਵੇਂ, ਆਪੇ ਗਾਵੇਂ ਆਪ ਬਜਾਵੇਂ
ਹੱਥੋਂ ਕੋਲ ਸਰੂਦ ਸੁਣਾਵੇਂ, ਕਿਤੇ ਜਾਹਲ ਹੋ ਕੇ ਨਸਦੇ ਹੋ

੫ ਤੇਰੀ ਵਹਦਤ ਤੂਹੋਂ ਬੁਝਾਵੇਂ, 'ਅਨਲਹੱਕ' ਦੀ ਤਾਰ ਹਿਲਾਵੇਂ
ਸੂਲੀ ਤੇ ਮਨਸੂਰ ਚੜ੍ਹਾਵੇਂ, ਉਥੇ ਕੋਲ ਖਲੋ ਕੇ ਹਸਦੇ ਹੋ

ਜਿਵੇਂ ਸਿਕੰਦਰ ਤਰਫ਼ ਨੁਸ਼ਾਬਾਂ, ਹੋ ਰਸੂਲ ਲੈ ਆਇਆ ਕਿਤਾਬਾਂ
ਯੁਸਫ਼ ਹੋ ਕੇ ਅੰਦਰ ਖ਼ਾਬਾਂ, ਜੁਲੈਖ਼ਾ ਦਾ ਦਿਲ ਖਸਦੇ ਹੋ

ਕਿਤੇ ਰੂਮੀ ਹੋ ਕਿਤੇ ਜ਼ੰਗੀ ਹੋ, ਕਿਤੇ ਟੇਪੀ ਪੋਸ਼ ਫਰੰਗੀ ਹੋ
ਕਿਤੇ ਮੈਖ਼ਾਨੇ ਵਿਚ ਭੰਗੀ ਹੋ, ਕਿਤੇ ਮਿਹਰ ਮਿਹਰੀ ਬਣ ਵਸਦੇ ਹੋ

ਬੁੱਲ੍ਹਾ ਸ਼ਹੁ ਇਨਾਇਤ ਆਰਫ਼ ਹੈ, ਉਹ ਦਿਲ ਮੇਰੇ ਦਾ ਵਾਰਸ ਏ
ਮੈਂ ਲੋਹਾ ਤੇ ਉਹ ਪਾਰਸ ਹੈ, ਤੁਸੀਂ ਉਸੇ ਦੇ ਸੰਗ ਖਸਦੇ ਹੋ

੫੬
ਕੀ ਕਰਦਾ ਨੀ ਕੀ ਕਰਦਾ ਨੀ, ਕੋਈ ਪੁੱਛੇ ਖਾਂ ਦਿਲਬਰ ਕੀ ਕਰਦਾ

ਇਕਸੇ ਘਰ ਵਿਚ ਵਸਦਿਆਂ ਰਸਦਿਆਂ, ਨਹੀਂ ਹੁੰਦਾ ਵਿਚ ਪਰਦਾ

100

Ask Adam this: Who brought him, where did he come
    from, and where does he go? Whom did he deal with
    there, when he ate the grain[3] and ran away?

You are the one who listens and the one who tells. You are
    the one who sings and the one who plays. You made
    the melody of the word sound from his hand, then as
    the ignorant one[4] you fled.

Unity is yours and you are the one who makes it                    5
    understood. You play the string of *I am God.*[5] You
    made Mansur mount the gallows, while you stood
    around and laughed.[6]

Like Sikandar coming to Nushaba,[7] you come as the
    Apostle with the scriptures. As Yusuf in her dreams,[8]
    you steal the heart of Zulaikha.

Now you are a Greek, now you are an African, now you are
    a European in a hat. Now you are a hashish addict in
    the tavern, now you live comfortably as a respectable
    married couple.

Bullha, Shah Inayat is a master mystic, he is the lord of my
    heart. I am iron and he is the philosopher's stone.[9] You
    snatch hold of me and make us touch.


### 56

What is he doing, what is he doing? Someone should ask
    what the beloved is doing.

Those who live happily together in one house do not need
    a screen between them.

ਵਿਚ ਮਸੀਤ ਨਮਾਜ਼ ਗੁਜ਼ਾਰੇ, ਬੁਤਖ਼ਾਨੇ ਜਾ ਵੜਦਾ

ਆਪ ਇੱਕੋ ਕਈ ਲੱਖ ਘਰਾਂ ਦੇ, ਮਾਲਕ ਇਹ ਘਰ ਘਰ ਦਾ

ਜਿਤ ਵਲ ਵੇਖਾਂ ਉਤ ਵਲ ਓਹੋ, ਹਰ ਦੀ ਸੰਗਤ ਕਰਦਾ

ਮੂਸਾ ਤੇ ਫ਼ਰਔਨ ਬਣਾ ਕੇ, ਦੋ ਹੋ ਕੇ ਕਿਉਂ ਲੜਦਾ

ਹਾਜ਼ਰ ਨਾਜ਼ਰ ਓਹੋ ਹਰ ਥਾਂ, ਸੂਚਕ[੧] ਕਿਸ ਨੂੰ ਖੜਦਾ

ਐਸੀ ਨਾਜ਼ੁਕ ਬਾਤ ਕਿਉਂ ਕਹਿੰਦਾ, ਨਾ ਕਹਿ ਸਕਦਾ ਨਾ ਜਰਦਾ

ਇਤ ਵੱਲ ਆਪੇ ਉਤ ਵੱਲ ਆਪੇ, ਆਪੇ ਸਾਹਿਬ ਬਰਦਾ

ਵਹਦਤ ਦਾ ਦਰਿਆ ਸਚਾਵਾਂ, ਓਥੇ ਦਿੱਸੇ ਹਰ ਕੋਈ ਤਰਦਾ

ਬੁੱਲ੍ਹਾ ਸ਼ਹੁ ਦਾ ਇਸ਼ਕ ਬਘੇਲਾ, ਰੱਤ ਪੀਦਾਂ ਗੋਸ਼ਤ ਚਰਦਾ

## ੫੭

ਕੀ ਕਰਦਾ ਬੇਪਰਵਾਹੀ ਜੇ

'ਕੁਨ' ਕਿਹਾ 'ਫ਼ਯਕੂਨ' ਕਹਾਇਆ, ਬਾਤਨ ਜ਼ਾਹਰ ਦੇ ਵਲ ਆਇਆ
ਬੇਚੂਨੀ ਦਾ ਚੂੰਨ ਬਣਾਇਆ, ਬਿਖੜੀ ਖੇਡ ਮਚਾਈ ਜੇ

ਸਿਰ ਮੁਖ਼ਫ਼ੀ ਦਾ ਜਿਸ ਦਮ ਬੋਲਾ, ਘੁੰਘਟ ਅਪਨੇ ਮੂੰਹ ਸੇ ਖੋਲਾ
ਹੁਣ ਕਿਉਂ ਕਰਦਾ ਸਾਥੋਂ ਓਹਲਾ, ਸਭ ਵਿਚ ਹਕੀਕਤ ਆਈ ਜੇ

He performs the prayer in the mosque, he goes into the
    idol temple.
There is just one of him and many hundreds of thousands
    of houses, but he is the master of every house.
Wherever I look, there is only him. He keeps company      5
    with everyone.
He created Moses and Pharaoh.[1] Why does he turn
    himself into two and fight?
Present and seeing, only he exists everywhere. Who does
    the informer seize?
How can I tell such a sensitive secret? I cannot utter it, nor
    can I bear it.
On this side and that side there is only him. He is the
    master and the slave.
The river of unity is true. Everyone can be seen swimming   10
    there.
Bullha, love for the lord is a young tiger. It drinks blood
    and it eats flesh.

## 57

What is this nonchalance he practices?
He said *Let it be* and made them say *and it was.*[1] The
    hidden proceeded to the manifest. He fashioned form
    from formlessness and set up a complex game.
At the moment he spoke of the hidden secret,[2] he removed
    the veil from his face. Now why does he conceal
    himself from us? True reality has entered everything.

'ਕੱਰਮਨਾ ਬਨੀ ਆਦਮ' ਕਿਹਾ, ਕੋਈ ਨਾ ਕੀਤਾ ਤੇਰੇ ਜਿਹਾ
ਸ਼ਾਨ ਬਜ਼ੁਰਗੀ ਦੇ ਸੰਗ ਇਹਾ, ਡਫ਼ਲੀ ਖੂਬ ਵਜਾਈ ਜੇ

੫     ਆਪੇ ਬੇਪਰਵਾਹੀਆਂ ਕਰਦੇ, ਅਪਣੇ ਆਪ ਸੇ ਆਪੇ ਡਰਦੇ
ਰਿਹਾ ਸਮਾ ਵਿਚ ਹਰ ਹਰ ਘਰ ਦੇ, ਭੁੱਲੀ ਫਿਰੇ ਲੁਕਾਈ ਜੇ

ਚੇਟਕ ਲਾ ਦੀਵਾਨਾ ਹੋਇਆ, ਲੈਲਾ ਬਣ ਕੇ ਮਜਨੂੰ ਮੋਹਿਆ
ਆਪੇ ਰੋਇਆ ਆਪੇ ਧੋਇਆ, ਕੇਹੀ ਕੀਤੀ ਅਸ਼ਨਾਈ ਜੇ

ਆਪੇ ਹੈਂ ਤੂੰ ਸਾਜਨ ਸਈਆਂ, ਅਕਲ ਦਲੀਲਾਂ ਸਭ ਉਠ ਗਈਆਂ
ਬੁੱਲ੍ਹੂ ਸ਼ਹੁ ਨੇ ਖੁਸ਼ੀਆ ਲਈਆਂ, ਹੁਣ ਕਰਦਾ ਕਿਉਂ ਜੁਦਾਈ ਜੇ


੫੮
ਕੀ ਜਾਣਾਂ ਮੈਂ ਕੋਈ ਵੇ ਅੜਿਆ, ਕੀ ਜਾਣਾ ਮੈਂ ਕੋਈ

ਜੋ ਕੋਈ ਅੰਦਰ ਬੋਲੇ ਚਾਲੇ, ਜ਼ਾਤ ਅਸਾਡੀ ਸੋਈ
ਜਿਸ ਦੇ ਨਾਲ ਮੈਂ ਨੇਹੁੰ ਲਗਾਇਆ, ਉਹੋ ਜੇਹੀ ਹੋਈ

ਚਿੱਟੀ ਚਾਦਰ ਲਾਹ ਸੁੱਟ ਕੁੜੀਏ, ਪਹਿਨ ਫ਼ਕੀਰਾਂ ਲੋਈ
ਚਿੱਟੀ ਚਾਦਰ ਦਾਗ਼ ਹਜ਼ਾਰਾਂ, ਲੋਈ ਨੂੰ ਦਾਗ਼ ਨਾ ਕੋਈ

ਅਲਫ਼ ਪਛਾਤਾ ਬੇ ਪਛਾਤੀ, ਤੇ ਤਲਾਵਤ ਹੋਈ
ਸੀਨ ਪਛਾਤਾ ਸ਼ੀਨ ਪਛਾਤਾ, ਸਾਦਕ ਸਾਬਰ ਹੋਈ

*We have honored the sons of Adam,*[3] for no one like you has
    been made. Such is the glory that goes with greatness;
    the drum was properly beaten.[4]
He is the one who acts nonchalantly, he is the one who is      5
    afraid of himself. He is present in every house, while
    people roam in confusion.
He displayed his charms and he became mad. He became
    Laila to make Majnun[5] fall in love. He was the one who
    wept, he was the one who wailed. What a wonderful
    kind of love he made.
You yourself are the beloved and the girls. All reason and
    logic have vanished. Bullha, the lord has taken away
    joys; why does he now inflict separation?

## 58

What[1] do I know of anyone, my friend, what do I know
    of anyone?
Whoever speaks and moves inside us is our essential
    being. I have become identical with the one I fell in
    love with.
Get rid of your white shawl, girl, and put on the fakirs'
    blanket. The white shawl will get covered with stains,
    but there is no stain on the blanket.[2]
I recognized *alif,*[3] I recognized *be,* then *te* began my
    scriptural recitation. I recognized *sīn,*[4] I recognized
    *shīn,* then I became sincere and patient.

ਪ ਕੂ ਕੂ ਕਰਦੀ ਕੁਮਰੀ ਆਹੀ, ਗਲ ਵਿਚ ਤੱਕ ਪਿਓਈ
ਬੱਸ ਨਾ ਕਰਦੀ ਕੂ ਕੂ ਕੋਲੋਂ, ਕੂ ਕੂ ਅੰਦਰ ਮੋਈ

ਜੋ ਕੁਝ ਕਰਸੀ ਅੱਲ੍ਹਾ ਭਾਣਾ, ਕਿਆ ਕੁਝ ਕਰਸੀ ਕੋਈ
ਜੋ ਕੁਝ ਲੇਖ ਮੱਥੇ ਦਾ ਲਿਖਿਆ, ਮੈਂ ਉਸ ਤੇ ਸ਼ਾਕਰ ਹੋਈ

ਆਸ਼ਕ ਬਕਰੀ ਮਾਸ਼ੂਕ ਕਸਾਈ, ਮੈਂ ਮੈਂ ਕਰਦੀ ਕੋਹੀ
ਜਿਉਂ ਜਿਉਂ ਮੈਂ ਮੈਂ ਬਹੁਤਾ ਕਰਦੀ, ਤਿਉਂ ਤਿਉਂ ਮੋਈ ਮੋਈ

ਬੁੱਲ੍ਹਾ ਸ਼ਾਹੁ ਇਨਾਇਤ ਕਰਕੇ, ਸ਼ੋਕ ਸ਼ਰਾਬ ਦਿਤੋਈ
ਭਲਾ ਹੋਇਆ ਅਸੀਂ ਦੂਰੋਂ ਛੁੱਟੇ, ਨੇੜੇ ਆਣ ਲੱਧੋਈ


ਪ੯

ਕੀ ਬੇਦਰਦਾਂ ਦੇ ਸੰਗ ਜਾਰੀ, ਰੋਵਣ ਅੱਖੀਆਂ ਜ਼ਾਰੋ ਜ਼ਾਰੀ

ਸਾਨੂੰ ਗਏ ਬੇਦਰਦੀ ਛੱਡ ਕੇ, ਸੀਨੇ ਸਾਂਗ ਹਿਜਰ ਦੀ ਗੱਡ ਕੇ
ਜਿਸਮੋਂ ਜਿੰਦ ਨੂੰ ਲੈ ਗਏ ਕੱਢ ਕੇ, ਇਹ ਗੱਲ ਕਰ ਗਏ ਹੈਸਿਆਰੀ

ਬੇਦਰਦਾਂ ਦਾ ਕੀ ਭਰਵਾਸਾ, ਖ਼ੋਛ ਨਹੀਂ ਦਿਲ ਅੰਦਰ ਮਾਸਾ
ਚਿੜੀਆਂ ਮੌਤ ਗਵਾਰਾਂ ਹਾਸਾ, ਮਗਰੋਂ ਹਸ ਹਸ ਤਾੜੀ ਮਾਰੀ

ਆਵਣ ਕਹਿ ਗਏ ਫੇਰ ਨਾ ਆਏ, ਆਵਣ ਦੇ ਸਭ ਕੌਲ ਭੁਲਾਏ
ਮੈਂ ਭੁੱਲੀ ਭੁਲ ਨੈਟ ਲਗਾਏ, ਕੇਹੇ ਮਿਲੇ ਸਾਨੂੰ ਠੱਗ ਬਪਾਰੀ

"Coo, coo," said the turtledove, with your ring around its    5
neck.[5] Its cooing never stops. It was still busy cooing
when it died.

Whatever he does, it is God's will; what can anyone do by
himself? I am grateful for whatever fate is written on
my forehead.

The lover is the goat and the beloved is the butcher. Saying
"Me, me,"[6] it is slaughtered. The more it says "Me,
me," the deader it is.

Bullha, the lord in his grace[7] gave me the wine of passion.
It is good that we have been set free from distant
separation and that you have come near and found us.

## 59

With those who are cruel, what love is possible? My eyes
are weeping bitterly.

The cruel ones abandoned us and went away, transfixing
our breast with the spear of separation and removing
the life from our body. This is what those murderers
did.

What trust can be placed in the cruel, who do not have an
ounce of fear in their hearts? The death of birds is a
joke to peasants; afterward they laugh and clap their
hands.

They said they would come but did not, forgetting all
their promises of coming. I wander lost but have fixed
my eyes on them. How will I get to see those robber
traders?

੫ ਬੁੱਲ੍ਹੇ ਸ਼ਾਹ ਇਕ ਸੌਦਾ ਕੀਤਾ, ਪੀਤਾ ਜ਼ਹਿਰ ਪਿਆਲਾ ਪੀਤਾ
    ਨਾ ਕੁਝ ਨਫ਼ਾ ਨਾ ਟੋਟਾ ਲੀਤਾ, ਦਰਦ ਦੁਖਾਂ ਦੀ ਗਠੜੀ ਭਾਰੀ

## ੬੦

ਕੇਹੇ ਲਾਰੇ ਦੇਨਾਂ ਏਂ ਸਾਨੂੰ, ਦੋ ਘੜੀਆਂ ਮਿਲ ਜਾਈਂ

ਨੇੜੇ ਵੱਸੇਂ ਥਾਂ ਨਾ ਦੱਸੇਂ, ਢੂੰਢਾਂ ਕਿਤ ਵਲ ਜਾਹੀਂ
ਆਪੇ ਝਾਤੀ ਪਾਈ ਅਹਿਮਦ, ਵੇਖਾਂ ਤਾਂ ਮੁੜ ਨਾਹੀਂ

ਆਖ ਗਿਓਂ ਮੁੜ ਆਇਓ ਨਾਹੀਂ, ਸੀਨੇ ਭੜਕਟ ਭਾਹੀਂ
ਇਕਸੇ ਘਰ ਵਿਚ ਵਸਦਿਆਂ ਰਸਿਦਾਂ, ਕਿਤ ਵਲ ਕੂਕ ਸੁਣਾਈਂ

ਪਾਂਧੀ ਜਾ ਮੇਰਾ ਦੇਹ ਸੁਨੇਹਾ, ਦਿਲ ਦੇ ਉਹਲੇ ਲੁਕਦਾ ਕੇਹਾ
ਨਾਮ ਅੱਲ੍ਹ ਦੇ ਨਾ ਹੋ ਵੈਰੀ, ਮੁਖ ਵੇਖਣ ਨੂੰ ਨਾ ਤਰਸਾਈਂ

੫ ਬੁੱਲ੍ਹਾ ਸ਼ਾਹੁ ਕੀ ਲਾਇਆ ਮੈਨੂੰ, ਅੱਧੀ ਰਾਤੇ ਤੇਰੀ ਮਹਿਮਾਂ
    ਊਝੜ ਬੇਲੇ ਸਭ ਕੋਈ ਡਰਦਾ, ਸੋ ਢੂੰਢਾਂ ਮੈਂ ਚਾਈਂ ਚਾਈਂ

Bullhe Shah did a deal, he drank the cup filled with the 5
poison of love. He got no profit and no loss; his bundle
of pains and sorrows is heavy.

### 60

What[1] are these false promises you offer? Meet me for just
a couple of moments.

You live near but do not tell me the place. In which
direction should I look for you? It is you who peep out
as Ahmad.[2] When I look, you are no longer there.

You promised when you went, but you have not returned.
Flames blaze in my breast. Living happily in the same
house, where else[3] should I cry out to you?

Go, traveler, and deliver my message. How can you hide in
the cover of the heart? In the name of God, do not be
hostile. Do not make me long to see your face.

Bullha, what has the lord done to me? In the middle of the 5
night I sing your praises. Everyone fears the wild river
glades, but that is where I search most happily.

੬੧

ਕੌਂਟ ਆਇਆ ਪਹਿਨ ਲਿਬਾਸ ਕੁੜੇ, ਤੁਸੀਂ ਪੁੱਛੋ ਨਾਲ ਇਖ਼ਲਾਸ ਕੁੜੇ

ਹੱਥ ਖੁੰਡੀ ਮੋਢੇ ਕੰਬਲ ਕਾਲਾ, ਅੱਖੀਆਂ ਦੇ ਵਿਚ ਵੱਸੇ ਉਜਾਲਾ
ਚਾਕ ਨਹੀਂ ਕੋਈ ਹੈ ਮਤਵਾਲਾ, ਪੁੱਛੋ ਬਿਠਾ ਕੇ ਪਾਸ ਕੁੜੇ

ਚਾਕਰ ਚਾਕ ਨਾ ਇਸ ਨੂੰ ਆਖੋ, ਇਹ ਨਾ ਖ਼ਾਲੀ ਗੁੱਝੜੀ ਘਾਤੋਂ
ਵਿਛੜਿਆ ਹੋਇਆ ਪਹਿਲੀ ਰਾਤੋਂ, ਆਇਆ ਕਰਨ ਤਲਾਸ਼ ਕੁੜੇ

ਨਾ ਇਹ ਚਾਕਰ ਚਾਕ ਕਹੀਂ ਦਾ, ਨਾ ਇਹ ਜ਼ੱਰਾ ਸ਼ੌਕ ਮਹੀਂ ਦਾ
ਨਾ ਮੁਸ਼ਤਾਕ ਹੈ ਦੁੱਧ ਦਹੀਂ ਦਾ, ਨਾ ਉਸ ਭੁੱਖ ਪਿਆਸ ਕੁੜੇ

੫  ਬੁੱਲ੍ਹਾ ਸ਼ਾਹੁ ਲੁਕ ਬੈਠਾ ਓਹਲੇ, ਦੱਸੇ ਭੇਤ ਨਾ ਮੁੱਖ ਸੇ ਬੋਲੇ
ਬਾਬਲ ਵਰ ਖੋੜਿਆਂ ਤੋਂ ਟੋਲੇ, ਵਰ ਮੈਂਡਾ ਮੈਂਡੇ ਪਾਸ ਕੁੜੇ

੬੨

ਖ਼ਾਕੀ ਖ਼ਾਕ ਸਿਉਂ ਰਲ ਜਾਣਾ, ਕੁਝ ਨਹੀਂ ਜ਼ੋਰ ਪਿੰਗਾਣਾ

ਗਏ ਸੋ ਗਏ ਫੇਰ ਨਹੀਂ ਆਏ, ਮੇਰੇ ਜਾਨੀ ਮੀਤ ਪਿਆਰੇ
ਮੇਰੇ ਬਾਝੋਂ ਰਹਿੰਦੇ ਨਾਹੀਂ, ਹੁਣ ਕਿਉਂ ਅਸਾਂ ਵਿਸਾਰੇ
ਵਿਚ ਕਬਰਾਂ ਦੇ ਖ਼ਬਰ ਨਾ ਕਾਈ, ਮਾਰੂ ਕੇਹਾ ਝੁਲਾਣਾ

## 61

Who[1] has come dressed up, my girl? Ask him straight,
    my girl.

A crook is in his hand and a black blanket on his shoulders;
    light dwells in the eyes. He is not a herdsman but
    a man of wisdom. Get him to sit beside you and
    question him, my girl.

Do not call him a menial herdsman.[2] He is not devoid of
    secret purpose. Separated since the first night,[3] he has
    come to search, my girl.

He is no one's menial herdsman, nor does he take the least
    pleasure in buffaloes. He has no desire for milk or
    yogurt, nor does he feel hunger or thirst, my girl.

Bullha, the lord sits hidden in concealment. He does    5
    not reveal the secret or speak with his mouth. My
    father seeks a bridegroom from the Kheras,[4] but my
    bridegroom is by my side, my girl.

## 62

Those made of dust must mingle with the dust. Force and
    might are of no avail.

Those who have gone have gone, they have not returned,
    my dear beloved friends. They could not bear to
    live without me, so now why have they forgotten
    us? There is no awareness in the grave, so why this
    anguished thrashing about?[1]

ਚਿਤ ਪਿਆਰ ਨਾ ਜਾਏ ਸਾਥੋਂ, ਉੱਥੇ ਸਾਹ ਨਾ ਰਹਿੰਦੇ
ਅਸੀਂ ਮੋਇਆਂ ਦੇ ਪਰਲੇ ਪਾਰ ਹਾਂ, ਜਿਊਂਦਿਆਂ ਦੇ ਵਿਚ ਬਹਿੰਦੇ
ਅੱਜ ਕਿ ਭਲਕੇ ਤੁਰਨ ਦਾ ਸਾਨੂੰ, ਹੋਸੀ ਬੜਾ ਖਪਾਟਾ

ਓਥੇ ਮਗਰ ਪਿਆਦੇ ਲੱਗੇ, ਤਾਂ ਅਸੀਂ ਏਥੇ ਆਏ
ਏਥੇ ਸਾਨੂੰ ਰਹਿਟ ਨਾ ਮਿਲਦਾ, ਅੱਗੇ ਕਿਤ ਵਲ ਧਾਏ
ਜੋ ਕੁਝ ਅਗਲਿਆਂ ਦੇ ਸਿਰ ਬੀਤੀ, ਅਸਾਂ ਵੀ ਓਹੋ ਟਿਕਾਟਾ

੫    ਬੁੱਲ੍ਹਾ ਏਥੇ ਰਹਿਟ ਨਾ ਮਿਲਦਾ, ਰੋਂਦੇ ਪਿਟਦੇ ਚੱਲੇ
ਇੱਕੋ ਨਾਮ ਓਸੇ ਦਾ ਖਰਚੀ, ਪੈਸਾ ਹੋਰ ਨਾ ਪੱਲੇ
ਮੈਂ ਸੁਪਨਾ ਸਭ ਜਗ ਵੀ ਸਪਨਾ, ਸੁਪਨਾ ਲੋਕ ਬਬਾਟਾ

## ੬੩

ਖੇਡ ਲੈ ਵਿਚ ਵਿਹੜੇ ਘੁੰਮੀ ਘੁੰਮ

ਏਸ ਵਿਹੜੇ ਵਿਚ ਆਲਾ ਸੋਹਦਾ, ਆਲੇ ਦੇ ਵਿਚ ਤਾਕੀ
ਤਾਕੀ ਦੇ ਵਿਚ ਸੇਜ ਵਿਛਾਵਾਂ, ਨਾਲ ਪੀਆ ਸੰਗ ਰਾਤੀ

ਏਸ ਵਿਹੜੇ ਦੇ ਨੌਂ ਦਰਵਾਜ਼ੇ, ਦਸਵਾਂ ਗੁਪਤ ਰਖਾਤੀ
ਓਸ ਗਲੀ ਦੀ ਮੈਂ ਸਾਰ ਨਾ ਜਾਣਾਂ, ਜਹਾਂ ਆਵੇ ਪੀਆ ਜਾਤੀ

ਏਸ ਵਿਹੜੇ ਵਿਚ ਚਰਖਾ ਸੋਹਦਾ, ਆਲੇ ਦੇ ਵਿਚ ਤਾਕੀ
ਆਪਣੇ ਪੀਆ ਨੂੰ ਯਾਦ ਕਰੇਸਾਂ, ਚਰਖੇ ਦੇ ਹਰ ਫੇਰੇ

Our memory and love for them do not leave us, and we
    cannot stop sobbing. We have passed far beyond
    the dead, even as we sit among the living. Today or
    tomorrow we shall experience the great distress of
    departure.
The constables pursued us there, so we came here. We do
    not get to stay here; where will we move in the future?
    We are headed for the fate that befell those who went
    before us.
Bullha, no one gets to stay here. They departed weeping    5
    and beating their breasts. It is only his name that
    is our provision for the journey, we carry no other
    money. I am a dream, the whole world is a dream,
    and my father's people are a dream.

## 63

Dance[1] around the courtyard and play.
In this courtyard the alcove looks good. In the alcove there
    is a little window. I make up the bed in the alcove for
    a night with my beloved.
This courtyard has nine doors;[2] the tenth is kept secret.
    I do not have a clue about the street along which my
    beloved comes.
In this courtyard the spinning wheel looks good. In the
    alcove there is a little window. I will remember my
    beloved with every turn of the spinning wheel.

ਪ  ਇਸ ਵਿਹੜੇ ਵਿਚ ਮਕਨਾਂ ਹਾਥੀ, ਸੰਗਲ ਨਾਲ ਕਹੇੜੇ
  ਬੁੱਲੇ ਸ਼ਾਹ ਫ਼ਕੀਰ ਸਾਈਂ ਦਾ, ਜਾਗਦਿਆਂ ਕੋ ਛੇੜੇ

## ੬੪

ਗੱਲ ਰੌਲੇ ਲੋਕਾਂ ਪਾਈ ਏ

ਸਚ ਆਖ ਮਨਾ ਕਿਉਂ ਡਰਨਾ ਏਂ, ਇਸ ਸਚ ਪਿੱਛੇ ਤੂੰ ਤਰਨਾ ਏਂ
ਸਚ ਸਦਾ ਆਬਾਦੀ ਕਰਨਾ ਏਂ, ਸਚ ਵਸਤ ਅਚੰਭਾ ਆਈ ਏ

ਬਾਹਮਣ ਆ ਜਜਮਾਨ ਡਰਾਏ, ਪਿੱਤਰ ਪੀੜ ਦਸ ਭਰਮ ਦੁੜਾਏ
ਆਪੇ ਦੱਸ ਕੇ ਜਤਨ ਕਰਾਏ, ਪੂਜਾ ਸ਼ੁਰੂ ਕਰਾਈ ਏ

ਪਿੱਤਰ ਤੁਸਾਂ ਦੇ ਉੱਪਰ ਪੀੜਾ, ਗੁੜ ਚਾਵਲ ਮਨਸਾਓ ਲੀੜਾ
ਜੰਝੁ ਪਾਓ ਲਾਹੋ ਬੀੜਾ, ਚੁਲੀ ਤੁਰਤ ਪਵਾਈ ਏ

ਪ  ਪੀੜ ਨਹੀਂ ਇਉਂ ਨਿਕਲਣ ਲੱਗੀ, ਰੋਕ ਰੁਪਈਆ ਭਾਂਡੇ ਫੱਗੀ
  ਹੋਵੇ ਲਾਖੀ ਦਰੁਸਤ ਨਾ ਬੱਗੀ, ਬੁੱਲ੍ਹਾ ਇਹ ਬਾਤ ਬਟਾਈ ਏ

ਪਿਰਥਮ ਚੰਡੀ ਮਾਤ ਬਟਾਈ, ਜਿਸ ਨੂੰ ਪੂਜੇ ਸਰਬ ਲੋਕਾਈ
ਪਾਛੇ ਵਡ ਕੀੰ ਜੰਜ ਚੜ੍ਹਾਈ, ਡੋਲੀ ਠੁਮ ਠੁਮ ਆਈ ਏ

In this courtyard there is a baby elephant[3] that strains 5
    against its chain. Bullhe Shah is a fakir of the lord;
    he disturbs those who are awake.


## 64

People have covered the whole thing[1] in confusion.

Tell me truly, my heart, why are you afraid? It is thanks
    to this truth that you are saved. Truth always makes
    things flourish. Truth has come as a wondrous
    treasure.

The Brahmans[2] have come to scare their patrons. They
    make them anxious by telling them how their
    ancestors suffer. You are the one who instructs them
    and makes them exert themselves. It is you who
    causes the worship to begin.

"Your ancestors are in pain. Make offerings of raw sugar,
    rice, and cloth. Undo your shirt and put on your
    sacred thread." Then they are quickly given a handful
    of Ganges water.

This is not how suffering is removed, with cash, rupees, 5
    vessels, and cattle. Something that is actually scarlet
    cannot become white.[3] Bullha, this is all make-believe.

First the image of the goddess Chandi[4] was made, the
    mother whom all the people worship. Then the great
    bridegroom's[5] procession went out. The palanquin
    has come with lots of loud noise.

ਭੁੱਲ ਖੁਦਾ ਨੂੰ ਜਾਣ ਖੁਦਾਈ, ਬੁੱਤਾਂ ਅੱਗੇ ਸੀਸ ਨਿਵਾਈ
ਜਿਹੜੇ ਘੜ ਕੇ ਆਪ ਬਣਾਈ, ਸ਼ਰਮ ਰਤਾ ਨਾ ਆਈ ਏ

ਵੇਖੋ ਤੁਲਸੀ ਮਾਤ ਬਣਾਈ, ਸਾਲਗਰਾਮੇ ਸੰਗ ਪਰਨਾਈ
ਹਸ ਰਸ ਡੋਲੀ ਚਾ ਚੜ੍ਹਾਈ, ਸਾਲਾ ਸਹੁਰਾ ਬਣੇ ਜਵਾਈ ਏ

ਪੀਆਂ ਭੈਣਾਂ ਸਭ ਵਿਆਹਵਣ, ਪਰਦੇ ਅਪਣੇ ਆਪ ਕਜਾਵਣ
ਬੁੱਲ੍ਹੂ ਸ਼ਾਹ ਕੀ ਆਖਣ ਆਵਣ, ਨਾ ਮਾਤਾ ਕਿਸੇ ਵਿਆਹੀ ਏ

੧੦ ਸ਼ਾਹ ਰਗ ਥੀਂ ਰੱਬ ਦਿਸਦਾ ਨੇੜੇ, ਲੋਕਾਂ ਪਾਏ ਲੰਮੇ ਝੇੜੇ
ਵਾ ਕੇ ਝਗੜੇ ਕੋਟ ਨਬੇੜੇ, ਭਜ ਭਜ ਉਮਰ ਗਵਾਈ ਏ

ਬਿਰਛ ਬਾਗ਼ ਵਿਚ ਨਹੀਂ ਜੁਦਾਈ, ਬੰਦਾ ਰੱਬ ਤਿਵੇਂ ਬਣ ਆਈ
ਪਿਛਲੇ ਸਰਤੇ ਤੇ ਖਿੜ ਆਈ, ਦੁਬਿਧਾ ਆਣ ਮਿਟਾਈ ਏ

ਬੁੱਲ੍ਹੂ ਆਪੇ ਭੁੱਲ ਭੁਲਾਇਆ ਏ, ਆਪੇ ਚਿਲਿਆਂ ਵਿਚ ਦਬਾਇਆ ਏ
ਆਪੇ ਹੋਕਾ ਦੇ ਸੁਣਾਇਆ ਏ, ਮੁੱਝ ਮੇ ਭੇਤ ਨਾ ਕਾਈ ਏ

ਗਰਮ ਸਰਦ ਹੋ ਜਿਸ ਨੂੰ ਪਾਲਾ, ਹਰਕਤ ਕੀਤਾ ਚਿਹਰਾ ਕਾਲਾ
ਤਿਸ ਨੂੰ ਆਖਣ ਜੀ ਸੁਖਾਲਾ, ਇਸ ਦੀ ਕਰੋ ਦਵਾਈ ਏ

ਅੱਖੀਆਂ ਪੱਕੀਆਂ ਆਖਣ ਆਈਆਂ, ਐਸੀ ਸਮਝ ਕੇ ਆਓ ਨੀ ਮਾਈਆਂ
ਆਪੇ ਭੁੱਲ ਗਈਆਂ ਹੁਣ ਸਾਈਆਂ, ਹੁਣ ਤੀਰਥ ਪਾਸ ਸੁਧਾਈ ਏ

People mistakenly think they are divine and bow their
   heads before the idols. They were the ones who made
   them, yet they feel no shame at all.

See how the sacred basil is made the mother. It is married
   to the ammonite sacred to Vishnu. It is put into the
   bridal palanquin with rejoicing. The brother-in-law
   and the father-in-law become the son-in-law.[6]

Daughters and sisters all get married. They cover
   themselves in their veils. Bullha, what do they come
   to say? No one has married the mother.

The lord appears nearer than the jugular vein.[7] People      10
   have created lengthy disputes. Who can settle these
   contentions about him? They have wasted their lives
   in running around.

There is no separation between the tree and the garden.
   That is the relationship of creature and lord. After last
   autumn they blossom again. Duality is destroyed.

Bullha, you have gone astray, and have led others astray.
   You have disciplined yourself with lengthy vigils. You
   have made loud proclamations. But in no way are you
   distinct from me.[8]

Someone catches a chill and is feverish. His evil deeds
   have blackened his face. People ask him if he is feeling
   all right and say, "Give him some medicine."

They say that their eyesight is good. Come, mothers,[9] if
   that is what you think. They are lost in error, lord.
   Now the place of pilgrimage is correctly placed right
   beside us.

੧੫ ਪੋਸਤ ਆਖੇ ਮਿਲੇ ਅਫ਼ੀਮ, ਬੰਦਾ ਭਾਲੇ ਕਾਦਰ ਕਰੀਮ
ਨਾ ਕੋਈ ਦੱਸੇ ਗਿਆਨ ਹਕੀਮ, ਅਕਲ ਤੁਹਾਡੀ ਜਾਈ ਏ

ਜੋ ਕੋਈ ਦਿਸਦਾ ਏਹੋ ਪਿਆਰਾ, ਬੁੱਲੁ ਆਪੇ ਵੇਖਣਹਾਰਾ
ਆਪੇ ਬੇਦ ਕੁਰਆਨ ਪੁਕਾਰਾ, ਜੋ ਸੁਫਨੇ ਵਸਤ ਭੁਲਾਈ ਏ


੬੫

ਗੁਰ ਜੋ ਚਾਹੇ ਸੋ ਕਰਦਾ ਏ

ਮੇਰੇ ਘਰ ਵਿਚ ਚੋਰੀ ਹੋਈ, ਸੁੱਤੀ ਰਹੀ ਨਾ ਜਾਗਿਆ ਕੋਈ
ਮੈਂ ਗੁਰ ਫੜਿਆ ਸੋਝੀ ਹੋਈ, ਜੋ ਮਾਲ ਗਿਆ ਸੋ ਤਰਦਾ ਏ

ਪਹਿਲੇ ਮੁਖ਼ਫ਼ੀ ਆਪ ਖਜ਼ਾਨਾ ਸੀ, ਓਥੇ ਹੈਰਤ ਹੈਰਤਖ਼ਾਨਾ ਸੀ
ਫਿਰ ਵਹਦਤ ਦੇ ਵਿਚ ਆਣਾ ਸੀ, ਕੁਲ ਜੁਜ਼ ਦਾ ਮੁਜਮਲ ਪਰਦਾ ਏ

'ਕੁਨ ਫ਼ਯਕੂਨ' ਅਵਾਜ਼ਾ ਦੇਂਦਾ, ਵਹਦਤ ਵਿਚੋਂ ਕਸਰਤ ਲੈਂਦਾ
ਪਹਿਨ ਲਿਬਾਸ ਬੰਦਾ ਬਣ ਬਹਿੰਦਾ, ਕਰ ਬੰਦਗੀ ਮਸਜਿਦ ਵੜਦਾ ਏ

੫ ਰੋਜ਼ ਮੀਸਾਕ 'ਅਲਸਤ' ਸੁਣਾਵੇ, 'ਕਾਲੂ ਬਲਾ ਸ਼ਹਿਦਨਾ' ਚਾਹਵੇ
ਫਿਰ ਕੁਝ ਅਪਣਾ ਆਪ ਛੁਪਾਵੇ, ਉਹ ਗਿਣ ਗਿਣ ਵਸਤਾਂ ਧਰਦਾ ਏ

ਗੁਰ ਅੱਲੂ ਆਪ ਕਹੇਂਦਾ ਏ, ਗੁਰ ਅਲੀ ਨਬੀ ਹੋ ਬਹਿੰਦਾ ਏ
ਘਰ ਹਰ ਦੇ ਦਿਲ ਵਿਚ ਰਹਿੰਦਾ ਏ, ਉਹ ਖ਼ਾਲੀ ਭਾਂਡੇ ਭਰਦਾ ਏ

118

Like addicts after opium, creatures search for God the 15
    almighty and the merciful. No philosopher can tell
    you what true knowledge is. The intellect is your
    child.[10]
Should someone appear to be the true beloved, Bullha,
    he is the one who sees him. It is he who has proclaimed
    the Veda and the Qur'an. The whole thing[11] is lost in
    a dream.

## 65

The guru does whatever he wants.
There was a burglary in my house. I remained asleep and
    no one woke up. When I clung to the guru, I became
    aware that the goods that were lost had been regained.
First he was a hidden treasure.[1] There was a place of
    perfect wonderment there. Then he had to enter
    unity. The business of whole and part is a veil.
He proclaims *Let it be, and it was.*[2] From unity he assumes
    multiplicity. He gets dressed and becomes a creature,
    and enters the mosque and worships.
On the day of the covenant he announces *Am I not?* He 5
    desires *They said, "Yes, we testify."*[3] Then he conceals
    himself somewhat, he counts things out and places
    them.
The guru calls himself God. The guru appears as Ali[4]
    and the Prophet. The guru dwells in the hearts of
    everyone. He fills empty vessels.

ਬੁੱਲ੍ਹੂ ਸ਼ਹੁ ਨੂੰ ਘਰ ਵਿਚ ਪਾਇਆ, ਜਿਸ ਸਾਂਗੀ ਇਹ ਸਾਂਗ ਬਟਾਇਆ
ਲੋਕਾਂ ਕੋਲੋਂ ਭੇਤ ਛੁਪਾਇਆ, ਉਹ ਦਰਸ ਪਰਮ ਦਾ ਪੜਦਾ ਏ

## ੬੬

ਘਰ ਮੇ ਗੰਗਾ ਆਈ ਸੰਤੋ, ਘਰ ਮੇ ਗੰਗਾ ਆਈ

ਆਪੇ ਮੁਰਲੀ ਆਪ ਕਨ੍ਹਈਆ, ਆਪੇ ਜਾਦਵਰਾਈ

ਆਪ ਗੋਬਰੀਆ ਆਪ ਗਡਰੀਆ, ਆਪੇ ਦੇਤ ਰਖਾਈ

ਅਨਹਦ ਦੁਆਰ ਕਾ ਆਜਾ ਗੰਵਰੀਆ, ਕੰਗਟ ਦਸਤ ਚੜ੍ਹਾਈ

੫    ਮੁੰਡ ਮੁੰਡਾ ਮੋਹੇ ਪਰੀਤੀ, ਕੌਰੀਅਨ ਕੰਨਾਂ ਮੇ ਪਾਈ

ਅੰਮ੍ਰਿਤ ਫਲ ਖਾ ਲਿਓ ਰੇ ਗੋਸਾਈਂ, ਥੋੜੀ ਕਰੋ ਬਡਾਈ੧

## ੬੭

ਘੜਿਆਲੀ ਦਿਓ ਨਿਕਾਲ ਨੀ, ਅਜ ਪੀ ਘਰ ਆਇਆ ਲਾਲ ਨੀ

ਘੜੀ ਘੜੀ ਘੜਿਆਲ ਬਜਾਵੇ, ਰੈਨ ਵਸਲ ਦੀ ਪਿਆ ਘਟਾਵੇ
ਮੇਰੇ ਮਨ ਦੀ ਬਾਤ ਜੇ ਪਾਵੇ, ਹੱਥੋਂ ਚਾ ਸੁੱਟੇ ਘੜਿਆਲ ਨੀ

120

Bullha, I have found the lord in my house. He is the actor
who put on the show.[5] He hid the secret from people.
He recites the teaching of supreme truth.

## 66

The[1] Ganges has come into the house,[2] oh holy men, the
Ganges has come into the house.

It is he who is the flute, he who is Krishna, he who is the
lord of the Yadavs.[3]

It is he who collects the cow dung, he who is the herdsman,
he who pays the wages for herding.

He has come as the young peasant at the door that leads to
the unstruck,[4] wearing a bracelet on his wrist.

He has shaved his head[5] and has entranced me in love. He          5
wears cowrie shells[6] in his ears.

Eat the nectar fruit, oh lord of the cattle. Dare to advance
a little.

## 67

Get rid of the gong beater.[1] Today the beloved has come
to my house.

He strikes the gong at every quarter.[2] He is shortening
our night together. If he understood my thoughts, he
would throw the gong away.

ਅਨਹਦ ਵਾਜਾ ਵਜੇ ਸੁਹਾਨਾ, ਮੁਤਰਿਬ ਸੁਘੜਾ ਤਾਨ ਤਰਾਨਾ
ਨਮਾਜ਼ ਰੋਜ਼ਾ ਭੁੱਲ ਗਿਆ ਦੁਗਾਨਾ, ਮਦ ਪਿਆਲਾ ਦੇਣ ਕਲਾਲ ਨੀ

ਮੁਖ ਵੇਖਣ ਦਾ ਅਜਬ ਨਜ਼ਾਰਾ, ਦੁੱਖ ਦਲਿੱਦਰ ਉਠ ਗਿਆ ਸਾਰਾ
ਰੈਣ ਵਡੀ ਕਿਆ ਕਰੇ ਪਸਾਰਾ, ਦਿਨ ਅੱਗੇ ਧਰੇ ਦੀਵਾਲ ਨੀ

੫   ਮੈਨੂੰ ਆਪਣੀ ਖ਼ਬਰ ਨਾ ਕਾਈ, ਕਿਆ ਜਾਣਾਂ ਮੈਂ ਕਿਤ ਗਵਾਈ
ਇਹ ਗੱਲ ਕਿਉਂਕਰ ਛੁਪੇ ਛੁਪਾਈ, ਹੁਣ ਹੋਇਆ ਫ਼ਜ਼ਲ ਕਮਾਲ ਨੀ

ਟੂਟੇ ਕਾਮਣ ਕਰੇ ਬਘੇਰੇ, ਸਿਹਰੀ ਆਏ ਵਡੇ ਵਡੇਰੇ
ਹੁਣ ਘਰ ਆਇਆ ਜਾਨੀ ਮੇਰੇ, ਰਹਾਂ ਲਖ ਵਰ੍ਹੇ ਇਹਦੇ ਨਾਲ ਨੀ

ਬੁੱਲ੍ਹੂ ਸ਼ਹੁ ਦੀ ਸੇਜ ਪਿਆਰੀ, ਨੀ ਮੈਂ ਤਾਰਨਹਾਰੇ ਤਾਰੀ
ਕਿਵੇਂ ਕਿਵੇਂ ਹੁਣ ਆਈ ਵਾਰੀ, ਹੁਣ ਵਿਛੜਨ ਹੋਇਆ ਮੁਹਾਲ ਨੀ

### ੬੮

ਘੁੰਗਟ ਓਹਲੇ ਨਾ ਲੁਕ ਸੋਹਣਿਆ, ਮੈਂ ਮੁਸ਼ਤਾਕ ਦੀਦਾਰ ਦੀ ਹਾਂ ।

ਜਾਨੀ ਬਾਝ ਦੀਵਾਨੀ ਹੋਈ, ਟੇਕਾਂ ਕਰਦੇ ਲੋਕ ਸਭੋਈ
ਜੇਕਰ  ਯਾਰ ਕਰੇ ਦਿਲਜੋਈ, ਮੈਂ ਤਾਂ ਫ਼ਰਿਆਦ ਪੁਕਾਰਦੀ ਹਾਂ

ਮੁਫ਼ਤ ਵਿਕਾਂਦੀ ਜਾਂਦੀ ਬਾਂਦੀ, ਮਿਲ ਮਾਹੀਆ ਜਿੰਦ ਐਵੇਂ ਜਾਂਦੀ
ਇਕਦਮ ਹਿਜਰ ਨਹੀਂ ਮੈਂ ਸਹਿੰਦੀ, ਮੈਂ ਬੁਲਬੁਲ ਇਸ ਗੁਲਜ਼ਾਰ ਦੀ ਹਾਂ

The unstruck music[3] plays sweetly. The capable musician
plays the melody and the tune. Praying and fasting
and prayers of two prostrations[4] are forgotten, when
the distiller[5] gives me a cup of liquor.

How amazing things appear when I behold his face. All my
pain and misery are removed. How the long night is
extended. Oh, put up a wall against the day.

I am completely unaware of myself. I do not know where 5
I became lost. How can this mystery be hidden? Now
I have been granted perfect grace.

I performed many spells and charms, and many great
magicians came. Now my dear beloved has come to
my house. May I live with him for a hundred thousand
years.

Bullha, the lord's bed is dear. See, I have been saved by the
savior. Somehow or other, my turn has now arrived.
Now parting has become impossible.


### 68

Do not hide behind a veil, my lovely. I desire a vision of
you.

Without my beloved I have become mad, and people all
taunt me. If the beloved is solicitous, then I will call
to him as a suppliant.

I am your slave girl who is being sold for nothing. Come
to me, beloved, my life is going for nothing. I am not
suffering some sudden separation. I am a nightingale
of this garden.[1]

## ੬੯

ਘੁੰਗਟ ਚੁੱਕ ਓ ਸਜਣਾ, ਹੁਣ ਸ਼ਰਮਾਂ ਕਾਹਨੂੰ ਰੱਖੀਆਂ ਵੇ

ਜ਼ੁਲਫ ਕੁੰਡਲ ਨੇ ਘੇਰਾ ਪਾਇਆ, ਬਿਸੀਅਰ ਹੋ ਕੇ ਡੰਗ ਚਲਾਇਆ
ਵੇਖ ਅਸਾਂ ਵੱਲ ਤਰਸ ਨਾ ਆਇਆ, ਕਰਕੇ ਖੂਨੀ ਅੱਖੀਆਂ ਵੇ

ਦੋ ਨੈਣਾਂ ਦਾ ਤੀਰ ਚਲਾਇਆ, ਮੈਂ ਆਜਿਜ਼ ਦੇ ਸੀਨੇ ਲਾਇਆ
ਘਾਇਲ ਕਰਕੇ ਮੁੱਖ ਛੁਪਾਇਆ, ਚੋਰੀਆਂ ਇਹ ਕਿਨ ਦੱਸੀਆਂ ਵੇ

ਬਿਰਹੁੰ ਕਟਾਰੀ ਤੂੰ ਕਸ ਮਾਰੀ, ਤਦ ਮੈਂ ਹੋਈ ਬੇਦਿਲ ਭਾਰੀ
ਮੁੜ ਨਾ ਲਈ ਤੈਂ ਸਾਰ ਹਮਾਰੀ, ਪੱਤੀਆਂ ਤੇਰੀਆਂ ਕੱਚੀਆਂ ਵੇ

੫ ਨੇਹੁੰ ਲਗਾ ਕੇ ਮਨ ਹਰ ਲੀਤਾ, ਫੇਰ ਨਾ ਅਪਣਾ ਦਰਸ਼ਨ ਦੀਤਾ
ਜ਼ਹਿਰ ਪਿਆਲਾ ਆਪੇ ਪੀਤਾ, ਸਾਂ ਅਕਲੋਂ ਮੈਂ ਲੱਚੀਆਂ ਵੇ

ਸ਼ਾਹ ਇਨਾਇਤ ਮੁਖੋਂ ਨਾ ਬੋਲੇ, ਸੂਰਤ ਤੇਰੀ ਹਰ ਵਲ ਟੋਲਾਂ
ਸਾਬਤ ਹੋ ਕੇ ਫੇਰ ਕਿਉਂ ਡੋਲਾਂ, ਅਜ ਕੱਲੋਂ ਮੈਂ ਸੱਚੀਆਂ ਵੇ


## ੧੦

ਚਲੋ ਦੇਖੀਏ ਉਸ ਮਸਤਾਨੜੇ ਨੂੰ, ਜਿਹਦੀ ਤ੍ਰਿੰਝਟਾਂ ਦੇ ਵਿਚ ਪਈ ਏ ਧੁੰਮ
ਉਹ ਤੋਂ ਮੈਂ ਵਹਦਤ ਵਿਚ ਰੰਗਦਾ ਏ, ਨਹੀਂ ਪੁੱਛਦਾ ਜ਼ਾਤ ਦੇ ਕੀ ਹੋ ਤੁਮ

ਜਿਹਦਾ ਸ਼ੋਰ ਚੁਫੇਰੇ ਪੈਂਦਾ ਏ, ਉਹ ਕੋਲ ਤੇਰੇ ਨਿੱਤ ਰਹਿੰਦਾ ਏ
ਨਾਲੇ 'ਨਹੁਨ ਅਕਰਬ' ਕਹਿੰਦਾ ਏ, ਨਾਲੇ ਆਖੇ 'ਵੜੀ ਅਨਫ਼ੁਸਿਕੁਮ'

## 69

Lift your veil, beloved. Now why have you put on these
    modest airs?

Your curling tresses coiled around me. They turned into
    serpents and stung me. You looked at me pitilessly
    with murderous eyes.

You fired your two eyes' arrows and struck the breast of
    this poor wretch. After wounding me, you hid your
    face. Who showed you these clandestine ways?

When you struck me hard with the dagger of separation,
    I became deeply distraught. You did not ask after me
    anymore. Your messages proved to be untrue.

You made me fall in love and stole my heart, but then you   5
    did not show yourself. I was the one who drank the
    cup of poison. My mind was unsteady.

I do not just speak of Shah Inayat with my lips, I search for
    your face in every direction. Now that I have become
    resolute, why should I waver? Today I am true to my
    promise.

## 70

Let us go and see that wild one, of whom there is so much
    talk in the spinning parties.[1] He dyes you and me in
    the ocean of unity, and does not ask what your caste[2]
    is.

The one who creates such clamor everywhere remains
    beside you always. He also says *We are nearer,*[3] as well
    as *And in your own selves.*[4]

ਛਡ ਝੂਠ ਭਰਮ ਦੀ ਬਸਤੀ ਨੂੰ, ਕਰ ਇਸ਼ਕ ਦੀ ਕਾਇਮ ਮਸਤੀ ਨੂੰ
ਗਏ ਪਹੁੰਚ ਸਜਣ ਦੀ ਹਸਤੀ ਨੂੰ, ਜਿਹੜੇ ਹੋ ਗਏ 'ਸੁੰਮੁਨ ਬੁਕਮੁਨ ਉਮ'

ਨਾ ਤੇਰਾ ਏ ਨਾ ਮੇਰਾ ਏ, ਜਗ ਫ਼ਾਨੀ ਝਗੜਾ ਝੇੜਾ ਏ
ਬਿਨਾਂ ਮੁਰਸ਼ਦ ਰਹਿਬਰ ਕਿਹੜਾ ਏ, ਪੜ੍ਹ 'ਫ਼ਜ਼ਕੁਰੂਨੀ ਅਜ਼ਕੁਰਕੁਮ'

੫  ਬੁੱਲ੍ਹੇ ਸ਼ਾਹ ਇਹ ਬਾਤ ਇਸ਼ਾਰੇ ਦੀ, ਜਿਨ੍ਹਾਂ ਲੱਗ ਗਈ ਤਾਂਘ ਨਜ਼ਾਰੇ ਦੀ
ਦਸ ਪੈਂਦੀ ਘਰ ਵਟਜਾਰੇ ਦੀ, ਹੈ 'ਯਦੁੱਲਾਹਿ ਫ਼ੌਕ ਐਦੀਕੁਮ'


## ੧੧

ਚੁਪ ਕਰਕੇ ਕਰੀਂ ਗੁਜ਼ਾਰੇ ਨੂੰ

ਸੱਚ ਸੁਣਕੇ ਲੋਕ ਨਾ ਸਹਿੰਦੇ ਨੀ, ਸੱਚ ਆਖੀਏ ਤਾਂ ਗਲ ਪੈਂਦੇ ਨੀ
ਫਿਰ ਸੱਚੇ ਪਾਸ ਨਾ ਬਹਿੰਦੇ ਨੀ, ਸੱਚ ਮਿੱਠਾ ਆਸ਼ਕ ਪਿਆਰੇ ਨੂੰ

ਸੱਚ ਸ਼ੁਰੂ ਕਰੇ ਬਰਬਾਦੀ ਏ, ਸੱਚ ਆਸ਼ਕ ਦੇ ਘਰ ਸ਼ਾਦੀ ਏ
ਸੱਚ ਕਰਦਾ ਨਵੀਂ ਆਬਾਦੀ ਏ, ਜਿਹਾ ਸ਼ਰ੍ਹਾ ਤਰੀਕਤਹਾਰੇ ਨੂੰ

ਚੁਪ ਆਸ਼ਕ ਤੋਂ ਨਾ ਹੁੰਦੀ ਏ, ਜਿਸ ਆਈ ਸੱਚ ਸੁਗੀਧੀ ਏ
ਜਿਸ ਮਾਲੂ ਸੁਹਾਗ ਦੀ ਗੁੰਦੀ ਏ, ਛਡ ਦੁਨੀਆਂ ਕੁਝ ਪਸਾਰੇ ਨੂੰ

੫  ਬੁੱਲ੍ਹਾ ਸ਼ਹੁ ਸੱਚ ਹੁਣ ਬੋਲੇ ਹੈ, ਸੱਚ ਸ਼ਰ੍ਹਾ ਤਰੀਕਤ ਫੋਲੇ ਹੈ
ਗੱਲ ਚੌਥੇ ਪਦ ਦੀ ਖੇਲੇ ਹੈ, ਜਿਹਾ ਸ਼ਰ੍ਹਾ ਤਰੀਕਤ ਹਾਰੇ ਨੂੰ

Leave this habitation of falseness and delusion, and adhere
firmly to the intoxication of love. The essence of the
beloved has been reached by those who have become
*deaf, dumb, and blind.*[5]

It is not mine, it is not yours. This transitory world is a
quarrelsome altercation. Who but the guide directs
us? Recite *Remember me, and I will remember you.*[6]

Bullha, this is a hint to those who have felt the desire to
see him. A sign of the trader's[7] house is *The hand of
God is over their hands.*[8]

5

## 71

Get along by keeping silent.

When they hear the truth, people cannot endure it. If
you tell the truth, they fall on you. Then they do not
sit beside a truthful person. Truth is sweet to the dear
lover.

Truth destroys the law. Truth is the delight of the lover's
house. Truth makes things flourish anew. It is like the
law for the follower of the way.

Silence is impossible for the lover who has experienced
the perfume of truth, and who has plaited the garland
of married bliss. Forsake the world's false expanse.

Bullhe Shah now speaks of reality.[1] He examines the
truth of the law and the way. He reveals the secret of
the fourth state.[2] It is like the law for the follower of
the way.[3]

5

੧੨

ਜਾਤਾ ਹੈ ਮੈਂ ਜਾਤਾ ਹੈ,੧ ਇਸ਼ਕ ਸ਼ਰੂ ਕੀ ਨਾਤਾ ਹੈ

ਪੜ੍ਹ ਪੜ੍ਹ ਪੰਡਿਤ ਮੁੱਲਾਂ ਹਾਰੇ, ਕਿਸੇ ਨਾ ਭੇਤ ਪਛਾਤਾ ਹੈ

ਇੱਕੋ ਹਰਫ਼ ਪਰੇਮ ਦਾ ਪੜ੍ਹਿਆ, ਭੁੱਲਿਆ ਰੱਬ ਪਛਾਤਾ ਹੈ

ਨਮਾਜ਼ ਰੋਜ਼ਾ ਓਸ ਕੀ ਕਰਨਾ, ਜਿਸ ਮਧ ਪੀਤੀ ਮਧਮਾਤਾ ਹੈ

੫  ਸੂਰਤ ਤੇਰੀ ਜ਼ਾਹਰ ਹੋਈ, ਹੁਣ ਹੌਂਮੀ ਗਿਆ ਗਵਾਤਾ ਹੈ

ਜ਼ਰੀਬਾਫ਼ ਦੀ ਕਦਰ ਕੀ ਜਾਣੇ, ਛਟ ਓਨਾ ਜਤ ਕਾਤਾ ਹੈ

ਐਨ ਗ਼ੈਨ ਦੀ ਖ਼ਬਰ ਕੀ ਜਾਣੇ, ਪੜ੍ਹਿਆ ਇਲਮ ਭੁਲਾਤਾ ਹੈ

ਕਨਜ਼ ਕਦੂਰੀ ਮੰਤਕ ਮਾਅਨੇ, ਸਾਰਾ ਇਲਮ ਗਵਾਤਾ ਹੈ

ਬੁੱਲ੍ਹਾ ਸ਼ਹੁ ਦੀ ਮਜਲਸ ਬਹਿ ਕੇ, ਹੋ ਗਿਆ ਗੁੰਗਾ ਬਾਤਾ ਹੈ

੧੩

ਜਿਸ ਤਨ ਲਗਿਆ ਇਸ਼ਕ ਕਮਾਲ, ਨਾਚੇ ਬੇਸੁਰ ਤੇ ਬੇਤਾਲ

ਦਰਦਮੰਦਾਂ ਨੂੰ ਕੋਈ ਨਾ ਛੇੜੇ, ਆਪੇ ਅਪਣਾ ਦੁੱਖ ਸਹੇੜੇ
ਜੰਮ ਨਾ ਜੀਓ ਨਾ ਮੂਲ ਉਧੇੜੇ, ਆਪਟਾ ਬੁੱਝੇ ਆਪ ਖ਼ਿਆਲ

128

## 72

I[1] have realized, ah, I have realized the relationship
between love and the law.

For all their learning, the Brahmans and mullahs are
defeated. No one has recognized the secret.

When I studied the single word of love, I recognized the
lord whom I had mistaken.

Are prayer and fasting to be performed by one who has
drunk wine and become intoxicated?

Now that your form has become manifest, all sense of
self is lost and destroyed.

How can the craft of the worker in gold lace be appreciated
by one who produces sacking from wool and goat's
hair?

How can one know about 'ain and ġhain[2] when all the
learning one has studied is forgotten?

The Kanz and the Qudūrī,[3] logic and semantics—all this
knowledge is lost.

Bullha, through sitting in the company of the lord, all talk
is struck dumb.

## 73

The body smitten by perfect love dances without a tune,
without a beat.

No one can torment those who are in pain, and who have
invited suffering upon themselves. They have passed
beyond birth and life and are absorbed in their own
thoughts.

ਜਿਸ ਨੇ ਵੇਸ ਇਸ਼ਕ ਦਾ ਕੀਤਾ, ਧੁਰ ਦਰਬਾਰੋਂ ਫਤਵਾ ਲੀਤਾ
ਜਦੋਂ ਹਜ਼ੂਰੋਂ ਪਿਆਲਾ ਪੀਤਾ, ਕੁਝ ਨਾ ਰਿਹਾ ਜਵਾਬ ਸਵਾਲ

ਜਿਸਦੇ ਅੰਦਰ ਵਸਿਆ ਯਾਰ, ਉੱਠਿਆ ਯਾਰੋ ਯਾਰ ਪੁਕਾਰ
ਨਾ ਉਹ ਚਾਹੇ ਰਾਗਾ ਨਾ ਤਾਰ, ਐਵੇਂ ਬੈਠਾ ਖੇਡੇ ਹਾਲ

੫    ਬੁੱਲ੍ਹਾ ਸ਼ਾਹੁ ਨਗਰ ਸਚ ਪਾਇਆ, ਝੂਠਾ ਰੌਲਾ ਸਭ ਮੁਕਾਇਆ
ਸੱਚਿਆਂ ਕਾਰਨ ਸੱਚ ਸੁਣਾਇਆ, ਪਾਇਆ ਉਸਦਾ ਪਾਕ ਜਮਾਲ

## ੧੪
ਜਿਚਰ ਨਾ ਇਸ਼ਕ ਮਜਾਜ਼ੀ ਲਾਗੇ, ਸੂਈ ਸੀਵੇ ਨਾ ਬਿਨ ਧਾਗੇ੧

ਇਸ਼ਕ ਮਜਾਜ਼ੀ ਦਾਤਾ ਹੈ, ਜਿਸ ਪਿੱਛੇ ਮਸਤ ਹੋ ਜਾਤਾ
ਇਸ਼ਕ ਜਿਨ੍ਹਾਂ ਦੇ ਹੱਡੀਂ ਪੈਂਦਾ, ਸੋਈ ਨਰ ਜੀਵਤ ਮਰ ਵੈਂਦਾ
ਇਸ਼ਕ ਪਿਤਾ ਤੇ ਮਾਤਾ ਹੈ, ਜਿਸ ਪਿੱਛੇ ਮਸਤ ਹੋ ਜਾਤਾ ਹੈ

ਆਸ਼ਕ ਦਾ ਤਨ ਸੁਕਦਾ ਜਾਏ, ਮੈਂ ਖੜੀ ਜਿੰਦਬੜ ਕੇ ਸਾਏ
ਵੇਖ ਮਸ਼ੂਕਾਂ ਖਿੜ ਖਿੜ ਹਾਸੇ, ਇਸ਼ਕ ਬੇਤਾਲ ਪੜ੍ਹਾਤਾ ਹੈ

ਜਿਸ ਉੱਤੇ ਇਸ਼ਕ ਇਹ ਆਇਆ ਹੈ, ਉਹ ਬੇਬਸ ਕਰ ਦਿਖਲਾਇਆ ਹੈ
ਨਸ਼ਾ ਰੋਮ ਰੋਮ ਮੇਂ ਆਇਆ ਹੈ
ਇਸ ਵਿਚ ਨਾ ਰੱਤੀ ਉਹਲਾ ਹੈ, ਹਰ ਤਰਫ਼ ਦਿਸੀਂਦਾ ਮੌਲਾ ਹੈ

Whoever has adopted the appearance of love obtained
a license from the primal court. When he drank the
cup from the divine presence, there was no more
question or debate.
The one in whom the beloved dwells gets up and calls out:
"My beloved, my beloved!" He does not desire any
music or instrument, he just sits and plays in ecstasy.
Bullha has found truth in the city of the lord. All false     5
confusion is brought to an end. He has announced the
truth for those who are true. He has discovered his
perfect beauty.

## 74

So[1] long as human love[2] has not been felt, the needle
cannot sew without thread.[3]
Human love is the giver who sends me into ecstasy. They
whose bones are pervaded by love die while they are
still alive. Love is our father and our mother. It sends
us into ecstasy.
The lover's body dries up. I stand in the shade of the castor
tree.[4] See, the beloveds laugh out loud, taught by the
demon love.[5]
Whoever experiences this love is rendered powerless.
Every bit of his body is filled with ecstasy. There is not
the slightest concealment in him. The lord appears in
every direction.

੫ ਬੁੱਲ੍ਹਾ ਆਸ਼ਕ ਵੀ ਹੁਣ ਤਰਦਾ ਹੈ, ਜਿਸ ਫ਼ਿਕਰ ਪੀਆ ਦੇ ਘਰ ਦਾ ਹੈ
ਰੱਬ ਮਿਲਦਾ ਵੇਖ ਉਚਰਦਾ ਹੈ
ਮਨ ਅੰਦਰ ਹੋਇਆ ਝਾਤਾ ਹੈ, ਜਿਸ ਪਿਛੇ ਮਸਤ ਹੋ ਜਾਤਾ ਹੈ

## ੧੫

ਜਿੰਦ ਕੁੜਿੱਕੀ ਦੇ ਮੂੰਹ ਆਈ

ਆਪੇ ਹੈਂ ਤੂੰ 'ਲਹਮਕ ਲਹਮੀ', ਆਪੇ ਹੈਂ ਤੂੰ ਨਿਆਰਾ
ਗੱਲਾਂ ਸੁਣ ਸੁਣ ਤੇਰੀਆਂ ਮੇਰਾ, ਅਕਲ ਗਿਆ ਉੱਡ ਸਾਰਾ
ਸ਼ਰੀਅਤ ਤੋਂ ਬੇਸ਼ਰੀਅਤ ਕਰਕੇ, ਭਲੀ ਖੁਭਣ ਵਿਚ ਪਾਈ

ਜ਼ੱਰਾ ਇਸ਼ਕ ਤੁਸਾਡਾ ਦਿਸਦਾ, ਪਰਬਤ ਕੋਲੋਂ ਭਾਰਾ
ਇਕ ਘੜੀ ਦੇ ਵੇਖਟ ਕਾਰਨ, ਚੁੱਕ ਲਿਆ ਜਗ ਸਾਰਾ
ਕੀਤੀ ਮਿਹਨਤ ਮਿਲਦੀ ਨਾਹੀਂ, ਡਾਢੇ ਦੀ ਅਸ਼ਨਾਈ

ਵਾਵੇਲਾ ਕੀ ਕਰਨਾ ਜਿੰਦੇ, ਜੋ ਸਾੜੇ ਸੋ ਸਾੜੇ
ਸੁੱਖਾਂ ਦਾ ਇਕ ਪੁਲਾ ਨਾਹੀਂ, ਦੁੱਖਾਂ ਦੇ ਖਲਵਾੜੇ
ਹੋਣੀ ਸੀ ਜੋ ਉਸ ਦਿਨ ਹੋਈ, ਹੁਣ ਕੀ ਕਰੀਏ ਭਾਈ

੫ ਸੁਲੂ ਨਾ ਮੰਨਦਾ ਬਾਤ ਨਾ ਪੁੱਛਦਾ, ਆਖ ਵੇਖਾਂ ਕੀ ਕਰਦਾ
ਕਲ ਮੈਂ ਕਮਲੀ ਤੇ ਉਹ ਕਮਲਾ, ਹੁਣ ਕਿਉਂ ਮੈਥੋਂ ਡਰਦਾ
ਉਹਲੇ ਬਹਿ ਕੇ ਰਮਜ਼ ਚਲਾਈ, ਦਿਲ ਨੂੰ ਚੋਟ ਲਗਾਈ

132

Now even Bullha the lover is saved. For those who are
 anxious to know where the beloved lives, see, the lord
 comes and speaks. From inside the heart, he peeps
 out, the one who sends me into ecstasy.

## 75

My heart is caught in a net.

It is you who are a case of *Your flesh is my flesh*,[1] it is you
 who are distinct. Listening to all you say, my mind is in
 a complete whirl. Taking me from the law to freedom
 from the law, you have cast me into a wonderful mire.

A fragment of your love seems heavier than a mountain. In
 order to see you for a single instant, I have taken the
 whole world on my head. In spite of all my efforts, I
 have not obtained that cruel one's love.

Why, oh heart, do you lament so? Let him destroy me
 if he will. I do not have a single sheaf of joys, only
 whole threshing floors of griefs. Whatever happened
 that day was fated to happen. Now what can we do,
 brother?

He does not agree to peace, nor does he ask after me. Let
 me speak and see what he does. Yesterday I was crazy
 and he was crazy. Now why does he fear me? Sitting in
 concealment, he has fired his glance and wounded my
 heart.

ਸੀਨੇ ਬਾਟ ਦੰਦਾਲ ਗਲੇ ਵਿਚ, ਇਸ ਹਾਲਤ ਵਿਚ ਜਾਲਾਂ
ਚਾ ਚਾ ਸਿਰ ਭੇਂ ਤੇ ਮਾਰਾਂ, ਰੋ ਰੋ ਯਾਰ ਕੂੰ ਭਾਲਾਂ
ਅਗੇ ਵੀ ਸਈਆਂ ਨੇਹੁੰ ਲਗਾਇਆ, ਕਿ ਮੈਂ ਹੀ ਪ੍ਰੀਤ ਲਗਾਈ

ਜਗ ਵਿਚ ਰੌਸ਼ਨ ਨਾਮ ਤੁਸਾਡਾ, ਆਸ਼ਕ ਤੋਂ ਕਿਉਂ ਨਸਦੇ ਹੋ
ਵੱਸੋ ਰੱਸੋ ਵਿਚ ਬੁੱਕਲ ਦੇ, ਅਪਣਾ ਭੇਤ ਨਾ ਦਸਦੇ ਹੋ
ਵਿਚਕੜੇ ਵਿਚਕਾਰੋਂ ਫੜ, ਮੈਂ ਕਰ ਉਲਟੀ ਲਟਕਾਈ

ਅੰਦਰ ਵਾਲਿਆ ਬਾਹਰ ਆਵੀਂ, ਬਾਹੋਂ ਪਕੜ ਖਲੋਵਾਂ
ਜ਼ਾਹਰਾ ਮੈਥੋਂ ਲੁੱਕਟ ਛੁੱਪਟ, ਬਾਤਨ ਕੋਲੇ ਹੋਵਾਂ
ਏਸੇ ਬਾਤਨ ਫਟੀ ਜ਼ੁਲੈਖ਼ਾ, ਮੈਂ ਬਾਤਨ ਬਰਲਾਈ

ਆਖਟੀਆਂ ਸੀ ਆਖ ਸੁਟਾਈਆਂ, ਮਹਲਾ ਸੁਟਦਾ ਨਾਹੀਂ
ਹੱਥ ਮਰੋੜਾਂ ਫੋੜਾਂ ਤਲੀਆਂ, ਰੋਵਾਂ ਢਾਹੀਂ ਢਾਹੀਂ
ਲੈਟੇ ਬੀਂ ਮੁੜ ਦੇਟਾ ਆਇਆ, ਇਹ ਤੇਰੀ ਭਲਿਆਈ

੧੦ ਇਕ ਇਕ ਲਹਿਰ ਅਜਿਹੀ ਆਵੇ, ਜੋ ਨਾ ਕਹਿਟੀਆਂ ਦੱਸਾਂ
ਸੱਚ ਆਖਾਂ ਤਾਂ ਸੂਲੀ ਫਾਹਾ, ਝੂਠ ਕਹਾਂ ਤਾਂ ਵੱਸਾਂ
ਐਸੀ ਨਾਜ਼ੁਕ ਬਾਤ ਕਿਉਂ ਆਖਾਂ, ਕਹਿੰਦਿਆਂ ਹੋਏ ਪਰਾਈ

ਵਹੀ ਵਸੀਲਾ ਪਾਕਾਂ ਦਾ, ਤੁਸੀਂ ਆਪੇ ਸਾਡੇ ਹੋਵੇ
ਜਾਗਦਿਆਂ ਸੰਗ ਸਾਡੇ ਜਾਗੋ, ਸਵਾਂ ਤਾਂ ਨਾਲੇ ਸੋਵੇ
ਜਿਸ ਨੇ ਤੈਂ ਸੰਗ ਪਰੀਤ ਲਗਾਈ, ਕਿਹੜੇ ਸੁੱਖ ਸੁਵਾਈ

ਐਸੀਆਂ ਲੀਕਾਂ ਲਾਈਆਂ ਮੈਨੂੰ, ਹੋਰ ਕਈ ਘਰ ਗਾਲੇ
ਉੱਪਰ ਵਾਰੋਂ ਪਾਵੇਂ ਝਾਤੀ, ਵੱਤੀ ਫਿਰੋਂ ਦੁਆਲੇ
ਲੁਕਟ ਛੁੱਪਟ ਤੇ ਛਲ ਜਾਵਟ, ਇਹ ਤੇਰੀ ਵਡਿਆਈ

With an arrow in my breast and an iron collar around my
neck, I am in a sorry state. Violently I dash my head
upon the ground. I weep and search for my beloved.
Have my girlfriends fallen in love before, or is it just
me who has become infatuated?

Your name is glorious in the world. Why do you flee from
your lover? You dwell in the folds of my veil,[2] but you
do not reveal your secret. Seizing me within by the
middle, you have hung me upside down.

Oh you who dwell within, come outside, let me stand and
hold on to your arm. Outwardly you play hide-and-
seek from me, but inside I am near. Zulaikha[3] was
wounded inwardly, and inwardly I am injured.

The things that had to be said were clearly proclaimed.
He deliberately will not hear me and does not listen.
I wring my hands and weep bitterly. Instead of
receiving, I had to give again. Such is your kindness.

Each wave comes on in such a way that I cannot describe    10
them. If I tell the truth, I face the gallows and the
noose. If I lie, I flourish. How can I utter such a
delicate thing? Once I speak, it belongs to others.

Revelation is the medium for the holy. Become ours of
your own accord. Remain awake with us when we
wake. If I sleep, then sleep with me. Do you allow
anyone who is in love with you to sleep peacefully?

You have so disgraced me, and have destroyed many other
houses. From above you glance down. All around you
roam about me. You deceive us with this hide-and-
seek. This is your greatness.

ਤੇਰਾ ਮੇਰਾ ਨਿਆਉਂ ਨਬੇੜੇ, ਰੂਮੋਂ ਕਾਜ਼ੀ ਆਵੇ
ਖੋਲ੍ਹ ਕਿਤਾਬਾਂ ਕਰੇ ਤੱਸਲੀ, ਦੋਹਾਂ ਇੱਕ ਬਤਾਵੇ
ਮੈਂ ਤੇ ਕਾਜ਼ੀ ਹੋਏ ਰਾਜ਼ੀ, ਕਰਸੀ ਕੀ ਲੋਕਾਈ

ਬੁੱਲ੍ਹਾ ਸ਼ਹੁ ਤੂੰ ਕੇਹਾ ਜੇਹਾ, ਹੁਣ ਕੇਹਾ ਮੈਂ ਕੇਹੀ
ਤੈਨੂੰ ਜੋ ਮੈਂ ਢੂੰਡਣ ਲੱਗੀ, ਮੈਂ ਭੀ ਆਪ ਨਾ ਰੇਹੀ
ਪਾਇਆ ਜ਼ਾਹਰ ਬਾਤਨ ਮੈਨੂੰ, ਬਾਰੂ ਅੰਦਰ ਰੁਸ਼ਨਾਈ

## ੧੯

ਜੁਮ੍ਹੇਂ ਦੀ ਹੋਰੋ ਹੋਰ ਬਹਾਰ

ਪੀਰ ਅਸਾਨੂੰ ਪੀੜਾਂ ਲਾਈਆਂ, ਮੰਗਲ ਮੂਲ ਨਾ ਸੁਰਤਾਂ ਆਈਆਂ
ਇਸ਼ਕ ਛਨਿਛਰ ਘੋਲ ਘੁਮਾਈਆਂ, ਬੁਧ ਸੁਧ ਲੈਂਦਾ ਨਹੀਓਂ ਯਾਰ

ਪੀਰ ਵਾਰ ਰੋਜ਼ੇ ਤੇ ਜਾਵਾਂ, ਸਭ ਪੈਗ਼ੰਬਰ ਪੀਰ ਮਨਾਵਾਂ
ਜਦ ਪੀਆ ਦਾ ਦਰਸ਼ਨ ਪਾਵਾਂ, ਕਰਦੀ ਹਾਰ ਸ਼ਿੰਗਾਰ

ਮੰਤਕ ਮਾਅਨੇ ਪੜ੍ਹਾਂ ਨ ਅਸਲਾਂ, ਵਾਜਬ ਫ਼ਰਜ਼ ਨ ਸੁੰਨਤ ਨਫ਼ਲਾਂ
ਕੰਮ ਕਿਸ ਆਈਆਂ ਸ਼ਰ੍ਹਾਂ ਦੀਆਂ ਅਕਲਾਂ, ਕੁਝ ਨਹੀਂ ਬਾਝੋਂ ਦੀਦਾਰ

ਸ਼ਾਹ ਇਨਾਇਤ ਦੀਨ ਅਸਾਂ ਦਾ, ਦੀਨ ਦੁਨੀ ਮਕਬੂਲ ਅਸਾਂ ਦਾ
ਖੁੱਥੀ ਮੀਢੀ ਦਸਤ ਪਰਾਂਦਾ, ਫਿਰਾਂ ਉਜਾੜ ਉਜਾੜ

To settle the case between us, the *qazi* comes from Rum.[4]
   Opening his books, he gives reassurance, saying both
   are one. I am happy with the *qazi*. How will he hide
   from me?
Bullha says: What are you like, lord? Now what are
   you like and what am I like? If I start seeking you,
   there is no me left. You found me both manifest and
   concealed. Your light is both outside and inside.

## 76

Friday[1] brings a special delight.
Monday[2] gave us pains; on Tuesday we gained no
   understanding. We were sacrificed to love on
   Saturday. Wednesday[3] removed our awareness when
   you were not there, beloved.
On Monday I go to the shrine and pray to the prophets
   and saints. When I gain a vision of the beloved, I
   adorn myself.
I do not study the principles of logic and semantics,
   obligations, duties, the law, and extra rituals. What
   use are minds trained in religious law? Nothing
   matters except seeing him.
Shah Inayat is my religion, the one whom we accept in this   5
   world and the next. My plait is undone and the ribbon
   is in my hand as I wander in the wilderness.

ਭੁੱਲੀ ਹੀਰ ਸਲੇਟੀ ਮਰਦੀ, ਬੇਲੇ ਮਾਹੀ ਮਾਹੀ ਕਰਦੀ
ਕੋਈ ਨਾ ਮਿਲਦਾ ਦਿਲ ਦਾ ਦਰਦੀ, ਮੈਂ ਮਿਲਸਾਂ ਰਾਂਝਣ ਨਾਲ

ਬੁੱਲ੍ਹਾ ਭੁੱਲਾ ਨਮਾਜ਼ ਦੁਗਾਨਾ, ਜਦ ਦਾ ਸੁਣਿਆ ਤਾਨ ਤਰਾਨਾ
ਅਕਲ ਕਹੇ ਮੈਂ ਜ਼ਰਾ ਨਾ ਮਾਨਾਂ, ਇਸ਼ਕ ਕੂਕੇਂਦਾ ਤਾਰੋ ਤਾਰ

## ੧੧

ਜੋ ਰੰਗ ਰੰਗਿਆ ਗੁੱਝਾ ਰੰਗਿਆ, ਮੁਰਸ਼ਦ ਵਾਲੀ ਲਾਲੀ ਓ ਯਾਰ

ਅਹਦ ਵਿਚੋਂ ਅਹਿਮਦ ਹੋਇਆ, ਵਿੱਚੋਂ ਮੀਮ ਨਿਕਾਲੀ ਓ ਯਾਰ
ਦੁੱਰੇ ਮਆਨੀ ਦੀ ਧੂਮ ਮਚੀ ਹੈ, 'ਨਹਨੁ' ਕਾ ਘੁੰਡ ਉਠਾਲੀ ਓ ਯਾਰ

ਜੁਲਫ਼ ਸਿਆਹ ਵਿਚ ਹੈ ਜਦ ਬੈਠਾ, ਓਹ ਚਮਕਾਰਾ ਵਿਖਾਲੀ ਓ ਯਾਰ
'ਕੁਨ ਫ਼ਯਕੂਨ' ਅਵਾਜ਼ਾ ਹੋਇਆ, ਦਿੱਤੀ ਮੀਮ ਵਿਖਾਲੀ ਓ ਯਾਰ

ਅਹਦ ਕੋਲੇ ਅਹਿਮਦ ਹੋਇਆ, ਬਿਸਮਿਲ ਮੀਮ ਨਿਕਾਲੀ ਓ ਯਾਰ
ਪਾਕ ਮੁਹੰਮਦ ਪੈਦਾ ਹੋਇਆ, ਚੌਦਾਂ ਤਬਕਾਂ ਦਾ ਵਾਲੀ ਓ ਯਾਰ

੫  'ਅਲਸਤੁ ਬਿਰੱਬਿਕੁਮ' ਨਾਜ਼ਲ ਹੋਇਆ, 'ਕਾਲੂ ਬਲਾ' ਗਲ ਡਾਲੀ
          ਓ ਯਾਰ
'ਕੁੱਲਿ ਸ਼ੈਇਨ' ਕੀ ਖੇਡ ਮਚੀ ਹੈ, ਅਪਣਾ ਆਪ ਸੰਭਾਲੀ ਓ ਯਾਰ

ਸੂਰਾ ਯਾਸੀਨ ਮੁਜ਼ੰਮਲ ਵਾਲਾ, ਬਦਲਾ ਕੁਝ ਦਵਾਲੀ ਓ ਯਾਰ
'ਸੁੰਮੁਨ ਬੁਕਮੁਨ ਉਮਯੁਨ' ਹੋਇਆ, ਲਾਈਆਂ ਦੀ ਲਜ ਪਾਲੀਂ ਓ ਯਾਰ

Hir the daughter of the Sials[4] is lost and on the point of
   death, crying out to her beloved in the river glade:
   "I can find no one who feels what is in my heart. I
   will meet with my dear Ranjha."
Bullha forgot the prayer of two prostrations[5] once he
   heard the music play. I have no belief at all in what
   the intellect says, when love cries out aloud.[6]


## 77

The[1] color that I have been dyed is a deep one, it is the
   crimson of the guide, my friend.
Ahmad emerged from Ahad,[2] God brought forth the
   *mīm* from himself, my friend. The fame of the pearl
   of meanings[3] was celebrated. Lift the veil of *We*,[4]
   my friend.
In your dark curls there is the white hand.[5] Display
   its brilliance, my friend. *Let it be, and it was*[6] was
   proclaimed. He displayed the *mīm*, my friend.
Ahmad emerged from Ahad, the *mīm* was brought forth
   in the beginning, my friend. Holy Muhammad was
   born, the lord of the fourteen spheres,[7] my friend.
*Am I not your lord?*[8] was revealed. *They said, "Yes"* was       5
   hung around their necks, my friend. The game of *Over
   all things*[9] has started. Control yourself, my friend.
Give me something for the sake of the *Yāsīn* and the
   *Muzammil*,[10] my friend. Protect the honor of those
   who seek refuge with you, having become *deaf, dumb,
   and blind*,[11] my friend.

'ਮੂਤੂ ਕਬਲ ਅਨ ਤਮੂਤੂ' ਹੋਇਆਂ, ਮੋਇਆਂ ਨੂੰ ਫੇਰ ਜਿਵਾਲੀਂ ਓ ਯਾਰ
'ਲਾ ਤਤਹੱਰਕੂ ਝੱਰਹੂ', ਦੋਜ਼ਖ਼ ਕਿਹਨੂੰ ਡਾਲੀਂ ਓ ਯਾਰ

'ਲਨ ਤਨਾਲੁਲਬਿੱਰ' ਕੋਲੋਂ, 'ਹੱਤਾ' ਦੀ ਰਮਜ਼ ਪਛਾਣੀਂ ਓ ਯਾਰ
ਔਖਾ ਝੇੜਾ ਇਸ਼ਕੇ ਵਾਲਾ, ਸੰਭਲ ਪੈਰ ਟਿਕਾਲੀਂ ਓ ਯਾਰ

ਹਰ ਸੈ ਅੰਦਰ ਤੂਹੀਂ ਆਪੇ, ਆਪੇ ਵੇਖ ਵਿਖਾਲੀਂ ਓ ਯਾਰ
ਸ਼ਬੇ ਮਿਅਰਾਜ ਨਬੀ ਜੀ ਵਾਲਾ, ਓਹਾ ਵਸਲ ਵਿਸਾਲੀਂ ਓ ਯਾਰ

੧੦   ਜਾ ਰੱਬ ਖ਼ਲਕਤ ਪੈਦਾ ਕੀਤੀ, ਦੁਨੀਆਂ ਖ਼ੂਬ ਖ਼ਿਆਲੀ ਓ ਯਾਰ
ਬੁੱਲ੍ਹਾ ਸ਼ਹੁ ਮੇਰੇ ਘਰ ਆਇਆ, ਕਰ ਕਰ ਨਾਚ ਵਿਖਾਲੀ ਓ ਯਾਰ

## ੧੮

ਟੁਕ ਬੁਝ ਕੌਣ ਆਇਆ ਏ, ਕਿਸੇ ਭੇਖੀ ਭੇਖ ਵਟਾਇਆ ਏ

ਜਿਸ ਨਾ ਦਰਦ ਦੀ ਬਾਤ ਕਹੀ, ਉਸ ਪਰੇਮ ਨਗਾਰ ਨਾ ਝਾਤ ਪਈ
ਉਹ ਡੁੱਬ ਮੋਈ ਸਭ ਘਾਤ ਗਈ, ਉਹ ਕਿਉਂ ਚੰਦਰੀ ਨੇ ਜਾਇਆ ਏ

ਮਾਨਿੰਦ ਪਲਾਸ ਬਣਾਇਓ ਈ, ਤਨ ਕਰ ਕਰ ਪਾਤ ਲੁਟਾਇਓ ਈ
ਮੁਖ ਕਾਲਾ ਕਰ ਦਿਖਲਾਇਓ ਈ, ਕਿਆ ਸਿਆਹੀ ਰੰਗ ਲਗਾਇਆ ਏ

ਇਕ ਰੱਬ ਦਾ ਨਾਂ ਖ਼ਜ਼ਾਨਾ ਏ, ਸੰਗ ਚੋਰਾਂ ਯਾਰਾਂ ਦਾਨਾ ਏ
ਇਸ ਰਹਿਮਤ ਦਾ ਖਸਮਾਨਾ ਏ, ਸੰਗ ਖ਼ੋਛ ਰਕੀਬ ਬਣਾਇਆ ਏ

Restore to life those who have died in accordance with *Die
before you die,*[12] my friend. You wrote, *You do not move
at all.*[13] Why cast them into hell, my friend?

In *You will not attain righteousness,* recognize the mystery
of *until,*[14] my friend. The quarrel of love is hard. Tread
carefully, my friend.

You are in everything. Display yourself, my friend. Grant
me the union that was given to the Prophet on the
night of the ascension,[15] my friend.

Oh Lord, you brought creation into being. The world is           10
a dream and a fancy, my friend. Bullha, the lord has
come to my house; show him your dancing,[16] my
friend.


## 78

Just guess who has come in disguise. A master of
concealment has transformed himself.

No one who has not spoken of pain has glimpsed the city
of love. She drowned[1] and died, with all opportunities
lost. Why was that unlucky wretch born?

You made yourself like the *palās* tree.[2] You turned your
body into leaves and destroyed them. You blackened
your face. What is this blackness you have colored
yourself with?

The only treasure is the name of the lord, although it is
reckoned a trifle by thieves and adulterers. Besides the
protection of this mercy, fear was created by the rival.[3]

੫ ਦੂਈ ਦੂਰ ਕਰੇ ਕੋਈ ਸ਼ੋਰ ਨਹੀਂ, ਇਹ ਤੁਰਕ ਹਿੰਦੂ ਕੋਈ ਹੋਰ ਨਹੀਂ
ਸਭ ਸਾਥ ਕਹੇ ਕੋਈ ਚੋਰ ਨਹੀਂ, ਹਰ ਘਟ ਘਟ ਆਪ ਸਮਾਇਆ ਏ

ਐਵੇਂ ਕਿੱਸੇ ਕਾਹਨੂੰ ਘੜਨਾ ਏਂ, ਤੇ ਗੁਲਸਤਾਂ ਬੋਸਤਾਂ ਪੜ੍ਹਨਾ ਏ
ਐਵੇਂ ਬੇਮੁਜਬ ਕਿਉਂ ਲੜਨਾ ਏਂ, ਕਿਸ ਉਲਟਾ ਵੇਦ ਪੜ੍ਹਾਇਆ ਏ

ਸ਼ਰੀਅਤ ਸਾਡੀ ਦਾਈ ਏ, ਤਰੀਕਤ ਸਾਡੀ ਮਾਈ ਏ
ਅੱਗੋਂ ਹੱਕ ਹਕੀਕਤ ਆਈ ਏ, ਅਤੇ ਮਾਰਫ਼ਤੋਂ ਕੁਝ ਪਾਇਆ ਏ

ਹੈ ਵਿਰਲੀ ਬਾਤ ਬਤਾਵਣ ਦੀ, ਤੁਸੀਂ ਸਮਝੋ ਦਿਲ ਤੇ ਲਾਵਣ ਦੀ
ਕੋਈ ਗਤ ਦੱਸੋ ਉਸ ਭਾਵਣ ਦੀ, ਇਹ ਕਾਹਨੂੰ ਭੇਤ ਬਣਾਇਆ ਏ

ਇਹ ਪੜ੍ਹਨਾ ਇਲਮ ਜਰੂਰ ਹੋਇਆ, ਪਰ ਦਸਣਾ ਨਾਮਨਜ਼ੂਰ ਹੋਇਆ
ਜਿਸ ਦਸਿਆ ਸੋ ਮਨਸੂਰ ਹੋਇਆ, ਇਸ ਸੂਲੀ ਪਕੜ ਚੜ੍ਹਾਇਆ ਏ

੧੦ ਤੁਝੇ ਕਸਬੇ ਫ਼ਕਰ ਤਾਕੀਦ ਕੀਆ, ਵਖ ਤਕ ਆਰਫ਼ ਬਾਜ਼ੀਦ ਕੀਆ
ਕਰ ਜ਼ੁਹਦੀ ਕੁਤਬ ਫ਼ਰੀਦ ਕੀਆ, ਕਿਸੇ ਬੇਮਿਹਨਤ ਨਹੀਂ ਪਾਇਆ ਏ

ਇਸ ਦੁੱਖ ਸੇ ਕਿਚਕਰ ਭਾਗੋਂਗਾ, ਰਹੋਂ ਸੁੱਤਾ ਕਦ ਤੂੰ ਜਾਗੋਂਗਾ
ਫੇਰ ਉਠਦਾ ਰੋਵਣ ਲਾਗੋਂਗਾ, ਕਿਸੇ ਗਫ਼ਲਤ ਮਾਰ ਸੁਲਾਇਆ ਏ

ਗ਼ੈਨ ਐਨ ਦੀ ਸੂਰਤ ਇਕ ਠਹਿਰਾ, ਇਕ ਨੁਕਤੇ ਦਾ ਹੈ ਫ਼ਰਕ ਪੜਾ
ਜੋ ਨੁਕਤਾ ਦਿਲ ਥੀਂ ਦੂਰ ਕਰਾ, ਫਿਰ ਗ਼ੈਨੋਂ ਐਨ ਜਿਤਾਇਆ ਏ

ਜਿਹੜਾ ਮਨ ਵਿਚ ਲੱਗਾ ਦੁਆ ਰੇ, ਇਹ ਕੌਣ ਕਹੇ ਮੈਂ ਮੂਆ ਰੇ
ਤਨ ਸਭ ਇਨਾਇਤ ਹੂਆ ਰੇ, ਫਿਰ ਬੁੱਲ੍ਹਾ ਨਾਮ ਧਰਾਇਆ ਏ

Get rid of duality, there is no confusion. He is both Turk    5
   and Hindu,[4] there is no one else. Call everyone a holy
   man, there is no thief. He is contained in every heart.

Why do you make up stories pointlessly, and read the
   *Gulistān* and the *Bostān*?[5] Why do you quarrel for no
   reason? Who has taught you this perverse Veda?[6]

The law[7] is our nurse, the way is our mother. Next came
   reality, and we gained something real from gnosis.

It is something seldom to be told. Realize that it is to be
   taken to heart. Show some way of pleasing him. What
   have you made a secret?[8]

It is necessary to study this science but unacceptable to
   reveal it. The one who did reveal it was Mansur,[9] who
   was seized and put on the gallows.

You were urged on by the practice of austerity. Bayazid[10]    10
   was separated from his body and became a perfect
   adept. Asceticism creates great saints. No one
   discovers it without effort.

How long will you flee from this suffering? You remain
   asleep; when will you awake? Then when you get
   up, you will burst out crying. A fit of obliviousness
   attacked you and made you sleep.

A single form was assigned to *'ain* and *ġhain*.[11] The only
   difference between them is a single dot. Once the dot
   is removed from the heart, *ġhain* is shown to be *'ain*.

While the heart is affected by duality, who can say "My
   ego is dead"? My whole being became Inayat; then it
   got the name Bullha.

੭੯

ਟੁੱਟੇ ਕਾਮਨ ਕਰਕੇ ਨੀ, ਮੈਂ ਪਿਆਰਾ ਯਾਰ ਮਨਾਵਾਂਗੀ

ਇਸ ਟੁੱਟੇ ਨੂੰ ਪੜ੍ਹ ਫੂਕਾਂਗੀ, ਸੂਰਜ ਅਗਨ ਜਲਾਵਾਂਗੀ

ਅੱਖੀਆਂ ਕਾਜਲ ਕਾਲੇ ਬਾਦਲ, ਭਵਾਂ ਸੇ ਆਗ ਲਗਾਵਾਂਗੀ

ਔਰ ਬਸਾਤ ਨਹੀਂ ਕੁਝ ਮੇਰੀ, ਜੋਬਨ ਧੜੀ ਗੁੰਦਾਵਾਂਗੀ

੫    ਸੱਤ ਸਮੁੰਦਰ ਦਿਲ ਦੇ ਅੰਦਰ, ਦਿਲ ਸੇ ਲਹਿਰ ਉਠਾਵਾਂਗੀ

ਬਿਜਲੀ ਹੋ ਕਰ ਚਮਕ ਡਰਾਵਾਂ, ਬਟ ਬਾਦਲ ਘਿਰ ਘਿਰ ਜਾਵਾਂਗੀ

ਇਸ਼ਕ ਅੰਗੀਠੀ ਹਰਮਲ ਤਾਰੇ, ਸੂਰਜ ਅਗਨ ਚੜ੍ਹਾਵਾਂਗੀ

ਨਾ ਮੈਂ ਵਿਆਹੀ ਨਾ ਮੈਂ ਕੁਆਰੀ, ਬੇਟਾ ਗੋਦ ਖਿਡਾਵਾਂਗੀ

ਬੁੱਲ੍ਹੂ ਮਕਾਨ ਦੀ ਪਟੜੀ ਉੱਤੇ, ਬਹਿਕੇ ਨਾਦ ਵਜਾਵਾਂਗੀ

੧੦    ਲਾ ਸੌਂਵਾਂ ਮੈਂ ਸ਼ਹੁ ਗਲ ਅਪਣੈ, ਤਦ ਮੈਂ ਨਾਰ ਕਹਾਵਾਂਗੀ

੮੦

ਢੋਲਾ ਆਦਮੀ ਬਟ ਆਇਆ, ਵਾਹ ਵਾਹ ਆਇਆ ਛੁਪਾ ਛੁਪਾਇਆ

ਆਪੇ ਆਹੂ ਆਪੇ ਚੀਤਾ, ਆਪੇ ਮਾਰਨ ਧਾਇਆ
ਆਪੇ ਸਾਹਿਬ ਆਪੇ ਬਰਦਾ, ਆਪੇ ਮੁੱਲ ਵਿਕਾਇਆ

## 79

I[1] will use spells and charms to win my dear beloved back.
I will recite and blow this spell.[2] I will use the sun to light
    the sacrificial fire.
The kohl on my eyes will be black clouds. With my
    eyebrows I will make fire.
Having no other resource, I will plait my youthful beauty.
Within my heart are the seven seas. I will stir up waves     5
    with my heart.
Becoming lightning, I will flash and frighten. I will become
    clouds and circle overhead.
With love as my brazier and the stars as wild rue,[3] I will
    offer the sun on the fire.
I am not married, nor am I a virgin. I will play with my son
    on my lap.
Bullha, I will sit on the stool of infinity and play the conch.
If I sleep in my lord's embrace, then I will be called a wife.   10

## 80

The beloved has come as man. How wonderfully he has
    come concealed.
It is he who is the deer, he who is the cheetah. It is he
    who moves fast to hunt them down. It is he who is
    the master, he who is the slave, he who lets himself
    be sold.

ਕਦੀ ਹਾਬੀ ਤੇ ਅਸਵਾਰ ਹੋਇਆ, ਕਦੀ ਠੂਠਾ ਡਾਂਗ ਭੁਵਾਇਆ
ਕਦੀ ਰਾਵਲ ਜੋਗੀ ਭੋਗੀ ਹੋ ਕੇ, ਸਾਂਗੀ ਸਾਂਗ ਬਟਾਇਆ

ਬਾਜ਼ੀਗਰ ਕਿਆ ਬਾਜ਼ੀ ਖੇਲੀ, ਮੈਨੂੰ ਪੁਤਲੀ ਵਾਂਗ ਨਚਾਇਆ
ਮੈਂ ਓਸੇ ਪੜਤਾਲੇ ਨਚਤਾ, ਜਿਸ ਰਾਤ ਯਾਰ ਲਖਾਇਆ

੫   ਹਾਬੀਲ ਕਾਬੀਲ ਆਦਮ ਦੇ ਜਾਏ, ਆਦਮ ਕਿਸ ਦਾ ਜਾਇਆ
ਬੁੱਲ੍ਹਾ ਉਨ੍ਹਾਂ ਤੋਂ ਭੀ ਅੱਗੇ ਆਹਾ, ਦਾਦਾ ਗੋਦ ਖਿਡਾਇਆ


੮੧

ਤਾਂਘ ਮਾਹੀ ਦੀ ਜਲੀ ਆਂ, ਨਿਤ ਕਾਂਗ ਉਡਾਵਾਂ ਖਲੀ ਆਂ

ਕੋਡੀ ਦਮੜੀ ਪੱਲੇ ਨਾ ਕਾਈ, ਪਾਰ ਵੰਞਣ ਨੂੰ ਮੈਂ ਸਧਰਾਈ
ਨਹੀਂ ਮਲਾਹਾਂ ਨਾਲ ਅਸ਼ਨਾਈ, ਝੇੜਾ ਕਰਾਂ ਵਲੱਲੀ ਆਂ

ਨੈ ਚੰਦਲ ਦੇ ਸ਼ੋਰ ਕਿਨਾਰੇ, ਘੁੰਮਣ ਘੇਰ ਵਿਚ ਠਾਠਾਂ ਮਾਰੇ
ਡੁਬ ਡੁਬ ਮੋਏ ਤਾਰੂ ਭਾਰੇ, ਜੋ ਸ਼ੋਰ ਕਰਾਂ ਤਾਂ ਝੱਲੀ ਆਂ

ਨੈ ਚੰਦਲ ਦੇ ਡੂੰਘੇ ਪਾਹੇ, ਤਾਰੂ ਗੋਤੇ ਖਾਂਦੇ ਆਏ
ਮਾਹੀ ਮੈਂਡੇ ਪਾਰ ਸਿਧਾਏ, ਮੈਂ ਕੇਵਲ ਰਹੀ ਆਂ ਕੱਲੀ ਆਂ

੫   ਨੈ ਚੰਦਲ ਦੀਆਂ ਤਾਰੂ ਫਾਟਾਂ, ਖਲੀ ਉਡੀਕਾਂ ਮਾਹੀ ਦੀਆਂ ਵਾਟਾਂ
ਇਸ਼ਕ ਮਾਹੀ ਦੇ ਲਾਈਆਂ ਚਾਟਾਂ, ਜੇ ਕੂਕਾਂ ਤਾਂ ਮੈਂ ਗਾਲੀ ਆਂ

Sometimes he is mounted on an elephant, sometimes he
  is sent around begging with earthen cup and staff.
  Sometimes he is a master yogi, sometimes a hedonist;
  he is an actor[1] who assumes different guises.
What a show the juggler has mounted; he has made me
  dance like a puppet. I must dance according to his
  measure, in the style that my beloved has shown me.
Abel and Cain were the sons of Adam, but who was          5
  Adam born from? Bullha, even before them, the
  grandfather[2] was dandled in his lap.


### 81

I[1] am consumed with desire for my beloved. I am
  anxiously standing in wait[2] for him.
I do not have even the smallest coin on me. I long to cross
  over to the other side. I am not on friendly terms with
  the boatmen. Foolishly, I get into quarrels with them.
There is a commotion on the banks of the river Chenab.
  The waves surge in the whirlpools. Strong swimmers
  keep drowning here. If I make a noise, I go crazy.
The tributaries of the river Chenab are deep. Swimmers
  dive deep into them. My beloved has gone across. I am
  left here alone.
The branches of the river Chenab can only be crossed by    5
  swimming. I stand waiting for my beloved to come.
  My love for my beloved has filled me with ecstasy. If
  I cry out, I am destroyed.

ਪਾਰ ਝਨਾਓਂ ਜੰਗਲ ਬੇਲੇ, ਓਬੇ ਖੂਨੀ ਸ਼ੋਰ ਬਘੇਲੇ
ਝਬ ਰੱਬ ਮੈਨੂੰ ਮਾਹੀ ਮੇਲੇ, ਮੈਂ ਏਸ ਫ਼ਿਕਰ ਵਿਚ ਗਾਲੀ ਆਂ

ਅੱਧੀ ਰਾਤੀ ਲਟਕਣ ਤਾਰੇ, ਇਕ ਲਟਕੇ ਇਕ ਲਟਕਣਹਾਰੇ
ਮੈਂ ਉੱਠ ਆਈ ਨਦੀ ਕਿਨਾਰੇ, ਹੁਣ ਪਾਰ ਲੰਘਣ ਨੂੰ ਖਲੀ ਆਂ

ਮੈਂ ਮਨਤਾਰੂ ਸਾਰ ਕੀ ਜਾਣਾਂ, ਵੰਝ ਨਾ ਚੱਪਾ ਤੁਲੂ ਪੁਰਾਣਾ
ਘੁੰਮਣ ਘੇਰ ਨਾ ਟਾਂਗ ਟਿਕਾਣਾ, ਰੋ ਰੋ ਫਾਟਾਂ ਤਲੀਆਂ

ਬੁੱਲ੍ਹੂ ਸ਼ਹੁ ਘਰ ਮੇਰੇ ਆਵੇ, ਹਾਰ ਸ਼ਿੰਗਾਰ ਮੇਰੇ ਮਨ ਭਾਵੇ
ਮੁੰਹ ਮੁਕਟਾ ਮੱਥੇ ਤਿਲਕ ਲਗਾਵੇ, ਜੇ ਵੇਖੇ ਤਾਣ ਮੈਂ ਭਲੀ ਆਂ

੮੨

ਤੁਸੀਂ ਆਓ ਮਿਲੋ ਮੇਰੀ ਪਿਆਰੀ, ਮੇਰੇ ਟੁਰਨੇ ਦੀ ਹੋਈ ਤਿਆਰੀ

ਸੱਭੇ ਰਲ ਕੇ ਟੋਰਨ ਆਈਆਂ, ਮਾਸੀਆਂ ਫੁੱਫੀਆ ਚਾਚੀਆਂ ਤਾਈਆਂ
ਸੱਭੇ ਰੋਂਦੀਆਂ ਜ਼ਾਰੋ ਜ਼ਾਰੀ

ਸੱਭੇ ਆਖਣ ਇਹ ਗੱਲ ਜਾਣੀਂ, ਹਰਦਮ ਹੋਕੇ ਰਹੀਂ ਨਿਮਾਣੀ
ਤਾਹੀਂ ਲੱਗੋਂਗੀ ਓਬੇ ਪਿਆਰੀ

ਸੱਭੇ ਟੋਰ ਘਰਾਂ ਨੂੰ ਮੁੜੀਆਂ, ਮੈਂ ਹੋ ਇਕ ਇਕੱਲੜੀ ਟੁਰੀ ਆਂ
ਹੋਈ ਆਂ ਡਾਰੋਂ ਕੁੰਜ ਨਿਆਰੀ

On the other side of the Chenab there are jungles and
thickets, where cruel tigers and panthers roam. May
the lord bring me quickly to my beloved. This anxiety
is killing me.

It is the middle of the night and the stars are waning. Some
have already waned; others are about to do so. I have
got up and come to the riverbank. Now I am standing
here waiting to cross.

I cannot swim and do not have a clue what to do. I have no
pole or oar, and my raft is old. There are whirlpools,
and no crossing place is marked. I weep and wring my
hands.

Bullha, if the lord comes to my house, all my finery pleases
me. He is wearing a diadem[3] and a forehead mark. If
he looks at me, I feel fine.


## 82

Come to me, my dears. My departure is prepared.

They have all come to see me off, all my various aunts on
both sides. They all weep bitterly.

They all say, "Just be aware of this. You must be humble at
every moment. That way you will be liked there."

After seeing me off, they all return to their houses. I have
departed alone. I am like the crane who is separated
from her flock.

੫ ਬੁੱਲ੍ਹ ਸ਼ਹੁ ਮੇਰੇ ਘਰ ਆਵੇ, ਮੈਂ ਕੁੱਚਜੀ ਨੂੰ ਗਲ ਲਾਵੇ
   ਇਕ ਸ਼ਹੁ ਦੀ ਬਾਤ ਨਿਆਰੀ

## ੮੩

ਤੁਸੀਂ ਕਰੋ ਅਸਾਡੀ ਕਾਰੀ, ਕੇਹੀ ਹੋ ਗਈ ਵੇਦਨ ਭਾਰੀ

ਉਹ ਮੇਰੇ ਘਰ ਅੰਦਰ ਆਇਆ, ਉਸ ਨੇ ਮੈਨੂੰ ਆ ਭਰਮਾਇਆ
ਪੁੱਛੇ ਜਾਦੂ ਹੈ ਕਿ ਸਾਇਆ, ਉਸ ਤੋਂ ਲਵੇ ਹਕੀਕਤ ਸਾਰੀ

ਉਹੋ ਦਿਲ ਮੇਰੇ ਵਿਚ ਵਸਦਾ, ਬੈਠਾ ਨਾਲ ਅਸਾਡੇ ਹਸਦਾ
ਪੁੱਛਾਂ ਬਾਤਾਂ ਤੇ ਉਠ ਨਸਦਾ, ਲੈ ਬਾਜ਼ਾਂ ਵਾਂਗ ਉਡਾਰੀ

ਮੈਂ ਸ਼ਹੁ ਦਰਿਆਵਾਂ ਪਈ ਆਂ, ਠਾਠਾਂ ਲਹਿਰਾਂ ਦੇ ਮੂੰਹ ਗਈ ਆਂ
ਫੜ੍ਹ ਕੇ ਘੁੰਮਣ ਘੇਰ ਭਵਈਆਂ, ਪੜ ਬਰਖਾ ਰੈਣ ਅੰਧਾਰੀ

੫ ਸਾਈਆਂ ਐੜ ਛਨਿੱਛਰ ਚਾਏ, ਤਾਰੇ ਖਾਰਿਆਂ ਹੇਠ ਛੁਪਾਏ
   ਮੁੰਜ ਦੀਆਂ ਰੱਸੀਆਂ ਨਾਗ ਬਣਾਏ, ਇਹਨਾਂ ਸਹਿਰਾਂ ਤੋਂ ਬਲਿਹਾਰੀ

ਇਹ ਜੋ ਮੁਰਲੀ ਕਾਨੂ ਵਜਾਈ, ਦਿਲ ਮੇਰੇ ਨੂੰ ਚੋਟ ਲਗਾਈ
ਆਹ ਦੇ ਨਾਅਰੇ ਕਰਦੀ ਆਹੀ, ਮੈਂ ਰੋਵਾਂ ਜ਼ਾਰੋ ਜ਼ਾਰੀ

ਇਸ਼ਕ ਦੀਵਾਨੇ ਲੀਕਾਂ ਲਾਈਆਂ, ਡਾਢੀਆਂ ਘਟੀਆਂ ਸੱਥਾਂ ਪਾਈਆਂ
ਹਾਂ ਮੈਂ ਬਕਰੀ ਵਿੱਚ ਕਸਾਈਆਂ, ਰਹਿੰਦਾ ਸਹਿਮ ਹਮੇਸ਼ਾ ਭਾਰੀ

150

Bullha, the lord may embrace me if he comes to my house,  5
    although I am so unaccomplished. The ways of the
    lord are strange.

## 83

Give me a cure that works. I suffer from a grievous pain.
He came inside my house. He came and bewitched me.
    Ask if it is magic or a shadow.[1] Get the whole truth
    from him.
It is he who dwells in my heart. He sits with me and laughs.
    If I ask him things, he runs away. He takes flight like
    a hawk.
Now, lord, I have fallen into the river.[2] I am engulfed by
    the waves and billows. I have been seized and spun
    around in the whirlpools. The rain is falling and the
    night is dark.
Oh lord, you have performed such great and powerful  5
    tricks. You have hidden the stars under baskets.[3] You
    have turned fiber ropes into snakes. I am sacrificed to
    all this magic.
This flute that Krishna played inflicted a wound on my
    heart. I sighed and uttered loud laments, while
    weeping bitter tears.
My mad love has brought me disgrace. It has brought me
    before harsh tribunals. I am a goat among butchers.
    I am always gripped by deep terror.

ਇਸ਼ਕ ਰੁਹੇਲਾ ਨਾਹੀਂ ਜਚਦਾ, ਅੰਦਰ ਧਰਿਆ ਬੰਨੇ ਨਚਦਾ
ਮੈਨੂੰ ਦਿਓ ਸੁਨੇਹੜਾ ਸਚ ਦਾ, ਮੇਰੀ ਕਰੋ ਕੋਈ ਗ਼ਮਖ਼ਾਰੀ

ਮੈਂ ਕੀ ਮਿਹਰ ਮੁਹੱਬਤ ਜਾਣਾਂ, ਸਈਆਂ ਕਰਦੀਆਂ ਜ਼ੋਰ ਪਿੰਗਾਣਾ
ਗਲਗਲ ਮੇਵਾ ਕੀ ਹਦਵਾਣਾ, ਕੀ ਕੋਈ ਵੈਦ ਪਸਾਰੀ

੧੦ ਨੌਸ਼ਹੁ ਜਿਸ ਦਾ ਬਾਂਸ ਬਰੇਲੀ, ਟੁੱਟੀ ਡਾਲੋਂ ਰਹੇ ਇਕੇਲੀ
ਕੂਕੇ ਬੇਲੇ ਬੇਲੀ ਬੇਲੀ, ਉਹਦੀ ਕਰੇ ਕੋਈ ਦਿਲਦਾਰੀ

ਬੁੱਲ੍ਹੂ ਸ਼ਹੁ ਦੇ ਜੇ ਮੈਂ ਜਾਵਾਂ, ਅਪਣਾ ਸਿਰ ਧੜ ਫੇਰ ਨਾ ਪਾਵਾਂ
ਓਬੇ ਜਾਵਾਂ ਫੇਰ ਨਾ ਆਵਾਂ, ਏਥੇ ਐਵੇਂ ਉਮਰ ਗੁਜ਼ਾਰੀ

੮੫

ਤੂੰ ਕਿਧਰੋਂ ਆਇਆ ਕਿਧਰ ਜਾਣਾ, ਅਪਣਾ ਦੱਸ ਟਿਕਾਣਾ

ਜਿਸ ਠਾਣੇ ਦਾ ਮਾਣ ਕਰੋਂ ਤੂੰ, ਤੇਰੇ ਨਾਲ ਨਾ ਜਾਸੀ ਠਾਣਾ

ਜ਼ੁਲਮ ਕਰੋਂ ਤੇ ਲੋਕ ਸਤਾਵੇਂ, ਕਸਬ ਫੜਿਓ ਲੁਟ ਖਾਣਾ

ਮਹਿਬੂਬ ਸੁਜਾਨੀ ਕਰੇ ਅਸਾਨੀ, ਖੋਂਢ ਜਾਏ ਮਲਕਾਣਾ

੫ ਸ਼ਹਿਰ ਖ਼ਮੋਸ਼ਾਂ ਦੇ ਚਲ ਵੱਸੀਏ, ਜਿੱਥੇ ਮੁਲਕ ਸਮਾਣਾ

152

Fierce love cannot be properly understood. If it is placed
    inside, it dances on the boundary wall. Give me a
    message from the true one. Let someone show me
    some sympathy.

What do I know of kindness and love? My girlfriends
    are violent toward me. I do not know the difference
    between a citron and a watermelon.[4] Is there any
    doctor or apothecary for me?

The girl whose bridegroom is like bamboo from Bareilly[5]    10
    has been broken off from the branch and is alone. In
    the river glade she cries, "Beloved, beloved." Will
    anyone console her?

Bullha, if I go to the lord's, I will not get my life back
    again.[6] If I go there, I will not return. Here my life has
    been passed for nothing.

## 84

Where have you come from, where are you going to? Tell
    us where you live.

The position of which you are so proud will not go with
    you.

You oppress people and torment them. You have stolen
    their food and snatched away their livelihood.

The wise beloved makes things easy, and makes the fear
    of the angel of death go away.

You must go and settle in the city of the silent,[1] into which    5
    the whole country is admitted.

ਭਰ ਭਰ ਪੁਰ ਲੰਘਾਵੇ ਡਾਢਾ, ਮਲਕੁਲਮੌਤ ਮੁਹਾਣਾ

ਕਰ ਲਏ ਚਾਵੜ ਚਾਰ ਦਿਹਾੜੇ, ਓੜਕ ਤੂੰ ਉੱਠ ਜਾਣਾ

ਇਨ੍ਹਾਂ ਸਭਨਾਂ ਥੀਂ ਏ ਬੁੱਲ੍ਹਾ, ਔਗਣਹਾਰ ਪੁਰਾਣਾ

<br>

੮੫

ਤੂੰਹੀਓ ਹੈਂ ਮੈਂ ਨਾਹੀਂ ਵੇ ਸੱਜਣਾ, ਤੂੰਹੀਓ ਹੈਂ ਮੈਂ ਨਾਹੀਂ

ਖੇਲੇ ਦੋਂ ਪਰਛਾਵੇਂ ਵਾਂਗੂੰ, ਰਿਹਾ ਮਨ ਮਾਹੀਂ

ਜਾਂ ਬੋਲਾਂ ਤੂੰ ਨਾਲੇ ਬੋਲੇਂ, ਚੁੱਪ ਕਰਾਂ ਮਨ ਮਾਹੀਂ

ਜਾਂ ਸੌਂਵਾਂ ਤੇ ਨਾਲੇ ਸੌਂਵੇਂ, ਜਾਂ ਟੁਰਾਂ ਤੂੰ ਰਾਹੀਂ

੫ ਬੁੱਲ੍ਹਾ ਸ਼ਾਹੁ ਘਰ ਆਇਆ ਸਾਡੇ, ਜਿੰਦੜੀ ਘੋਲ ਘੁਮਾਈਂ

<br>

੮੬

ਤੇਰਾ ਨਾਮ ਧਿਆਈਦਾ, ਸਾਈਂ ਤੇਰਾ ਨਾਮ ਧਿਆਈਦਾ

ਬੁੱਲ੍ਹੇ ਨਾਲੋਂ ਚੁੱਲ੍ਹਾ ਚੰਗਾ, ਜਿਸ ਪਰ ਤੁਆਮ ਪਕਾਈਦਾ

ਰਲ ਫ਼ਕੀਰਾਂ ਮਜਲਿਸ ਕੀਤੀ, ਥੋਰਾ ਥੋਰਾ ਖਾਈਦਾ

ਰੰਗੜ ਨਾਲੋਂ ਖੰਗਰ ਚੰਗਾ, ਜਿਸ ਪਰ ਪੈਰ ਘਸਾਈਦਾ

154

Full loads of passengers are taken across by the cruel
  ferryman, the angel of death.
You may enjoy yourself for a few days, but in the end you
  must get up and leave.
Bullha has long been more sinful than all these creatures.


### 85

There is only you, there is no me, beloved. There is only
  you, there is no me.
Like the shadows in a ruined house, I go around and
  around in my head.
When I speak, then you speak too. When I am silent, you
  are in my mind.
When I sleep, you sleep with me. When I walk, you are on
  my way.
Bullha, the lord has come to my house. My life is sacrificed     5
  to him.


### 86

Your[1] name is the focus of our meditation, lord, your name
  is the focus of our meditation.
Better than Bullha is a hearth[2] on which food is cooked.
The fakirs have come together and held a party, where
  every crumb is eaten.
Better than a Ranghar[3] is a lump of brick on which the foot
  is rubbed.

੫ ਬੁੱਲ੍ਹੂ ਸ਼ਹੁ ਨੂੰ ਸੋਈ ਪਾਵੇ, ਜੋ ਬਕਰਾ ਬਣੇ ਕਸਾਈ ਦਾ

## ੮੭

ਤੈਂ ਕਿਤ ਪਰ ਪਾਯੋਂ ਪਸਾਰਾ ਏ, ਕੋਈ ਦਮ ਕਾ ਈਹਾਂ ਗੁਜ਼ਾਰਾ ਏ

ਇਕ ਪਲਕ ਝਲਕ ਦਾ ਮੇਲਾ ਏ, ਕੁਝ ਕਰ ਲੈ ਏਹੋ ਵੇਲਾ ਏ
ਇਹ ਘੜੀ ਗ਼ਨੀਮਤ ਦਿਹਾੜਾ ਏ

ਇਕ ਰਾਤ ਸਰਾਂ ਦਾ ਰਹਿਣਾ ਏ, ਏਥੇ ਆ ਕਰ ਫੁੱਲ ਨਾ ਬਹਿਣਾ ਏ
ਕਲ ਸਭ ਦਾ ਕੂਚ ਨਕਾਰਾ ਏ

ਤੂੰ ਉਸ ਮਕਾਨੋਂ ਆਇਆ ਹੈਂ, ਏਥੇ ਆਦਮ ਬਣ ਸਮਾਇਆ ਹੈਂ
ਹੁਣ ਛੱਡ ਮਜਲਿਸ ਕੋਈ ਕਾਰਾ ਏ

੫ ਬੁੱਲ੍ਹੂ ਸ਼ਹੁ ਇਹ ਭਰਮ ਤੁਮ੍ਹਾਰਾ ਏ, ਸਿਰ ਚੁੱਕਿਆ ਪਰਬਤ ਭਾਰਾ ਏ
ਉਸ ਮੰਜ਼ਲ ਰਾਹ ਨਾ ਖਾਹੜਾ ਏ

## ੮੮

ਦਿਲ ਲੋਚੇ ਮਾਹੀ ਯਾਰ ਨੂੰ

ਇਕ ਹਸ ਹਸ ਗੱਲਾਂ ਕਰਦੀਆਂ, ਇਕ ਰੋਂਦੀਆਂ ਧੋਦੀਆਂ ਭਰਦੀਆਂ
ਕਹੋ ਫੁੱਲੀ ਬਸੰਤ ਬਹਾਰ ਨੂੰ, ਦਿਲ ਲੋਚੇ ਮਾਹੀ ਯਾਰ ਨੂੰ

ਮੈਂ ਨੂਤੀ ਧੋਤੀ ਰਹਿ ਗਈ, ਇਕ ਗੱਚ ਮਾਹੀ ਦਿਲ ਪੈ ਗਈ
ਭਾਹ ਲਾਈਏ ਹਾਰ ਸ਼ਿੰਗਾਰ ਨੂੰ, ਦਿਲ ਲੋਚੇ ਮਾਹੀ ਯਾਰ ਨੂੰ

Bullha, the lord is found by those who become a goat for          5
    the butcher.


## 87

What have you spread yourself out on? You are here for
    only a few moments.

It is a fair that is over in a flash. Do something, now is the
    time. This moment, this day is your opportunity.

You get one night's stay in this caravanserai. When you
    get here, do not spread yourself out. Tomorrow the
    departure drum sounds for everyone.

You have come from that abode. You have settled yourself
    here as a human being. Now leave the party—you have
    a task to perform.

Bullhe Shah, this is your delusion. You have loaded a          5
    heavy mountain on your head. This is not the road or
    passage to that destination.


## 88

My heart desires my dear beloved.

Some girls laugh and talk, some weep bitterly and suffer.
    Just tell the blossoming spring: "My heart desires my
    dear beloved."[1]

I am left here all bathed and washed. My beloved has taken
    against me. Into the fire with all this finery! My heart
    desires my dear beloved.

ਮੈਂ ਕਮਲੀ ਕੀਤੀ ਦੂਤੀਆਂ, ਦੁਖ ਘੇਰ ਚੁਫੇਰਿਓਂ ਲੀਤੀਆਂ
ਘਰ ਆ ਮਾਹੀ ਦੀਦਾਰ ਨੂੰ, ਦਿਲ ਲੋਚੇ ਮਾਹੀ ਯਾਰ ਨੂੰ

੫   ਬੁੱਲ੍ਹਾ ਸ਼ਾਹੁ ਮੇਰੇ ਘਰ ਆਇਆ, ਮੈਂ ਘੁਟ ਰਾਂਝਣ ਗਲ ਲਾਇਆ
ਦੁੱਖ ਗਏ ਸਮੁੰਦਰੋਂ ਪਾਰ ਨੂੰ, ਦਿਲ ਲੋਚੇ ਮਾਹੀ ਯਾਰ ਨੂੰ


੮੯
ਨਾ ਜੀਵਾਂ ਮਹਾਰਾਜ, ਮੈਂ ਤੇਰੇ ਬਿਨ ਨਾ ਜੀਵਾਂ

ਇਹਨਾਂ ਸੁਕਿਆਂ ਫੁਲਾਂ ਵਿਚ ਬਾਸ ਨਹੀਂ, ਪਰਦੇਸ ਗਿਆਂ ਦੀ ਕੋਈ ਆਸ
ਨਹੀਂ
ਜਿਹੜੇ ਸਾਈਂ ਸਾਜਨ ਪਾਸ ਨਹੀਂ

ਤੂੰ ਕੀ ਸੁੱਤਾ ਏਂ ਚਾਦਰ ਤਾਣ ਕੇ, ਸਿਰ ਤੇ ਮੌਤ ਖਲੋਤੀ ਆਣ ਕੇ
ਕੋਈ ਅਮਲ ਨਾ ਕੀਤਾ ਜਾਣ ਕੇ

ਕੀ ਮੈਂ ਖੱਟਿਆ ਤੇਰੀ ਹੋ ਕੇ, ਦੋਵੇਂ ਨੈਣ ਗਵਾਏ ਰੋ ਕੇ
ਤੇਰਾ ਨਾਮ ਲਈਏ ਮੁਖ ਧੋ ਕੇ

੫   ਬੁੱਲ੍ਹਾ ਸ਼ਾਹੁ ਬਦੇਸੋਂ ਆਉਂਦਾ, ਹੱਥ ਕੰਗਣਾ ਤੇ ਬਾਹੀਂ ਲਟਕਾਉਂਦਾ
ਸਿਰ ਸਦਕਾ ਤੇਰੇ ਨਾਉਂ ਦਾ

My enemies have made me mad. Griefs have surrounded
    me on all sides. Come home, beloved, and let me see
    you. My heart desires my dear beloved.
Bullha, the lord has come to my house. I have held Ranjha    5
    in a tight embrace. My griefs have vanished across the
    ocean. My heart desires my dear beloved.

## 89

Lord, I cannot live, I cannot live without you.
There is no fragrance in these withered flowers. There is
    no hope of his return from foreign parts. The one who
    is my beloved lord is not by my side.
Why have you covered yourself with a sheet and gone to
    sleep? Death has come to hover over your head. You
    have not consciously performed any good action.
What have I gained by becoming yours? I have destroyed
    both my eyes through weeping. I bathe my face in
    tears as I take your name.
Bullha, the lord comes from foreign parts, with a thread    5
    tied around his wrist and his arms hanging loose. My
    head is a sacrifice to your name.

੯੦

ਨਿੱਤ ਪੜ੍ਹਨਾ ਏਂ ਇਸਤਗ਼ਫ਼ਾਰ, ਕੈਸੀ ਤੋਬਾ ਹੈ ਇਹ ਯਾਰ

ਸਾਵੀਂ ਦੇ ਕੇ ਲਵੇਂ ਸਵਾਈ, ਵਿਧੀਆਂ ਦੀ ਤੂੰ ਬਾਜ਼ੀ ਲਾਈ
ਮੁਸਲਮਾਨੀ ਇਹ ਕਿਥੋਂ ਪਾਈ, ਇਹ ਤੇਰਾ ਕਿਰਦਾਰ

ਜਿਥੇ ਨਾ ਜਾਣਾ ਓਥੇ ਜਾਏਂ, ਮਾਲ ਪਰਾਇਆ ਮੂੰਹ ਧਰ ਖਾਏਂ
ਕੁਝ ਕਿਤਾਬਾਂ ਸਿਰ ਤੇ ਚਾਏਂ, ਇਹ ਤੇਰਾ ਇਤਬਾਰ

ਜ਼ਾਲਮ ਜ਼ੁਲਮੋਂ ਨਾਹੀਂ ਡਰਦੇ, ਅਪਣੀ ਅਮਲੀਂ ਆਪੇ ਮਰਦੇ
ਮੂੰਹੋਂ ਤੋਬਾ ਦਿਲੋਂ ਨਾ ਕਰਦੇ, ਏਥੇ ਓਥੇ ਹੋਣ ਖ਼ੁਆਰ

੫    ਸੋਂ ਦਿਨ ਜੀਵੇਂ ਇਕ ਦਿਨ ਮਰਸੇਂ, ਉਸ ਦਿਨ ਖ਼ੌਫ਼ ਖ਼ੁਦਾ ਦਾ ਕਰਸੇਂ
ਇਸ ਤੋਬਾ ਥੀਂ ਤੋਬਾ ਕਰਸੇਂ, ਉਹ ਤੋਬਾ ਕਿਸ ਕਾਰ

ਬੁੱਲ੍ਹਾ ਸ਼ਹੁ ਦੀ ਸੁਣੋ ਹਕਾਇਤ, ਹਾਦੀ ਫੜਿਆਂ ਹੋਈ ਹਦਾਇਤ
ਮੇਰਾ ਸਾਈਂ ਸ਼ਾਹ ਇਨਾਇਤ, ਉਹੋ ਲੰਘਾਵੇ ਪਾਰ

੯੧

ਨੀ ਸਈਓ ਮੈਂ ਗਾਈ ਗਵਾਚੀ, ਖੇਲ੍ਹ ਘੁੰਘਟ ਮੁਖ ਨਾਚੀ

ਜਿਤ ਵੱਲ ਵੇਖਾਂ ਉਤ ਵੱਲ ਓਹੀ, ਕਸਮ ਓਸੇ ਦੀ ਹੋਰ ਨਾ ਕੋਈ
'ਵਹੁਵ ਮਅਕੁਮ' ਫਿਰ ਗਈ ਧੌਣੀ, ਜਬ ਗੁਰ ਪਤਰੀ ਤੇਰੀ ਵਾਚੀ

## 90

You keep asking for God's forgiveness.[1] What sort of
    repentance is this, my friend?

On whatever you give, you charge an extra 25 percent.
    You play a tricky game. Where did you discover how
    to be this sort of Muslim? Is this how you behave?

You go where you should not go. You greedily consume the
    wealth that belongs to others. You load your head with
    books full of falsehood. Is this what you put your trust
    in?

Oppressors have no fear of being oppressive. They are the
    ones who die through their own actions. They profess
    repentance with their lips, not with their hearts. They
    are disgraced in this world and the next.

You may live for a hundred days, but one day you will die.   5
    On that day you will be afraid of God. You will repent
    of this repentance. What use is that repentance?

Hear the tale of Bullhe Shah. He found true guidance
    when he took hold of the true guide. My lord is Shah
    Inayat. It is he who delivers me across.

## 91

I am utterly lost, girls. I have removed the veil from my
    face and danced.

In whichever direction I look, he alone is there. By him
    I swear that there is no one else. The cry *And he is with
    you* [1] was proclaimed, oh master, when your manual[2]
    was read out.

ਨਾਮ ਨਿਸ਼ਾਨ ਨਾ ਮੇਰਾ ਸਈਓ, ਜੋ ਆਖਾਂ ਤੁਸੀਂ ਚੁੱਪ ਕਰ ਰਹੀਓ
ਇਹ ਗੱਲ ਮੂਲ ਕਿਸੇ ਨਾ ਕਹੀਓ, ਬੁੱਲ੍ਹਾ ਖ਼ੂਬ ਹਕੀਕਤ ਜਾਚੀ

੯੨

ਨੀ ਕੁਟੀਚਲ ਮੇਰਾ ਨਾਂ

ਮੁੱਲਾਂ ਮੈਨੂੰ ਸਬਕ ਪੜ੍ਹਾਇਆ, ਅਲੜ੍ਹੋਂ ਅੱਗੇ ਕੁਝ ਨਾ ਆਇਆ
ਉਸ ਦੀਆਂ ਜੁੱਤੀਆਂ ਖਾਂਦੀ ਸਾਂ

ਕਿਵੇਂ ਕਿਵੇਂ ਦੋ ਅੱਖੀਆਂ ਲਾਈਆਂ, ਰਲ ਕੇ ਸਈਆਂ ਮਾਰਨ ਆਈਆਂ
ਨਾਲੇ ਮਾਰੇ ਬਾਬਲ ਮਾਂ

ਸਹੁਰੇ ਸਾਨੂੰ ਵੜਨ ਨਾ ਦੇਂਦੇ, ਨਾਨਕ ਦਾਦਕ ਘਰੋਂ ਕਢੇਂਦੇ
ਮੇਰਾ ਪੇਕੇ ਨਹੀਓ ਥਾਂ

੫  ਪੜ੍ਹਨ ਸੇਤੀ ਸਭ ਮਾਰਨ ਆਹੀਂ, ਬਿਨ ਪੜ੍ਹਿਆਂ ਹੁਣ ਛਡਦਾ ਨਾਹੀਂ
ਨੀ ਮੈਂ ਮੁੜ ਕੇ ਕਿਤ ਵੱਲ ਜਾਂ

ਬੁੱਲ੍ਹਾ ਸ਼ਹੁ ਕੀ ਲਾਇਆ ਮੈਨੂੰ, ਮਤ ਕੁਝ ਲੱਗੇ ਉਹ ਹੀ ਤੈਨੂੰ
ਤਦ ਕਰੇਂਗਾ ਤੂੰ ਨਿਆਂ

੯੩

ਨੀ ਮੈਨੂੰ ਲਗੜਾ ਇਸ਼ਕ ਅਵਲ ਦਾ, ਅਵਲ ਦਾ ਰੋਜ਼ ਅਜ਼ਲ ਦਾ

ਵਿਚ ਕੜਾਹੀ ਤਲ ਤਲ ਜਾਵੇ, ਤਲਿਆਂ ਨੂੰ ਚਾ ਤਲਦਾ

I have no name or mark, girls. Keep silent when I speak.
Make sure you do not tell this to anyone. Bullha has
a firm sense of the truth.

## 92

"Dunce"[1] is my name, oh.
The mullah taught me the lesson, but I could not get
beyond *alif*.[2] I suffered a beating with his slippers.
Somehow or other our eyes met. My girlfriends have got
together to beat me. My father and mother beat me
too.
My in-laws do not let me in. My grandparents' people
throw me out of their homes. I have no place in my
father's house.
When they study, the class all heave sighs. Now, unless          5
I study, the teacher does not spare me. Oh, where can
I turn to?
Bullha, what did the lord do to me? Mind that something
does not happen to you too. Then you will be fair to
me.

## 93

Oh, I was smitten by love from the first. From the first,
from the day of pre-eternity.[1]
Love fries its victims in the pan. Those who are already
fried are fried some more.

ਮੋਇਆਂ ਨੂੰ ਇਹ ਦਲ ਦਲ ਮਾਰੇ, ਵਲਿਆਂ ਨੂੰ ਚਾ ਵਲਦਾ

ਕਿਆ ਜਾਣਾਂ ਮੈਂ ਚਿਟਗੋ ਕੱਖੀਂ, ਨਿਤ ਸੂਲ ਕਲੇਜੇ ਸਲਦਾ

੫ ਤੀਰ ਜਿਗਰ ਵਿਚ ਲੱਗਾ ਇਸ਼ਕੋਂ, ਨਹੀਂ ਹਲਾਇਆ ਹਲਦਾ

ਬੁੱਲ੍ਹਾ ਸ਼ਹੁ ਦਾ ਨੇਹੁੰ ਅਨੋਖਾ, ਨਹੀਂ ਰਲਾਇਆਂ ਰਲਦਾ


<br>

## ੫੪

ਪਤੀਆ ਲਿਖੂੰਗੀ ਮੈਂ ਸ਼ਾਮ ਨੂੰ, ਪੀਆ ਮੈਨੂੰ ਨਜ਼ਰ ਨ ਆਵੇ
ਆਂਗਨ ਬਨਾ ਡਰਾਵਣਾ, ਕਿਤ ਬਿਧ ਰੈਨ ਵਿਹਾਵੇ

ਕਾਗਜ਼ ਕਰੂੰ ਲਿਖ ਦਾਮਨੇ, ਨੈਣ ਆਂਸੂ ਲਾਊਂ
ਬਿਰਹੋਂ ਜਾਰੀ ਹੋ ਜਰੀ, ਦਿਲ ਫੂਕ ਜਲਾਊਂ

ਪਾਂਧੇ ਪੰਡਤ ਜਗਤ ਕੇ, ਪੁੱਛ ਰਹੀਆਂ ਸਾਰੇ
ਬੇਦ ਪੋਥੀ ਕਿਆ ਦੋਸ ਹੈ, ਹੀਣੇ ਭਾਗ ਹਮਾਰੇ

ਨੀਂਦ ਗਾਈ ਕਿਤੇ ਦੇਸ ਨੂੰ, ਉਹ ਭੀ ਵੈਰਨ ਮੇਰੀ
ਮਤ ਸੁਫਨੇ ਮੇਂ ਆ ਮਿਲੇ, ਉਹ ਨੀਂਦਰ ਕਿਹੜੀ

੫ ਰੋ ਰੋ ਜੀਉ ਵਲਾਉਂਦੀਆਂ, ਗ਼ਮ ਕਰਨੀ ਆਂ ਦੂਟਾ
ਨੈਣੋਂ ਨੀਰ ਨਾ ਚੱਲੇ, ਕਿਸ ਕੀਤਾ ਟੂਟਾ

Those who are already dead get smothered to death again
and again. Those who are already gripped are gripped
some more.

Somehow it is like a spark in the straw. Its sharp pain
continually pierces my heart.

Love struck my heart with an arrow. It cannot be shaken 5
loose, however hard I try.

Bullha, the love between me and my lord is strange. We
cannot be united, however hard I try.

## 94

I will write a note to my beloved. I cannot see the one I
love. The courtyard has become frightening. How will
I get through the night?

I will make my paper by writing on my hem. I use my eyes'
tears to write with. I am consumed by separation.
I will blow on my heart and make it burn.

I keep asking all the world's Brahmans and priests: "What
is wrong in the Vedas and holy books, for my luck to be
so bad?"

Sleep has departed to some other land. It too is my enemy.
Maybe he will come to me in a dream. What a sleep
that would be.

I try to divert myself by weeping, but I suffer a double 5
sorrow. No tears flow from my eyes. Who has cast
this spell?

ਪੀੜ ਪਰਾਈ ਜਰ ਰਹੀ, ਰੋਮ ਰੋਮ ਦੁਖ ਜਾਗੇ
ਬੇਦਰਦੀ ਬਾਂਹੀਂ ਟੋਹ ਕੇ, ਮੁੜ ਪਾਛੇ ਭਾਗੇ

ਭਾਈਆ ਵੇ ਜੋਤਸ਼ੀਆ, ਇਕ ਬਾਤ ਸੱਚੀ ਵੀ ਕਹੀਓ
ਜੋ ਮੈਂ ਹੀਣੀ ਕਰਮ ਦੀ, ਤੁਸੀਂ ਚੁੱਪ ਨਾ ਰਹੀਓ

ਇਕ ਹਨੇਰੀ ਕੋਠੜੀ, ਦੂਜਾ ਦੀਆ ਨਾ ਬਾਤੀ
ਬਾਹੋਂ ਫੜ੍ਹ ਕੇ ਲੈ ਚੱਲੇ, ਕੋਈ ਸੰਗ ਨਾ ਸਾਥੀ

ਭੱਜ ਸਕਾਂ ਨਾ ਭਜ ਜਾਂ, ਸੱਚਾ ਇਸ਼ਕ ਫ਼ਕੀਰੀ
ਦੁਲੜੀ ਤਿਲੜੀ ਚੌਲੜੀ, ਗਲ ਪਰੇਮ ਜੰਜੀਰੀ

੧੦  ਪਾਬੀ ਦੋਨੋਂ ਗੁੰਮ ਹੁਏ, ਸਿਰ ਲਾਗੀ ਜਾਣੇ
ਗਏ ਇਨਾਇਤ ਕਾਦਰੀ, ਫਿਰ ਕਠਨ ਕਹਾਣੇ

ਇਕ ਫ਼ਕਰਾਂ ਦੀ ਗੋਦੜੀ, ਲੱਗੇ ਪਰੇਮ ਦੇ ਧਾਗੇ
ਸੁੱਖੀਆ ਹੋਵੇ ਪੀ ਸਵੇਂ, ਕੋਈ ਦੁੱਖੀਆ ਜਾਗੇ

ਦਸਤ ਫੁੱਲਾਂ ਦੀ ਟੇਕਰੀ, ਕੋਈ ਲਿਓ ਬਪਾਰੀ
ਦਰ ਦਰ ਹੋਕਾ ਦੇ ਰਹੀ ਆਂ, ਸਭ ਚਲਟਹਾਰੀ

ਸਾਜਨ ਤੁਮਰੀ ਪ੍ਰੀਤ ਸੇ, ਮੁਝੇ ਹਾਥ ਕਿਆ ਆਇਆ
ਛਤਰ ਸੂਲਾਂ ਦਾ ਝੱਲਿਆ, ਤੇਰਾ ਪੰਥ ਨਾ ਪਾਇਆ

ਪਰੇਮ ਨਗਰ ਚਲ ਵਸੀਏ, ਜਿਥੇ ਕੰਤ ਹਮਾਰਾ
ਬੁੱਲ੍ਹਾ ਸ਼ਹੁ ਤੋਂ ਮੰਗਨੀ ਹਾਂ, ਜੇ ਦੇ ਨਜ਼ਾਰਾ

I suffer the pain caused by another. Suffering is awakened
in every part of my body. The cruel one takes my
pulse, but then he runs away from me.

Oh brother astrologer, just tell me the truth. Do not
remain silent just because my fortune is bad.

Not only is my room dark, but there is no wick in my lamp.
No friend or companion has taken me by the arm to
lead me away.

I try to run away but I cannot. This love and this life of a
fakir are true. Love has laid its chain of two, three, and
four strands around my neck.

The light in both my eyes is lost. I realize what has
happened to me. With the departure of Inayat
Qadiri,[1] my story has again become difficult.

10

The quilt of Sufi poverty has been stitched by the thread
of love. If the beloved is there, you may sleep happily;
let some other unhappy wretch remain awake.

In my hand there is a basket of flowers; bring a trader here.
At every door I keep crying out: "Everyone is about to
depart."

Dear friend, what did I get from your love? I suffered
overwhelming pain, but did not find the road that
leads to you.

Let us go and live in the city of love, where our bridegroom
lives. Bullha, I beg the lord to grant me a sight of him.

੪੫

ਪਰਦਾ ਕਿਸ ਤੋਂ ਰਾਖੀਦਾ, ਕਿਉਂ ਓਹਲੇ ਬਹਿ ਬਹਿ ਝਾਕੀਦਾ

ਪਹਿਲੋਂ ਆਪੇ ਸਾਜਨ ਸਾਜੀਦਾ, ਹੁਣ ਦਸਨਾ ਏਂ ਸਬਕ ਨਮਾਜੀ ਦਾ
ਹੁਣ ਆਇਆ ਆਪ ਨਜ਼ਾਰੇ ਨੂੰ, ਵਿਚ ਲੈਲਾ ਬਣ ਬਣ ਝਾਕੀਦਾ

ਸ਼ਾਹ ਸ਼ਮਸ ਦੀ ਖੱਲ ਲੁਹਾਇਓ, ਸੂਲੀ ਚਾ ਮਨਸੂਰ ਚੜ੍ਹਾਇਓ
ਜ਼ਕਰੀਏ ਸਿਰ ਕਲਵੱਤੂ ਧਰਾਇਓ, ਕੀ ਲੇਖਾ ਰਹਿ ਗਿਆ ਬਾਕੀ ਦਾ

'ਕੁਨ' ਕਿਹਾ 'ਫ਼ਯਕੂਨ' ਕਹਾਇਆ, ਬੇਚੂਨੀ ਦਾ ਚੂਨ ਬਣਾਇਆ
ਖ਼ਾਤਰ ਤੇਰੀ ਜਗਤ ਬਣਾਇਆ, ਸਿਰ ਪਰ ਛਤਰ 'ਲੌਲਾਕੀ' ਦਾ

੫    ਹੁਣ ਸਾਡੇ ਵਲ ਧਾਇਆ ਏ, ਨਾ ਰਹਿੰਦਾ ਛੁਪਾ ਛੁਪਾਇਆ ਏ
ਕਿਤੇ ਬੁੱਲ੍ਹੁ ਨਾਮ ਧਰਾਇਆ ਏ, ਵਿਚ ਓਹਲਾ ਰੱਖਿਆ ਖ਼ਾਕੀ ਦਾ

੪੬

ਪੜਤਾਲਿਓ ਹੁਣ ਆਸ਼ਕ ਕਿਹੜੇ

ਨੇਹੁੰ ਲੱਗਾ ਮਤ ਗਈ ਗਵਾਤੀ, 'ਨਹਨੁ ਅਕਰਬ' ਜ਼ਾਤ ਪਛਾਤੀ
ਸਾਈਂ ਭੀ ਸ਼ਾਹ ਰਗ ਤੋਂ ਨੇੜੇ

ਹੀਰੇ ਹੋ ਮੁੜ ਰਾਂਝਾ ਹੋਈ, ਇਹ ਗਲ ਵਿਰਲਾ ਜਾਣੈ ਕੋਈ
ਚੁੱਕ ਪਏ ਸਭ ਝਗੜੇ ਝੇੜੇ

## 95

From whom are you veiling yourself? Why do you sit in
    concealment and peep out?

First you created yourself as our beloved. Now you teach
    us as a pious performer of prayers. Now it is you who
    have come for the spectacle. You are within it and
    keep peeping out as Laila.[1]

You had Shah Shams[2] flayed alive. You had Mansur[3] sent
    to the gallows. You set the saw to Zakariya's[4] head.
    What account is there left to settle?

You said *Let it be,*[5] and caused *and it was* to be said. You
    gave form to formlessness. For your sake the world
    was made. The royal umbrella of *If it were not for you*[6]
    was placed over his head.

Now he has come quickly upon us. He cannot remain    5
    hidden. Here he is given the name of Bullha, with the
    screen of earthliness[7] placed between us.

## 96

Which lovers have you tested now?

All my sense was destroyed with the onset of love.
    I recognized the essential meaning of *We are nearer.*[1]
    The lord is nearer than the jugular vein.

He was Hir and then became Ranjha. Very rare are the
    people who realize this. Once they do so, all disputes
    are resolved.

ਲੈ ਬਰਾਤਾਂ ਰਾਤੀਂ ਜਾਗਣ, ਨੂਰ ਨਬੀ ਦੇ ਬਰਸਣ ਲਾਗਣ
ਉਹੋ ਵੇਖ ਅਸਾਡੇ ਬੇੜੇ

੫  'ਅਨਲਹੱਕ' ਆਪ ਕਹਾਇਆ ਲੋਕਾ, ਮਨਸੂਰ ਨਾ ਦੇਂਦਾ ਆਪੇ ਹੋਕਾ
ਮੁੱਲਾਂ ਬਣ ਬਣ ਆਵਣ ਨੇੜੇ

ਬੁੱਲ੍ਹਾ ਸ਼ਹੁ ਸ਼ਰ੍ਹਾ ਤੇ ਕਾਜ਼ੀ, ਹੱਕ ਹਕੀਕਤ ਤੇ ਭੀ ਰਾਜ਼ੀ
ਸਾਈਂ ਘਰ ਘਰ ਨਿਆਉਂ ਨਬੇੜੇ


੬੧
ਪਾਣੀ ਭਰ ਭਰ ਗਈਆਂ ਸੱਭੇ, ਆਪੇ ਅਪਣੀ ਵਾਰ
ਇਕ ਭਰ ਆਈਆਂ ਇਕ ਭਰ ਚਲੀਆਂ, ਇਕ ਖਲੀਆਂ ਬਾਂਹ ਪਸਾਰ
ਜਿਸ ਜਗ ਦਾ ਤੂੰ ਮਾਣ ਕਰੇਂ ਹੈ, ਸੋ ਜਗ ਤਾਰ ਬਤਾਰ

ਹਾਰ ਹਮੇਲਾਂ ਪਾਈਆਂ ਗਲ ਵਿਚ, ਬਾਹੀਂ ਛਟਕੇ ਚੂੜਾ
ਕੰਨੀਂ ਬੁਕ ਬੁਕ ਮਛਰੀਆਲੇ, ਸੱਭ ਅਡੰਬਰ ਕੂੜਾ
ਅਜੇ ਸ਼ਹੁ ਨੇ ਝਾਤ ਨਾ ਪਾਈ, ਐਵੇਂ ਗਿਆ ਸ਼ਿੰਗਾਰ

ਹੱਥੀਂ ਮਹਿੰਦੀ ਪੈਰੀਂ ਮਹਿੰਦੀ, ਸਿਰ ਤੇ ਧੜੀ ਗੁੰਦਾਈ
ਤੇਲ ਫੁਲੇਲ ਪਾਨਾਂ ਦਾ ਬੀੜਾ, ਦੰਦੀਂ ਮਿੱਸੀ ਲਾਈ
ਕੋਈ ਜੁ ਸਦ ਪਈਓਨੇ ਡਾਢੀ, ਵਿੱਸਰਿਆ ਘਰ ਬਾਰ


170

With letters of exemption,[2] they stay awake all night in
    vigil. The light of the Prophet begins to rain on them.
    See, he is in our courtyard.
It was you who made him say *I am God*.[3] It was not Mansur   5
    who cried out, people. Then you became the mullahs[4]
    who stood near.
Bullha, the lord is the law[5] and the judge. It is also he who
    delights in true reality. The lord dispenses justice in
    every house.

## 97

The women have all filled their vessels with water, each
    in their own turn. Some have got water and come,
    some have departed, while others are standing with
    outstretched arms. The world in which you take such
    pride crumbles into pieces.
You wear garlands and necklaces around your neck,
    bangles clink upon your wrists, and from your ears
    fine earrings hang clustered, but all this display is
    false. The lord has still not acknowledged you with a
    glance, so all this finery has been for nothing.
There is henna on your hands and feet, and your hair is
    tied in a bridal plait. Perfumed with oil and flower
    essence, you chew betel, and your teeth are decorated
    with *missī*.[1] But when you get the dread call, your
    family is forgotten.

ਬੁੱਲ੍ਹ ਸ਼ਹੁ ਦੇ ਪੰਧ ਪਵੇਂ ਜੇ, ਤਾਂ ਤੂੰ ਰਾਹ ਪਛਾਣੇਂ
ਪੌ ਬਾਰਾਂ ਪਾਸਿਓਂ ਮੰਗੋਂ, ਦਾਅ ਪਿਆ ਤੈ ਕਾਣੇ
ਗੁੰਗੀ ਡੋਰੀ ਕਮਲੀ ਹੋਈ, ਜਾਨ ਦੀ ਬਾਜ਼ੀ ਹਾਰ

## ੮੮

ਪਿਆਰਿਆ ਸੰਭਲ ਕੇ ਨੇਹੁੰ ਲਾ, ਪਿੱਛੋਂ ਪੱਛੋਤਾਵੇਂਗਾ

ਜਾਂਦਾ ਜਾਹ ਨਾ ਆਵੀਂ ਫੇਰ, ਓਥੇ ਬੇਪਰਵਾਹੀ ਫੇਰ
ਓਥੇ ਢਹਿਲ ਖਲੋਂਦੇ ਸ਼ੇਰ, ਤੂੰ ਵੀ ਫੱਦਿਆ ਜਾਵੇਂਗਾ

ਖੁਹ ਵਿਚ ਜੁਸਫ਼ ਪਾਇਓਨੇ, ਫਿਰ ਵਿਚ ਬਜ਼ਾਰ ਵਿਕਾਇਓਨੇ
ਇਕ ਅੱਟੀ ਮੁੱਲ ਪੁਰਾਇਓਨੇ, ਤੂੰ ਕੇਡੀ ਮੁੱਲ ਪਵਾਵੇਂਗਾ

ਨੇਹੁੰ ਲਾ ਵੇਖ ਜ਼ੁਲੈਖ਼ਾ ਲਏ, ਓਥੇ ਆਸ਼ਕ ਤੜਫਟ ਪਏ
ਮਜਨੂੰ ਕਰਦਾ ਹੈ ਹੈ ਹੈ, ਤੂੰ ਓਥੋਂ ਕੀ ਲਿਆਵੇਂਗਾ

੫ ਓਥੇ ਇਕਨਾਂ ਪੋਸ਼ ਲੁਹਾਈਦੇ, ਇਕ ਆਰਿਆਂ ਨਾਲ ਚਿਰਾਈਦੇ
ਇਕ ਸੂਲੀ ਪਕੜ ਚੜ੍ਹਾਈਦੇ, ਓਥੇ ਤੂੰ ਵੀ ਸੀਸ ਕਟਾਵੇਂਗਾ

ਘਰ ਕਲਾਲਾਂ ਤੇਰੇ ਪਾਸੇ, ਓਥੇ ਆਵਟ ਮਸਤ ਪਿਆਸੇ
ਭਰ ਭਰ ਪੀਵਟ ਪਿਆਲੇ ਕਾਸੇ, ਤੂੰ ਵੀ ਜੀ ਲਲਚਾਵੇਂਗਾ

ਦਿਲਬਰ ਹੁਣ ਗਿਓਂ ਕਿਤ ਲੋ, ਭਲਕੇ ਕੀ ਜਾਣਾਂ ਕੀ ਹੋ
ਮਸਤਾਂ ਦੇ ਨਾ ਕੋਲ ਖਲੋ, ਤੂੰ ਵੀ ਮਸਤ ਸਦਾਵੇਂਗਾ

Bullha, if you follow the path of the Lord, you will
    recognize the way. You want a winning throw, but
    you get three ones.[2] You have become dumb, deaf,
    and crazy,[3] having staked your life and lost.

### 98

Be careful how you fall in love, my dear. Later you will be
    sorry.
Go if you are going to go, do not come back again. There is
    great indifference over there.[1] Tigers stand still in fear
    over there. You too will get caught.
They put Yusuf in the well, then sold him in the bazaar. He
    was paid for in full with a hank of yarn.[2] You will be
    priced at a cowrie.[3]
Zulaikha[4] fell in love and bought him. Lovers are writhing
    in agony over there. Majnun[5] says, "Ah, ah, ah!" What
    will you bring back from over there?
Over there some have their skins flayed,[6] some are cut up    5
    with saws,[7] others are seized and put on the gallows.[8]
    You too will get your head cut off over there.
Right beside you is the distillers' house, where the thirsty
    drunks come. They drink full cups and goblets. You
    too will fill your heart with craving.
Which country have you gone to now, beloved? Who
    knows what will happen tomorrow? Do not stand near
    the drunks, or you will be called one too.

ਬੁੱਲ੍ਹਿਆ ਗ਼ੈਰ ਸ਼ਰ੍ਹਾ ਨਾ ਹੋ, ਸੁਖ ਦੀ ਨੀਂਦਰ ਭਰ ਕੇ ਸੋ
ਮੂੰਹੋਂ ਨਾ 'ਅਨਲਹੱਕ' ਬਗੋ, ਚੜ੍ਹ ਸੂਲੀ ਢੋਲੇ ਗਾਵੇਂਗਾ

<br>

## ੯੯

ਪਿਆਰਿਆ ਸਾਨੂੰ ਮਿਠੜਾ ਨਾ ਲਗਦਾ ਸ਼ੋਰ, ਸੁੰਨਮਈ ਤੇ ਰਾਜ਼ੀ ਰਹਿਣਾ

ਸਾਨੂੰ ਮਿਠੜਾ ਨਾ ਲਗਦਾ ਸ਼ੋਰ, ਮੈਂ ਘਰ ਖਿਲਾ ਸ਼ਗੂਫ਼ਾ ਹੋਰ
ਵੇਖੀਆਂ ਬਾਗ਼ ਬਹਾਰਾਂ ਹੋਰ, ਹੁਣ ਮੈਨੂੰ ਕੁਝ ਨਾ ਕਹਿਣਾ

ਹੁਣ ਮੈਂ ਮੋਈ ਨੀ ਮੇਰੀਏ ਮਾਂ, ਪੂਟੀ ਮੇਰੀ ਲੈ ਗਿਆ ਕਾਂ
ਡੋ ਡੋ ਕਰਦੀ ਮਗਰੇ ਜਾਂ, ਪੂਟੀ ਦੇ ਦਈਂ ਸਾਈਂ ਦੇ ਨਾਂ

ਬੁੱਲ੍ਹਾ ਸਾਈਂ ਦੇ ਨਾਲ ਪਿਆਰ, ਮਿਹਰ ਇਨਾਇਤ ਕਰੇ ਹਜ਼ਾਰ
ਇਹੋ ਕੌਲ ਤੇ ਇਹੋ ਕਰਾਰ, ਦਿਲਬਰ ਦੇਹ੍ਹ ਵਿਚ ਰਹਿਣਾ

<br>

## ੧੦੦

ਪਿਆਰੇ ਬਿਨ ਮਸਲੂਤ ਉਠ ਜਾਣਾ, ਤੂੰ ਕਦੀਏ ਹੋ ਸਿਆਣਾ

ਕਰਕੇ ਚਾਵੜ ਚਾਰ ਦਿਹਾੜੇ, ਥੀਸੋਂ ਅੰਤ ਨਿਮਾਣਾ
ਜ਼ੁਲਮ ਕਰੇਂ ਤੇ ਲੋਕ ਸਤਾਵੇਂ, ਛਡ ਦੇ ਜ਼ੁਲਮ ਕਮਾਣਾ

ਜਿਸ ਜਿਸ ਦਾ ਵੀ ਮਾਣ ਕਰੇਂ ਤੂੰ, ਸੋ ਵੀ ਸਾਥ ਨਾ ਜਾਣਾ
ਸ਼ਹਿਰ ਖ਼ਮੋਸ਼ਾਂ ਵੇਖ ਹਮੇਸ਼ਾਂ, ਜਿਸ ਵਿਚ ਜਗ ਸਮਾਣਾ

Bullha, do not act outside the law, and sleep undisturbed.
    Do not come out with *I am God*,[9] or you will be singing
    merrily up on the gallows.


## 99

My dear, this noise is not agreeable to me. I would live in
    peaceful contentment.
This noise is not agreeable to me. Another blossom has
    opened in my house. I have seen new delights. Do not
    say anything to me now.
Now I am dead, Mother. The crow has taken away my
    cotton roll. I go to shoo it, saying, "In the name of the
    lord, give me back my cotton roll."
Bullha loves the lord, who bestows thousands of favors
    and blessings. All I vow and promise is that the
    beloved should dwell in my body.


## 100

My dear, you will have to get up and go without having
    done anything good. Will you ever become sensible?
For a few days you will have a good time, but you will be
    humbled in the end. You are cruel and oppress people.
    Give up this practice of cruelty.
Whatever you are proud of will not go with you. Always
    keep your eyes on the city of the silent,[1] into which the
    whole world is admitted.

ਭਰ ਭਰ ਪੁਰ ਲੰਘਾਵੇ ਡਾਢਾ, ਮਲਕੁਲਮੌਤ ਮੁਹਾਣਾ
ਏਥੇ ਜਿਤਨੇ ਹੈਂ ਸਭ ਤਨਤੇ, ਮੈਂ ਔਗਟਹਾਰ ਨਿਮਾਣਾ

੫  ਬੁੱਲ੍ਹਾ ਦੁਸ਼ਮਨ ਨਾਲ ਬੁਰੇ ਵਿਚ, ਹੈ ਦੁਸ਼ਮਨ ਬਲ ਢਾਣਾ
ਮਹਿਬੂਬ ਰਬਾਨੀ ਕਰੇ ਅਸਾਨੀ, ਖੋੱਫ ਜਾਏ ਮਲਕਾਣਾ

## ੧੦੧

ਪੀਆ ਪੀਆ ਕਰਤੇ ਹਮੀ ਪੀਆ ਹੋਏ, ਅਬ ਪੀਆ ਕਿਸ ਨੂੰ ਕਹੀਏ

ਹਿਜਰ ਵਸਲ ਹਮ ਦੋਨੋਂ ਛੋੜੇ, ਅਬ ਕਿਸ ਕੇ ਹੋ ਰਹੀਏ

ਮਜਨੂੰ ਲਾਲ ਦੀਵਾਨੇ ਵਾਂਗੂੰ, ਅਬ ਲੈਲਾ ਹੋ ਰਹੀਏ

ਬੁੱਲ੍ਹਾ ਸ਼ਹੁ ਘਰ ਮੇਰੇ ਆਏ, ਅਬ ਕਿਉਂ ਤਾਅਨੇ ਸਹੀਏ

## ੧੦੨

'ਫਸੀਮ ਵਜਹੁੱਲ੍ਹੁ' ਦਸਨਾ ਏਂ ਅੱਜ ਓ ਯਾਰ

ਘੁੰਘਟ ਖੋਲ ਮੁੱਖ ਵੇਖ ਨਾ ਮੇਰਾ, ਐਬ ਨਮਾਣੀ ਦੇ ਕੱਜ ਓ ਯਾਰ

ਮੈਂ ਅਟਜਾਣੀ ਤੇਰਾ ਨੇਹੁੰ ਕੀ ਜਾਣਾਂ, ਲਾਵਣ ਦਾ ਨਹੀਂ ਚੱਜ ਓ ਯਾਰ

ਹਾਜੀ ਲੋਕ ਮੱਕੇ ਨੂੰ ਜਾਂਦੇ, ਸਾਡਾ ਹੈਂ ਤੂੰ ਹੱਜ ਓ ਯਾਰ

Filling his boat with loads of passengers, the relentless
    ferryman who is the angel of death takes them across.
    Everyone here is flourishing, but I am full of faults and
    wretched.
Bullha, the enemy[2] who is present in evil must be       5
    destroyed by force. When the divine beloved makes
    things easy, fear of the angel of death departs.

## 101

By repeating "Beloved, beloved," we too have become the
    beloved. Whom should we call "Beloved" now?
We have abandoned both separation and union. Now to
    whom should we belong?
Like Majnun[1] the mad lover, now let us live as Laila.
Bullha, the lord has come to my house. So why should we
    put up with reproaches?

## 102

*Then there is the face of God*[1] is what you tell us today,
    my beloved.
Do not lift the veil and look at my face. Hide the faults
    of this poor wretch, my beloved.
I am ignorant; what do I know of your love? I am not
    clever enough to practice it, my beloved.
Hajjis go to Mecca.[2] You are our pilgrimage, my beloved.

ਪ ਡੂੰਘੀ ਨਦੀ ਤੇ ਤੁਲ੍ਹਾ ਪੁਰਾਣਾ, ਮਿਲਸਾਂ ਕਿਹੜੇ ਪੱਜ ਓ ਯਾਰ

ਬੁੱਲ੍ਹੂ ਸ਼ਹੁ ਮੈਂ ਜ਼ਾਹਰ ਡਿਠਾ, ਲਾਹ ਮੂੰਹੋਂ ਤੋਂ ਲੱਜ ਓ ਯਾਰ

## ੧੦੩
ਬਸ ਕਰ ਜੀ ਹੁਣ ਬਸ ਕਰ ਜੀ, ਕਾਈ ਬਾਤ ਅਸਾਂ ਨਾਲ ਹਸ ਕਰ ਜੀ

ਤੁਸੀਂ ਦਿਲ ਮੇਰੇ ਵਿਚ ਵਸਦੇ ਹੋ, ਐਵੇਂ ਸਾਥੋਂ ਦੂਰ ਕਿਉਂ ਨਸਦੇ ਹੋ
ਨਾਲੇ ਘੱਤ ਜਾਦੂ ਦਿਲ ਖਸਦੇ ਹੋ, ਹੁਣ ਕਿਤ ਵਲ ਜਾਸੋ ਨਸ ਕਰ ਜੀ

ਤੁਸੀਂ ਮੋਇਆਂ ਨੂੰ ਮਾਰ ਨਾ ਖੁਟਦੇ ਸੀ, ਖਿੰਦੋ ਵਾਂਗ ਖੁੰਢੀ ਨਿਤ ਕੁਟਦੇ ਸੀ
ਗੱਲ ਕਰਦਿਆਂ ਦਾ ਗਲ ਘੁਟਦੇ ਸੀ, ਹੁਣ ਰਹੁ ਪਿੰਜਰ ਵਿਚ
        ਫਸ ਕਰ ਜੀ੧

ਤੁਸੀਂ ਛੁਪਦੇ ਹੋ ਅਸੀਂ ਪਕੜੇ ਹੋ, ਅਸਾਂ ਹਿਰਦੇ ਅੰਦਰ ਜਕੜੇ ਹੋ
ਤੁਸੀਂ ਅਜੇ ਛੁਪਣ ਨੂੰ ਤਕੜੇ ਹੋ, ਹੁਣ ਕਿੱਧਰ ਜਾਸੋ ਨਸ ਕਰ ਜੀ

ਪ ਮੈਂ ਬੁੱਲ੍ਹੂ ਸ਼ਹੁ ਦੀ ਬਰਦੀ ਹਾਂ, ਤੇਰਾ ਮੁਖ ਵੇਖਣ ਨੂੰ ਮਰਦੀ ਹਾਂ
ਨਿਤ ਸੌ ਸੌ ਮਿੰਨਤਾਂ ਕਰਦੀ ਹਾਂ, ਕਿਆ ਤੀਰ ਚਲਾਇਓ ਕਸ ਕਰ ਜੀ

The river[3] is deep and the raft is old. On what pretext can    5
    I meet you, my beloved?
Bullha, I have seen the lord in manifest form. Remove this
    modesty from your face, my beloved.

## 103

That is enough now, that is enough. Please say something
    to us with a laugh.
You dwell in my heart; what makes you run far away from
    me like this? At the same time you cast your spell and
    seize my heart. Which way will you run off now?
You do not stop killing those who are already dead. You
    keep hitting them, like a stick striking the ball. You
    throttle those who speak. Now let yourself be caught
    and caged.
You were hiding, but I caught you. You are still full of
    energy to hide. I have pinioned you in my heart.
    Where will you run away to now?
I, Bullha, am the slave girl of the lord. Now I am dying to    5
    see your face. I keep offering hundreds of pleas. How
    carefully you aimed your arrow at me!

੧੦੪

ਬੰਸੀ ਕਾਹਨ ਅਚਰਜ ਬਜਾਈ

ਬੰਸੀ ਵਾਲਿਆ ਚਾਕਾ ਰਾਂਝਾ, ਤੇਰਾ ਸੁਰ ਸਭ ਨਾਲ ਹੈ ਸਾਂਝਾ
ਤੇਰੀਆਂ ਮੌਜਾਂ ਸਾਡਾ ਮਾਂਝਾ, ਸਾਡੀ ਸੁਰ ਤੈਂ ਆਪ ਮਿਲਾਈ

ਬੰਸੀ ਵਾਲਿਆ ਕਾਹਨ ਕਹਾਵੇਂ, ਸ਼ਬਦ ਅਨੇਕ ਅਨੂਪ ਸੁਣਾਵੇਂ
ਅੱਖੀਆਂ ਦੇ ਵਿਚ ਨਜ਼ਰ ਨਾ ਆਵੇਂ, ਕੈਸੀ ਬਿਖੜੀ ਖੇਲ ਰਚਾਈ

ਬੰਸੀ ਸਭ ਕੋਈ ਸੁਣੇ ਸੁਣਾਵੇ, ਅਰਥ ਇਸ ਦਾ ਕੋਈ ਵਿਰਲਾ ਪਾਵੇ
ਜੋ ਕੋਈ ਅਨਹਦ ਕੀ ਸੁਰ ਪਾਵੇ, ਸੋ ਇਸ ਬੰਸੀ ਕਾ ਸੌਦਾਈ

੫   ਸੁਣੀਆਂ ਬੰਸੀ ਦੀਆਂ ਘੰਗੋਰਾਂ, ਕੂਕੇ ਤਨ ਮਨ ਵਾਂਗੂੰ ਮੋਰਾਂ
ਡਿਠੀਆਂ ਇਸ ਦੀਆਂ ਤੋੜਾਂ ਜੋੜਾਂ, ਇਕ ਸੁਰ ਦੀ ਸਭ ਕਲਾ ਉਠਾਈ

ਇਸ ਬੰਸੀ ਦਾ ਲੰਮਾ ਲੇਖਾ, ਜਿਸ ਨੇ ਢੂੰਡਾ ਤਿਸ ਨੇ ਦੇਖਾ
ਸਾਵੀ ਇਸ ਬੰਸੀ ਦੀ ਰੇਖਾ, ਏਸ ਵਜੂਦੋਂ ਸਿਫ਼ਤ ਉਠਾਈ

ਇਸ ਬੰਸੀ ਦੇ ਪੰਜ ਸਤ ਤਾਰੇ, ਆਪ ਅਪਣੀ ਸੁਰ ਭਰਦੇ ਸਾਰੇ
ਇਕ ਸੁਰ ਸਭ ਦੇ ਵਿਚ ਦਮ ਮਾਰੇ, ਸਾਡੀ ਇਸ ਨੇ ਹੋਸ਼ ਭੁਲਾਈ

ਬੁੱਲ੍ਹੂ ਪੁੱਜ ਪਏ ਤਕਰਾਰ, ਬੂਹੇ ਆਣ ਖਲੋਤੇ ਯਾਰ
ਰੱਖੀਂ ਕਲਮੇ ਨਾਲ ਬਿਉਪਾਰ, ਤੇਰੀ ਹਜ਼ਰਤ ਭਰੇ ਗਵਾਹੀ

## 104

How wonderfully Krishna has played his flute.[1]

Flute player, herdsman, Ranjha, your notes are shared
with everyone. Your delights are my time of gloom.[2]
It is you who have mingled my tune with yours.

Flute player, you call yourself Krishna. You perform so
many beautiful hymns. My eyes cannot see you. What
a tangled game you have set up.

The flute is something that everyone can hear or play, but
very few grasp its meaning.[3] Anyone who discovers
the note of the unstruck music[4] becomes passionate
for this flute.

Hearing the flute's high notes, the body and soul scream        5
like a peacock. The way it is put together, the whole
art of a single note is created.

This flute has a long story. Whoever searched for it has
seen it. The stem of this flute is green. Its qualities
have been created by the divine being.

This instrument has five or seven holes.[5] All are filled
with their own notes. Amid them all, one note sounds
loudly. It has completely transported us.

Bullha, his promises have been fulfilled. The beloved has
come to stand at my door. Transact your business[6] in
the name of the word. The lord will be your witness.

੧੦੫

ਬਹੁੜੀਂ ਵੇ ਤਬੀਬਾ ਮੈਂਡੀ ਖ਼ਬਰ ਗਈਆ
ਤੇਰੇ ਇਸ਼ਕ ਨਚਾਇਆ ਕਰ ਥਈਆ ਥਈਆ

ਇਸ਼ਕੇ ਡੇਰਾ ਮੇਰੇ ਅੰਦਰ ਕੀਤਾ
ਭਰ ਕੇ ਜ਼ਹਿਰ ਪਿਆਲਾ ਮੈਂ ਆਪੇ ਪੀਤਾ
ਝਬਦੇ ਆਵੀਂ ਵੇ ਤਬੀਬਾ ਨਹੀਂ ਤੇ ਮੈਂ ਮਰ ਗਈਆ

ਛੁਪ ਗਿਆ ਸੂਰਜ ਬਾਹਰ ਰਹਿ ਗਈ ਲਾਲੀ
ਵੇ ਮੈਂ ਸਦਕੇ ਜਾਵਾਂ ਜੇ ਮੁੜ ਦਿਓਂ ਵਖਾਲੀ
ਭੁੱਲ ਗਈਆ ਮੈਂ ਪੀੜਾ ਤੇਰੇ ਨਾਲ ਨਾ ਗਈਆ

ਤੇਰੇ ਇਸ਼ਕ ਦੀ ਸਾਰ ਵੇ ਮੈਂ ਨਾ ਜਾਣਾਂ
ਇਹ ਸਿਰ ਆਇਆ ਏ ਮੇਰਾ ਹੇਠ ਵਦਾਣਾਂ
ਸੱਟ ਪਈ ਇਸ਼ਕ ਦੀ ਤਾਂ ਕੂਕਾਂ ਦਈਆ

੫  ਏਸ ਇਸ਼ਕ ਦੇ ਕੋਲੋਂ ਸਾਨੂੰ ਹਟਕ ਨਾ ਮਾਏ
ਜਾਂਦੜੇ ਬੇੜੇ ਮੋੜ ਕੌਣ ਹਟਾਏ
ਮੇਰੀ ਅਕਲ ਭੁੱਲੀ ਨਾਲ ਮੁਹਾਟਿਆਂ ਦੇ ਗਈਆ

ਏਸ ਇਸ਼ਕੇ ਦੀ ਝੰਗੀ ਵਿਚ ਮੋਰ ਬੁਲੇਂਦਾ
ਸਾਨੂੰ ਕਾਬਾ ਕਿਬਲਾ ਪਿਆਰਾ ਯਾਰ ਦਸੇਂਦਾ
ਸਾਨੂੰ ਘਾਇਲ ਕਰਕੇ ਫੇਰ ਖ਼ਬਰ ਨਾ ਲਈਆ

ਬੁੱਲ੍ਹਾ ਸ਼ਾਹ ਇਨਾਇਤ ਦੇ ਚੱਲ ਬਹੀਏ ਬੂਹੇ
ਜਿਸਨੇ ਪੁਆਏ ਸਾਨੂੰ ਸਾਵੇ ਤੇ ਸੂਹੇ
ਜਾਂ ਮੈਂ ਮਾਰੀ ਹੈ ਅੱਡੀ ਮਿਲ ਪਿਆ ਹੈ ਵਹੀਆ

## 105

Come to my assistance, doctor, I have lost my senses. Your
love has set me dancing in rhythm.[1]

Love has taken up its lodging inside me. I am the one who
has drunk a cup full of poison. Come quickly, doctor,
or else I shall be dead.

The sun has set,[2] but outside the sky is still red. Oh, I will
sacrifice myself, if only you will show yourself again.
It was my fault, master, that I did not go with you.

I did not realize what your love was like. It hit my head
and crushed me like a mighty hammer. When I felt the
blow of love, I screamed aloud.

Mother, do not stop me from this love. Who can turn     5
around a boat that is drifting away and bring it back?
My brain is confused and has gone with the boatmen.

The peacock cries in the thicket of this love. My dear
friend shows me the Kaaba and the Qibla.[3] After
wounding me, he does not ask how I am.

Bullha, let us go and sit at the gate of Shah Inayat, who
made me dress in green and red.[4] When I started
dancing, I found my way to him.

## ੧੦੬

ਬੁੱਲ੍ਹੂ ਕੀ ਜਾਣਾਂ ਮੈਂ ਕੌਣ

ਨਾ ਮੈਂ ਮੋਮਨ ਵਿਚ ਮਸੀਤਾਂ, ਨਾ ਮੈਂ ਵਿਚ ਕੁਫ਼ਰ ਦੀਆਂ ਰੀਤਾਂ
ਨਾ ਮੈਂ ਪਾਕਾਂ ਵਿਚ ਪਲੀਤਾਂ, ਨਾ ਮੈਂ ਮੂਸਾ ਨਾ ਫ਼ਰਔਨ

ਨਾ ਮੈਂ ਅੰਦਰ ਬੇਦ ਕਿਤਾਬਾਂ, ਨਾ ਵਿਚ ਭੰਗਾਂ ਨਾ ਸ਼ਰਾਬਾਂ
ਨਾ ਵਿਚ ਰਿੰਦਾਂ ਮਸਤ ਖ਼ਰਾਬਾਂ, ਨਾ ਵਿਚ ਜਾਗਣ ਨਾ ਵਿਚ ਸੌਣ

ਨਾ ਵਿਚ ਸ਼ਾਦੀ ਨਾ ਗ਼ਮਨਾਕੀ, ਨਾ ਮੈਂ ਵਿਚ ਪਲੀਤੀ ਪਾਕੀ
ਨਾ ਮੈਂ ਆਬੀ ਨਾ ਮੈਂ ਖ਼ਾਕੀ, ਨਾ ਮੈਂ ਆਤਿਸ਼ ਨਾ ਮੈਂ ਪੌਣ

੫    ਨਾ ਮੈਂ ਅਰਬੀ ਨਾ ਲਾਹੌਰੀ, ਨਾ ਮੈਂ ਹਿੰਦੀ ਸ਼ਹਿਰ ਨਗੌਰੀ
ਨਾ ਹਿੰਦੂ ਨਾ ਤੁਰਕ ਪਸ਼ੌਰੀ, ਨਾ ਮੈਂ ਰਹਿੰਦਾ ਵਿਚ ਨਦੌਨ

ਨਾ ਮੈਂ ਭੇਤ ਮਜ਼੍ਹਬ ਦਾ ਪਾਇਆ, ਨਾ ਮੈਂ ਆਦਮ ਹੱਵਾ ਜਾਇਆ
ਨਾ ਮੈਂ ਆਪਣਾ ਨਾਮ ਧਰਾਇਆ, ਨਾ ਵਿਚ ਬੈਠਣ ਨਾ ਵਿਚ ਭੌਣ

ਅੱਵਲ ਆਖ਼ਰ ਆਪ ਨੂੰ ਜਾਣਾਂ, ਨਾ ਕੋਈ ਦੂਜਾ ਹੋਰ ਪਛਾਣਾਂ
ਮੈਥੋਂ ਹੋਰ ਨਾ ਕੋਈ ਸਿਆਣਾ, ਬੁੱਲ੍ਹੂ ਸ਼ਹੁ ਖੜਾ ਹੈ ਕੌਣ

## ੧੦੭

ਬੁੱਲ੍ਹੂ ਕੀ ਜਾਣੇ ਜ਼ਾਤ ਇਸ਼ਕ ਦੀ ਕੌਣ
ਨਾਉਂ ਸੁਹਾਣਾ ਕੰਮ ਬਖੇੜੇ, ਵੰਢੇ ਜਾਗਣ ਸੌਣ

ਰਾਂਝੇ ਨੂੰ ਮੈਂ ਗਾਲੀਆਂ ਦੇਵਾਂ, ਮਨ ਵਿਚ ਕਰਾਂ ਦੁਆਈਂ

ਮੈਂ ਤੇ ਰਾਂਝਾ ਇਕੋ ਕੋਈ, ਲੋਕਾਂ ਨੂੰ ਅਜ਼ਮਾਈਂ

## 106

Bullha,[1] what do I know about who I am?

I am not a believer in the mosques, nor do I follow the rites
of unbelief. I am not among the pure or the polluted.
I am not Moses or Pharaoh.[2]

I am not in the Vedas or in the scriptures;[3] I am not in
drugs or in liquor. I am not among the drunken
reprobates. I am not in waking, nor am I in sleep.

I am not in joy or in sadness, nor am I in pollution or
purity. I am not of water[4] or of earth, nor am I fire
or air.

I am neither an Arab nor from Lahore, nor an Indian from      5
the city of Nagaur.[5] I am not a Hindu, nor a Turk[6]
from Peshawar. Nor do I live in Nadaun.[7]

I have not discovered the secret of religion; nor am I born
of Adam and Eve. I have not given myself a name; nor
am I found in sitting or moving about.

I know myself to be first and last, I do not recognize
anyone else. No one is wiser than I am. Bullha, who
is the lord[8] standing here?

## 107

Bullha, does anyone know the true nature of love? It is
beautiful by name, but its actions are troublesome,
destroying both waking hours and sleep.

I curse Ranjha, but in my heart I offer prayers for him.
Ranjha and I are one; I am simply testing people.[1]

ਜਿਸ ਬੇਲੇ ਵਿਚ ਬੇਲੀ ਦਿੱਸੇ, ਉਸ ਦੀਆਂ ਲਵਾਂ ਬਲਾਈਂ

੫ ਬੁੱਲ੍ਹਾ ਸ਼ਹੁ ਨੂੰ ਪਾਸੇ ਛੱਡ ਕੇ, ਜੰਗਲ ਵਲ ਨਾ ਜਾਈਂ


### ੧੦t

ਬੁੱਲ੍ਹੇ ਨੂੰ ਸਮਝਾਵਟ ਆਈਆਂ, ਭੈਣਾਂ ਤੇ ਭਰਜਾਈਆਂ

ਮੰਨ ਲੈ ਬੁੱਲ੍ਹਿਆ ਸਾਡਾ ਕਹਿਣਾ, ਛੱਡ ਦੇ ਪੱਲਾ ਰਾਈਆਂ
ਆਲ ਨਬੀ ਔਲਾਦ ਅਲੀ ਨੂੰ, ਤੂੰ ਕਿਉਂ ਲੀਕਾਂ ਲਾਈਆਂ

ਜਿਹੜਾ ਸਾਨੂੰ ਸੱਯਦ ਸੱਦੇ, ਦੋਜ਼ਖ ਮਿਲਣ ਸਜ਼ਾਈਆਂ
ਜੇ ਕੋਈ ਸਾਨੂੰ ਰਾਈ ਆਖੇ, ਬਹਿਸ਼ਤੀਂ ਪੀਂਘਾਂ ਪਾਈਆਂ

ਰਾਈਂ ਸਾਈਂ ਸਭਨੀਂ ਥਾਈਂ, ਰੱਬ ਦੀਆਂ ਬੇਪਰਵਾਈਆਂ
ਸੋਹਣੀਆਂ ਪਰੇ ਹਟਾਈਆਂ, ਕੋਝੀਆਂ ਲੈ ਗਲ ਲਾਈਆਂ

੫ ਜੇ ਤੂੰ ਲੋੜੇਂ ਬਾਗ਼ ਬਹਾਰਾਂ, ਚਾਕਰ ਹੋ ਜਾ ਰਾਈਆਂ
ਬੁੱਲ੍ਹੇ ਸ਼ਾਹ ਦੀ ਜ਼ਾਤ ਕੀ ਪੁੱਛਨੈਂ, ਸ਼ਾਕਰ ਹੋ ਰਜ਼ਾਈਆਂ

The river glade where the beloved appears is the place
    to which I am devoted.
Bullha, do not leave the lord who is beside you and go off    5
    toward the jungle.

### 108

Bullha's[1] sisters and his brothers' wives have come to give
    him their advice.
"Listen to what we say, Bullha, stop clinging to the Arain's
    skirt. Why have you brought disgrace on the family of
    the Prophet and the descendants of Ali?"[2]
"May anyone who calls us a Sayyid suffer the punishments
    of hell. Swings are set up in paradise for anyone who
    calls us an Arain."
The Arain lord is in all places. The lord is supremely
    indifferent. The beautiful are set aside and the ugly are
    embraced.
If you desire the joys of spring, become the servant of the    5
    Arains. Why do you ask what Bullhe Shah's caste is?
    Just be grateful for whatever pleases Him.

੧੦੯

ਬੇਹਦ ਰਮਜ਼ਾਂ ਦਸਦਾ ਨੀਂ, ਚੋਲਣ ਮਾਹੀ
ਮੀਮ ਦੇ ਉਹਲੇ ਵਸਦਾ ਨੀਂ, ਚੋਲਣ ਮਾਹੀ

ਔਲੀਆ ਮਨਸੂਰ ਕਹਾਵੇ, ਰਮਜ਼ 'ਅਨਲਹੱਕ' ਆਪ ਬਤਾਵੇ
ਆਪੇ ਆਪ ਨੂੰ ਸੂਲੀ ਚੜ੍ਹਾਵੇ, ਤੇ ਕੋਲ ਖਲੋਕੇ ਹੱਸਦਾ ਨੀ, ਚੋਲਣ ਮਾਹੀ

੧੧੦

ਭਰਵਾਸਾ ਕੀ ਅਸ਼ਨਾਈ ਦਾ, ਡਰ ਲਗਦੈ ਬੇਪਰਵਾਹੀ ਦਾ

ਇਬਰਾਹੀਮ ਚਿਖਾ ਵਿਚ ਪਾਇਓ, ਸੁਲੇਮਾਨ ਤੋਂ ਭੱਠ ਝੁਕਾਇਓ
ਯੂਨਸ ਮੱਛੀ ਤੋਂ ਨਿਗਲਾਇਓ, ਫੜ ਯੂਸਫ਼ ਮਿਸਰ ਵਿਕਾਈਦਾ

ਜ਼ਕਰੀਆ ਸਿਰ ਕਲਵੱਤੂ ਚਲਾਇਓ, ਸਾਬਰ ਦੇ ਤਨ ਕੀੜੇ ਪਾਇਓ
ਸੁਨਾਂ ਗਲ ਜੁੱਨਾਰ ਪਵਾਇਓ, ਕਿਤੇ ਉਲਟਾ ਪੋਸ਼ ਲੁਹਾਈਦਾ

ਪੈਗ਼ੰਬਰ ਤੋਂ ਨੂਰ ਉਪਾਇਓ, ਨਾਮ ਇਮਾਮ ਹੁਸੈਨ ਧਰਾਇਓ
ਝੂਲਾ ਜਬਰਾਈਲ ਝੁਲਾਇਓ, ਫਿਰ ਪਿਆਸਾ ਗਲਾ ਕਟਾਈਦਾ

੫ ਜਾਂ ਜ਼ਕਰੀਆ ਰੁੱਖ ਛੁਪਾਇਆ, ਛੁਪਟਾ ਉਸ ਦਾ ਬੁਰਾ ਮਨਾਇਆ
ਆਰਾ ਸਿਰ ਤੇ ਚਾ ਵਗਾਇਆ, ਸਟੇ ਰੁੱਖ ਚਰਾਈਦਾ

ਯਹੀਆ ਉਸ ਦਾ ਯਾਰ ਕਹਾਇਆ, ਨਾਲ ਉਸੇ ਦੇ ਨੇਹੁੰ ਲਗਾਇਆ
ਰਾਹ ਸ਼ਰ੍ਹਾ ਦਾ ਉਨ ਬਤਲਾਇਆ, ਸਿਰ ਉਸ ਦਾ ਥਾਲ ਟਿਕਾਈਦਾ

## 109

He tells of countless mysteries, my dear beloved.
    He dwells concealed in *mīm*,[1] my dear beloved.
He calls himself the saint Mansur,[2] and it is he who reveals
    the secret of *I am God*. He puts himself upon the
    gallows, and standing nearby he laughs,[3] my dear
    beloved.

## 110

What trust is there in love? I fear its indifference.
You put Ibrahim[1] on the pyre, and made Sulaiman[2] stoke
    the furnace. You had Yunus[3] swallowed by the fish,
    and seized Yusuf[4] and had him sold in Egypt.
You set the saw to Zakariya's[5] head, and put worms in the
    body of Ayub the patient.[6] You made Sanaan[7] put
    on the girdle, and on another occasion had someone
    hanged upside down and flayed.[8]
You created light from the Prophet, and gave it the name
    of Imam Husain.[9] You had his cradle swung by Jibrail,
    then had his throat cut in his thirst.
When the tree hid Zakariya,[10] you made them take his      5
    concealment amiss. You had the saw set on his head,
    so he was split along with the tree.
You called Yahya[11] his friend,[12] and it was with him that
    he fell in love. You made him proclaim the path of the
    law, then had his head put on the salver.

ਬੁੱਲ੍ਹੂ ਸ਼ਹੁ ਹੁਟ ਸਹੀ ਸੰਵਾਤੇ ਹੈਂ, ਹਰ ਸੂਰਤ ਨਾਲ ਪਛਾਤੇ ਹੈਂ
ਕਿਤੇ ਆਤੇ ਹੈਂ ਕਿਤੇ ਜਾਤੇ ਹੈਂ, ਹੁਟ ਮੈਥੋਂ ਭੁੱਲ ਨਾ ਜਾਈਦਾ


੧੧੧

ਭਾਵੇਂ ਤੂੰ ਜਾਣ ਨਾ ਜਾਣ ਵੇ, ਵਿਹੜੇ ਆ ਵੜ ਮੇਰੇ
ਮੈਂ ਤੇਰੇ ਕੁਰਬਾਨ ਵੇ, ਵਿਹੜੇ ਆ ਵੜ ਮੇਰੇ

ਤੇਰੇ ਜਿਹਾ ਮੈਨੂੰ ਹੋਰ ਨਾ ਕੋਈ, ਢੂੰਡਾਂ ਜੰਗਲ ਬੇਲਾ ਰੋਹੀ
ਢੂੰਡਾਂ ਤਾਂ ਸਾਰਾ ਜਹਾਨ ਵੇ

ਲੋਕਾਂ ਦੇ ਭਾਣੇ ਚਾਕ ਮਹੀਂ ਦਾ, ਰਾਂਝਾ ਲੋਕਾਂ ਵਿਚ ਕਹੀਂਦਾ
ਸਾਡਾ ਤਾਂ ਦੀਨ ਈਮਾਨ ਵੇ

ਮਾਪੇ ਛੇੜ ਲਗੀ ਲੜ ਤੇਰੇ, ਸ਼ਾਹ ਇਨਾਇਤ ਸਾਈਂ ਮੇਰੇ
ਲਾਈਆਂ ਦੀ ਲਜ ਪਾਲ ਵੇ


੧੧੨

ਬੈਠਾਂ ਮੈਂ ਕਤਦੀ ਕਤਦੀ ਹੁੱਟੀ

ਪਿੜੀ ਪੱਛੀ ਪਛਵਾੜੇ ਰਹਿ ਗਈ, ਹੱਥ ਵਿਚ ਰਹਿ ਗਈ ਜੁੱਟੀ
ਅੱਗੇ ਚਰਖਾ ਪਿੱਛੇ ਪੀਹੜਾ, ਮੇਰੇ ਹੱਥੋਂ ਤੰਦ ਤਰੁੱਟੀ

ਦਾਜ ਦਹੇਜ ਅਸਾਂ ਕੀ ਕਰਨਾ, ਜਿਸ ਪਰੇਮ ਕਟੋਰੀ ਮੁੱਠੀ
ਓਹ ਚੋਰ ਮੇਰਾ ਪਕੜ ਮੰਗਾਓ, ਜਿਸ ਮੇਰੀ ਜਿੰਦ ਕੁੱਠੀ

Bullha says: Lord, now you have been truly recognized.
    You are familiar in every guise. Here you come and
    there you go. Do not go away now and forget me.


### 111

Whether you know me or not, come into my courtyard.
    I am sacrificed to you; come into my courtyard.
I have seen no one like you, though I search jungle,
    thickets, and desert, even if I search the entire world.
In people's eyes he is a herdsman of the buffaloes; among
    them he is called Ranjha. But he is our religion and
    our faith.
Leaving my parents, I have clung to your skirt, oh my lord
    Shah Inayat. Protect the honor of the one who clings
    to you.


### 112

Sister, I am exhausted with all this spinning.
The wicker baskets for the thread are at the back of the
    house. I am left with the cotton roll in my hand. In
    front of me is the spinning wheel, behind me is the
    stool. The thread in my hand is broken.
Why should I work on preparing my dowry? I hold the
    cup of love in my hand. Summon that thief who has
    destroyed my life, and arrest him.

ਭੋਂਦਾ ਭੋਂਦਾ ਮੇਰਾ ਊੜਾ ਡਿੱਗਾ, ਛਿਬ ਉਲੜੀ ਤੰਦ ਟੁੱਟੀ
ਆਸ਼ਕ ਬਕਰਾ ਮਸ਼ੂਕ ਕਸਾਈ, ਮੈਂ ਮੈਂ ਕਰਦੀ ਕੁੱਠੀ

੫    ਭਲਾ ਹੋਇਆ ਮੇਰਾ ਚਰਖਾ ਟੁੱਟਾ, ਜਿੰਦ ਅਡ਼ਾਬੋਂ ਛੁੱਟੀ
ਬੁੱਲ੍ਹੂ ਸ਼ਹੁ ਨੇ ਨਾਚ ਨਚਾਇਆ, ਪ੍ਰੇਮ ਪਈ ਕੜਕੁੱਟੀ


੧੧੩

ਮਨ ਅਟਕਿਓ ਸ਼ਾਮ ਸੁੰਦਰ ਸੂੰ

ਕਹੂੰ ਵੇਖੂੰ ਬਾਹਮਣ ਕਹੂੰ ਸ਼ੇਖਾ, ਆਪੇ ਆਪ ਕਰਨ ਸਭ ਭੇਖਾ
ਕਿਆ ਕਿਆ ਖੇਲਿਆ ਹੁਨਰ ਸੂੰ

ਸੁਝ ਪੜੀ ਤਬ ਰਾਮ ਦੁਹਾਈ, ਹਮ ਤੁਮ ਏਕ ਨਾ ਦੂਜਾ ਕਾਈ
ਇਸ ਪ੍ਰੇਮ ਨਗਾਰ ਕੇ ਘਰ ਸੂੰ

ਪੰਡਿਤ ਗਾਵਟ ਕਿਤ ਲਖ ਸਣਾਏ, ਨਾ ਕਹੀਂ ਜਾਏ ਨਾ ਕਹੀਂ ਆਏ
ਜੈਸੇ ਕਰ ਕਾ ਕੰਗਟ ਕਰ ਸੂੰ

੫    ਬੁੱਲ੍ਹੂ ਸ਼ਹੁ ਦੀ ਪੈਰੀਂ ਪੜੀਏ, ਸੀਸ ਕਾਟ ਕਰ ਆਗੇ ਧਰੀਏ
ਹੁਣ ਮੈਂ ਹਰਿ ਦੇਖਾ ਹਰ ਹਰ ਸੂੰ

As it spins around and around, my spindle has fallen off.
    My spool of thread has got tangled and the yarn is
    broken. The beloved is the butcher and the lover is
    the goat. It calls out "Me, me,"[1] and is slaughtered.
It would be good if my spinning wheel broke, then my life    5
    would be delivered from this torment. Bullha, the lord
    has made me dance, and the sound is very loud.

## 113

My[1] mind is fixed on my dark beloved.[2]

Sometimes I see a Brahman, sometimes a Shaikh. He is
    the one who creates all these guises. How skillfully he
    has played.

When I realized this, I appealed to Ram: you and I are one,
    there is no one else in this house in the city of love.

How many hundreds of thousands of kinds of existence
    the pandit describes. But the soul does not go
    anywhere and does not come anywhere. It is like a
    bracelet worn on the wrist.[3]

Bullha, let us fall at the lord's feet. Let us cut off our    5
    head and lay it before him. Now I have seen God in
    everything.

੧੧੪

ਮਾਏ ਨਾ ਮੁੜਦਾ ਇਸ਼ਕ ਦੀਵਾਨਾ, ਸ਼ਹੁ ਨਾਲ ਪਰੀਤਾਂ ਲਾ ਕੇ

ਇਸ਼ਕ ਸ਼ਰ੍ਹਾ ਦੀ ਲੱਗ ਗਈ ਬਾਜ਼ੀ, ਖੇਡਾਂ ਮੈਂ ਦਾਉ ਲਗਾ ਕੇ
ਮਾਰਨ ਬੋਲੀ ਬੋਲ ਨਾ ਬੋਲਾਂ, ਸੁਣਾਂ ਨਾ ਕੰਨ ਲਾ ਕੇ

ਵਿਹੜੇ ਵਿਚ ਸ਼ੈਤਾਨ ਨਚੋਂਦਾ, ਇਸ ਨੂੰ ਰੱਖ ਸਮਝਾ ਕੇ
ਤੋੜ ਸ਼ਰ੍ਹਾ ਨੂੰ ਜਿਤ ਲਈ ਬਾਜ਼ੀ, ਫਿਰਦੀ ਨੱਕ ਵਢਾ ਕੇ

ਮੈਂ ਅੰਜਾਣੀ ਖੇਡ ਵਗੁੱਚੀ ਆਂ, ਖੇਡਾਂ ਆਕੇ ਬਾਕੇ
ਇਹ ਖੇਡਾਂ ਹੁਣ ਲਗਦੀਆਂ ਝੇੜਾਂ, ਘਰ ਪੀਆ ਦੇ ਆ ਕੇ

੫    ਸਈਆਂ ਨਾਲ ਮੈਂ ਪਾਵਾਂ ਗਿੱਧਾ, ਦਿਲਬਰ ਲੁਕ ਲੁਕ ਝਾਕੇ
ਪੁੱਛੇ ਨੀ ਇਹ ਕਿਉਂ ਸ਼ਰਮਾਂਦਾ, ਜਾਏ ਨਾ ਭੇਤ ਬਤਾ ਕੇ

ਕਾਫ਼ਰ ਕਾਫ਼ਰ ਆਖਣ ਤੈਨੂੰ, ਸਾਰੇ ਲੋਕ ਸੁਣਾ ਕੇ
ਮੋਮਨ ਕਾਫ਼ਰ ਮੈਨੂੰ ਦੋਵੇਂ ਨਾ ਦਿਸਦੇ, ਵਹਦਤ ਦੇ ਵਿਚ ਆ ਕੇ

ਚੋਲੀ ਚੁੰਨੀ ਝੁਕਿਆ ਝੁੱਗਾ, ਪੁਟੀ ਸ਼ਿਰਕ ਜਲਾ ਕੇ
ਵਾਰਿਆ ਕੁੱਫਰ ਵੱਡਾ ਮੈਂ ਦਿਲ ਬੀਂ, ਤਲੀ ਤੇ ਸੀਸ ਟਿਕਾ ਕੇ

ਮੈਂ ਵਡਭਾਗੀ ਮਾਰਿਆ ਖ਼ਾਵਿੰਦ, ਹੱਥੀਂ ਜ਼ਹਿਰ ਪਿਲਾ ਕੇ
ਵਸਲ ਕਰਾਂ ਮੈਂ ਨਾਲ ਸੱਜਣ ਦੇ, ਸ਼ਰਮ ਹਜਾ ਗਵਾ ਕੇ

ਵਿਚ ਚਮਨ ਮੈਂ ਪਲੰਘ ਵਿਛਾਇਆ, ਯਾਰ ਸੁਤੀ ਗਲ ਲਾ ਕੇ
ਸਿਰੋਹੀ ਨਾਲ ਮਿਲ ਗਈ ਸਿਰੋਹੀ,੧ ਬੁੱਲ੍ਹਾ ਸ਼ਹੁ ਨੂੰ ਪਾ ਕੇ

194

## 114

Mother,[1] this mad love does not turn aside, ever since I fell
in love with the lord.

The game between love and law has started. I roll the dice
and play. They utter taunts, but I say nothing back,
nor do I listen carefully.

"Satan makes her dance in the courtyard. Talk to her and
make her stop."[2] I have broken the law and won the
game. I go around in disgrace.

I was a silly girl who was lost in her game. I played at
making things out of mud.[3] These games now seem
ridiculous, since I entered my beloved's house.

I clap and dance[4] with my girlfriends, while the beloved          5
hides and peeps. Ask him why he is embarrassed. He
goes without revealing the secret.

"Unbeliever, unbeliever" is what they call you when the
people all cry out. Neither believer nor unbeliever is
apparent to me when I enter unity.

I destroyed my blouse and scarf and my hut, after burning
duality on the fire. I have sacrificed great unbelief
from my heart, with my head placed on my palm.

How lucky I am to have killed my master,[5] handing it
poison to drink. I will be together with my beloved,
abandoning all shame and reserve.

I have spread a bed in the garden, and sleep in my
beloved's embrace. We are united as one, now that
Bullha has found the lord.

१९५

ਮਾਹੀ ਵੇ ਤੈਂ ਮਿਲਿਆਂ ਸਭ ਦੁੱਖ ਹੋਵਣ ਦੂਰ

ਲੋਕਾਂ ਦੇ ਭਾਣੇ ਚਾਕ ਚਕੇਟਾ, ਸਾਡਾ ਰੱਬ ਗ਼ਫ਼ੂਰ

ਜੈਂ ਦੇ ਮਿਲਣ ਦੀ ਖ਼ਾਤਰ ਚਸ਼ਮਾਂ, ਬਹਿੰਦੀਆਂ ਸੀ ਨਿਤ ਝੂਰ

ਉਠ ਗਈ ਹਿਜਰ ਜੁਦਾਈ ਜਿਗਰੋਂ, ਜ਼ਾਹਰ ਦਿਸਦਾ ਨੂਰ

੫  ਬੁੱਲ੍ਹੂ ਰਮਜ਼ ਸਮਝ ਦੀ ਪਾਈਆ, ਨਾ ਨੇੜੇ ਨਾ ਦੂਰ


੧੧੬

ਮਿੱਤਰ ਪਿਆਰੇ ਕਾਰਨ ਨੀ, ਮੈਂ ਲੋਕ ਉਲ੍ਹਾਮੇਂ ਲੈਨੀ ਹਾਂ

ਲੱਗਾ ਨੇਹੁੰ ਮੇਰਾ ਜਿਸ ਸੇਤੀ, ਵੇਖ ਸਰਹਾਣੇ ਪਲੰਘ ਦੇ ਜੀਤੀ
ਆਲਮ ਕਿਉਂ ਸਮਝਾਵੇ ਰੀਤੀ, ਮੈਂ ਡਿੱਠੇ ਬਾਝ ਨਾ ਰਹਿਨੀ ਹਾਂ

ਤੁਸੀਂ ਸਮਝਾਓ ਵੀਰੋ ਭੋਰੀ, ਰਾਝਣ ਵੈਂਦਾ ਮੈਥੋਂ ਚੋਰੀ
ਜੈਂਦੇ ਇਸ਼ਕ ਕੀਤੀ ਮੈਂ ਭੋਰੀ, ਮੈਂ ਨਾਲ ਅਰਾਮ ਨਾ ਬਹਿਨੀ ਹਾਂ

ਬਿਰਹੋਂ ਆ ਵੜਿਆ ਵਿਚ ਵਿਹੜੇ, ਰੋਜ਼ ਅਜ਼ਾਰ ਦੇਵੇ ਤਨ ਘੇਰੇ
ਦਾਰੂ ਦਰਦ ਨਾ ਬਾਝੋਂ ਤੇਰੇ, ਮੈਂ ਸਜਨਾਂ ਬਾਝ ਮਰੇਨੀ ਹਾਂ

੫  ਬੁੱਲ੍ਹੇ ਸ਼ਾਹ ਘਰ ਰਾਂਝਣ ਆਵੇ, ਮੈਂ ਤੱਤੀ ਨੂੰ ਲੈ ਗਲ ਲਾਵੇ
ਨਾਲ ਖ਼ੁਸ਼ੀ ਦੇ ਰੈਣ ਵਿਹਾਵੇ, ਨਾਲ ਖ਼ੁਸ਼ੀ ਦੇ ਰਹਿਨੀ ਹਾਂ

## 115

Beloved, through meeting you, all my sorrows are
     removed.

In people's eyes he is a humble herdsman. For me he is the
     all-forgiving lord.

My yearning to meet him meant that my eyes were always
     downcast in distress.

Separation and parting have been removed from my heart.
     His light is made manifest to me.

Bullha, I have discovered the secret of understanding.          5
     He is neither near nor far.

## 116

For the sake of my dear friend, I suffer people's
     reproaches.

When I see my beloved on the pillow of my bed, I rejoice.
     Why do people tell me how I should behave? I cannot
     rest without seeing him.

Just explain things to me, brothers. Ranjha goes away from
     me by stealth. My love for him has driven me mad.
     I cannot sit in comfort.

Separation has come into the courtyard. Every day it
     envelopes my body and torments me. There is no
     remedy for my pain except you. Without my beloved
     I will die.

Bullha, may the lord come to my house, may he embrace          5
     me in my suffering, and may he spend the night in joy.
     Then I will live happily.

੧੧੭

ਮੁਰਲੀ ਬਾਜ ਉਠੀ ਅਟਘਾਤਾਂ, ਸੁਣ ਕੇ ਭੁੱਲ ਗਈਆਂ ਸਭ ਬਾਤਾਂ

ਲਗ ਗਏ ਅਨਹਦ ਬਾਣ ਨਿਆਰੇ, ਛੁੱਟ ਗਏ ਦੁਨੀਆਂ ਕੁੜ ਪਸਾਰੇ
ਸਾਈਂ ਮੁਖ ਵੇਖਣ ਵਟਜਾਰੇ, ਮੈਨੂੰ ਭੁੱਲ ਗਈਆਂ ਸਭ ਬਾਤਾਂ

ਹੁਣ ਮੈਂ ਚੈਂਚਲ ਮਿਰਗ ਫਹਾਇਆ, ਓਸੇ ਮੈਨੂੰ ਬੰਨ੍ਹ ਬਹਾਇਆ
ਸਿਰਫ ਦੁਗਾਨਾ ਇਸ਼ਕ ਪੜ੍ਹਾਇਆ, ਰਹਿ ਗਈਆਂ ਤ੍ਰੈ ਚਾਰ ਰਕਾਤਾਂ

ਬੂਹੇ ਆਣ ਖਲੋਤਾ ਯਾਰ, ਬਾਬਲ ਪੂਜ ਪਿਆ ਤਕਰਾਰ
ਕਲਮੇ ਨਾਲ ਜੇ ਰਹਿ ਵਿਹਾਰ, ਨਬੀ ਮੁਹੰਮਦ ਭਰੇ ਸ਼ਫਾਤਾਂ

੫  ਬੁੱਲ੍ਹੇ ਸ਼ਹੁ ਮੈਂ ਹੁਣ ਭਰਮਾਈ, ਜਦ ਦੀ ਮੁਰਲੀ ਕਾਹਨ ਬਜਾਈ
ਬੌਰੀ ਹੋ ਤੁਸਾਂ ਵਲ ਧਾਈ, ਖੋਜੀਆਂ ਕਿਤ ਵਲ ਦਸਤ ਬਰਾਤਾਂ

੧੧੮

ਮੁੱਲਾਂ ਮੈਨੂੰ ਮਾਰਦਾ ਈ

ਮੁੱਲਾਂ ਮੈਨੂੰ ਸਬਕ ਪੜ੍ਹਾਇਆ, ਅਲੜ੍ਹੋਂ ਅੱਗੇ ਕੁਝ ਨਾ ਆਇਆ
ਉਹ ਬੇ ਈ ਬੇ ਪੁਕਾਰਦਾ ਈ

## 117

The flute has begun to play mysteriously.[1] When I hear it,
I forget everything.

I have been pierced by the wonderful arrows of the
unstruck music.[2] I have escaped from the world's false
displays. The traders[3] behold the face of the lord.[4]
I have forgotten everything.

Restless as a deer, I have now been trapped. It is he who
has tied me up and made me sit still. Love taught me
only the prayer of two prostrations,[5] omitting those of
three and four.

My beloved has come and stood at my door. Father, his
promise has been fulfilled. If your dealings are in
accordance with the profession of faith, the prophet
Muhammad will intercede[6] for you.

Bullha, I have been beguiled ever since Krishna played his       5
flute. Madly I rushed toward you. Which way can the
stolen goods[7] be tracked?

## 118

The[1] mullah beats me.

The mullah taught me the lesson. I could not understand
anything beyond *alif*, but all he keeps shouting is
*"Be, be!"*[2]

## ੧੧੯

ਮੂੰਹ ਆਈ ਬਾਤ ਨਾ ਰਹਿੰਦੀ

ਝੂਠ ਆਖਾਂ ਤੇ ਕੁਝ ਬਚਦਾ ਏ, ਸੱਚ ਆਖਿਆਂ ਭਾਂਬੜ ਮਚਦਾ ਏ
ਜੀ ਦੋਹਾਂ ਗੱਲਾਂ ਤੋਂ ਜਰਦਾ ਏ, ਜਚ ਜਚ ਕੇ ਜੀਭਾ ਕਹਿੰਦੀ ਏ

ਜਿਸ ਪਾਇਆ ਭੇਤ ਕਲੰਦਰ ਦਾ, ਰਾਹ ਖੋਜਿਆ ਆਪਣੇ ਅੰਦਰ ਦਾ
ਉਹ ਵਾਸੀ ਹੈ ਸੁਖ ਮੰਦਰ ਦਾ, ਜਿਥੇ ਕੋਈ ਨਾ ਚੜ੍ਹਦੀ ਲਹਿੰਦੀ ਏ

ਇਕ ਲਾਜ਼ਮ ਬਾਤ ਅਦਬ ਦੀ ਏ, ਸਾਨੂੰ ਬਾਤ ਮਲੂਮੀ ਸਭ ਦੀ ਏ
ਹਰ ਹਰ ਵਿਚ ਸੂਰਤ ਰਬ ਦੀ ਏ, ਕਿਤੇ ਜ਼ਾਹਰ ਕਿਤੇ ਛੁਪੇਂਦੀ ਏ

੫  ਇਹ ਤਿਲਕਣ ਬਾਜ਼ੀ ਵਿਹੜਾ ਏ, ਤੁਰੋ ਥਮ ਥਮ ਪੈਰ ਅੰਧੇਰਾ ਏ
ਵੜ੍ਹ ਅੰਦਰ ਵੇਖੇ ਕਿਹੜਾ ਏ, ਕਿਉਂ ਖ਼ੁਫਤਣ ਬਾਹਰ ਢੂੰਡੇਂਦੀ ਏ

ਏਥੇ ਭੇਖਾ ਪਾਓ ਪਸਾਰਾ ਏ, ਇਹਦਾ ਲਖਣਾ ਬਹੁਤ ਨਿਆਰਾ ਏ
ਇਕ ਸੂਰਤ ਦਾ ਚਮਕਾਰਾ ਏ, ਜਿਵੇਂ ਚਿਟਗ ਦਾਰੂ ਵਿਚ ਪੈਂਦੀ ਏ

ਕਿਤੇ ਨਾਜ਼ ਅਦਾ ਦਿਖਲਾਈਦਾ, ਕਿਤੇ ਹੋ ਰਸੂਲ ਮਿਲਾਇਦਾ
ਕਿਤੇ ਆਸ਼ਕ ਬਣ ਬਣ ਆਈਦਾ, ਕਿਤੇ ਜਾਨ ਜੁਦਾਈ ਸਹਿੰਦੀ ਏ

ਕਿਉਂ ਮਿੱਟੀ ਲਾਲ ਬਣਾਨਾ ਹੈਂ, ਤੂੰ ਆਪੇ ਦੂੱਰ ਜਗਾਨਾ ਹੈਂ
ਇਕ ਨੁਕਤੇ ਲਾਲ ਬੇਗਾਨਾ ਹੈਂ, ਅਜੇ ਮੁਰਸ਼ਦ ਪੀਰ ਢੂੰਡੇਂਦੀ ਏ

ਜਦੋਂ ਜ਼ਾਹਰ ਹੋਏ ਨੂਰ ਹੁਰੀਂ, ਜਲ ਗਏ ਪਹਾੜ ਕੋਹ ਤੁਰ ਹੁਰੀਂ
ਤਦੋਂ ਦਾਰ ਚੜ੍ਹੇ ਮਨਸੂਰ ਹੁਰੀਂ, ਓਥੇ ਸ਼ੇਖੀ ਪੇਸ਼ ਨਾ ਵੈਂਦੀ ਏ

੧੦  ਜੇ ਜ਼ਾਹਰ ਕਰਾਂ ਇਸਰਾਰ ਤਾਈਂ, ਸਭ ਭੁੱਲ ਜਾਵਣ ਤਕਰਾਰ ਤਾਈਂ
ਫਿਰ ਮਾਰਨ ਬੁੱਲ੍ਹੇ ਯਾਰ ਤਾਈਂ, ਏਥੇ ਮਖ਼ਫੀ ਗੱਲ ਸੋਹੇਂਦੀ ਏ

## 119

I[1] cannot help saying what comes onto my tongue.

If I tell lies, then something is omitted. Telling the truth
    sets things alight. Both alternatives make my heart
    hesitate. As it hesitates, my tongue speaks.[2]

Anyone who has discovered the fakir's secret has tracked
    the path within himself. He is an inhabitant of the
    temple of joy, where there is no rise or fall.

All that is necessary is to be respectful. I know the
    universal rule. All things contain the form of the lord,
    sometimes manifest, sometimes hidden.

This courtyard[3] is a slippery business. Tread carefully, for   5
    it is dark. Go in and see who it is. Why do you seek
    delusion outside?

Appearance extends itself here. Understanding things is
    a strange business. There is the flash of a single form,
    like a spark that falls into gunpowder.

Sometimes he displays airs and graces. Sometimes
    he becomes the Prophet and brings about union.
    Sometimes he turns himself into a lover and comes.
    Sometimes the soul suffers in separation.

Why do you make earth and rubies? You yourself are a
    unique pearl. You are made distinct with a dot. Still
    you seek your director and guide.

When the exalted light was manifested, the holy mountain
    of Sinai[4] was burned up. The saintly Mansur[5]
    ascended the gallows. Boasting is of no use.

If I reveal the mystery, all disputes will be forgotten. Then   10
    they would kill friend Bullha. Veiled expression[6] is
    suitable here.

ਅਸਾਂ ਪੜਿਆ ਇਲਮ ਤਕੀਕੀ ਏ, ਉੱਥੇ ਇਕੋ ਹਰਫ਼ ਹਕੀਕੀ ਏ
ਸਭ ਝਗੜਾ ਹੋਰ ਵਧੀਕੀ ਏ, ਐਵੇਂ ਰੌਲਾ ਪਾ ਪਾ ਬਹਿੰਦੀ ਏ

ਐ ਸ਼ਾਹ ਅਕਲ ਤੂੰ ਆਇਆ ਕਰ, ਸਾਨੂੰ ਅਦਬ ਅਦਾਬ ਸਿਖਾਇਆ ਕਰ
ਮੈਂ ਝੂਠੀ ਨੂੰ ਸਮਝਾਇਆ ਕਰ, ਜੋ ਮੂਰਖ ਮਾਤੂ ਕਹਿੰਦੀ ਏ

ਵਾਹ ਵਾਹ ਕੁਦਰਤ ਬੇਪਰਵਾਹੀ ਏ, ਦੇਵੇ ਕੈਦੀ ਦੇ ਸਿਰ ਸ਼ਾਹੀ ਏ
ਇਕ ਬੇਟਾ ਜਾਇਆ ਮਾਈ ਏ, ਸਭ ਕਲਮਾ ਇਸ ਦਾ ਕਹਿੰਦੀ ਏ

ਇਸ ਆਜਿਜ਼ ਦਾ ਕੀ ਹੀਲਾ ਏ, ਰੰਗ ਜ਼ਰਦ ਤੇ ਮੁਖੜਾ ਪੀਲਾ ਏ
ਜਿੱਥੇ ਆਪੇ ਆਪ ਵਸੀਲਾ ਏ, ਉੱਥੇ ਕੀ ਅਦਾਲਤ ਕਹਿੰਦੀ ਏ

੧੫ ਤੈਂ ਆਪੇ ਪੁਲ ਸਿਰਾਤ ਬਟਾਈ, ਤੈਂ ਅੱਗੇ ਕਿਸ ਢਾਲ ਢਵਾਈ
ਸਭ ਕਲਮਾ ਤੱਜਬ ਪਾਰ ਲੰਘਾਈ, ਉੱਥੇ ਕੌਣ ਦੋਜ਼ਖ਼ ਵਿਚ ਰਹਿੰਦੀ ਏ

ਬੁੱਲ੍ਹਾ ਸ਼ਹੁ ਅਸਾਂ ਬੀ ਵੱਖ ਨਹੀਂ, ਬਿਨ ਸ਼ਹੁ ਬੀ ਦੂਜਾ ਕੱਖ ਨਹੀਂ
ਪਰ ਵੇਖਣ ਵਾਲੀ ਅੱਖ ਨਹੀਂ, ਤਾਹੀਂ ਜਾਨ ਜੁਦਾਈਆਂ ਸਹਿੰਦੀ ਏ

## ੧੨੦

ਮੇਰਾ ਰਾਂਝਣ ਹੁਣ ਕੋਈ ਹੋਰ

ਤਖ਼ਤ ਮੁਨੱਵਰ ਬਾਂਗਾਂ ਮਿਲੀਆਂ, ਸੁਟੀਆਂ ਤਖ਼ਤ ਲਹੌਰ

ਇਸ਼ਕੇ ਮਾਰੇ ਐਵੇਂ ਫਿਰਦੇ, ਜਿਊਂ ਜੰਗਲ ਵਿਚ ਢੋਰ

ਰਾਂਝ ਤਖ਼ਤ ਹਜ਼ਾਰੇ ਦਾ ਸਾਈਂ, ਹੁਣ ਉੱਥੋਂ ਹੋਇਆ ਚੋਰ

I have studied the science of certainty, where only one
letter[7] is real. All other disputation is superfluous.
A tumult is created for nothing.

Oh lord reason, keep coming, and keep teaching me
respect and decorum. Keep correcting me, for I am
untruthful, saying that man is foolish.

The divine power is wonderfully nonchalant. It bestows
royalty on the prisoner's head. It is a son born of a
mother. Everyone professes faith in him.[8]

What resource does this helpless one possess, whose color
is yellow and whose face is pale? Where he is himself
the intercessor,[9] who can speak of the court of justice?

It is you who made the Sirat bridge.[10] Who can shield 15
themselves against you? It is the excellent word[11] that
delivers us safely across. Who then remains in hell?

Bullha, the lord is not separate from us; without him
there is nothing else, not even a straw. But you do not
possess the eye of vision. That is why the soul suffers
its separations.

## 120

My Ranjha is now someone else.

When the calls came from the throne of light, they were
heard in royal Lahore.[1]

Those who are smitten by love wander like cattle in the
forest.

Ranjha, the lord of Takht Hazara,[2] has now come from
there as a thief.

੫    ਬੁੱਲ੍ਹ ਸ਼ਾਹ ਅਸਾਂ ਮਰਨਾ ਨਾਹੀਂ, ਕਬਰ ਪਏ ਕੋਈ ਹੋਰ

## ੧੨੧

ਮੇਰੀ ਬੁੱਕਲ ਦੇ ਵਿਚ ਚੋਰ, ਨੀ ਮੇਰੀ ਬੁੱਕਲ ਦੇ ਵਿਚ ਚੋਰ

ਸਾਏ ਕਿਸਨੂੰ ਕੂਕ ਸੁਟਾਵਾਂ, ਨੀ ਮੇਰੀ ਬੁੱਕਲ ਦੇ ਵਿਚ ਚੋਰ
ਚੋਰੀ ਚੋਰੀ ਨਿਕਲ ਗਿਆ, ਜਗ ਵਿਚ ਪੈ ਗਿਆ ਸ਼ੋਰ

ਮੁਸਲਮਾਨ ਸਿਵਿਆਂ ਤੋਂ ਡਰਦੇ, ਹਿੰਦੂ ਡਰਦੇ ਗੋਰ
ਦੋਵੇਂ ਏਸੇ ਦੇ ਵਿਚ ਮਰਦੇ, ਇਹੋ ਦੋਹਾਂ ਦੀ ਖੋਰ

ਕਿਤੇ ਰਾਮ ਦਾਸ ਕਿਤੇ ਫ਼ਤਿਹ ਮੁਹੰਮਦ, ਏਹੋ ਕਦੀਮੀ ਸ਼ੋਰ
ਮਿਟ ਗਿਆ ਦੋਹਾਂ ਦਾ ਝਗੜਾ, ਨਿਕਲ ਪਿਆ ਕੁਝ ਹੋਰ

੫    ਅਰਸ਼ ਮੁਨੱਵਰੋਂ ਬਾਂਗਾਂ ਮਿਲੀਆਂ, ਸੁਣੀਆਂ ਤਖ਼ਤ ਲਹੋਰ
ਸ਼ਾਹ ਇਨਾਇਤ ਕੁੰਡੀਆਂ ਪਾਈਆਂ, ਲੁਪ ਛੁਪ ਖਿਚਦਾ ਡੋਰ

ਜਿਸ ਛੁੰਡਿਆ ਤਿਸ ਪਾਇਓ ਨਾਹੀਂ, ਝੂਰ ਝੂਰ ਹੋਇਆ ਮੋਰ
ਪੀਰ ਪੀਰਾਂ ਬਗਦਾਦ ਅਸਾਡਾ, ਮੁਰਸ਼ਦ ਤਖ਼ਤ ਲਹੋਰ

ਏਹੋ ਤੁਸੀਂ ਵੀ ਆਖੋ ਸਾਰੇ, ਆਪ ਗੁੱਡੀ ਆਪ ਡੋਰ
ਮੈਂ ਦਸਨਾ ਤੁਸੀ ਪਕੜ ਲਿਆਓ, ਬੁੱਲ੍ਹੇ ਸ਼ਾਹ ਦਾ ਚੋਰ

Bullhe Shah, we are not going to die; let someone else fall    5
    into the grave.

## 121

There is a thief in the folds of my scarf.[1] Oh, there is a thief
    in the folds of my scarf.

Good people, to whom shall I utter my cry? Oh, there is a
    thief in the folds of my scarf. Stealthily he got out, and
    havoc was caused in the world.

Muslims fear the burning grounds, Hindus fear the grave.
    Both of them die in this dispute. This is the enmity
    between the two.

Sometimes he is Ram Das, sometimes he is Fateh
    Muhammad,[2] hence all this long-standing uproar.
    The quarrel between them was removed, when
    someone else emerged.

When the calls came from the heavenly throne of light,    5
    they were heard in royal Lahore.[3] Shah Inayat has set
    out his hooks, and without being seen he tugs the line.

Whoever did not find the one he was looking for cried out
    in grief like the peacock. Baghdad is the place of the
    Pir of Pirs;[4] our guide is in royal Lahore.

This is what you all should say: it is he who is the kite, he
    who is the string. I am telling you to arrest Bullhe
    Shah's thief and bring him here.

੧੨੨

ਮੇਰੇ ਕਿਉਂ ਚਿਰ ਲਾਇਆ ਮਾਹੀ, ਨੀ ਮੈਂ ਉਸ ਤੋਂ ਘੋਲ ਘੁਮਾਈ

ਦਰਦ ਫ਼ਰਾਕ ਬਘੇਰਾ ਕਰਿਆ, ਇਹ ਦੁਖ ਮੈਬੋਂ ਜਾਏ ਨਾ ਜਰਿਆ
ਟਮਕ ਅਸਾਡੇ ਸਿਰ ਤੇ ਧਰਿਆ, ਮੋਢੋ ਬੁਗਚਾ ਲੋਹ ਕੜਾਹੀ

ਜਾਗਦਿਆਂ ਮੈਂ ਘਰ ਵਿਚ ਮੁੱਠੀ, ਕਦੀ ਨਹੀਂ ਸਾਂ ਬੈਠੀ ਉੱਠੀ
ਜਿਸ ਦੀ ਸਾਂ ਮੈਂ ਓਸੇ ਕੁੱਠੀ, ਹੁਣ ਕੀ ਕਰ ਲਿਆ ਬੇਪਰਵਾਹੀ

ਬੁੱਲ੍ਹੂ ਸ਼ਹੁ ਤੇਰੇ ਤੋਂ ਵਾਰੀ, ਮੈਂ ਬਲਿਹਾਰੀ ਲਖ ਲਖ ਵਾਰੀ
ਤੇਰੀ ਸੂਰਤ ਬਹੁਤ ਪਿਆਰੀ, ਮੈਂ ਬੇਚਾਰੀ ਘੋਲ ਘੁਮਾਈ

੫    ਮਾਹੀ ਦੇ ਪੰਜ ਪੀਰ ਪਨਾਹੀ, ਝੁੰਡਟ ਉਸ ਨੂੰ ਵਿਚ ਲੋਕਾਈ
ਮੇਰੇ ਮਾਹੀ ਤੇ ਫ਼ਜ਼ਲ ਇਲਾਹੀ, ਜਿਸ ਨੇ ਗ਼ੈਬੋਂ ਤਾਰ ਹਿਲਾਈ

'ਕੁਨ ਫ਼ਯਕੂਨ' ਅਵਾਜ਼ਾ ਆਇਆ, ਤਖ਼ਤ ਹਜ਼ਾਰਿਓਂ ਰਾਂਝਾ ਧਾਇਆ
ਚੁਚਕ ਦਾ ਓਹ ਚਾਕ ਸਦਾਇਆ, ਉਹ ਆਹਾ ਸਾਹਿਬ ਸਫ਼ਾਈ

ਚੱਲ ਰਾਂਝਾ ਮੁਲਤਾਨ ਚਲਹੋਂ, ਗ਼ੌਸ ਬਹਾਵਲ ਪੀਰ ਮਨਾਵੇਂ
ਆਪਟੀ ਤੁਰਤ ਮੁਰਾਦ ਲਿਆਵੇਂ, ਮੇਰਾ ਜੀ ਰੱਬ ਮੌਲਾ ਚਾਹੀ

ਜਿੱਥੇ ਇਸ਼ਕ ਡੇਰਾ ਘਤ ਬਹਿੰਦਾ, ਓਥੇ ਸਬਰ ਕਰਾਰ ਨਾ ਰਹਿੰਦਾ
ਕੋਈ ਛੁੱਟਕਟ ਐਵੇਂ ਕਹਿੰਦਾ, ਗਾਲ ਪਈ ਪ੍ਰੇਮ ਦੀ ਫਾਹੀ

ਜੀਵ ਖੇੜਿਆਂ ਦੀ ਆਕੇ ਢੁੱਕੀ, ਮੈਂ ਹੁਣ ਹੀਰ ਨਿਮਾਣੀ ਮੁੱਕੀ
ਮੇਰੀ ਰੱਤ ਸਰੀਰੋਂ ਸੁੱਕੀ, ਵਲ ਵਲ ਮਾਰੇ ਬਿਰਹੋਂ ਖਾਈ

੧੦    ਖੇੜਾ ਫੁੱਲ ਘੋੜੇ ਤੇ ਚੜ੍ਹਿਆ, ਫੱਕਰ ਧੂੜ ਗਰਦ ਵਿਚ ਰਲਿਆ
ਏਡ ਮਾਣ ਕਿਉਂ ਕੂੜਾ ਕਰਿਆ, ਉਸ ਕੀਤੀ ਬੇਪਰਵਾਹੀ

## 122

Why[1] has my beloved taken so long? Oh, I am devoted
to him.

Separation has given me much pain; I cannot endure this
suffering. It has put a large drum on my head and
placed a sack with an iron pot on my shoulders.

At home I am ravaged as soon as I wake up. I am never able
to get up or to sit down. It is the one I belonged to who
has slain me; how can he be so indifferent now?

Bullha offers himself to you, oh lord. I am sacrificed
thousands of times over. Your appearance is very dear.
I am a poor creature who is devoted to you.

The Five Pirs[2] protect my beloved, they search for him        5
among people. Divine grace is upon my beloved, who
has played the string from the unseen world.

The call came: *Let it be, and it was*.[3] Ranjha came quickly
from Takht Hazara. He was called Chuchak's[4]
herdsman, but he was the lord of purity.

Come, Ranjha, let us go to Multan, to pay homage to
the great saint Bahaval Haq.[5] Let us gain our desire
immediately. My heart longs for the lord.

Wherever love sets up camp, all patience and resolve
disappear. They may claim to be free, but the noose of
love has fallen around their neck.

The bridegroom's procession of the Kheras has come. I,
poor Hir, am finished now. The blood has evaporated
from my body. Separation keeps burying me in a pit.

The Khera is proudly mounted on his horse. The poor        10
fakir[6] is mingled with the dust. Why put on such a
false show of pride? He has shown his indifference.

ਚੜ੍ਹ ਕੇ ਪੀਰ ਖੇੜਿਆਂ ਦਾ ਆਇਆ, ਉਸ ਨੇ ਕੇਹਾ ਸ਼ੋਰ ਮਚਾਇਆ
ਮੈਨੂੰ ਮਾਹੀ ਨਜ਼ਰ ਨਾ ਆਇਆ, ਤਾਹੀਓਂ ਕੀਤੀ ਹਾਲ ਦੁਹਾਈ

ਮੈਂ ਮਾਹੀ ਦੀ ਮਾਹੀ ਮੇਰਾ, ਗੋਸ਼ਤ ਪੋਸਤ ਬੇਰਾ ਬੇਰਾ
ਦਿਨ ਹਸ਼ਰ ਦੇ ਕਰਸਾਂ ਝੇੜਾ, ਜਦ ਦੇਸੀ ਦਾਦ ਇਲਾਹੀ

ਚੁਚਕ ਕਾਜ਼ੀ ਸੱਦ ਬਹਾਇਆ, ਮੈਂ ਮਨ ਰਾਂਝੂ ਮਾਹੀ ਭਾਇਆ
ਧੱਕੋ ਧੱਕ ਨਿਕਾਹ ਪੜ੍ਹਾਇਆ, ਉਸ ਕੀਤਾ ਫ਼ਰਜ਼ ਅਦਾਈ

ਤੇਲ ਵਟਣਾ ਕੰਧੇ ਤੇ ਮਲਿਆ, ਚੋਇਆ ਚੰਨਣ ਮੱਥੇ ਰਲਿਆ
ਮਾਹੀ ਮੇਰਾ ਬੇਲੇ ਵੜਿਆ, ਮੈਂ ਕੀ ਕਰਨੇ ਕੰਗਣ ਬਾਹੀ

੧੫  ਟਮਕ ਸੁੱਟ ਟਿੱਲੇ ਵਲ ਜਾਵੇ, ਬੈਠਾ ਉਸ ਦਾ ਨਾਮ ਧਿਆਵੇ
ਕੰਨ ਪੜਵਾ ਕੇ ਮੁੰਦਰਾਂ ਪਾਵੇ, ਗੁਰ ਲੈ ਕੇ ਦੋ ਸਿਰ ਸਾਹੀਏ

ਗੁਰ ਗੋਰਖ ਨੂੰ ਪੀਰ ਮਨਾਵੇ, ਹੀਰੇ ਹੀਰੇ ਕਰ ਕੁਰਲਾਵੇ
ਜਿਸ ਦੇ ਕਾਰਨ ਮੁੰਡ ਮੰਡਾਵੇ, ਉਹ ਮੂੰਹ ਪੀਲਾ ਜ਼ਰਦ ਕਪਾਹੀ

ਜੋਗੀ ਜੋਗ ਸਿਧਾਰਨ ਆਇਆ, ਸਿਰ ਦਾੜ੍ਹੀ ਮੂੰਹ ਮੋਨ ਮੁਨਾਇਆ
ਇਸਨੇ ਭਗਵਾਂ ਭੇਸ ਵਟਾਇਆ, ਕਾਲੀ ਸੇਲ੍ਹੀ ਗਲ ਵਿਚ ਪਾਈ

ਜੋਗੀ ਸ਼ਹਿਰ ਖੇੜਿਆਂ ਦੇ ਆਵੇ, ਜਿਸ ਘਰ ਮਤਲਬ ਸੋ ਘਰ ਜਾਵੇ
ਬੂਹੇ ਜਾ ਕੇ ਨਾਦ ਵਜਾਵੇ, ਆਪੇ ਹੋਇਆ ਫ਼ਜ਼ਲ ਇਲਾਹੀ

The Pir of the Kheras[7] has come mounted; what an uproar
   he has created. I have not seen my beloved, and that is
   why I have lamented my condition.
I am the beloved's, the beloved is mine, in flesh and skin
   and every single part. On the day of resurrection I will
   create a dispute, when divine justice is dispensed.
Chuchak called for the *qazi* and sat him down. My beloved
   Ranjha is the one who has pleased my heart. Forcibly,
   the marriage ceremony was recited and the ritual was
   performed.
Oil and lotion[8] were rubbed on his shoulders, and sandal
   paste was smeared on his forehead. My beloved has
   gone into the river glade. What use to me are the
   bangles on my arm?
Casting aside his drum,[9] he goes toward Tilla,[10] he sits and
   meditates on his name.[11] He has his ears split and the
   earrings inserted, and is initiated by the guru.
My Pir gains the approval of guru Gorakh.[12] He keeps
   crying "Hir, Hir." The one for whom he had his head
   shaven has a face as pale as the cotton boll.
The yogi came to practice yoga, with his head and beard
   and face clean-shaven. He has put on ochre-colored
   clothing, and has a yogi's coarse black thread around
   his neck.
The yogi comes to the city of the Kheras, going to the
   house where his purpose lies. He goes to the door
   and sounds his horn. All this has happened by
   divine grace.

15

ਬੂਹੇ ਪੈਖੜ ਪਿਆ ਪਿੰਗਾਲੇ, ਟੁਟ ਗਿਆ ਖੱਪਰ ਡੁਲ੍ਹ ਪਏ ਦਾਣੇ
ਇਸ ਦੇ ਵਲ ਛਲ ਕੋਟ ਪਛਾਣੇ, ਚੀਟਾ ਹੁੱਲ ਗਿਆ ਵਿਚ ਪਾਹੀ

੨੦ ਚੀਟਾ ਹੁਣ ਹੁਣ ਝੋਲੀ ਪਾਵੇ, ਬੈਠਾ ਹੀਰੇ ਤਰਫ਼ ਤਕਾਵੇ
ਜੋ ਕੁਝ ਲਿਖਿਆ ਲੇਖ ਸੋ ਪਾਵੇ, ਰੋ ਰੋ ਲੜਦੇ ਨੈਣ ਸਿਪਾਹੀ

ਇਹ ਗੱਲ ਸਹਿਤੀ ਨਾਦ ਪਛਾਤੀ, ਦੋਹਾਂ ਦੀ ਵੇਦਨ ਇੱਕੋ ਜਾਤੀ
ਉਹ ਵੀ ਆਹੀ ਸਹੀ ਮਦਮਾਤੀ, ਉੱਤੇ ਧੁਆਂ ਸੱਥਰ ਪਾਈ

ਬੁੱਲੂ ਸਹਿਤੀ ਫੰਦ ਮਚਾਇਆ, ਹੀਰ ਸਲੇਟੀ ਨਾਂਗ ਲੜਾਇਆ
ਜੋਗੀ ਮੰਤਰ ਝਾੜਨ ਆਇਆ, ਦੋਹਾਂ ਆਸ ਮੁਰਾਦ ਪੁਚਾਈ

## ੧੨੩

ਮੇਰੇ ਘਰ ਆਇਆ ਪੀਆ ਹਮਰਾ

ਵਾਹ ਵਾਹ ਵਹਦਤ ਕੀਨਾ ਸ਼ੋਰ, ਅਨਹਦ ਬੰਸੀ ਦੀ ਘਟ੍ਯਘੋਰ
ਅਸਾਂ ਹੁਣ ਪਾਇਆ ਤਖ਼ਤ ਲਹੌਰ

ਜਲ ਗਏ ਮੇਰੇ ਘੇਟ ਨਿਘੇਟ, ਲਗ ਗਈ ਪ੍ਰੇਮ ਸੱਚੇ ਦੀ ਚੋਟ
ਸਾਨੂੰ ਉਸ ਖ਼ਸਮ ਦੀ ਓਟ

ਹੁਣ ਕਿਆ ਗਿਣੀਏ ਸਾਲੇ ਸਾਇਤ, ਲਗ ਗਿਆ ਮਸਤ ਪਿਆਲਾ ਹਾਤ
ਹੁਣ ਮੈਂ ਭੁੱਲ ਗਈ ਜ਼ਾਤ ਸਿਫ਼ਤ

੫ ਹੁਣ ਕਿਆ ਕੀਨੇ ਬੀਸ ਪਚਾਸ,[੧] ਪੀਤਮ ਪਾਈ ਅਸਾਂ ਵਲ ਚਾਸ
ਹੁਣ ਸਾਨੂੰ ਸਭ ਜਗ ਦਿਸਦਾ ਲਾਸ

At the door he is violently seized. His bowl is broken and
his beads scattered. Who recognizes his deceit? The
grains of millet[13] are scattered on the path.

Picking up the millet grains, he puts them in his pouch.   20
He sits and looks intently at Hir. He discovers the fate
that is written there. Their eyes weep and engage with
each other like soldiers.

Hir's sister-in-law Sahti realizes what is going on, she
knows the secret pain they share. She too was truly
intoxicated with love, and added straw to the smoke.

Bullha, Sahti devised a trick.[14] She caused Hir of the Sials
to fight with the snake. The yogi came to cast his
spells. Both their desires were fulfilled.


### 123

Our beloved has come to our house.

Unity has created a wonderful uproar. The unstruck flute
plays its high notes. Now I have found royal Lahore.[1]

The false and the true within me have been consumed.
I have felt the blow of true love. I have found refuge
with the lord.

Now why reckon years and hours? I have got hold of an
intoxicating cup. I have forgotten my essence and
attributes.

Now what is the point of counting? The beloved has   5
looked[2] kindly upon me. Now the world looks dead[3]
to me.

ਹੁਣ ਅਸਾਨੂੰ ਆਸ ਦੀ ਫਾਸ, ਬੁੱਲੂ ਸ਼ਹੁ ਆਇਆ ਹਮਰੇ ਪਾਸ
ਸਾਈਂ ਪੁਜਾਈ ਸਾਡੀ ਆਸ

## ੧੨੪

ਮੇਰੇ ਨੌਸ਼ਹੁ ਦਾ ਕਿਤ ਮੇਲ

ਅਗਲੇ ਵੱਲ ਦੀ ਖ਼ਬਰ ਨਾ ਕੋਈ, ਰਹਿ ਕਿਤਾਬਾਂ ਫੋਲ

ਸੱਚੀਆਂ ਨੂੰ ਪਏ ਵੱਜਣ ਪੌਲੇ, ਝੂਠੀਆਂ ਕਰਨ ਕਲੋਲ

ਚੰਗ ਚੰਗੇਰੇ ਪਰੇ ਪਰੇਰੇ, ਅਸੀਂ ਆਈਆਂ ਸੀ ਅਟਭੋਲ

੫   ਬੁੱਲੂ ਸ਼ਾਹ ਜੇ ਬੋਲਾਂਗਾ, ਹੁਣ ਕੌਣ ਸੁਣੇ ਮੇਰੇ ਬੋਲ

## ੧੨੫

ਮੇਰੇ ਮਾਹੀ ਕਿਉਂ ਚਿਰ ਲਾਇਆ ਏ

ਕਹਿ ਬੁੱਲੂ ਹੁਣ ਪ੍ਰੇਮ ਕਹਾਣੇ, ਜਿਸ ਤਨ ਲਾਗੇ ਸੋ ਜਨ ਜਾਣੇ
ਅੰਦਰ ਝਿੜਕਾਂ ਬਾਹਰ ਤਾਅਨੇ, ਨੇਹੁੰ ਲਾ ਕੇ ਸੁਖ ਪਾਇਆ ਏ

ਨੈਟਾਂ ਕਾਰ ਰੋਵਣ ਦੀ ਪਕੜੀ, ਇਕ ਮਰਨਾਂ ਦੂਜਾ ਜਗ ਦੀ ਫਕੜੀ
ਬਿਰਹੋਂ ਜਿੰਦ ਅਵੱਲੀ ਜਕੜੀ, ਨੀ ਮੈਂ ਰੋ ਰੋ ਹਾਲ ਵੰਜਾਇਆ ਏ

Now we are ensnared by hope. Bullha, the lord has come
to our side. The lord has fulfilled our hope.

## 124

How precious my bridegroom is.

No clue as to what lies ahead can be gained from studying
books.

The true get beaten with slippers, while the false have a
merry time.

The comfortably off are far from the truth; we have come
without presuppositions.

Bullhe Shah, if I speak, who will listen to what I say?          5

## 125

My beloved, why have you taken so long?

Now tell the stories of love, Bullha. The body that has
experienced it is the one that knows. Rebukes at home
and reproaches outside are the comfort I have found
through falling in love.

My eyes have assumed the task of weeping. First there is
death, then there is the world's taunting. The pain of
love has gripped my unhappy heart. Oh, I have wept
and bewailed my condition.

ਅਸਾਂ ਪਿਆਲਾ ਉਹ ਤਹਿਕੀਕ ਕੀਆ, ਜੋ ਭਰਕੇ ਸ਼ਾਹ ਮਨਸੂਰ ਪੀਆ
ਉਹ ਪੀਆ ਨੇ ਤਾਜ ਮਿਅਰਾਜ ਦੀਆ, ਮੈਂ ਖੁਹ ਥੀਂ ਵੂਜ਼ੂ ਕਰਾਇਆ ਏ

੫  ਇਸ਼ਕ ਮੁਅੱਜ਼ਨ ਬਾਂਗ ਦਿਵਾਈ, ਸ਼ਹੁ ਰਾਵਟ ਦੀ ਗੱਲ ਸੁਣਾਈ
ਕਰ ਨੀਯਤ ਸਜਦੇ ਵਲ ਧਾਈ, ਨੀ ਮੈਂ ਮੂੰਹ ਮਹਿਰਾਬ ਲਗਾਇਆ ਏ

ਬੁੱਲ੍ਹਾ ਸ਼ਹੁ ਗੁਰ ਲਪਟ ਲਗਾਈਂ, ਰਸਤੇ ਮੋਂ ਸਭ ਬਣ ਠਣ ਆਈਂ
ਵੇਖਾਂ ਮੈਂ ਇਨਾਇਤ ਸਾਈਂ, ਜਿਸ ਮੈਨੂੰ ਸ਼ਹੁ ਮਿਲਾਇਆ ਏ

## ੧੨੬

ਮੈਂ ਉਡੀਕਾਂ ਕਰ ਰਹੀ, ਕਦੀ ਆ ਕਰ ਫੇਰਾ

ਮੈਂ ਜੋ ਤੈਨੂੰ ਆਖਿਆ, ਕੋਈ ਘੱਲ ਸੁਨੇਹੜਾ
ਚਸ਼ਮਾਂ ਸੇਜ ਵਿਛਾਇਆਂ, ਦਿਲ ਕੀਤਾ ਡੇਰਾ
ਤੂੰ ਲਟਕੇਂਦਾ ਆ ਵੜੇਂ, ਸ਼ਾਹ ਇਨਾਇਤ ਮੇਰਾ

ਉਹ ਅਜੇਹਾ ਕੌਣ ਹੈ, ਜਾ ਆਖੇ ਜਿਹੜਾ
ਮੈਂ ਵਿਚ ਕੀ ਤਕਸੀਰ ਹੈ, ਮੈਂ ਬਰਦਾ ਤੇਰਾ
ਤੈਂ ਬਾਝੋਂ ਮੇਰਾ ਕੌਣ ਹੈ, ਦਿਲ ਢਾ ਨਾ ਮੇਰਾ

ਦਸਤ ਕੰਗਣ ਬਾਹੀਂ ਚੁੜੀਆਂ, ਗਾਲ ਨੌਰੰਗ ਚੋਲਾ
ਮਾਹੀ ਮੈਨੂੰ ਕਰ ਗਿਆ, ਕੋਈ ਰਾਵਲ ਰੋਲਾ
ਜਲ ਬਲ ਆਹੀਂ ਮਾਰੀਆਂ, ਦਿਲ ਪੱਥਰ ਤੇਰਾ

We have fully investigated the cup that Shah Mansur[1]
    filled and drank from. The beloved gave me the crown
    of the ascension[2] and made me perform my ablution
    from the well.[3]
Love made the muezzin give the call to prayer.[4] He        5
    proclaimed the message of giving pleasure to the lord.
    Forming my intention, I went quickly to perform the
    prostration. Oh, I have turned my face toward the
    *mihrab*.
 Bullha, embrace the lord and master. On the way all the
    girls have dressed up. Let me see Shah Inayat, who has
    made me meet my lord.


## 126

I keep waiting, do come and visit me some time.
Remember what I said to you and send me a message. I
    have spread out my eyes as a bed for you, I have made
    my heart your lodging. Come on in with your swaying
    movement, my Shah Inayat.
Is there anyone who will go and tell you this message from
    me? "What fault is there in me? I am your slave. Who
    do I have besides you? Do not destroy my heart."
I have a bracelet on my wrist and bangles on my arms,[1] and
    I am wearing a tunic of many colors. The beloved has
    made me some sort of yogi. I am consumed and heave
    bitter sighs. Your heart is made of stone.

੫ ਕਿਆ ਤੇਰੀ ਮਾਂਗ ਸੰਧੂਰ ਭਰੀ, ਸੋਹੇ ਰਤੜਾ ਚੋਲਾ
ਪਈ ਸੀਮੀ ਵਾਂਗ ਮੈਂ ਕੂਕਦੀ, ਕਰ ਢੋਲਾ ਢੋਲਾ
ਅਟਗਿਟਵੀਆਂ ਸੂਲਾਂ ਪਾ ਲਿਆ, ਸੂਲਾਂ ਦਾ ਘੇਰਾ

ਮੈਂ ਜਾਤਾ ਦੁੱਖ ਘਰ ਆਪਣੇ, ਦੁੱਖ ਪਏ ਘਰ ਕਈਆਂ
ਜਿਹਾ ਸਿਰ ਸਿਰ ਭਾਂਬੜ ਭੜਕਿਆ, ਸਭ ਪਿਟਦੀਆਂ ਗਈਆਂ
ਹੁਣ ਆਣ ਪਈ ਸਿਰ ਆਪਣੇ, ਸਭ ਚੁੱਕ ਗਿਆ ਝੇੜਾ

ਜਿਹੜੀਆਂ ਸਾਹਵਰੇ ਮੁੱਤੀਆਂ, ਸੋਈ ਪੇਕੇ ਹੋਵਣ
ਸ਼ਹੁ ਜਿਨਾਂ ਤੇ ਮਾਇਲ ਏ, ਚੜੂ ਸੇਜੇ ਸੋਵਣ
ਜਿਸ ਘਰ ਕੌਂਤ ਨ ਬੋਲਿਆ, ਸੋਈ ਖ਼ਾਲੀ ਵਿਹੜਾ

ਮੈਂ ਢੂੰਡ ਸ਼ਹਿਰ ਸਭ ਭਾਲਿਆ, ਘੱਲਾਂ ਕਾਸਦ ਕਿਹੜਾ
ਹੁਣ ਚੜ੍ਹਿਆਂ ਡੋਲੀ ਪਰੇਮ ਦੀ, ਦਿਲ ਧੜਕੇ ਮੇਰਾ
ਦਿਲਦਾਰ ਮੁੰਹਮਦ ਆਰਬੀ, ਹੱਥ ਪਕੜੀਂ ਮੇਰਾ

ਪਹਿਲੀ ਪੌੜੀ ਉਤਰੀ, ਪੁਲ ਸਰਾਤੇ ਡੇਰਾ
ਹਾਜੀ ਲੋਕ ਮੱਕੇ ਨੂੰ ਜਾਵਣ, ਮੈਂ ਮੁਖ ਵੇਖਾਂ ਤੇਰਾ
ਆ ਇਨਾਇਤ ਕਾਦਰੀ, ਦਿਲ ਚਾਹੇ ਮੇਰਾ

੧੦ ਪਹਿਲੀ ਰਾਤ ਵਸਾਲ ਦੀ, ਦਿਲ ਖੌਂਢੇ ਮੇਰਾ
ਡੂੰਘੀ ਗੋਰ ਖਟੋਂਦਿਆਂ, ਹੋਇਆ ਲਹਦੋਂ ਤੇੜਾ
ਪਹਿਲਾ ਬੰਦ ਖੁਲੇਂਦਿਆਂ, ਮੂੰਹ ਕਾਅਬੇ ਮੇਰਾ

ਮਿਲੀ ਹੈ ਬਾਂਗ ਰਸੂਲ ਦੀ, ਫੁਲ ਖਿੜਿਆ ਮੇਰਾ
ਸਦਾ ਹੋਇਆ ਮੈਂ ਹਾਜ਼ਰੀ, ਹਾਂ ਹਾਜ਼ਰ ਤੇਰਾ
ਹਰ ਪਲ ਤੇਰੀ ਹਾਜ਼ਰੀ, ਇਹੋ ਸਜਦਾ ਮੇਰਾ

216

What is the parting in your hair marked with vermilion?     5
     Your red tunic looks good on you. I keep crying out
     like Sammi,[2] saying, "Oh, my beloved Dhola!" I have
     experienced innumerable torments. Those torments
     have enveloped me.

I thought it was just my home that suffered, but suffering
     has affected many people's houses. All those upon
     whose heads the flame of love blazed have gone away
     in mourning. Now it has come upon my head, and my
     quarrel with them is finished.

Those who were sent to their in-laws are back home.
     Those whom the lord favored have climbed into bed
     and sleep there. The courtyard of the house where the
     bridegroom has not spoken is empty.

I have searched the entire city. Who shall I send as my
     messenger? Now I have climbed into the palanquin
     of love, and my heart is beating. Oh my beloved
     Muhammad the Arabian, take hold of my hand.

I have gone down the first stair and am stationed on the
     Sirat bridge.[3] Hajjis go to Mecca,[4] but I gaze on your
     face. Come, Inayat Qadiri,[5] my heart desires you.

On the first night of being together,[6] my heart is full of     10
     fear. After the deep grave was dug, the tomb was split
     open. When the first tie of my winding sheet was
     undone, my face was turned toward the Kaaba.

I have heard the call of the Apostle, and I blossom like a
     flower. I am in permanent attendance upon you, and
     I am present before you. My permanent attendance
     upon you is my humble act of prostration.

ਬੁੱਲ੍ਹੁ ਭੜਕਟ ਸ਼ਹੁ ਲਈ, ਸੀਨੇ ਵਿਚ ਭਾਹੀਂ
ਔਖਾ ਪੈਡਾ ਪਰੇਮ ਦਾ, ਸੋ ਘਟਦਾ ਨਾਹੀਂ
ਪਏ ਰਾਹ ਵਿਚ ਬਾਘੇ ਚਿਤਰੇ, ਸਿਰ ਧਾੜੀਂ ਬੇੜ੍ਹਾ

## ੧੨੧

ਮੈਂ ਕਸੁੰਬੜਾ ਚੁਣ ਚੁਣ ਹਾਰੀ

ਏਸ ਕਸੁੰਭੇ ਦੇ ਕੰਡੇ ਭਲੇਰੇ, ਅੜ ਅੜ ਚੁਨਰੀ ਪਾੜੀ
ਏ ਕਸੁੰਭੇ ਦਾ ਹਾਕਮ ਕਰੜਾ, ਜ਼ਾਲਮ ਏ ਪਟਵਾਰੀ

ਏਸ ਕਸੁੰਭੇ ਦੇ ਚਾਰ ਮੁਕੱਦਮ, ਮਲਬਾ ਮੰਗਦੇ ਭਾਰੀ
ਹੋਰਨਾਂ ਚੁਗਿਆ ਫੂਹੀ ਫੂਹੀ, ਮੈਂ ਭਰ ਲਈ ਪਟਾਰੀ

ਚੁਗ ਚੁਗ ਕੇ ਮੈਂ ਢੇਰੀ ਕੀਤਾ, ਲੱਥੇ ਆਣ ਬਪਾਰੀ
ਔਖੀ ਘਾਟੀ ਮੁਸ਼ਕਿਲ ਪੈਡਾ, ਸਿਰ ਪਰ ਗਠੜੀ ਭਾਰੀ

੫   ਅਮਲਾਂ ਵਾਲੀਆਂ ਸਭ ਲੰਘ ਗਈਆਂ, ਰਹਿ ਗਈ ਔਗਣਹਾਰੀ
ਸਾਰੀ ਉਮਰਾ ਖੇਡ ਗਵਾਈ, ਉਜਕ ਬਾਜ਼ੀ ਹਾਰੀ

'ਅਲਸਤ' ਕਿਹਾ ਜਦ ਅੱਖੀਆਂ ਲਾਈਆਂ, ਹੁਣ ਕਿਉਂ ਯਾਰ ਵਿਸਾਰੀ
ਇੱਕੋ ਘਰ ਵਿਚ ਵਸਦੀਆਂ ਰਸਦੀਆਂ, ਹੁਣ ਕਿਉਂ ਰਹੀ ਨਿਆਰੀ

ਮੈਂ ਕਮੀਨ ਕੁਚੱਜੀ ਕੋਝੀ, ਬੇਗੁਣ ਕੋਟ ਵਿਚਾਰੀ
ਬੁੱਲ੍ਹਾ ਸ਼ਹੁ ਦੇ ਲਾਇਕ ਨਾਹੀਂ, ਸ਼ਾਹ ਇਨਾਇਤ ਤਾਰੀ

218

Bullha, fires of longing for the lord burn fiercely in my
breast. The journey of love is difficult, and it does not
get less so. There are tigers and leopards on the way,
and I am surrounded by bandits.

## 127

I have had enough of picking safflowers.[1]

This safflower has rather fine thorns. They keep catching
in my veil and tearing it. The master of this safflower
is harsh, and his accountant is cruel.

This safflower has four officers.[2] They demand a hefty
sum. The other girls[3] have picked very little. I have
filled my basket.

I have picked and picked, and have accumulated a pile.
The merchants have come to stay. The passage is
difficult and the way is hard. I have a heavy bundle on
my head.

The girls who have performed good deeds have all got          5
safely across. I am full of faults and am left here. My
whole life has been wasted in playing about. The game
is finally lost.

*Am I not your lord?*[4] he said, when he set his eyes on me.
Now why has the beloved forgotten me? We lived
happily together in the same house. Why have I now
been abandoned?

I am lowly, clumsy, and ugly. Who is going to think of me,
who am without any good qualities? Bullha, I am not
worthy of the lord. Shah Inayat has delivered me.

## ੧੨੮

ਮੈਂ ਕਿਉਂ ਕਰ ਜਾਵਾਂ ਕਾਅਬੇ ਨੂੰ, ਦਿਲ ਲੋਚੇ ਤਖ਼ਤ ਹਜ਼ਾਰੇ ਨੂੰ

ਲੋਕੀ ਸਜਦਾ ਕਾਅਬੇ ਨੂੰ ਕਰਦੇ, ਸਾਡਾ ਸਜਦਾ ਯਾਰ ਪਿਆਰੇ ਨੂੰ

ਔਗੁਣ ਵੇਖ ਨਾ ਭੁੱਲ ਮੀਆਂ ਰਾਂਝਾ, ਯਾਦ ਕਰੀਂ ਉਸ ਕਾਰੇ ਨੂੰ

ਮੈਂ ਮਨਤਾਰੂ ਤਰਨ ਨਾ ਜਾਣਾਂ, ਸ਼ਰਮ ਪਈ ਤੁੱਧ ਤਾਰੇ ਨੂੰ

੫ ਤੇਰਾ ਸਾਨੀ ਕੋਈ ਨਹੀਂ ਮਿਲਿਆ, ਢੂੰਡ ਲਿਆ ਜਗ ਸਾਰੇ ਨੂੰ

ਬੁੱਲ੍ਹੂ ਸ਼ਹੁ ਦੀ ਪ੍ਰੀਤ ਅਨੋਖੀ, ਤਾਰੇ ਔਗੁਣਹਾਰੇ ਨੂੰ


## ੧੨੯

ਮੈਂ ਗਾਲ ਓਥੇ ਦੀ ਕਰਦਾ ਹਾਂ, ਪਰ ਗਾਲ ਕਰਦਾ ਵੀ ਡਰਦਾ ਹਾਂ

ਨਾਲ ਤੁਹਾਂ ਦੇ ਲਾਰਾ ਲਾਇਆ, ਤੁਸੀਂ ਚਲੇ ਮੈਂ ਨਾਲੇ ਆਇਆ
ਏਥੇ ਬਰਦਾ ਚਾ ਬਣਾਇਆ, ਮੈਂ ਭਰਮ ਭੁਲਾਇਆ ਭਰਦਾ ਹਾਂ

ਹਾਕਮ ਨਾਲ ਹੈ ਖੇਲ ਅਸਾਡੀ, ਮੀਰੀ ਹੋ ਕੇ ਵੀ ਮੈਂ ਫਾਡੀ
ਧਰੀ ਧਰਾਈ ਪੂੰਜੀ ਤੁਹਾਡੀ, ਮੈਂ ਅਗਲਾ ਲੇਖਾ ਭਰਦਾ ਹਾਂ

ਦੇ ਪੂੰਜੀ ਮੂਰਖ ਝੁੰਝਲਾਇਆ, ਮਗਰ ਚੋਰਾਂ ਦੇ ਪੈੜਾ
ਚੋਰਾਂ ਦੀ ਮੈਂ ਪੈੜ ਲਿਆਇਆ, ਹਰ ਸ਼ਬ ਧਾੜੇ ਪੜਦਾ ਹਾਂ

## 128

Why should I go to the Kaaba?[1] My heart longs for Takht
   Hazara.

People prostrate themselves toward the Kaaba; my
   prostration is to my dear beloved.

Sir Ranjha, do not let the sight of my defects mislead you.
   Just remember your promise.

I am not a swimmer and do not know how to swim.[2] It
   is your responsibility to save me.

No one has ever encountered anyone like you, though          5
   they search the entire world.

Bullha, the lord's love is strange. He saves one who is full
   of faults.


## 129

I speak of that place. But even as I speak I am afraid.

You made a false promise to the souls, saying: "You go,
   and I will come too."[1] You made me a slave here.
   I was deluded and am paying for it.

I am playing with a stern despot. Even if I am the top
   player, I am placed bottom. All the money I have
   staked falls to you. I am settling a long-standing
   account.

Giving over the money, I was foolishly upset. I started
   tracking thieves. I tracked down the thieves, but I
   am robbed every night.

੫ ਨਾ ਨਾਲ ਮੇਰੇ ਉਹ ਰਚਦਾ ਏ, ਨਾ ਮਿੰਨਤ ਕੀਤੀ ਸਜਦਾ ਏ
ਜਾਂ ਮੁੜ ਬੈਠਾਂ ਤਾਂ ਭਜਦਾ ਏ, ਮੁੜ ਮਿੰਨਤ ਜ਼ਾਰੀ ਕਰਦਾ ਹਾਂ

ਕੀ ਸੁਖ ਪਾਇਆ ਮੈਂ ਆਣ ਇੱਥੇ, ਨਾ ਮੰਜ਼ਲ ਨਾ ਡੇਰੇ ਜਿੱਥੇ
ਘੰਟਾ ਕੁਝ ਸੁਟਾਵਾਂ ਕਿੱਥੇ, ਨਿਤ ਉਠ ਕਚਾਵੇ ਕੜਦਾ ਹਾਂ

ਬੁੱਲ੍ਹੇ ਸ਼ਹੁ ਬੇਅੰਤ ਡੂੰਘਾਈ, ਦੋ ਜਗ ਬੀਚ ਨਾ ਲਗਦੀ ਕਾਈ
ਪਾਰ ਉਰਾਰ ਦੀ ਖ਼ਬਰ ਨਾ ਕਾਈ, ਮੈਂ ਬੇ ਸਿਰ ਪੈਰੀਂ ਤਰਦਾ ਹਾਂ


੧੩੦
ਮੈਂ ਚੁਹੜੇਟੜੀ ਹਾਂ ਸੱਚੇ ਸਾਹਿਬ ਦੀ ਸਰਕਾਰੋਂ

ਧਿਆਨ ਕੀ ਛਜਲੀ ਗਿਆਨ ਕਾ ਝਾੜੂ, ਕਾਮ ਕ੍ਰੋਧ ਨਿਤ ਝਾੜੂੰ
ਮੈਂ ਚੁਹੜੇਟੜੀ ਹਾਂ ਸੱਚੇ ਸਾਹਿਬ ਦੀ ਸਰਕਾਰੋਂ

ਕਾਜ਼ੀ ਜਾਣੇ ਹਾਕਮ ਜਾਣੇ, ਫ਼ਾਰਗ ਖ਼ਤੀ ਬੇਗਾਰੋਂ
ਦਿਨੇ ਰਾਤ ਮੈਂ ਏਹੋ ਮੰਗਦੀ, ਦੂਰ ਨਾ ਕਰ ਦਰਬਾਰੋਂ

ਤੁੱਧ ਬਾਝੋਂ ਮੇਰਾ ਹੋਰ ਨਾ ਕੋਈ, ਕੈਂ ਵੱਲ ਕਰੂੰ ਪੁਕਾਰੋਂ
ਬੁੱਲ੍ਹਾ ਸ਼ਹੁ ਇਨਾਇਤ ਕਰਕੇ, ਬਖ਼ਰਾ ਮਿਲੇ ਦੀਦਾਰੋਂ

He does not make up with me. My entreaties have no                    5
    effect. When I return, he runs away. Then once again
    I entreat him piteously.
What joy have I found through coming here, where there
    is no stage or stopping place? Where should I ring the
    bell of departure? I keep tying the litter tightly on my
    camel.
Bullha, the depth of the lord is bottomless. There is no
    plumbing the gap between the two worlds. I have no
    clue about the near bank or the far one. I swim about
    helplessly.

## 130

I[1] am a poor sweeper girl from the establishment of the
    true lord.
With the fan of attention and the broom of knowledge
    I keep sweeping up lust and anger. I am a poor
    sweeper-girl from the establishment of the true lord.
The *qazi* knows, the governor knows, I have a certificate
    freeing me from forced labor. By day and night all I ask
    is this: "Do not send me away from this court."
I have no one else except for you. So to whom should I cry
    out, saying: "Bullha, may the lord graciously give me
    a chance to see him"?

## ੧੩੧

ਮੈਂ ਚੁਹਝੇਟੜੀ ਹਾਂ ਸੱਚੇ ਸਾਹਿਬ ਦੀ ਦਰਬਾਰੋਂ

ਪੈਰੋਂ ਨੰਗੀ ਸਿਰੋਂ ਝੰਡੋਲੀ, ਸਨੇਹਾ ਆਇਆ ਪਾਰੋਂ
ਤੜਬਰਾਟ ਕੁਝ ਬਟਦਾ ਨਾਹੀ, ਕੀ ਲੈਸਾਂ ਸੰਸਾਰੋਂ
ਪਕੜਾਂ ਫਜਲੀ ਹਿਰਸ ਉਡਾਵਾਂ, ਛੁੱਟਾਂ ਮਾਲਗੁਜ਼ਾਰੋਂ

ਹਿੰਦੂ ਤੁਰਕ ਨਾ ਹੁੰਦੇ ਐਸੇ, ਦੋ ਜਰਮੇ ਤ੍ਰੈ ਜਰਮੇ
ਹਰਾਮ ਹਲਾਲ ਪਛਾਤਾ ਨਾਹੀਂ, ਅਸੀਂ ਦੋਹਾਂ ਤੇ ਨਹੀਂ ਭਰਮੇ
ਗੁਰੂ ਪੀਰ ਪਰਖ ਅਸਾਂ ਨੂੰ, ਸਭਨਾਂ ਤੋਂ ਸਿਰ ਵਾਰੋਂ

ਖੁੰਡੀ ਮੁੰਡੀ ਦਾ ਬੋਹਲ ਬਹਾਇਆ, ਬਖ਼ਰਾ ਲਿਆ ਦੀਦਾਰੋਂ
ਝੁੰਡ ਮੁੱਖ ਪੀਆ ਤੋਂ ਲਾਹਿਆ, ਸ਼ਰਮ ਰਹੀ ਦਰਬਾਰੋਂ
ਬੁੱਲ੍ਹਾ ਸ਼ਾਹੁ ਦੇ ਹੋ ਕੇ ਰਹੀਏ, ਛੁੱਟ ਗਏ ਬੇਗਾਰੋਂ

## ੧੩੨

ਮੈਂ ਪਾ ਪੜ੍ਹਿਆਂ ਤੋਂ ਨਸਨਾਂ ਹਾਂ

ਕੋਈ ਮੁਨਸਿਫ਼ ਹੋ ਨਿਰਵਾਰੇ, ਤਾਂ ਮੈਂ ਦਸਨਾਂ ਹਾਂ
ਮੈਂ ਪਾ ਪੜ੍ਹਿਆਂ ਤੋਂ ਨਸਨਾਂ ਹਾਂ

ਆਲਮ ਫਾਜ਼ਲ ਮੇਰੇ ਭਾਈ, ਪਾ ਪੜ੍ਹਿਆਂ ਮੇਰੀ ਅਕਲ ਗਵਾਈ
ਦੇ ਇਸ਼ਕ ਦੇ ਹੁਲਾਰੇ, ਤਾਂ ਮੈਂ ਵਸਨਾ ਹਾਂ¹

## 131

I[1] am a poor sweeper girl from the court of the true lord.

With bare feet and unkempt hair, I have received a
message from the other side. It is no good my being
hasty.[2] What will I take from the world? If I take hold
of my fan and make greed fly away, I am exempted
from being taxed.

I am not a Hindu or a Turk.[3] I am not twice-born, nor am
I thrice-born.[4] I do not recognize pure and impure,
nor do I believe in either of these. My teacher[5] has
given me the power of discernment, and I am devoted
to everyone.

I have made a pile of grain[6] from my gleanings. I removed
the veil from the face of the beloved, preserving
modesty in the court. Bullha, if I am owned by the
lord, I am released from forced labor.


## 132

I flee from those who have studied a little bit.[1]

If someone discerning judges me, I tell him: "I flee from
those who have studied a little bit."

Learned scholars are my brothers; those who have studied
a little bit drive me mad. If I am transported by love,
I flourish.

## ੧੩੩

ਮੈਂ ਪਾਇਆ ਏ ਮੈਂ ਪਾਇਆ ਏ, ਤੈਂ ਆਪ ਸਰੂਪ ਵਟਾਇਆ ਏ

ਕਹੂੰ ਤੁਰਕ ਕਿਤਾਬਾਂ ਪੜ੍ਹਤੇ ਹੋ, ਕਹੂੰ ਭਗਤ ਹਿੰਦੂ ਜਪ ਕਰਤੇ ਹੋ
ਕਹੂੰ ਗੁੜੂ ਕੁੰਡੇ ਮੇਂ ਪੜ੍ਹਤੇ ਹੋ, ਹਰ ਘਰ ਘਰ ਲਾਡ ਲਡਾਇਆ ਏ

ਕਿਤੇ ਬੈਰੀ ਹੋ ਕਿਤੇ ਬੇਲੀ ਹੋ, ਕਿਤੇ ਆਪ ਗੁਰੂ ਕਿਤੇ ਚੇਲੀ ਹੋ
ਕਿਤੇ ਮਜਨੂੰ ਹੋ ਕਿਤੇ ਲੇਲੀ ਹੋ, ਹਰ ਘਟ ਘਟ ਬੀਚ ਸਮਾਇਆ ਏ

ਕਹੂੰ ਗ਼ਾਫ਼ਲ ਕਹੂੰ ਨਮਾਜ਼ੀ ਹੋ, ਕਹੂੰ ਮਿੰਬਰ ਤੇ ਬਹਿ ਵਾਅਜ਼ੀ ਹੋ
ਕਹੂੰ ਤੇਗ਼ ਬਹਾਦਰ ਗ਼ਾਜ਼ੀ ਹੋ, ਕਹੂੰ ਆਪਣਾ ਪੰਥ ਬਣਾਇਆ ਏ

੫  ਕਹੂੰ ਮਸਜਦ ਕਾ ਵਰਤਾਰਾ ਏ, ਕਹੂੰ ਬਣਿਆ ਠਾਕੁਰ ਦੁਆਰਾ ਏ
ਕਹੂੰ ਬੈਰਾਗੀ ਜਟ ਧਾਰਾ ਏ, ਕਹੂੰ ਸ਼ੇਖਨ ਬਣ ਬਣ ਆਇਆ ਏ

ਬੁੱਲ੍ਹਾ ਸ਼ਾਹ ਦਾ ਮੈਂ ਮੁਹਤਾਜ ਹੋਇਆ, ਮਹਾਰਾਜ ਮਿਲੇ ਮੇਰਾ ਕਾਜ ਹੋਇਆ
ਮੁਝੇ ਪੀਆ ਕਾ ਦਰਸ ਮਿਅਰਾਜ ਹੋਇਆ, ਲੱਗਾ ਇਸ਼ਕ ਤਾਂ ਏਹ ਗੁਣ
ਗਾਇਆ ਏ

## 133

I have found out, I have found out, that it is you who have
changed your form.

Here you are a Muslim and recite the scriptures. Here you
are a devout Hindu and repeat your muttered prayers.
Here you are plunged into a deep pit. You have
displayed your affection in every house.

Here you are an enemy, here you are a friend. Here you are
a guru, here you are a disciple. Here you are Majnun,
here you are Laila.[1] You are contained in every body.

Here you are careless, here you are punctilious in prayer.
Here you ascend the pulpit and preach a sermon. Here
you are Tegh Bahadur,[2] the warrior for faith. Here you
have created your own way.[3]

Here there is the business of the mosque. Here you have            5
become a Hindu temple. Here you are an ascetic
wearing matted locks. Here you have come as a female
Shaikh.[4]

Bullha, I need the lord. If I meet my sovereign, my task
is fulfilled. The sight of my beloved is my heavenly
ascension.[5] I have fallen in love, so I sing this praise
to him.

## ੧੩੪

ਮੈਂ ਪੁੱਛਾਂ ਸ਼ਹੁ ਦੀਆਂ ਵਾਟਾਂ ਨੀ, ਕੋਈ ਕਰੇ ਅਸਾਂ ਨਾਲ ਬਾਤਾਂ ਨੀ

ਭੁੱਲੇ ਰਹੇ ਨਾਮ ਨਾ ਜਪਿਆ, ਗ਼ਾਫਲਤ ਅੰਦਰ ਯਾਰ ਹੈ ਛਪਿਆ
ਉਹ ਸਿੱਧ ਪੁਰਖਾ ਤੇਰੇ ਅੰਦਰ ਵਸਿਆ, ਲਗੀਆਂ ਨਫ਼ਸ ਦੀਆਂ ਚਾਟਾਂ ਨੀ

ਜਪ ਲੈ ਨਾ ਹੋ ਭੋਲੀ ਭਾਲੀ, ਮਤ ਸਦੀਏਂ ਮੂੱਖ ਮੁਕਾਲੀ
ਉਲਟੀ ਪਰੇਮ ਨਗਰ ਦੀ ਚਾਲੀ, ਭੜਕਟ ਇਸ਼ਕ ਦੀਆਂ ਲਾਟਾਂ ਨੀ

ਭੋਲੀ ਨਾ ਹੋ ਹੋ ਸਿਆਣੀ, ਇਸ਼ਕ ਨੂਰ ਦਾ ਭਰ ਲੈ ਪਾਟੀ
ਇਸ ਦੁਨੀਆਂ ਦੀ ਛੋੜ ਕਹਾਣੀ, ਇਹ ਯਾਰ ਮਿਲਣ ਦੀਆਂ ਘਾਤਾਂ ਨੀ

੫  ਬੁੱਲੂ ਰੱਬ ਬਣਾ ਬੈਠੋਂ ਆਪੇ, ਤਦ ਦੁਨੀਆਂ ਦੇ ਪਏ ਸਿਆਪੇ
ਦੂਤੀ ਵਿਹੜਾ ਦੁਸ਼ਮਣ ਮਾਪੇ, ਸਭ ਕੜਕ ਪਈਆਂ ਆਫ਼ਾਤਾਂ ਨੀ

## ੧੩੫

ਮੈਂ ਬੇਕੈਦ ਮੈਂ ਬੇਕੈਦ, ਨਾ ਰੋਗੀ ਨਾ ਵੈਦ

ਨਾ ਮੈਂ ਮੋਮਨ ਨਾ ਮੈਂ ਕਾਫ਼ਰ, ਨਾ ਸੈਦੀ ਨਾ ਸੈਦ

ਚੌਪੀਂ ਤਬਕੀਂ ਸੈਰ ਅਸਾਡਾ, ਕਿਤੇ ਨਾ ਹੁੰਦਾ ਕੈਦ

ਖ਼ਰਾਬਾਤ ਮੇਂ ਜਾਲ ਅਸਾਡੀ, ਨਾ ਸ਼ੋਭਾ ਨਾ ਕੈਦ

## 134

I ask about the ways to the lord. I hope someone will speak
  to me.

You have been led astray and have not recited his name.
  Through your heedlessness, the beloved has been
  hidden. The divine being dwelled within you. You
  were seduced by the delights of the lower self.

Recite his name and do not be foolish. Otherwise you will
  be called disgraceful. The ways of the city of love are
  contrary. The flames of love are blazing.

Do not be foolish, be sensible. Be filled with the light of
  love. Abandon the tale of this world. These are the
  opportunities to meet the beloved.

Bullha, it was the lord who created you. Then the                 5
  sorrows of the world overtook you. My household is
  treacherous, my parents are my enemies. All these
  calamities have burst upon me.

## 135

I am without limit or restriction. I am not a patient, nor
  a doctor.

I am not a believer, nor an unbeliever. I am not the hunter,
  nor the prey.

I travel through the fourteen spheres[1] of the universe.
  I have no limits anywhere.

My life is passed in the tavern.[2] I am given no honor and
  no blame.

੫ ਬੁੱਲੂ ਸ਼ਹੁ ਦੀ ਜ਼ਾਤ ਕੀ ਪੁੱਛਨੈਂ, ਨਾ ਪੈਦਾ ਨਾ ਪੈਦ


## ੧੩੬

ਮੈਂ ਵਿਚ ਹਮੀਂ ਰਹੀ ਨਾ ਰਾਈ, ਜਬ ਕੀ ਤੁਮ ਸੰਗ ਪ੍ਰੀਤ ਲਗਾਈ

ਜਦ ਵਸਲ ਵਸਾਲ ਬਟਾਈਏਗਾ, ਤਦ ਗੁੰਗੇ ਦਾ ਗੁੜ ਖਾਈਏਗਾ
ਸਿਰ ਪੈਰ ਨਾ ਅਪਣਾ ਪਾਈਏਗਾ, ਮੈਂ ਇਹ ਹੋਰ ਨਾ ਕਿਸੇ ਬਟਾਈ

ਹੋਏ ਨੈਣ ਨੈਣਾਂ ਦੇ ਬਰਦੇ, ਦਰਸ਼ਨ ਸੈ ਕੋਹਾਂ ਤੋਂ ਕਰਦੇ
ਪਲ ਪਲ ਦੇੜਨ ਮਾਰੇ ਡਰ ਦੇ, ਤੈਂ ਕੋਈ ਲਾਲਚ ਘਤ ਭਰਮਾਈ

ਹੁਣ ਅਸਾਂ ਵਹਦਤ ਵਿਚ ਘਰ ਪਾਇਆ, ਵਾਸਾ ਹੈਰਤ ਦੇ ਸੰਖ ਲਾਹਿਆ
ਜੀਵਨ ਜੰਮਣ ਮਰਨ ਵੰਜਾਇਆ, ਆਪਣੀ ਸੁਧ ਬੁਧ ਰਹੀ ਨਾ ਕਾਈ

੫ ਮੈਂ ਜਾਤਾ ਸੀ ਇਸ਼ਕ ਸੁਖਾਲਾ, ਚਹੁੰ ਨਦੀਆਂ ਦਾ ਵਹਿਣ ਉਡਾਲਾ
ਕਦੀ ਤੇ ਅੰਗ ਭੜਕੇ ਕਦੀ ਪਾਲਾ, ਨਿਤ ਬਿਰਹੋਂ ਅੱਗ ਲਗਾਈ

ਡੋਂ ਡੋਂ ਇਸ਼ਕ ਨਕਾਰੇ ਵਜਦੇ, ਆਸ਼ਕ ਵੇਖ ਉੱਤੇ ਵਲ ਭਜਦੇ
ਤੜ ਤੜ ਤਿੜਕ ਗਏ ਲੜ ਲਜ ਦੇ, ਲਗ ਗਿਆ ਨੇਹੁੰ
    ਤਾਂ ਸ਼ਰਮ ਸਿਧਾਈ

ਪਿਆਰੇ ਬਸ ਕਰ ਬਹੁਤੀ ਹੋਈ, ਤੇਰਾ ਇਸ਼ਕ ਮੇਰੀ ਦਿਲਜੋਈ
ਤੈਂ ਬਿਨ ਮੇਰਾ ਸੱਕਾ ਨਾ ਕੋਈ, ਅੰਮਾਂ ਬਾਬਲ ਭੈਟ ਨਾ ਭਾਈ


230

Why do you ask what Bullha is like? He does not create,     5
    nor is he created.


## 136

Not the least bit of "I" is left in me, since I fell in love with
    you.
When I achieve union with you, it is like raw sugar that is
    eaten by the dumb.[1] I cannot find my own head and
    feet; no one else made this "I."[2]
Eyes became the slaves of eyes.[3] They behold you from a
    hundred leagues away. They run after you all the time
    in fear.[4] You have enticed them with great desire.
Now we have set up home in unity. My repose has been
    swallowed up by wonderment. I have eliminated life
    and birth and death. I am left with no consciousness
    or awareness.
I thought that love was easy, but it is as turbulent as a     5
    current fed by four rivers. Sometimes it erupts as fire,
    sometimes as ice. The blaze of separation rages all the
    time.
"Boom, boom" roll the drums of love. When they see it,
    the lovers run in that direction. The skirt of shame is
    torn to shreds. Once love is experienced, all sense of
    shame departs.
Enough, my dear, that is quite enough. My love for you
    is my comfort. Apart from you I have no family, no
    mother or father, no sister or brother.

ਕਦੀ ਜਾ ਅਸਮਾਨੀ ਬਹਿੰਦੇ ਹੋ, ਕਦੀ ਇਸ ਦਾ ਦੁਖ ਸਹਿੰਦੇ ਹੋ
ਕਦੀ ਪੀਰੇ ਮੁਗਾਂ ਬਣ ਬਹਿੰਦੇ ਹੋ, ਮੈਂ ਤਾਂ ਇਕਸੇ ਨਾਚ ਨਚਾਈ

ਤੇਰੇ ਹਿਜਰੇ ਵਿਚ ਮੇਰਾ ਹੁਜਰਾ ਏ, ਦੁਖ ਡਾਢਾ ਮੈਂ ਪਰ ਗੁਜ਼ਰਾ ਏ
ਕਦੇ ਹੋ ਮਾਇਲ ਮੇਰਾ ਮੁਜਰਾ ਏ, ਮੈਂ ਤੈਬੋਂ ਗੋਲ ਘੁਮਾਈ

੧੦  ਤੁਧ ਕਾਰਨ ਮੈਂ ਹਬਸੀ ਹੋਇਆ, ਨੌ ਦਰਵਾਜ਼ੇ ਬੰਦ ਕਰ ਸੋਇਆ
ਦਰ ਦਸਵੇਂ ਤੇ ਆਣ ਖਲੋਇਆ, ਕਦੇ ਮੰਨ ਮੇਰੀ ਅਸ਼ਨਾਈ

ਬੁੱਲ੍ਹਾ ਸ਼ਹੁ ਮੈਂ ਤੇਰੇ ਵਾਰੇ ਹਾਂ, ਮੁਖ ਵੇਖਣ ਦੇ ਵਟਜਾਰੇ ਹਾਂ
ਕੁਝ ਅਸੀਂ ਵੀ ਤੈਨੂੰ ਪਿਆਰੇ ਹਾਂ, ਕਿਹ ਮੈਂ ਐਵੇਂ ਘੋਲ ਘੁਮਾਈ


੧੩੭

ਮੈਂ ਵੈਸਾਂ ਜੋਗੀ ਦੇ ਨਾਲ ਨੀ, ਮੱਥੇ ਤਿਲਕ ਲਗਾ ਕੇ

ਮੈ ਵੈਸਾਂ ਨਾ ਰਹਿਸਾਂ ਹੋੜੇ, ਕੋਟ ਜਾਂਦੀ ਨੂੰ ਮੋੜੇ
ਮੈਨੂੰ ਮੁੜਨਾ ਹੋਇਆ ਮੁਹਾਲ ਨੀ, ਸਿਰ ਤੇ ਮਿਹਣਾ ਚਾ ਕੇ

ਜੋਗੀ ਨਹੀਂ ਇਹ ਦਿਲ ਦਾ ਮੀਤਾ, ਭੁੱਲ ਗਈ ਮੈਂ ਪਿਆਰ ਕਿਉਂ ਕੀਤਾ
ਮੈਨੂੰ ਰਹੀ ਨਾ ਕੱਝ ਸੰਭਾਲ ਨੀ, ਉਸ ਦਾ ਦਰਸ਼ਨ ਪਾ ਕੇ

ਏਸ ਜੋਗੀ ਮੈਨੂੰ ਕੇਹੀਆ ਲਾਈਆਂ, ਹਾਉਂ ਕਲੇਜੇ ਕੁੰਡੀਆਂ ਪਾਈਆਂ
ਇਸ਼ਕ ਦਾ ਪਾਇਓਸ ਜਾਲ ਨੀ, ਮਿੱਠੀ ਬਾਤ ਸੁਣਾ ਕੇ

੫  ਮੈਂ ਜੋਗੀ ਨੂੰ ਖ਼ੂਬ ਪਛਾਤਾ, ਲੋਕਾਂ ਮੈਨੂੰ ਕਮਲੀ ਜਾਤਾ
ਲੁਟਿਓ ਝੰਗ ਸਿਆਲ ਨੀ, ਕੰਨੀ ਮੁੰਦਰਾ ਪਾ ਕੇ

Sometimes you take your seat in the heavens, sometimes
you suffer this world's pain. Sometimes you sit as the
Magian elder.[5] You have made me dance to a single
tune.[6]

Separation from you is my cell. I have experienced great
suffering. Do be kind to me sometime, this is the
performance I offer you. I am a sacrifice to you.

For your sake I became a prisoner. I shut the nine doors[7]     10
and slept. You came and stood at the tenth door. Do
at some time acknowledge my love.

Bullha is devoted to you, lord. I am a trader whose
business is to see your face. Do you feel any affection
for me, or have I sacrificed myself for nothing?


### 137

I will go with the yogi, having put a mark on my forehead.[1]

I will go, I will not be stopped from leaving. Who is going
to turn me back as I go? It has become impossible
for me to turn back, now that I have experienced
reproaches for being in love.

He is not a yogi, but my heart's beloved. I have forgotten
why I fell in love. I lost all control, once I gained a sight
of him.

What did this yogi do to me? He put his hooks in my heart.
He cast the net of love when he uttered his sweet talk.

I recognized the yogi well. People thought me mad. You     5
looted Jhang[2] of the Sials when you put the earrings in
your ears.

ਜੇ ਜੋਗੀ ਘਰ ਆਵੇ ਮੇਰੇ, ਚੁਕ ਜਾਵਣ ਸਭ ਝਗੜੇ ਝੇੜੇ
ਲਾਵਾਂ ਸੀਨੇ ਨਾਲ ਨੀ, ਲਖ ਲਖ ਸ਼ਗਾਨ ਮਨਾ ਕੇ

ਮਾਏ ਨੀ ਇਕ ਜੋਗੀ ਆਇਆ, ਦਰ ਸਾਡੇ ਉਸ ਧੂਆਂ ਪਾਇਆ
ਮੰਗਦੈ ਹੀਰ ਸਿਆਲ ਨੀ, ਬੈਠਾ ਭੇਸ ਵਟਾ ਕੇ

ਤਾਅਨੇ ਨਾ ਦੇ ਫੁੱਠੀ ਤਾਈ, ਜੋਗੀ ਏਥੇ ਕਿਸਮਤ ਲਿਆਈ
ਹੁਣ ਹੋਇਆ ਫ਼ਜ਼ਲ ਕਮਾਲ ਨੀ, ਆਇਆ ਜੋਗ ਸੁਧਾ ਕੇ

ਮਾਹੀ ਨਹੀਂ ਕੋਈ ਨੂਰ ਇਲਾਹੀ, ਅਨਹਦ ਦੀ ਜਿਸ ਮੁਰਲੀ ਵਾਹੀ
ਮੁੱਠਿਓਸ ਹੀਰ ਸਿਆਲ ਨੀ, ਡਾਢੇ ਕਾਮਣ ਪਾ ਕੇ

੧੦  ਲੱਖਾਂ ਗਏ ਹਜ਼ਾਰਾਂ ਆਏ, ਉਸ ਦੇ ਭੇਤ ਕਿਸੇ ਨਾ ਪਾਏ
ਗੱਲਾਂ ਤਾ ਮੂਸਾ ਨਾਲ ਨੀ, ਪਰ ਕੋਹ ਤੁਰ ਚੜ੍ਹਾ ਕੇ

ਅਬਦੁਹ ਰਸੂਲ ਕਹਾਇਆ, ਵਿਚ ਮਿਅਰਾਜ ਬੁਰਾਕ ਮੰਗਾਇਆ
ਜਬਰਾਈਲ ਕਾਰਨ ਇਸਤਕਬਾਲ ਨੀ,੧ ਹੂਰਾਂ ਮੰਗਲ ਗਾ ਕੇ

ਏਸ ਜੋਗੀ ਦੇ ਸੁਟੇ ਅਖਾੜੇ, ਹਮਨ ਹੁਸੈਨ ਨਬੀ ਦੇ ਪਿਆਰੇ
ਮਾਰਿਓਸ ਵਿਚ ਜਦਾਲ ਨੀ, ਪਾਣੀ ਬਿਨ ਤਰਸਾ ਕੇ

ਏਸ ਜੋਗੀ ਦੀ ਸੁਣੈ ਕਹਾਣੀ, ਸੋਹਣੀ ਡੁੱਬੀ ਡੂੰਘੇ ਪਾਣੀ
ਫਿਰ ਗੁਲਿਆ ਮਹੀਂਵਾਲ ਨੀ, ਸਾਰਾ ਰਕਤ ਲੁਟਾ ਕੇ

ਡੋਲੀ ਲੈ ਚੱਲੇ ਨੇ ਖੇੜੇ, ਮੁੱਢ ਕਦੀਮੀ ਦੁਸ਼ਮਨ ਜਿਹੜੇ
ਰਾਂਝਾ ਤਾਂ ਹੋਇਆ ਨਾਲ ਨੀ, ਸਿਰ ਤੇ ਟੱਮਕ ਚਾ ਕੇ

If the yogi comes to my house, all my quarrels and troubles
are finished. May I hold him to my breast, having cast
the omens thousands of times.

Mother, a yogi has come. He has set up his fire[3] at our
door. He asks for Hir the Sial. He sits there having
altered his appearance.

Do not taunt him, aunts.[4] Fate has brought the yogi here.
Now divine grace has been perfectly shown. He has
come practicing yoga with a pure heart.

He is not my beloved herdsman, but some divine light.
He has played the unstruck music[5] on his flute. He
has ruined Hir the Sial, wreaking his powerful magic.

Millions have gone and thousands have come, but no one   10
has discovered his secret. He spoke with Moses after
he had made him climb Mount Sinai.[6]

*His slave*[7] was called the Apostle. At the time of his
ascension[8] he asked for Buraq, whom Jibrail led in
welcome. The houris sang joyful songs.

Hear about this yogi's arenas. He slew the Prophet's
darlings, Hasan and Husain,[9] in battle, depriving
them of water and making them thirst.

Hear the story of this yogi. Sohni[10] drowned in the deep
water. Then Mahinval was cast adrift after losing all
his goods.

The Kheras took me away in the bridal palanquin. They
were my old enemies from the beginning. Ranjha was
nearby, with the drum[11] on his head.

੧੫ ਜੋਗੀ ਨਹੀਂ ਕੋਈ ਜਾਦੂ ਸਾਇਆ, ਭਰ ਭਰ ਪਿਆਲਾ ਜ਼ੱਕ ਪਿਲਾਇਆ
ਮੈਂ ਪੀ ਪੀ ਹੋਈ ਨਿਹਾਲ ਨੀ, ਅੰਗ ਭਭੂਤ ਰਮਾ ਕੇ

ਜੋਗੀ ਨਾਲ ਕਰੌਂਦੇ ਝੇੜੇ, ਕੇਹੇ ਪਾ ਬੈਠੇ ਕਾਜ਼ੀ ਘੇਰੇ
ਵਿਚ ਕੈਦੋਂ ਪਾਈ ਮੁਕਾਲ ਨੀ, ਕੁੜਾ ਬਰਾ ਲਗਾ ਕੇ

ਬੁੱਲ੍ਹੂ ਮੈਂ ਜੋਗੀ ਨਾਲ ਵਿਆਹੀ, ਲੋਕਾਂ ਕਮਲਿਆਂ ਖ਼ਬਰ ਨਾ ਕਾਈ
ਮੈਂ ਜੋਗੀ ਦਾ ਮਾਲ ਨੀ, ਪੰਜੇ ਪੀਰ ਮਨਾ ਕੇ


੧੩੮
ਮੈਨੂੰ ਇਸ਼ਕ ਹੁਲਾਰੇ ਦੇਂਦਾ ਏ, ਮੂੰਹ ਚੜ੍ਹਿਆ ਯਾਰ ਭੁਲੇਂਦਾ ਏ

ਪੁੱਛਦਾ ਹੈਂ ਕੀ ਜ਼ਾਤ ਸਫ਼ਾਤ ਮੇਰੀ, ਉਹੋ ਆਦਮ ਵਾਲੀ ਜ਼ਾਤ ਮੇਰੀ
'ਨਹਨੁ ਅਕਰਬ' ਦੇ ਵਿਚ ਖ਼ਾਤ ਮੇਰੀ, ਵਿਚ ਰੱਬ ਦਾ ਸਿੱਰ ਝੁਲੇਂਦਾ ਏ

ਕਿਤੇ ਸ਼ੀਆ ਏ ਕਿਤੇ ਸੁੰਨੀ ਏ, ਕਿਤੇ ਜਟਾਧਾਰ ਕਿਤੇ ਮੁੰਨੀ ਏ
ਮੇਰੀ ਸਭ ਸੇ ਫ਼ਾਰਗ਼ ਕੁੰਨੀ ਏ, ਜੋ ਕਹਾਂ ਸੋ ਯਾਰ ਮਨੇਂਦਾ ਏ

ਬੁੱਲ੍ਹੂ ਦੂਰੋਂ ਚਲ ਕੇ ਆਇਆ ਜੀ, ਉਹਦੀ ਸੂਰਤ ਨੇ ਭਰਮਾਇਆ ਜੀ
ਓਸੇ ਪਾਕ ਜਮਾਲ ਵਿਖਾਇਆ ਜੀ, ਉਹ ਹਿਕ ਦਮ ਨਾ ਭੁਲੇਂਦਾ ਏ

236

He is not a yogi but some magic or shadow. He fills the       15
    cup of ecstasy and gives it to me to drink. I have kept
    drinking it and become ecstatic, smearing the yogi's
    ash on my limbs.

They dispute with the yogi. What entanglements the
    *qazi*[12] created. Kaido intervened with his slanders
    and false accusations.

Bullha, I am married to the yogi. These foolish people do
    not have the slightest idea. I belong to the yogi, after
    propitiating the Five Pirs.[13]

## 138

I am transported by love. The beloved I am always talking
    about is calling me.

Why do you ask my essence and attributes? I share the
    same essential being as Adam. *We are nearer*[1] is where
    I lie in wait. Within myself, the secret of the lord
    delights me.

Somewhere there is a Shia, somewhere there is a Sunni.
    Somewhere there is a yogi with matted locks,
    somewhere there is one whose head is shaved.
    My being[2] is free from them all. The lord agrees to
    whatever I say.

Bullha, he has come from far. His appearance has
    entranced me. He has revealed his pure beauty.
    He never misleads me.

੧੩੯

ਮੈਨੂੰ ਸੁਖ ਦਾ ਸੁਨੇਹੜਾ ਤੂੰ ਝਬ ਲਿਆਵੀਂ, ਵੇ ਪਾਂਧੀਆ ਹੋ

ਮੈਂ ਕੁਬੜੀ ਮੈਂ ਦੁਬੜੀ ਹੁਈ ਆਂ
ਮੇਰੇ ਸਭ ਦੁਖੜੇ ਬਤਲਾਵੀਂ, ਵੇ ਪਾਂਧੀਆ ਹੋ

ਖੁਲੀਆਂ ਲਿਟਾਂ ਗਲ ਦਸਤ ਪਰਾਂਦਾ
ਇਹ ਗਲ ਆਖ ਸੁਣਾਵੀਂ, ਵੇ ਪਾਂਧੀਆ ਹੋ

ਇਕ ਲਖ ਦੇਂਦੀ ਮੈਂ ਦੋ ਲਖ ਦੇਸਾਂ
ਮੈਨੂੰ ਪਿਆਰਾ ਆਣ ਮਿਲਾਵੀਂ, ਵੇ ਪਾਂਧੀਆ ਹੋ

੫     ਯਾਰਾਂ ਲਿਖ ਕਿਤਾਬਤ ਭੇਜੀ
ਕਿਤੇ ਗੋਸ਼ੇ ਬਹਿ ਸਮਝਾਵੀਂ, ਵੇ ਪਾਂਧੀਆ ਹੋ

ਬੁੱਲ੍ਹਾ ਸ਼ਹੁ ਦੀਆਂ ਮੁੜਨ ਮੁਹਾਰਾਂ
ਲਿਖ ਪੱਤੀਆਂ ਤੂੰ ਝਬ ਧਾਵੀਂ, ਵੇ ਪਾਂਧੀਆ ਹੋ

੧੪੦

ਮੈਨੂੰ ਕੀ ਹੋਇਆ, ਹੁਣ ਮੈਥੋਂ ਗਈ ਗਵਾਤੀ ਮੈਂ

ਮੈਨੂੰ ਕੀ ਹੋਇਆ, ਕਿਉਂ ਮੈਨੂੰ ਕਮਲੀ ਕਹਿੰਦੇ ਹੈਂ

ਮੈਂ ਵਿਚ ਵੇਖਾਂ ਤਾਂ ਮੈਂ ਨਹੀਂ ਹੁੰਦੀ, ਮੈਂ ਵਿਚ ਦਿਸਨਾ ਏਂ ਤੈਂ

ਸਿਰ ਤੋਂ ਪੈਰ ਤੀਕਰ ਵੀ ਤੂੰ ਹੈਂ, ਅੰਦਰ ਬਾਹਰ ਹੈਂ ਤੈਂ

੫     ਛੁੱਟ ਪਈ ਉਰਾਰੋਂ ਪਾਰੋਂ, ਨਾ ਬੇੜੀ ਨਾ ਨੈਂ

238

## 139

Quick, traveler, bring me a message of joy.

I am bent and bowed. Traveler, describe all my sufferings
to him.

My hair hangs loose, the ribbon is in my hand. Traveler,
tell him this.

I give you one lakh,[1] I will give you two lakhs. Traveler,
get my beloved to come to me.

I have written a letter to the beloved and sent it. Traveler, 5
sit somewhere private and go through it with him.

Bullha, may the lord turn back to me. Traveler, go quickly
with the letters I have written.

## 140

What has happened to me? The "I" in me is lost and gone.

What has happened to me? Why do they call me crazy?

When I look into myself, there is no "I." Only you can be
seen in me.

From head to foot, there is only you. You are inside and
outside.

I am free from the far bank and the near bank. There is no 5
boat, there is no river.[1]

ਮਨਸੂਰ ਪਿਆਰੇ ਕਿਹਾ 'ਅਨਲਹੱਕ', ਕਹੇ ਕਹਾਇਆ ਕੈਂ

ਬੁੱਲ੍ਹਾ ਸ਼ਹੁ ਉਸੇ ਦਾ ਆਸ਼ਕ, ਅਪਟਾ ਆਪ ਵੰਞਾਇਆ ਜੈਂ

## ੧੪੧

ਮੈਨੂੰ ਛੱਡ ਗਏ ਆਪ ਲੱਦ ਗਏ, ਮੈਂ ਵਿਚ ਕੀ ਤਕਸੀਰ

ਰਾਤੀਂ ਨੀਂਦ ਨਾ ਦਿਹੁੰ ਸੁਖ ਸੁੱਤੀ, ਅੱਖੀਂ ਪਲਟਿਆ ਨੀਰ

ਛਵ੍ਹੀਆਂ ਤੇ ਤਲਵਾਰਾਂ ਕੋਲੋਂ, ਇਸ਼ਕ ਦੇ ਤਿੱਖੇ ਤੀਰ

ਇਸ਼ਕੇ ਜੇਡ ਨਾ ਜ਼ਾਲਮ ਕੋਈ, ਇਹ ਜ਼ਹਿਮਤ ਬੇਪੀਰ

੫    ਇਕ ਪਲ ਸਾਇਤ ਆਰਾਮ ਨਾ ਆਵੇ, ਬੁਰੀ ਬਿਹੁੰ ਦੀ ਪੀੜ

ਬੁੱਲ੍ਹਾ ਸ਼ਹੁ ਜੇ ਕਰ ਇਨਾਇਤ, ਦੁੱਖ ਹੋਵਣ ਤਗਸੀਰ

## ੧੪੨

ਮੈਨੂੰ ਦਰਦ ਅਵੱਲੜੇ ਦੀ ਪੀੜ

ਆ ਮੀਆਂ ਰਾਂਝਾ ਦੇ ਦੇ ਨਜ਼ਾਰਾ, ਮੁਆਫ਼ ਕਰੀਂ ਤਕਸੀਰ

ਤਖ਼ਤ ਹਜ਼ਾਰਿਓਂ ਰਾਂਝਾ ਟੁਰਿਆ, ਹੀਰ ਨਿਮਾਣੀ ਦਾ ਪੀਰ

ਹੋਰਨਾਂ ਦੇ ਨੌਂਸ਼ਹੁ ਆਵੇ ਜਾਵੇ, ਕੀ ਬੁੱਲ੍ਹੇ ਵਿਚ ਤਕਸੀਰ

240

Dear Mansur said *I am God*.[2] But who was the one who
    made him say it?
Bullhe, the lord is the lover of those who have destroyed
    their selves.

### 141

He has left me, he has packed up and gone.[1] What fault is
    there in me?
I get no sleep at night or rest by day. Tears stream from my
    eyes.
The arrows of love are sharper than choppers or swords.
No tyrant is crueler than love. It is a vicious affliction.
I am not at ease for a moment or an instant. The pain of     5
    separation is bad.
Bullha, if the lord is gracious, my pains will be
    transformed.

### 142

I am suffering the pain of my mad grief.
Come, Sir Ranjha, grant me a sight of you. Forgive
    my faults.
Ranjha went from Takht Hazara, the master of poor Hir.
The other women's bridegrooms visit them. What fault
    is there in Bullha?

## ੧੪੨

ਰਹੁ ਰਹੁ ਵੇ ਇਸ਼ਕਾ ਮਾਰਿਆ ਈ, ਕਹੁ ਕਿਸ ਨੂੰ ਪਾਰ ਉਤਾਰਿਆ ਈ

ਆਦਮ ਕਟਕੋਂ ਮਨੂ ਕਰਾਇਆ, ਆਪੇ ਮਗਰ ਸ਼ੈਤਾਨ ਦੁੜਾਇਆ
ਕਢ ਬਹਿਸ਼ਤੋ ਜ਼ਿਮੀਂ ਰੁਲਾਇਆ, ਕੇਡ ਪਸਾਰ ਪਸਾਰਿਆ ਈ

ਈਸਾ ਨੂੰ ਬਿਨ ਬਾਪ ਜੰਮਾਇਆ, ਨੂਹੇ ਪਰ ਤੂਫ਼ਾਨ ਮੰਗਾਇਆ
ਨਾਲ ਪਿਊ ਦੇ ਪੁੱਤ ਲੜਾਇਆ, ਡੋਬ ਉਹਨਾਂ ਨੂੰ ਮਾਰਿਆ ਈ

ਮੂਸਾ ਨੂੰ ਕੋਹ ਤੂਰ ਚੜ੍ਹਾਇਓ, ਇਸਮਾਈਲ ਨੂੰ ਜ਼ਿਬ੍ਹਾ ਕਰਾਇਓ
ਯੂਨਸ ਮੱਛੀ ਤੋਂ ਨਿਗਲਾਇਓ, ਕੀ ਉਨ੍ਹਾਂ ਨੂੰ ਰੁਤਬੇ ਚਾੜ੍ਹਿਆ ਈ

੫  ਖ਼ਾਬ ਜ਼ੁਲੈਖ਼ਾ ਨੂੰ ਦਿਖਲਾਇਓ, ਯੁਸਫ਼ ਖੂਹ ਦੇ ਵਿਚ ਪਵਾਇਓ
ਭਾਈਆਂ ਨੂੰ ਇਲਜ਼ਾਮ ਦਿਵਾਇਓ, ਤਾਂ ਮਰਾਤਬ ਚਾੜ੍ਹਿਆ ਈ

ਭੱਠ ਸੁਲੇਮਾਂ ਤੋਂ ਝੁਕਾਇਓ, ਇਬਰਾਹੀਮ ਚਿਖ਼ਾ ਵਿਚ ਪਾਇਓ
ਸਾਬਰ ਦੇ ਤਨ ਕੀੜੇ ਪਾਇਓ, ਹਸਨ ਜ਼ਹਿਰ ਦੇ ਮਾਰਿਆ ਈ

ਮਨਸੂਰ ਨੂੰ ਚਾ ਸੂਲੀ ਦਿੱਤਾ, ਰਾਹਬ ਦਾ ਕਢਵਾਇਆ ਪਿੱਤਾ
ਜ਼ਕਰੀਆ ਸਿਰ ਕਲਵੱਤਰ ਦਿੱਤਾ, ਫੇਰ ਉਨ੍ਹਾਂ ਕੰਮ ਸਾਰਿਆ ਈ

ਸ਼ਾਹ ਸਰਮਦ ਦਾ ਗਲਾ ਕਟਾਇਓ, ਸ਼ਮਸ ਨੇ ਜਾਂ ਸੁਖ਼ਨ ਅਲਾਇਓ
'ਕੁਮ ਬਿਇਜ਼ਨੀ' ਆਪ ਕਹਾਇਓ, ਸਿਰ ਪੈਰੋਂ ਖੱਲ ਉਤਾਰਿਆ ਈ

## 143

Hey love, stop, stop. You have destroyed me. Tell me who
 you have delivered safely across.

You had Adam banned from the wheat;[1] it was you who
 set Satan running after him. You expelled him from
 paradise and made him wander over the earth. What
 a great display you put on!

You caused Jesus to be born without a father; you
 summoned the flood over Nuh.[2] You set the son
 quarreling with the father; you drowned and killed
 them.[3]

You made Moses climb Mount Sinai,[4] you had Ismail[5]
 slaughtered, you had Yunus[6] swallowed by the fish.
 What a rank you raised them to!

You made Zulaikha see her dream and had Yusuf[7] put          5
 down the well. You caused his brothers to be blamed,
 then raised them high in rank.

You made Sulaiman[8] stoke the furnace; you put Ibrahim[9]
 on the pyre. You put the worms in the body of Ayub
 the patient;[10] you gave Hasan[11] poison and killed him.

You put Mansur[12] on the gallows and had the gall bladder
 removed from the monk.[13] You sawed Zakariya's[14]
 head. So how did you take care of them?

You had Shah Sarmad's[15] throat cut. When Shams[16]
 uttered his famous words, it was you who made him
 say, *Arise by my permission.* You had his skin flayed
 from head to foot.

ਏਸ ਇਸ਼ਕ ਦੇ ਬੜੇ ਅਡੰਬਰ, ਇਸ਼ਕ ਨਾ ਛੁਪਦਾ ਬਾਹਰ ਅੰਦਰ
ਇਸ਼ਕ ਕੀਤਾ ਸ਼ਾਹ ਸ਼ਰਫ਼ ਕਲੰਦਰ, ਬਾਰਾਂ ਵਰ੍ਹੇ ਦਰਿਆ ਵਿਚ
    ਠਾਰਿਆ ਈ

੧੦ ਇਸ਼ਕ ਲੈਲਾ ਦੇ ਧੁੰਮਾਂ ਪਾਈਆਂ, ਤਾਂ ਮਜਨੂੰ ਨੇ ਅੱਖੀਆਂ ਲਾਈਆਂ
    ਉਹਨੂੰ ਧਾਰਾਂ ਇਸ਼ਕ ਚੁੰਘਾਈਆਂ, ਖੁਹੇ ਬਰਸ ਗੁਜ਼ਾਰਿਆ ਈ

ਇਸ਼ਕ ਹੋਰੀਂ ਹੀਰ ਵਲ ਧਾਏ, ਤਾਂ ਮੀਏਂ ਰਾਂਝੇ ਕੰਨ ਪੜਵਾਏ
ਸਾਹਿਬਾਂ ਨੂੰ ਜਦ ਵਿਆਹਵਟ ਆਏ, ਸਿਰ ਮਿਰਜ਼ੇ ਦਾ ਵਾਰਿਆ ਈ

ਸੱਸੀ ਚਾ ਥੱਲੀਂ ਰੁਲਾਇਓ, ਸੋਹਣੀ ਕੱਚੇ ਘੜੇ ਰੁੜ੍ਹਾਇਓ
ਰੋਡੇ ਦੇ ਸਿਰ ਗਿਲਾ ਜੋ ਆਇਓ, ਪੁਰਜ਼ੇ ਕਰ ਕਰ ਮਾਰਿਆ ਈ

ਢੋਜਾਂ ਕਤਲ ਕਰਾਈਆਂ ਭਾਈਆਂ, ਮਸ਼ਕਾਂ ਚੁਹਿਆਂ ਤੋਂ ਟੁਕਵਾਈਆਂ
ਡਿੱਠੀ ਕੁਦਰਤ ਤੇਰੀ ਸਾਈਆਂ, ਸਿਰ ਤੈਥੋਂ ਬਲਿਹਾਰਿਆ ਈ

ਕੋਰੇ ਪਾਂਡੇ ਕਰਨ ਲੜਾਇਆਂ, ਅਠਾਰਾਂ ਖੂਹਟੀਆਂ ਤਦੋਂ ਖਪਾਈਆਂ
ਮਾਰਨ ਭਾਈ ਸਕਿਆਂ ਭਾਈਆਂ, ਕੀ ਓਥੇ ਨਿਆਉਂ ਨਿਤਾਰਿਆ ਈ

੧੫ ਨਮਰੂਦ ਨੇ ਵੀ ਖੁਦਾਇ ਸਦਾਇਆ, ਉਸ ਨੇ ਰੱਬ ਨੂੰ ਤੀਰ ਚਲਾਇਆ
    ਮੱਛਰ ਤੋਂ ਉਸ ਨੂੰ ਮਰਵਾਇਆ, ਕਾਲੂੰ ਜ਼ਮੀਂ ਨਿਘਾਰਿਆ ਈ

ਫ਼ਿਰਔਨ ਨੇ ਜਦੋਂ ਖੁਦਾਇ ਕਹਾਇਆ, ਓਸੇ ਨਾਲ ਅਸ਼ਟੰਡ ਜਗਾਇਆ
ਨੀਲ ਨਦੀ ਦੇ ਵਿਚ ਡੁਬਾਇਆ, ਖੁਦੀਓ ਕਰ ਤੁਧ ਮਾਰਿਆ ਈ

ਲੰਕਾ ਚੜ੍ਹ ਕੇ ਨਾਦ ਬਜਾਇਓ, ਲੰਕਾ ਰਾਮ ਕੋਲੋਂ ਲੁਟਵਾਇਓ
ਹਰਨਾਕਸ਼ ਕਿਤਾ ਬਹਿਸ਼ਤ ਬਣਾਇਓ, ਉਹ ਵਿਚ ਦਰਵਾਜ਼ੇ ਮਾਰਿਆ ਈ

This love has put on great displays. Without or within,
    love is not hidden. When love made Shah Sharaf[17]
    a wandering dervish, you chilled him in the river for
    twelve years.

When Laila's[18] love was publicly proclaimed, Majnun      10
    locked eyes with her. You made him suck streams of
    love's milk when he spent a year in the well.

When love rushed toward Hir, Ranjha had his ears split.[19]
    Mirza[20] sacrificed his head when he arrived to marry
    Sahiban.

You made Sassi[21] wander in the deserts and cast Sohni[22]
    adrift on an unbaked pot. Later Roda's[23] reputation
    was ruined, and you cut him to pieces.

You had the brothers' armies[24] slaughtered and had the
    water skins chewed by rats.[25] I have seen your power,
    oh lord, and my head is sacrificed to you.

When the Kauravs and Pandavs[26] fought, you had
    eighteen great hosts destroyed. Brothers killed full
    brothers. What justice did you practice there?

Namrud[27] called himself God and fired an arrow at the      15
    lord. You caused Namrud to be killed by a mosquito
    and had Qarun[28] swallowed up by the earth.

When Pharaoh[29] called himself God, you made him put on
    a great show of pomp. You drowned him in the river
    Nile, where you slew him because of his arrogance.

You sounded the conch when attacking Lanka,[30] and you
    had Lanka plundered by Ram. You made Harnakash[31]
    create a stretch of paradise; you slew him at the gate.

ਸੀਤਾ ਦਹਿਸਰ ਲਈ ਬੇਚਾਰੀ, ਤਦ ਹਨੂਵੰਤ ਲੰਕਾ ਸਾੜੀ
ਰਾਵਣ ਦੀ ਸਭ ਢਾਹ ਅਟਾਰੀ, ਉੜਕ ਰਾਵਣ ਮਾਰਿਆ ਈ

ਗੋਪੀਆਂ ਨਾਲ ਕੀ ਚੱਜ ਕਮਾਇਓ, ਮੱਖਣ ਕਾਹਨ ਤੋਂ ਲੁਟਵਾਇਓ
ਰਾਜੇ ਕੰਸ ਨੂੰ ਪਕੜ ਮੰਗਾਇਓ, ਬੋਦੀਓਂ ਪਕੜ ਪਛਾੜਿਆ ਈ

੨੦   ਆਪੇ ਚਾ ਇਮਾਮ ਬਣਾਇਆ, ਉਸ ਦੇ ਨਾਲ ਯਜ਼ੀਦ ਲੜਾਇਆ
ਚੌਂਹੀਂ ਤਬਕੀਂ ਸ਼ੋਰ ਮਚਾਇਆ, ਸਿਰ ਨੇੜੇ ਤੇ ਚਾੜ੍ਹਿਆ ਈ

ਮੁਗ਼ਲਾਂ ਜ਼ਹਿਰ ਪਿਆਲੇ ਪੀਤੇ, ਭੂਰੀਆਂ ਵਾਲੇ ਰਾਜੇ ਕੀਤੇ
ਸਭ ਅਸ਼ਰਾਫ਼ ਫਿਰਨ ਚੁੱਪ ਕੀਤੇ, ਭਲਾ ਉਨ੍ਹਾਂ ਨੂੰ ਝਾੜਿਆ ਈ

ਬੁੱਲ੍ਹਾ ਸ਼ਾਹ ਫ਼ਕੀਰ ਵਿਚਾਰਾ, ਕਰ ਕਰ ਚੱਲਿਆ ਕੂਚ ਨਗਾਰਾ
ਰੋਸ਼ਨ ਜਗ ਵਿਚ ਨਾਮ ਹਮਾਰਾ, ਨੂਰੋਂ ਸਿਰਜ ਉਤਾਰਿਆ ਈ

# ੧੪੪

ਰਾਂਝਾ ਜੋਗੀੜਾ ਬਣ ਆਇਆ, ਵਾਹ ਵਾਹ ਸਾਂਗੀ ਸਾਂਗ ਰਚਾਇਆ

ਇਸ ਜੋਗੀ ਦੇ ਨੈਣ ਕਟੋਰੇ, ਬਾਜ਼ਾਂ ਵਾਂਗੂੰ ਲੈਂਦੇ ਡੋਰੇ
ਮੁਖ ਡਿਠਿਆਂ ਦੁਖ ਜਾਵਣ ਝੋਰੇ, ਇਨ੍ਹਾਂ ਅਖੀਆਂ ਲਾਲ ਲਖਾਇਆ।

ਏਸ ਜੋਗੀ ਦੀ ਕੀ ਨਿਸ਼ਾਨੀ, ਕੰਨ ਵਿਚ ਮੁੰਦਰਾਂ ਗਾਲ ਵਿਚ ਗਾਨੀ
ਸੂਰਤ ਇਸ ਦੀ ਯੂਸਫ਼ ਸਾਨੀ, ਇਸ ਅਲਫ਼ੋਂ ਅਹਦ ਬਣਾਇਆ

When Ravan the ten-headed abducted poor Sita,[32]
    Hanuman burned Lanka. Ravan was completely
    humiliated, and finally you killed him.
What tricks you performed with the Gopis.[33] You
    caused Krishna to steal the butter. You arrested and
    summoned Kans the king, seizing him by the topknot
    and throwing him down.
It was you who created the Imam[34] and made Yazid fight    20
    with him. Uproar broke out in the fourteen spheres,
    when you stuck his head upon a spear.
The Mughals drank cups of poison; you made men in
    rough blankets[35] into kings. The nobles all go about in
    silence; you have truly disgraced them.
Bullhe Shah is a poor fakir; he has departed, proclaiming
    to the sound of the drum: "Our name is glorious in the
    world; you have created us from light and saved us!"

## 144

Ranjha has come as a yogi. What a show the actor[1] has put
    on!
This yogi's eyes are goblets. They hunt like hawks. With
    the sight of his face, sorrows and worries disappear.
    These eyes have shown me something precious.
What is the mark of this yogi? He has rings in his ears and
    beads around his neck. In appearance he is a second
    Yusuf.[2] He has turned *alif* into Ahad.[3]

ਰਾਂਝਾ ਜੋਗੀ ਤੇ ਮੈਂ ਜੋਗਿਆਨੀ, ਇਸ ਦੀ ਖ਼ਾਤਰ ਭਰਸਾਂ ਪਾਣੀ
ਐਵੇਂ ਪਿਛਲੀ ਉਮਰ ਵਿਹਾਣੀ, ਏਸ ਹੁਣ ਮੈਨੂੰ ਭਰਮਾਇਆ

੫    ਬੁੱਲ੍ਹੂ ਸ਼ਹੁ ਦੀ ਇਹ ਗਤ ਪਾਏ, ਪ੍ਰੀਤ ਪੁਰਾਣੀ ਸ਼ੋਰ ਮਚਾਏ
ਇਹ ਗੱਲ ਕੀਕੁੰ ਛੁਪੇ ਛੁਪਾਏ, ਇਹ ਤਖ਼ਤ ਹਜ਼ਾਰਿਓਂ ਧਾਇਆ

## ੧੪੫

ਰਾਂਝਾ ਰਾਂਝਾ ਕਰਦੀ, ਹੁਣ ਮੈਂ ਆਪੇ ਰਾਂਝਾ ਹੋਈ
ਸੱਦੋ ਮੈਨੂੰ ਧੀਦੋ ਰਾਂਝਾ, ਹੀਰ ਨਾ ਆਖੋ ਕੋਈ

ਰਾਂਝਾ ਮੈਂ ਵਿਚ ਮੈਂ ਰਾਂਝੇ ਵਿਚ, ਹੋ ਖ਼ਿਆਲ ਨਾ ਕੋਈ
ਮੈਂ ਨਾਹੀਂ ਉਹ ਆਪੇ ਅਪਟੀ, ਆਪ ਕਰੇ ਦਿਲਜੋਈ

ਜੋ ਕੋਈ ਸਾਡੇ ਅੰਦਰ ਵੱਸੇ, ਜਾਤ ਅਸਾਡੀ ਸੋਈ
ਜਿਸ ਦੇ ਨਾਲ ਮੈਂ ਨੇਹੁੰ ਲਗਾਇਆ, ਓਹੋ ਜੇਹੀ ਹੋਈ

ਹੱਥ ਖੁੰਡੀ ਮੇਰੇ ਅੱਗੇ ਮੰਗੂ, ਮੋਢੇ ਭੂਰਾ ਲੋਈ
ਤਖ਼ਤ ਹਜ਼ਾਰੇ ਲੈ ਚੱਲ ਬੁੱਲ੍ਹਿਆ, ਸਿਆਲੀਂ ਮਿਲੇ ਨਾ ਢੋਈ

Ranjha is a yogi and I am his yogini. For his sake I will fetch
    water. I wasted my former life to no purpose. Now he
    has entranced me.

Bullha finds this ecstasy in the lord. Our love of long       5
    standing has created havoc. How can this be
    concealed? He has come here quickly from Takht
    Hazara.

## 145

Through[1] repeating "Ranjha, Ranjha," I have myself now
    become Ranjha. Call me Dhido[2] Ranjha, let no one call
    me Hir.

Ranjha is in me and I am in Ranjha, this is my only
    thought. There is no me, there is only him, and he is
    the one who shows tender care for himself.

Whoever dwells within us determines who we are. I have
    become just like the one I love.

With a staff in my hand I drive the buffaloes before me,
    wearing a rough blanket around my shoulders. Take
    me to Takht Hazara, Bullha, I can find no refuge with
    the Sials.

## ੧੪੬

ਰੈਣ ਗਈ ਲਟਕੇ ਸਭ ਤਾਰੇ, ਅਬ ਤੋ ਜਾਗ ਮੁਸਾਫ਼ਰ ਪਿਆਰੇ

ਆਵਾਗੋਂਟ ਸਰਾਈਂ ਡੇਰੇ, ਸਾਥ ਤਿਆਰ ਮੁਸਾਫ਼ਰ ਤੇਰੇ
ਅਜੇ ਨਾ ਸੁਣਿਓ ਕੂਚ ਨਕਾਰੇ

ਕਰ ਲੈ ਅਜ ਕਰਨੀ ਦੀ ਬੇਰਾ, ਬਹੁੜ ਨਾ ਹੋਸੀ ਆਵਣ ਤੇਰਾ
ਸਾਥੀ ਚੱਲੇ ਚੱਲ ਪੁਕਾਰੇ

ਕਿਆ ਸਰਧਨ ਕਿਆ ਨਿਰਧਨ ਪੌੜੇ, ਅਪਟੇ ਅਪਟੇ ਦੇਸ਼ ਕੋ ਦੌੜੇ
ਲਾਹਾ ਨਾਮ ਲੈ ਲਿਓ ਸੰਭਾਰੇ

੫   ਮੋਤੀ ਚੂਨੀ ਪਾਰਸ ਪਾਸੇ, ਪਾਸ ਸਮੁੰਦਰ ਮਰੋ ਪਿਆਸੇ
ਖੋਲ੍ਹ ਅੱਖੀਂ ਉੱਠ ਬਹੁ ਬਿਕਾਰੇ

ਬੁੱਲ੍ਹੂ ਸ਼ਹੁ ਦੀ ਪੈਰੀਂ ਪੜੀਏ, ਗ਼ਫ਼ਲਤ ਛਡ ਕੁਝ ਹੀਲਾ ਕਰੀਏ
ਮਿਰਗ ਜਤਨ ਬਿਨ ਖੇਤ ਉਜਾੜੇ

## ੧੪੭

ਰੋਜ਼ੇ ਹੱਜ ਨਮਾਜ਼ ਨੀ ਮਾਏ, ਮੈਨੂੰ ਪੀਆ ਨੇ ਆਣ ਭੁਲਾਏ

ਜਾਂ ਪੀਆ ਦੀਆਂ ਖ਼ਬਰਾਂ ਪਾਈਆਂ, ਮੱਤਕ ਨਹਵ ਸੱਭੇ ਭੁੱਲ ਗਈਆਂ
ਉਸ ਅਨਹਦ ਤਾਰ ਵਜਾਏ

## 146

The night is over, all the stars are dim. Now is the time to
    wake up, dear traveler.

You are encamped in the caravanserai of the cycle of birth
    and death. Your fellow travelers are ready. You have
    still not heard the departure drum.

Take action, for now is the time to act. You will not be
    coming here again. Your companions call out: "Come
    on, let us go."

Both rich and poor are weak. They have all run off to their
    own countries. Take the name as your profit, and
    guard it carefully.

Pearls and jewels and the philosopher's stone[1] are right     5
    next to you. The ocean is near, but you are dying of
    thirst.[2] Open your eyes and get up, you useless wretch.

Bullha, let us fall at the lord's feet. Let us abandon
    heedlessness and take active steps. If you make no
    effort, the deer[3] will wreck the field.

## 147

Fasts and pilgrimage and prayer, Mother, are all forgotten
    when my beloved comes.

When I got news of the beloved, I forgot all about logic
    and syntax. He played the unstruck music[1] on his
    string.

ਜਾਂ ਮੈਂ ਪੀਆ ਮੇਰੇ ਘਰ ਆਇਆ, ਭੁਲ ਗਿਆ ਮੈਨੂੰ ਸ਼ਰਹ ਵਕਾਇਆ
ਹਰ ਮਜ਼ਹਰ ਵਿਚ ਉਹਾ ਦਿਸਦਾ, ਅੰਦਰ ਬਾਹਰ ਜਲਵਾ ਜਿਸ ਦਾ ਲੋਕਾਂ
     ਖ਼ਬਰ ਨਾ ਕਾਏ

੧੪੮

'ਲਨ ਤਰਾਨੀ' ਦੱਸ ਕੇ ਜਾਨੀ, ਹੁਣ ਕਿਉਂ ਮੂੰਹ ਛੁਪਾਇਆ ਈ

ਮੈਂ ਢੋਲਣ ਵਿਚ ਫ਼ਰਕ ਨਾ ਕੋਈ, 'ਐਨ ਮਾ' ਫ਼ਰਮਾਇਆ ਈ
ਆਓ ਸਜਣ ਗਲ ਲੱਗ ਸਵਾਂ ਮੈਂ, ਹੁਣ ਕੀ ਘੁੰਗਟ ਪਾਇਆ ਈ

ਤਨ ਸਾਬਰ ਦੇ ਕੀੜੇ ਪਾਏ, ਜੋ ਝੜਿਆ ਸੋ ਪਾਇਆ ਈ
ਮਨਸੂਰ ਕੋਲੋਂ ਕੁਝ ਜ਼ਾਹਰ ਹੋਇਆ, ਸੂਲੀ ਪਕੜ ਚੜ੍ਹਾਇਆ ਈ

ਦੱਸੋ ਨੁਕਤਾ ਜ਼ਾਤ ਇਲਾਹੀ, ਸਜਦਾ ਕਿਸ ਕਰਾਇਆ ਈ
ਬੁੱਲ੍ਹਾ ਸ਼ਹੁ ਦਾ ਹੁਕਮ ਨਾ ਮੰਨਿਆ, ਸ਼ੈਤਾਨ ਖ਼ੁਆਰ ਕਰਾਇਆ ਈ

When the beloved came to my house, I forgot the
  *Commentary on the Wiqāya*.[2] In every scene, he alone
  appears, the one whose glory is inside and outside.
  People know nothing at all.

### 148

My love, you told me *You shall not see me*.[1] Now why have
  you hidden your face?
There is no difference between me and my beloved. You
  ordained *Wherever*.[2] Come, beloved, and let me sleep
  in your embrace. Why have you veiled yourself?
You put the worms in the body of Ayub the patient.[3] You
  put back any that dropped off him. Something was
  revealed by Mansur.[4] You had him arrested and put on
  the gallows.
Explain this point about the divine essence. Whom did
  you cause to prostrate themselves?[5] Bullha, when
  Satan[6] did not obey the lord's command, you brought
  about his disgrace.

## ੧੪੯

वत ना करसां माट रੁੱझੇटੇ यार दा वे अੜिआ

जान करां कुरबान भेत ना दसना ऐं वे अੜिआ
ਛੁੱडां तਕीਏ दुआर तੈनੂੰ ਉੱਠ नसना ऐं वे अੜिआ
रल मिल सਈआं ਪੁੱਫਟ गਈआं, ਹੋਇआ वਕਤ ਭੰडार दा
    वे अੜिआ

इਸ਼ਕ ਅੱला दी ज़ात लੋਕां दा ਮਿहਟਾ वे अੜिआ
ਕਿहनੂੰ करां पुਕार ਕਿसे नहीं रहਟਾ वे अੜिआ
ਓਸੇ दी गੱल ਉहੋ जाਣੇ, ਕੋਟ ਕੋਈ दम मारदा वे अੜिआ

ਅੱज ਅਜੋਕੜੀ रात मेरे घर वੱस खां वे अੜिआ
ਦਿल दीआं ਘੁੰਢੀਆं ਖੋਲੂ असां नाल हੱस खां वे अੜिआ
ਦਿलबर यार इकरार कीਤੋਈ, की इਤबार ਸੋहਣੇ यार दा
    वे अੜिआ

੫    इक करदीआं ਖੁਦी हੰकार ਉहनां नੂੰ ਤਾरना ऐं वे अੜिआ
इक ਪਿੱਛੇ ਫਿरन ਖ਼ੁआर सਖੀਆं नੂੰ साਜਨा ऐं वे अੜिआ
मੈਂडੇ ਸੋहਣੇ यार की इਤबार ਤੇरे ਪਿआर दा वे अੜिआ

ਚਿੱਕੜ भरीआं नाल ਉੱਠ ਭੁੰबर ਘੱਟना ऐं वे अੜिआ
मੈਂ लਾਇआ हार ਸ਼ਿੰगार मੈਬੋਂ ਉੱਠ नसना ऐं वे अੜिआ
ਬੁੱਲੂ ਸ਼हੁ घर ਆਇआ ਹੋਇआ वਕਤ दीदार दा वे अੜिआ

254

## 149

Never again will I boast about my beloved Ranjha, oh.[1]
I sacrifice my life, but you do not reveal your secret.

I search for you at the gate of the shrine, but you get
up and flee. My girlfriends have got together and have
gone to ask: "Is it time for the spinning party, oh?"

Love is the divine essence, but people reproach me for it.
To whom shall I cry out, when no one is going to stand
by me? He is the one who knows about himself; who
else dares open his mouth, oh?

Spend today, this very night, in my house. Undo the knots[2]
in your heart and laugh with me. You gave me your
promise, darling, but what trust can there be in my
beautiful beloved, oh?

Some are full of selfish pride, but you deliver them across.  5
Some follow you in disgrace, but you consume those
who are already consumed. My beautiful beloved,
what trust can there be in your love, oh?

You get up and join in the dance[3] with those who are
covered in mud. I am beautifully dressed, but you run
away from me. Bullha, the beloved has come to my
house, and the time when I see him is dear to me, oh.

१५०

ਵਲ ਪਰਦੇ ਵਿਚ ਪਾਇਆ ਯਾਰ, ਆਪੇ ਮੇਲ ਮਿਲਾਇਆ ਏ

ਹੁਣ ਮੈਂ ਮੋਈ ਨੀ ਮੇਰੀਏ ਮਾਂ, ਮੇਰੀ ਪੂਟੀ ਲੈ ਗਿਆ ਕਾਂ
ਪਿੰਡ ਡੋਂ ਡੋਂ ਕਰਦੀ ਜਾਂ, ਜਿਸ ਮੇਰਾ ਵਤਨ ਛੁਡਾਇਆ ਏ

ਕਾਂਵਾਂ ਪੂਟੀ ਦਈਂ ਪੀਆ ਦੇ ਨਾਂ, ਤੇਰੀਆਂ ਮਿੰਨਤਾਂ ਕਰਦੀ ਹਾਂ
ਜ਼ਰਬਾਂ ਤੇਰੀਆਂ ਜਰਨੀ ਹਾਂ, ਜਿਸ ਮੈਨੂੰ ਦੂਰ ਕਰਾਇਆ ਏ

ਹੁਣ ਮੈਨੂੰ ਭਲਾ ਨ ਲਗਦਾ ਸ਼ੋਰ, ਮੈਂ ਘਰ ਖਿੜਿਆ ਸ਼ਗੂਫ਼ਾ ਹੋਰ
ਬੇ ਨਾ ਤੇ ਨਾ ਸੇ ਨਾ ਹੋਰ, ਇੱਕੋ ਅਲਫ਼ ਪੜ੍ਹਾਇਆ ਏ

੫ ਹੁਣ ਮੈਨੂੰ ਮਜਨੂੰ ਆਖੇ ਨਾ, ਦਿਨ ਦਿਨ ਲੈਲਾ ਹੁੰਦਾ ਜਾਂ
ਡੇਰਾ ਯਾਰ ਬਟਾਏ ਤਾਂ, ਇਹ ਤਨ ਬੰਗਲਾ ਬਟਾਇਆ ਏ

ਬੁੱਲ੍ਹਾ ਇਨਾਇਤ ਕਰੇ ਹਜ਼ਾਰ, ਇਹੋ ਕੌਲ ਇਹੋ ਤਕਰਾਰ
ਵਲ ਪਰਦੇ ਵਿਚ ਪਾਇਆ ਯਾਰ, ਆਪੇ ਮੇਲ ਮਿਲਾਇਆ ਏ

१५१

ਵਾਹ ਸੋਹਣਿਆ ਤੇਰੀ ਚਾਲ ਅਜਾਇਬ, ਲਟਕਾਂ ਨਾਲ ਚਲੇਂਦੇ ਓ

ਆਪੇ ਜ਼ਾਹਰ ਆਪੇ ਬਾਤਨ, ਆਪੇ ਲੁਕ ਲੁਕ ਬਹਿੰਦੇ ਓ
ਆਪੇ ਮੁੱਲਾਂ ਆਪੇ ਕਾਜ਼ੀ, ਆਪੇ ਇਲਮ ਪੜ੍ਹੇਂਦੋ ਓ

## 150

My beloved set me behind a veil.[1] He is the one who has
    brought us together.

Oh Mother, now I am dead. The crow has taken away my
    cotton roll.[2] Then I create a loud noise over the one
    who made me leave my homeland.

Oh crow, give me my cotton roll in the name of the
    beloved, I entreat you. I suffer the blows given by you,
    who have set me at a distance.

Now I do not like all this noise. Another bud has
    blossomed in my house. He has not taught me *be* or *te*
    or *se* or anything else, only *alif*.[3]

Now do not call me Majnun,[4] when I am Laila every day.    5
    The beloved created this body of mine as a bungalow
    for him to stay in.

If Inayat creates thousands of Bullhas, all that they will say
    and all that they will repeat is this: "My beloved put
    me behind a veil. He is the one who has brought
    us together."

## 151

How wonderfully you move, beloved. Your movements are
    full of grace.

It is you who are manifest and you who are concealed. It
    is you who sit there after concealing yourself. It is you
    who are the mullah and you who are the *qazi*. It is you
    who impart instruction.

ਘੱਤ ਜੁੰਨਾਰ ਕੁਫਰ ਦਾ ਗਲ ਵਿਚ, ਬੁਤਖਾਨੇ ਵੜ ਬਹਿੰਦੇ ਓ
'ਲੌਲਾਕ ਲਮਾ ਅਫਲਾਕ' ਵਿਚਾਰੋ, ਆਪੇ ਪ੍ਰੇਮ ਮਚੌਂਦੇ ਓ

ਜਾਤ ਤੋਂ ਹੈ ਅਸ਼ਰਾਫ ਰੰਝੇਟਾ, ਲਾਇਆਂ ਦੀ ਲਾਜ ਰਖੰਦੇ ਓ
ਬੁੱਲ੍ਹੂ ਸ਼ਹੁ ਇਨਾਇਤ ਮੈਨੂੰ, ਪਲ ਪਲ ਦਰਸ਼ਨ ਦੇਂਦੇ ਓ

## ੧੫੨

ਵਾਹ ਵਾਹ ਛਿੜ ਪਈ ਦਰਬਾਰ, ਖਲਕ ਤਮਾਸ਼ੇ ਆਈ ਯਾਰ

ਅਸਾਂ ਅਜ ਕੀ ਕੀਤਾ ਕਲ ਕੀ ਕਰਨਾ, ਭੱਠ ਅਸਾਡਾ ਆਇਆ
ਐਸੀ ਵਾਹ ਕਿਆਰੀ ਬੀਜੀ, ਚਿੜੀਆਂ ਖੇਤ ਵੰਜਾਇਆ
ਜਿਹੜੇ ਮਗਰ ਪਿਆਦੇ ਲੱਗੇ, ਉਠ ਚੱਲੇ ਪੁਤਾ ਤਾਰ

ਇਕ ਉਲਾਮ੍ਹਾ ਸਈਆਂ ਦਾ ਹੈ, ਦੂਜਾ ਹੈ ਸੰਸਾਰ
ਨੰਗ ਨਾਮੂਸ ਏਥੋਂ ਦੇ ਏਥੇ, ਲਾਹ ਪਗੜੀ ਭੋਏਂ ਮਾਰ
ਨਾਮ ਸਾਈਂ ਦੇ ਕੰਢੇ ਬਵਾਏ, ਖਿਲ ਪਈ ਗੁਲਜ਼ਾਰ

ਨੱਢਾ ਗਿਰਦਾ ਬੁੱਢਾ ਗਿਰਦਾ, ਆਪੇ ਅਪਟੀ ਵਾਰੀ
ਕੀ ਬੀਵੀ ਕੀ ਬਾਂਦੀ ਲੌਂਡੀ, ਕੀ ਧੋਬਟ ਭਠਿਆਰੀ
ਅਮਲਾਂ ਸੇਤੀ ਹੋਣ ਨਬੇੜੇ, ਨਬੀ ਲੰਘਾਵੇ ਪਾਰ

258

You wrap the girdle[1] of unbelief around your neck. You
 go into the idol temple[2] and sit there. Think on *If
 it were not for you . . . the heavens*.[3] This is the loud
 message you proclaim.
Ranjha is noble by caste.[4] You protect those who seek
 protection from you. As Shah Inayat, you show
 yourself to Bullha all the time.


## 152

What a wonderful contest[1] there is at the court. People
 have come to the show, my friend.
What have we done today, and what must we do
 tomorrow? Our coming has been of no avail. What
 a wonderful flower bed was planted, but the birds have
 destroyed the field. The constables[2] who pursued us
 have gone off to pay in our taxes.
Not only do I have to endure the taunting of my
 girlfriends, but there is also the world. Worldly
 reputation belongs here. Take off your turban and
 throw it on the ground.[3] Since I planted thorns in
 the name of the lord, the garden has blossomed.
The youngster falls,[4] the old man falls, each in their
 turn. Mistress or handmaiden, washerwoman or
 innkeeper's wife, all have their fate decided according
 to their deeds. The Prophet delivers us.

੫    ਬੁੱਲ੍ਹਾ ਸ਼ਾਹ ਨੂੰ ਵੇਖਣ ਜਾਵੇ, ਅਪਣਾ ਭਾਣਾ ਕਰਦਾ
ਗੁਨੋ ਗੁਨੀ ਭਾਂਡੇ ਘੜ ਕੇ, ਠੀਕਰੀਆਂ ਕਰ ਧਰਦਾ
ਇਹ ਤਮਾਸ਼ਾ ਵੇਖ ਕੇ ਚਲ, ਤੇ ਅਗਲਾ ਵੇਖ ਬਜ਼ਾਰ

## ੧੫੩

ਵਾਹ ਵਾਹ ਮਾਟੀ ਦੀ ਗੁਲਜ਼ਾਰ, ਮਾਟੀ ਕੁਦਮ ਕਰੋਂਦੀ ਯਾਰ

ਮਾਟੀ ਜੋੜਾ ਮਾਟੀ ਘੋੜਾ, ਮਾਟੀ ਦਾ ਅਸਵਾਰ
ਮਾਟੀ ਮਾਟੀ ਨੂੰ ਦੌੜਾਏ, ਮਾਟੀ ਦਾ ਖੜਕਾਰ

ਮਾਟੀ ਮਾਟੀ ਨੂੰ ਮਾਰਨ ਲੱਗੀ, ਮਾਟੀ ਦੇ ਹਥਿਆਰ
ਜਿਸ ਮਾਟੀ ਪਰ ਬਹੁਤੀ ਮਾਟੀ, ਤਿਸ ਮਾਟੀ ਹੰਕਾਰ

ਮਾਟੀ ਬਾਗ਼ ਬਗ਼ੀਚਾ ਮਾਟੀ, ਮਾਟੀ ਦੀ ਗੁਲਜ਼ਾਰ
ਮਾਟੀ ਮਾਟੀ ਨੂੰ ਵੇਖਣ ਆਈ, ਮਾਟੀ ਦੀ ਏ ਬਹਾਰ

੫    ਹਸ ਖੇਡ ਮੁੜ ਮਾਟੀ ਹੋਈ, ਮਾਟੀ ਪਾਓ ਪਸਾਰ
ਬੁੱਲ੍ਹਾ ਇਹ ਬੁਝਾਰਤ ਬੁੱਝੋ, ਲਾਹ ਸਿਰੋਂ ਭੋਏਂ ਮਾਰ

Bullha goes to see the lord, according to his will.[5] He
    fashions pots of many kinds, then breaks them into
    pieces. Look at this show, then move on and look at
    the next bazaar.

## 153

This flower bed of earth is wonderful. Earth goes strutting
    along, my friend.
The costume is earth, the horse is earth, and the rider
    is earth. Earth drives earth along, and the clatter it
    makes is earth.
Earth starts to strike earth, using weapons of earth. The
    earth, which has plenty of earth on it, is proud.
The garden is earth, the orchard is earth, the flower bed
    is earth. Earth comes out to look at earth, this spring
    is made of earth.
After laughing and playing, it turns to earth, and earth
    stretches itself out. Bullha, if you guess this riddle,
    remove it[1] from your head and throw it on the ground.

੧੫੪

ਵਾਹ ਵਾਹ ਰਮਜ਼ ਸਜਣ ਦੀ ਹੋਰ, ਆਸ਼ਕ ਬਿਨਾਂ ਨਾ ਸਮਝੇ ਕੋਰ

ਕੋਠੇ ਤੇ ਚੜ੍ਹ ਦੇਵਾਂ ਹੋਕਾ, ਇਸ਼ਕ ਵਿਹਾਜ਼ਿਓ ਕੋਈ ਨਾ ਲੋਕਾ
ਇਸ ਦਾ ਮੂਲ ਨਾ ਖਾਟਾ ਧੋਖਾ, ਜੰਗਲ ਬਸਤੀ ਮਿਲੇ ਨਾ ਠੋਰ

ਆਸ਼ਕ ਦੋਹੀਂ ਜਹਾਨੀਂ ਮੁੱਠੇ, ਨਾਜ਼ ਮਾਸ਼ੂਕਾਂ ਦੇ ਉਹ ਕੁੱਠੇ
ਇਸ਼ਕ ਦਾ ਫੱਟਿਆ ਕੋਈ ਨਾ ਛੁੱਟੇ, ਕੀਤੇਸੁ ਬਾਂਦਾ ਫੱਟ ਬਲੋਰ

ਦੇ ਦੀਦਾਰ ਹੋਇਆ ਜਦ ਰਾਹੀ, ਅਚਣਚੇਤ ਪਈ ਗਲ ਫਾਹੀ
ਡਾਢੀ ਕੀਤੀ ਲਾਪਰਵਾਹੀ, ਮੈਨੂੰ ਮਿਲ ਗਿਆ ਠੱਗ ਲਹੋਰ

੫  ਸ਼ੀਰੀਂ ਹੈ ਬਿਰਹੋਂ ਦਾ ਖਾਣਾ, ਕੋਹ ਚੋਟੀ ਫ਼ਰਹਾਦ ਨਿਮਾਣਾ
ਯੂਸਫ਼ ਮਿਸਰ ਬਜ਼ਾਰ ਵਿਕਾਣਾ, ਉਸ ਨੂੰ ਨਾਹੀਂ ਵੇਖਣ ਕੋਰ

ਲੈਲਾ ਮਜਨੂੰ ਦੋਵੇਂ ਬਰਦੇ, ਸੋਹਣੀ ਡੁੱਬੀ ਵਿਚ ਬਹਰ ਦੇ
ਹੀਰ ਵੰਜਾਏ ਸੱਥੇ ਘਰ ਦੇ, ਇਸ ਦੀ ਛਿੱਕੀ ਮਾਹੀ ਡੋਰ

ਆਸ਼ਕ ਫਿਰਦੇ ਚੁੱਪ ਚੁਪਾਤੇ, ਜੈਸਾ ਮਸਤ ਸਦਾ ਮਧ ਮਾਤੇ
ਦਾਮ ਜ਼ੁਲਫ਼ ਦੇ ਅੰਦਰ ਫਾਥੇ, ਓਥੇ ਚੱਲੇ ਵੱਸ ਨਾ ਜ਼ੋਰ

ਜੇ ਉਹ ਆਣ ਮਿਲੇ ਦਿਲਜਾਨੀ, ਉਸ ਤੋਂ ਜਾਨ ਕਰਾਂ ਕੁਰਬਾਨੀ
ਸੂਰਤ ਦੇ ਵਿਚ ਯੂਸਫ਼ ਸਾਨੀ, ਆਲਮ ਦੇ ਵਿਚ ਜਿਸ ਦਾ ਸ਼ੋਰ

ਬੁੱਲ੍ਹਾ ਸ਼ਾਹੁ ਨੂੰ ਕੋਈ ਨਾ ਵੇਖੇ, ਜੋ ਵੇਖੇ ਸੋ ਕਿਸੇ ਨਾ ਲੇਖੇ ਏ
ਉੱਸ ਦਾ ਰੰਗ ਨਾ ਰੂਪ ਨਾ ਰੇਖ ਏ, ਉਹ ਈ ਹੋਵੇ ਹੋ ਕੇ ਚੋਰ

## 154

The hints that the beloved sends out are something
wonderfully different. Except for the lover, all are
blind and unable to understand them.

I climb up to the roof terrace and cry: Oh people, no one
should purchase love. Make sure you are not deceived
by it. No refuge from it can be found in the jungle or in
the village.

Lovers are destroyed in both worlds. They are slain by the
airs and graces of their beloveds. No one who has been
wounded by love is healed. It tears open wounds that
have been bound up.

He let me see him, then went on his way. Suddenly a
noose slipped around my neck. He displayed supreme
indifference. I encountered the robber from Lahore.[1]

Shirin suffered separation. Farhad[2] was in a sorry state on    5
the mountaintop. Yusuf[3] was sold in the bazaars of
Egypt. They were blind and did not see who he was.

Laila and Majnun[4] were both enslaved. Sohni[5] drowned in
the river. Hir destroyed her whole family. Her beloved
was pulling her string.

Lovers roam in silence. They are drunk, like those who
are always intoxicated with wine. Those caught in the
tress's curl have no strength or power to act.

If my beloved comes to me, I will sacrifice my life to him.
In appearance he is a second Yusuf,[6] because of whom
the whole world is in uproar.

Bullha, no one sees the lord. Those who do so can hardly
be counted. He has no color, form, or mark. He is the
one who exists as a thief.

१५५

ਵੇਖੋ ਨੀ ਸ਼ਹੁ ਇਨਾਇਤ ਸਾਈਂ, ਮੈਂ ਨਾਲ ਕਰਦਾ ਕਿਵੇਂ ਅਦਾਈਂ

ਕਦੀ ਆਵੇ ਕਦੀ ਆਵੇ ਨਾਹੀਂ, ਤਿਉਂ ਤਿਉਂ ਮੈਨੂੰ ਭੜਕਟ ਭਾਹੀਂ
ਨਾਮ ਅੱਲ੍ਹ ਪੈਗ਼ਾਮ ਸੁਣਾਈਂ, ਮੁਖ ਵੇਖਣ ਨੂੰ ਨਾ ਤਰਸਾਈਂ

ਬੁੱਲ੍ਹਾ ਸ਼ਹੁ ਕੇਹੀ ਲਾਈ ਮੈਨੂੰ, ਰਾਤ ਹਨੇਰ ਉੱਠ ਟੁਰਦੀ ਨੈਂ ਨੂੰ
ਜਿਸ ਉੱਝੜ ਤੋਂ ਸਭ ਕੋਈ ਡਰਦਾ, ਸੋ ਮੈਂ ਢੂੰਡਾਂ ਚਾਈਂ ਚਾਈਂ

१५६

ਵੇਖੋ ਨੀ ਕੀ ਕਰ ਗਿਆ ਮਾਹੀ, ਲੈ ਦੇ ਕੇ ਦਿਲ ਹੋ ਗਿਆ ਰਾਹੀ

ਅੰਮਾਂ ਝਿੜਕੇ ਬਾਬਲ ਮਾਰੇ, ਤਾਅਨੇ ਦੇਂਦੇ ਵੀਰ ਪਿਆਰੇ
ਮੈਂ ਜੇਹੀ ਬੁਰੀ ਬੁਰਿਆਰ ਵੇ ਲੋਕਾ, ਮੈਨੂੰ ਦਿਓ ਉਤੇ ਵੱਲ ਤੂਹੀ

ਆ ਬੂਹੇ ਤੇ ਨਾਦ ਵਜਾਇਆ, ਅਕਲ ਫ਼ਿਕਰ ਸਭ ਚਾ ਗਵਾਇਆ
ਅੱਲ੍ਹ ਦੀ ਸਹੁੰ ਅੱਲ੍ਹ ਜਾਣੇ, ਹਸਦਿਆਂ ਗਲ ਵਿਚ ਪੈ ਗਈ ਫਾਹੀ

ਰਹੁ ਇਸ਼ਕਾ ਕੀ ਕਰੇਂ ਅਖਾੜੇ, ਸ਼ਾਹ ਮਨਸੂਰ ਸੂਲੀ ਤੇ ਚਾੜ੍ਹੇ
ਆਣ ਬਟੀ ਜਦ ਨਾਲ ਅਸਾਡੇ, ਬੁੱਲ੍ਹੇ ਮੂੰਹ ਤੋਂ ਲੋਈ ਲਹੀ

੫  ਬੁੱਲ੍ਹੂ ਸ਼ਹੁ ਦੇ ਇਸ਼ਕ ਰੰਜਾਣੀ, ਡੰਗੀ ਆਂ ਮੈਂ ਕਿਸੇ ਨਾਂਗ ਇਞਾਣੀ
ਅੱਜ ਅਜੋਕੀ ਪ੍ਰੀਤ ਨਾ ਜਾਣੀ, ਲੱਗੀ ਰੋਜ਼ ਅਜ਼ਲ ਦੀ ਆਹੀ

## 155

See how my lord Shah Inayat flirts with me.
Sometimes he comes, sometimes he does not. And so I am
set ablaze. In the name of God, tell me your message.
Do not make me long to see your face.
Bullha, what has the lord done to me? In the dark of the
night I get up and go to the river.[1] In the wild country
that everyone fears, I seek him eagerly.

## 156

Just look and see what the beloved has gone and done.
After dealing in hearts, he has set off on his way.
My mother scolds me, my father beats me. My dear
brothers reproach me. Oh people, is there anyone so
bad and such an evildoer as I am? Chase me away in
the same direction.[1]
He came to the door and sounded his horn.[2] He has totally
destroyed reason and straight thinking. I swear
by God that God alone knows my condition. Our
merriment tied a noose around my neck.
Stop, love. Why do you set up these contests? You put
Lord Mansur[3] up on the gallows. When it happened to
me, Bullha lost all inhibition.[4]
Bullha, I am tormented by love. I am a poor wretch and     5
have been bitten by a snake.[5] This is not a love of this
moment. It started on the first day.

੧੫੭

ਵੇਖੋ ਨੀ ਪਿਆਰਾ ਮੈਨੂੰ ਸੁਫਨੇ ਮੇਂ ਛਲ ਗਿਆ

ਮੈਂ ਸੋਈ ਹੋਈ ਮੁੱਠੀ ਆਂ, ਮੈਂ ਵਾਂਗ ਜ਼ੁਲੈਖ਼ਾ ਕੁੱਠੀ ਆਂ
ਚਾ ਇਸ਼ਕ ਨੇ ਮੈਂ ਫੁੱਟੀ ਆਂ, ਮੇਰਾ ਬੰਦ ਬੰਦ ਹਲ ਗਿਆ

ਮੈਂ ਸਿਆਣੀਆਂ ਸਭ ਬੁਲਾਈਆਂ, ਮੈਂ ਔਸੀਆਂ ਸਭ ਪਵਾਈਆਂ
ਜਵਾਬ ਦਿੱਤਾ ਨਜ਼ੁਮਾਈਆਂ, ਮੇਰੀ ਨੈਟੀਂ ਨੀਰ ਉਛਲ ਗਿਆ

ਨੇੜੇ ਕਿਊਂ ਨਹੀਂ ਆਈਦਾ, ਸਾਨੂੰ ਦੂਰੋਂ ਨਹੀਂ ਦਿਖਲਾਈਦਾ
ਨੱਜ਼ਾਰੇ ਤੋਂ ਡਰਾਈਦਾ, ਕੋਹ ਤੁਰ ਪਹਾੜ ਜਲ ਗਿਆ

੫   ਪੀਆ ਨੇ ਨੈਟ ਬਾਟ ਲਾ ਕੇ, ਬਿਰਹੋਂ ਸੁੰ ਚੁਹਚੁਹਾ ਕੇ
    ਫ਼ਰਹਾਦ ਤੋਂ ਕੋਹ ਕਟਾ ਕੇ, ਸ਼ੀਰੀਂ ਸੁੰ ਰਲ ਗਿਆ

ਬੁੱਲ੍ਹੂ ਆਪ ਤੋਂ ਲਭਾਈਦਾ, ਸ਼ਹੁ ਇਨਾਇਤ ਹੈ ਪਾਈਦਾ
ਨੇੜੇ ਹੀ ਪਛਤਾਈਦਾ, ਬੁੱਲ੍ਹੂ ਅੱਜ ਸ਼ਹੁ ਮਿਲਿਆ ਗਿਆ

## 157

Look, my love has tricked me in a dream.

I slept and was deceived.[1] I have been slaughtered like
Zulaikha.[2] I have exploded with love. My body has
fallen apart.

I have called on the wise women and got them all to
draw figures.[3] The astrologers have given me a blunt
answer. My eyes are overflowing with tears.

Why should he not come near me? Why should he not
show himself from afar? Why should I be made to fear
a sight of him? Mount Sinai[4] is on fire.

My beloved shoots darts from his eyes, after steeping       5
me in the dye of separation. He gets Farhad[5] to cut
through the mountain before he is joined with Shirin.

Bullha, he lets himself be found. Shah Inayat is
discovered. Very soon I may be filled with regrets, but
today the lord has come to me.

*Other Poems*

# ਅਠਵਾਰਾ

## ਅ੧ ਸ਼ਨਿਚਰਵਾਰ

ਛਨਿਛਰ ਵਾਰ ਉਤਾਵਲੇ, ਵੇਖ ਸਜਣ ਦੀ ਸੋ
ਅਸਾਂ ਮੁੜ ਘਰ ਫੇਰ ਨਾ ਆਵਣਾ, ਜੋ ਹੋਟੀ ਹੋਗ ਸੋ ਹੋ
ਵਾਹ ਵਾਹ ਛਨਿਛਰਵਾਰ ਵਹੇਲੇ, ਦੁੱਖ ਸਜਣ ਦੇ ਮੈਂ ਵਲ ਪੇਲੇ
ਚੁੰਡਾਂ ਔਝੜ ਜੰਗਲ ਬੇਲੇ, ਅਧਰੀ ਰੈਣ ਕਵਲੜੇ ਵੇਲੇ
ਬਿਰਹੋਂ ਘੇਰੇ
ਕਿਹੜੇ ਟਾਂਗ ਤੁਸਾਡੀਆਂ ਤਾਂਘਾਂ, ਰਾਤੀਂ ਸੁਤੜੇ ਸ਼ੋਰ ਉਲਾਂਘਾਂ
ਉੱਚੀ ਚੜ੍ਹ ਕੇ ਕੂਕਾਂ ਚਾਂਘਾਂ, ਸੀਨੇ ਅੰਦਰ ਰਿੜਕਟ ਸਾਂਗਾਂ
ਪਿਆਰੇ ਤੇਰੀਆਂ

## ਅ੨ ਐਤਵਾਰ

ਐਤਵਾਰ ਸੁਣੈਤ ਹੈਂ, ਜੋ ਜੋ ਕਦਮ ਧਰੇ
ਉਹ ਵੀ ਆਸ਼ਕ ਨਾ ਕਹੋ, ਸਿਰ ਦੋਂਦਾ ਉਜ਼ਰ ਕਰੇ
ਸੋ ਆਇਤ ਐਤਵਾਰ ਭਾਇਤ, ਵਿੱਚੋਂ ਜਾਏ ਹਿਜਰ ਦੀ ਸਾਇਤ
ਮੇਰੇ ਦੁਖ ਦੀ ਸੁਣੈ ਹਿਕਾਇਤ, ਆ ਇਨਾਇਤ ਕਰੇ ਹਿਦਾਇਤ
ਤਾਂ ਮੈਂ ਤਾਰੀ ਆਂ
ਤੇਰੀ ਯਾਰੀ ਜਹੀ ਨਾ ਯਾਰੀ, ਤੇਰੇ ਪਕੜ ਵਿਛੋੜੇ ਮਾਰੀ
ਇਸ਼ਕ ਤੁਸਾਡਾ ਕਿਆਮਤ ਸਾਰੀ, ਤਾਂਹੀਂ ਹੋਈ ਆਂ ਵੇਦਨ ਭਾਰੀ
ਕਰ ਕੁਝ ਕਾਰੀਆਂ

270

# The Seven Days

## A1 SATURDAY

On Saturday, I am impatient to get news of my beloved.
I will not return home again, no matter what may
happen.

Ah, ah, Saturday is painful. Sufferings on account of my
beloved oppress me. I search the wilderness, the
jungle, and the thickets, in the middle of the night and
at bad times. I am beset by the pain of separation.

In my longing for you, it is as if I jump over sleeping tigers
in the night. I climb up high and shriek and scream.
Because of you, my love, spears churn in my breast.

## A2 SUNDAY

Sunday is a suitable time for whoever steps forward. Do
not call him a lover who excuses himself from offering
up his head.

Sunday is pleasing. The time of separation goes away. He
hears the story of my pain. If Inayat comes and gives
me guidance, I am saved.

There is no love like yours. Separation from you has seized
me and killed me. Your love is completely devastating,
and that is why I am filled with suffering. At least offer
me some remedy.

## ਅ੩ ਸੋਮਵਾਰ

ਬੁੱਲ੍ਹੂ ਰੋਜ਼ ਸੋਮਵਾਰ ਦੇ, ਕਿਆ ਚਲ ਚਲ ਕਰੇ ਪੁਕਾਰ

ਅਗੇ ਲਖ ਕਰੋੜ ਸਹੇਲੀਆਂ, ਮੈਂ ਕਿਸ ਦੀ ਪਾਟੀਹਾਰ

ਮੈਂ ਦੁਖਿਆਰੀ ਦੁੱਖ ਸਵਾਰ, ਰੋਟਾ ਅੱਖੀਆਂ ਦਾ ਰੁਜ਼ਗਾਰ

ਮੇਰੀ ਖ਼ਬਰ ਨਾ ਲੈਂਦਾ ਯਾਰ, ਹੁਣ ਮੈਂ ਜਾਤਾ ਮੁਰਦੇ ਮਾਰ

ਮੋਇਆਂ ਨੂੰ ਮਾਰਦਾ

ਮੇਰੀ ਉਸੇ ਨਾਲ ਲੜਾਈ, ਜਿਸ ਨੇ ਮੈਨੂੰ ਬਰਛੀ ਲਾਈ

ਸੀਨੇ ਅੰਦਰ ਭਾਹ ਭੜਕਾਈ, ਕਟ ਕਟ ਖਾਏ ਬਿਰੋਂ ਕਸਾਈ

ਭੜਕਾਇਆ ਯਾਰ ਦਾ

## ਅ੪ ਮੰਗਲਵਾਰ

ਮੰਗਲ ਮੈਂ ਗਾਲ ਪਾਟੀ ਆ ਗਿਆ, ਲਬਾਂ ਤੇ ਆਵਟਹਾਰ

ਮੈਂ ਘੁੰਮਟ ਘੇਰਾਂ ਘੇਰੀਆਂ, ਉਹ ਵੇਖੇ ਖਲਾ ਕਿਨਾਰ

ਮੰਗਲ ਬੰਦੀਵਾਨ ਦਿਲਾਂ ਦੇ, ਬੁੱਢੇ ਸ਼ਹੁ ਦਰਿਆਈਂ ਜਾਂਦੇ

ਕੱਪੜ ਕੜਕ ਦੁਪਹਿਰੀਂ ਖਾਂਦੇ, ਵਲ ਵਲ ਗੋਤਿਆਂ ਦੇ ਮੂੰਹ ਆਂਦੇ

ਮਾਰੇ ਯਾਰ ਦੇ

ਕੰਢੇ ਵੇਖ ਖਲਾ ਤਮਾਸ਼ਾ, ਸਾਡੀ ਮਰਗ ਉਹਨਾਂ ਦਾ ਹਾਸਾ

ਦਿਲ ਮੇਰੇ ਵਿਚ ਆਇਆ ਸੂ ਆਸਾ, ਵੇਖਾਂ ਦੇਸੀ ਕਦੋਂ ਦਿਲਾਸਾ

ਨਾਲ ਪਿਆਰ ਦੇ

## A3  MONDAY

Bullha, on Monday, what a cry of departure arises.
Thousands and millions of girls have preceded me.
What do I count for?[1]
I am grief-stricken and am overtaken by suffering.
Weeping is my eyes' daily occupation. The beloved
does not ask after me. Now I realize he is a corpse
slayer who kills those who are already dead.
My struggle is with the one who has speared me. Fire rages
in my breast. Separation is a butcher who cuts me up
and eats me. I am fed to my beloved.

## A4  TUESDAY

On Tuesday the water has come up to my neck; it is about
to come up to my lips. I am surrounded by whirlpools.
He stands on the bank and watches.
On Tuesday[2] the hearts are prisoners who drown in the
rivers of the lord. The shoals roar at midday, coming
toward the mouths of the divers, who are slain by the
beloved.
He stands on the bank and watches the spectacle. My
death is a joke to him. The hope of seeing him has
entered my heart. Let me see when he will comfort
me with love.

## ਅਪ  ਬੁੱਧਵਾਰ

ਬੁੱਧ ਸੁੱਧ ਰਹੀ ਮਹਿਬੂਬ ਦੀ, ਸੁੱਧ ਆਪਣੀ ਰਹੀ ਨਾ ਹੋਰ
ਮੈਂ ਬਲਿਹਾਰੀ ਉਸ ਦੇ, ਜੋ ਖਿਚਦਾ ਮੇਰੀ ਡੋਰ
ਬੁੱਧ ਸੁੱਧ ਆ ਗਿਆ ਬੁੱਧਵਾਰ, ਮੇਰੀ ਖ਼ਬਰ ਨਾ ਲਏ ਦਿਲਦਾਰ
ਸੁਖ ਦੁਖ ਤੋਂ ਘੱਤਾਂ ਵਾਰ, ਦੁੱਖਾਂ ਆਣ ਮਿਲਾਇਆ ਯਾਰ
ਪਿਆਰੇ ਤਾਰੀ ਆਂ
ਪਿਆਰੇ ਚੱਲਣ ਨ ਦੇਸਾਂ ਚਲਿਆ, ਲੈ ਕੇ ਨਾਲ ਜੁਲਫ਼ ਦੇ ਵਲਿਆ
ਉਹ ਚਲਿਆ ਤਾਂ ਮੈਂ ਛਲਿਆ, ਜਾਂ ਮੈਂ ਰਖਸਾਂ ਦਿਲ ਵਿਚ ਰਲਿਆ
ਲੈਸਾਂ ਵਾਰੀਆਂ

## ਅਓ  ਜੁਮੇਰਾਤ

ਜੁਮੇਰਾਤ ਸੁਹਾਵਣੀ, ਦੁੱਖ ਦਰਦ ਨਾ ਆਹਾ ਪਾਪ
ਉਹ ਜਾਮਾ ਸਾਡਾ ਪਹਿਨ ਕੇ, ਆਇਆ ਤਮਾਸ਼ੇ ਆਪ
ਅੱਗੋਂ ਆ ਗਈ ਜੁਮੇਰਾਤ, ਸ਼ਰਾਬੋਂ ਗਾਗਰ ਮਿਲੀ ਬਰਾਤ
ਲਗ ਗਿਆ ਮਸਤ ਪਿਆਲਾ ਹਾਥ, ਮੈਨੂੰ ਭੁਲ ਗਈ ਜ਼ਾਤ ਸਫ਼ਾਤ
ਦੀਵਾਨੀ ਹੋ ਰਹੀ
ਐਸੀ ਜ਼ਹਿਮਤ ਲੋਕ ਨਾ ਪਾਵਟ, ਮੁੱਲਾਂ ਘੋਲ ਤਵੀਜ਼ ਪਿਲਾਵਟ
ਪੜ੍ਹਨ ਅਜ਼ੀਮਤ ਜਿੰਨ ਬੁਲਾਵਟ, ਸਈਆਂ ਸ਼ਾਹ ਮਦਾਰ ਖਿਡਾਵਟ
ਮੈਂ ਚੁਪ ਹੋ ਰਹੀ

## A5  WEDNESDAY

On Wednesday I was left aware only of the beloved, with
    no consciousness of myself. He tugs my string, and I
    am devoted to him.

Wednesday has brought awareness.[3] My beloved takes no
    notice of me. I sacrifice my happiness for suffering.
    My beloved has come and united me with grief. I am
    saved by my beloved.

I will not let my beloved depart. May he take me and
    ensnare me in his tresses. If he leaves I am deceived,
    but I will still keep him close in my heart. I will
    sacrifice myself to him.

## A6  THURSDAY

Thursday is pleasant. There is no pain or suffering, no
    sighs or sin. He dresses himself as us and comes
    himself to watch the spectacle.

Thursday has come upon me. The wedding procession has
    come with flagons of wine. I am drunk with the cup in
    my hand. I have forgotten essence and attributes. I am
    crazy.

People should not trouble me. Mullahs prepare charms for
    me to drink. They recite spells and invoke jinns. My
    friends make Shah Madar[4] play. I am silent.

## ੧ ਜੁਮਾਂ

ਰੋਜ਼ ਜੁਮੇ ਦੇ ਬਖ਼ਸ਼ੀਆਂ, ਮੈਂ ਜਹੀਆਂ ਔਗਟਹਾਰ

ਫਿਰ ਉਹ ਕਿਉਂ ਨ ਬਖ਼ਸ਼ਸੀ, ਜਿਹੜੀ ਪੰਜ ਮੁਕੀਮ ਗੁਜ਼ਾਰ

ਜੁਮੇ ਦੀ ਹੋਰੋ ਹੋਰ ਬਹਾਰ, ਹੁਣ ਮੈਂ ਜਾਤਾ ਸਹੀ ਸਤਾਰ

ਬੀਬੀ ਬਾਂਦੀ ਬੇੜਾ ਪਾਰ, ਸਿਰ ਤੇ ਕਦਮ ਧਰੇਂਦਾ ਯਾਰ

ਸੁਹਾਗਣ ਹੋ ਰਹੀ

ਆਸ਼ਕ ਹੋ ਹੋ ਗੱਲਾਂ ਦੱਸੋਂ, ਛੋੜ ਮਸ਼ੂਕਾਂ ਕੈਂ ਵਲ ਨੱਸੇ

ਬੁੱਲ੍ਹਾ ਸ਼ਹੁ ਅਸਾਡੇ ਵੱਸੋਂ, ਨਿਤ ਉਠ ਖੇਡੇ ਨਾਲੇ ਹੱਸੋਂ

ਗਾਲ ਲਗਾ ਸੋ ਰਹੀ

276

## A7 FRIDAY

On Friday sinners like me are forgiven. So why should
forgiveness not be granted to those who recite all five
prayers?

Friday brings a special delight.[5] Now I have truly known
the pardoner. Whether mistress or maid, the whole
boatload is safely across. When the beloved puts his
foot on my head, I am a happily married bride.

You become our lover and tell us many things. To whom
will you flee after leaving those who love you? Bullha,
you dwell with us, lord. You always get up to play and
joke with us. I embrace you.

# ਬਾਰਾਂ ਮਾਹ

## ੫੧  ਅੱਸੂ

ਅੱਸੂ ਲਿਖੂੰ ਸੰਦੇਸਵਾ, ਮਤ ਵਾਚੇ ਮੇਰਾ ਪੀ
ਰਾਮਨ ਕੀਆ ਤੁਮ ਕਾਹੇ ਕੋ, ਜੋ ਕਲਮਲ ਆਇਆ ਜੀ
ਅੱਸੂ ਅਸਾਂ ਤੁਸਾਡੀ ਆਸ, ਸਾਡੀ ਜਿੰਦ ਤੁਸਾਡੇ ਪਾਸ
ਜਿਗਰੇ ਮੁੱਢ ਪਰੇਮ ਦੀ ਲਾਸ, ਦੁੱਖਾਂ ਹੱਡ ਸੁਕਾਏ ਮਾਸ
ਸੂਲਾਂ ਸਾੜੀਂ ਆਂ
ਸੂਲਾਂ ਸਾੜੀ ਰਹੀ ਬੇਹਾਲ, ਮੁੱਠੀ ਤਦੋਂ ਨਾ ਗਈਆਂ ਨਾਲ
ਉਲਟੀ ਪਰੇਮ ਨਗਰ ਦੀ ਚਾਲ, ਬੁੱਲ੍ਹੂ ਸ਼ਹੁ ਦੀ ਕਰਮਾਂ ਭਾਲ
ਪਿਆਰੇ ਮਾਰੀ ਆਂ

# The Twelve Months

## B1  ASSU (SEPTEMBER–OCTOBER)

In Assu I will write a message; perhaps my beloved will
    read it. Why did you set out when I was restless to see
    you?

In Assu my hope is in you, and my heart is in your
    keeping. The core of my heart bears the marks of love.
    From the beginning it has been scarred by love. My
    sufferings have consumed my flesh and bones. I am
    destroyed by pains.

Destroyed by pains, I am beside myself. I was ruined when
    I did not go with you. The ways of the city of love are
    perverse. Bullha, I will search for the lord. I am slain
    by the beloved.

## ੮੨  ਕਤਕ

ਕਹੋ ਕਤਕ ਕੈਸੀ, ਜੋ ਬਟਿਓ ਕਠਨ ਸੋ ਭੇਗ
ਸੀਸ ਕਪਰ ਹਥ ਜੋੜ ਕੇ, ਮਾਂਗੋ ਭੀਖ ਸੰਜੋਗ
ਕਤਕ ਗਿਆ ਤੁੰਬਟ ਕੱਟਣ, ਲੱਗੀ ਚਾਟ ਤਾਂ ਹੋਈ ਅੱਟਣ
ਦਰ ਦਰ ਲੱਗੀ ਧੁੰਮਾਂ ਘੱਟਣ, ਔਖੀ ਘਾਟ ਪੁਚਾਏ ਪੱਟਣ
ਸ਼ਾਮ ਦੇ ਵਾਸਤੇ
ਹੁਣ ਮੈਂ ਮੋਈ ਬੇਦਰਦਾ ਲੇਕਾ, ਕੋਈ ਦਿਓ ਉੱਚੀ ਚੜ੍ਹ ਹੋਕਾ
ਮੇਰਾ ਉਨ ਸੰਗ ਨੇਹੁੰ ਚਿਰੋਕਾ, ਬੁੱਲ੍ਹ ਸ਼ਹੁ ਬਿਨ ਜੀਵਨ ਔਖਾ
ਜਾਂਦਾ ਪਾਸ ਤੇ

## ੮੩  ਮੱਘਰ

ਮੱਘਰ ਮੈਂ ਘਰ ਰਹੀਆਂ ਸੋਧ ਕੇ, ਸਭ ਉੱਚੇ ਨੀਚੇ ਵੇਖ
ਪੜ੍ਹ ਪੰਡਤ ਪੋਥੀ ਭਾਲ ਰਹੇ, ਹਰਿ ਹਰਿ ਸੇ ਰਹੇ ਅਲੇਖ
ਮੱਘਰ ਮੈਂ ਘਰ ਕਿੱਧਰ ਜਾਂਦਾ, ਰਾਕਸ਼ ਨੇਹੁੰ ਹੱਡਾਂ ਨੂੰ ਖਾਂਦਾ
ਸੜ ਸੜ ਜੀਆ ਪਿਆ ਕੁਰਲਾਂਦਾ, ਆਵੇ ਲਾਲ ਕਿਸੇ ਦਾ ਆਂਦਾ
ਬਾਂਦੀ ਹੋ ਰਹਾਂ
ਜੋ ਕੋਈ ਸਾਨੂੰ ਯਾਰ ਮਿਲਾਵੇ, ਸੋਜ਼ੇ ਅਲਮ ਥੀਂ ਸਰਦ ਕਰਾਵੇ
ਚਿਖ਼੍ਹਾ ਤੋਂ ਬੈਠੀ ਸਤੀ ਉਠਾਵੇ, ਬੁੱਲ੍ਹੂ ਸ਼ਹੁ ਬਿਨ ਨੀਂਦ ਨ ਆਵੇ
ਭਾਵੇਂ ਸੋ ਰਹਾਂ

## B2  KATTAK (OCTOBER–NOVEMBER)

Say, what is Kattak like? Endure whatever difficulties
befall you. Use your head as a begging bowl and ask
for union as alms.

In Kattak I went to card cotton and to spin. When I fell
in love, the spinning party assembled. I went from
door to door, loudly crying, "This is a difficult place.
Deliver me to a crossing place, for the sake of the dark
lord."[1]

Oh cruel people, now I am dead. Let someone arise and
loudly shout: "My love for him began long ago. Bullha,
life is hard without the lord. He leaves my side."

## B3  MAGGHAR (NOVEMBER–DECEMBER)

In Magghar I go through the house, looking from top to
bottom. The learned Brahmans search their holy
books, but without finding God, who cannot be seen.

Where can I go home to in Magghar? Love is a demon[2]
that devours my bones. My heart is consumed and
keeps moaning, "I am a captive to anyone who brings
my beloved to me."

Whoever brings the beloved to me relieves me from my
burning pain. He removes the corpse of the suttee
from the pyre on which it lies. Bullha, I cannot rest
without my beloved, even though I am sleeping.

## ੪੪ ਪੋਹ

ਪੋਹ ਹੁਣ ਪੁੱਛੂੰ ਜਾ ਕੇ, ਤੁਮ ਨਿਆਰੇ ਰਹੋ ਕਿਉਂ ਮੀਤ
ਕਿਸ ਮੋਹਨ ਮਨ ਮੋਹ ਲਿਆ, ਜੋ ਪੱਥਰ ਕੀਨੇ ਚੀਤ
ਪਾਪੀ ਪੋਹ ਪਵਨ ਭੱਠ ਪਈਆਂ, ਲੱਦੇ ਹੋਤ ਤਾਂ ਉਡਝ ਗਈਆਂ
ਨਾਂ ਸੰਗ ਮਾਪੇ ਸੱਜਨ ਸਈਆਂ, ਪਿਆਰੇ ਇਸ਼ਕ ਜੁਆਲੇ ਲਈਆਂ
ਦੁੱਖਾਂ ਰੋਲੀ ਆਂ
ਕੜ ਕੜ ਕੱਪਰ ਕੜਕ ਡਰਾਏ, ਮਾਰੂ ਥਲ ਵਿਚ ਡੇਰੇ ਪਾਏ
ਜੀਉਂਦੀ ਮੋਈ ਨੀ ਮੇਰੀ ਮਾਏ, ਬੁੱਲ੍ਹਾ ਸ਼ਾਹ ਕਿਉਂ ਅਜੇ ਨਾ ਆਏ
ਹੰਢੂੰ ਡੋਹਲੀਆਂ

## ੪੫ ਮਾਘ

ਮਾਘੀ ਨ੍ਹਾਵਣ ਮੈਂ ਚਲੀ, ਜੋ ਤੀਰਥ ਕਰ ਸਮਿਆਨ
ਗਜ ਗਜ ਬਰਸੇ ਮੇਘਲਾ, ਮੈਂ ਰੋ ਰੋ ਕਰਾਂ ਇਸ਼ਨਾਨ
ਮਾਘ ਮਹੀਨੇ ਗਏ ਉਲਾਂਘ, ਨਵੀਂ ਮੁਹੱਬਤ ਬਹੁਤੀ ਤਾਂਘ
ਇਸ਼ਕ ਮੁਅੱਜ਼ਨ ਦਿੱਤੀ ਬਾਂਗ, ਪੜ੍ਹਾਂ ਨਮਾਜ਼ ਪੀਆ ਦੀ ਤਾਂਘ
ਦੁਆਈਂ ਕੀ ਕਰਾਂ
ਆਖਾਂ ਪਿਆਰੇ ਮੈਂ ਵਲ ਆ, ਤੇਰੇ ਮੁੱਖ ਵੇਖਣ ਦਾ ਚਾਅ
ਭਾਵੇਂ ਹੋਰ ਤਤੀ ਨੂੰ ਤਾਅ, ਬੁੱਲ੍ਹਾ ਸ਼ਾਹ ਨੂੰ ਆਣ ਮਿਲਾ
ਤੇਰੀ ਹੋ ਰਹਾਂ

## B4  POH (DECEMBER–JANUARY)

Now in Poh I go and ask: "Why do you stay away from me,
   my friend? Who is the lovely girl who has entranced
   you and turned your heart to stone?"

In the wretched season of Poh, I have fallen into the
   furnace. They had taken the Hot[3] away by the time
   my eyes opened. I do not have my parents or my
   girlfriends with me, beloved. Love for my dear one
   has burned me with its flame. My sufferings have
   destroyed me.

With loud noises, the whirlpools roar and terrify me.[4] I am
   put into the Maru Thal.[5] I am dead though still alive,
   Mother. Bullha, why has the lord still not come? I shed
   copious tears.

## B5  MAGH (JANUARY–FEBRUARY)

I went to bathe at the Maghi festival,[6] making
   preparations at the sacred bathing place. The cloud
   thunders and rains. I weep and bathe in my tears.

In Magh the months pass on. I am filled with new love
   and great yearning. Love is the muezzin who has
   announced the call to prayer. The regular prayer that
   I recite is my yearning for my beloved. What other
   prayers can I offer?

I say: "Come to me, beloved. I desire to see your face, even
   though you make my sufferings still more intense.
   Bullha, come and bring the lord to me. I am yours."

## ੬੪ ਫੱਗਣ

ਫੱਗਣ ਫੁਲੇ ਖੇਤ, ਜਿਉਂ ਬਣ ਤਣ ਫੁਲ ਸ਼ਿੰਗਾਰ
ਹਰ ਡਾਲੀ ਫੁਲ ਪੱਤੀਆਂ, ਗਲ ਫੁਲਨ ਕੇ ਹਾਰ
ਹੋਰੀ ਖੇਲਣ ਸਈਆਂ ਫੱਗਣ, ਮੇਰੇ ਨੈਣ ਝਲਾਰੀਂ ਵੱਗਣ
ਔਖੇ ਜੀਉਦਿਆਂ ਦੇ ਦਿਨ ਤੱਗਣ, ਸੀਨੇ ਬਾਣ ਪਰੇਮ ਦੇ ਲੱਗਣ
ਹੋਰੀ ਹੋ ਰਹੀ
ਜੋ ਕੁਝ ਰੋਜ਼ ਅਜ਼ਲ ਬੀਂ ਹੋਈ, ਲਿਖੀ ਕਲਮ ਨਾ ਮੇਟੇ ਕੋਈ
ਦੁੱਖਾਂ ਸੂਲਾਂ ਦਿੱਤੀ ਢੋਈ, ਬੁੱਲ੍ਹੂ ਸ਼ਾਹ ਨੂੰ ਆਖੇ ਕੋਈ
ਜਿਸ ਨੂੰ ਰੋ ਰਹੀ

## ੬੧ ਚੇਤ

ਚੇਤ ਚਮਨ ਵਿਚ ਕੋਇਲਾਂ, ਨਿਤ ਕੂ ਕੂ ਕਰਨ ਪੁਕਾਰ
ਮੈਂ ਸੁਟ ਸੁਟ ਝੂਰ ਝੂਰ ਮਰ ਰਹੀ, ਕਬ ਘਰ ਆਵੇ ਯਾਰ
ਹੁਣ ਕੀ ਕਰਾਂ ਜੋ ਆਇਆ ਚੇਤ, ਬਣ ਬਣ ਫੁਲ ਰਹੇ ਸਭ ਖੇਤ
ਦੇਂਦੇ ਆਪਣਾ ਅੰਤ ਨਾ ਭੇਤ, ਸਾਡੀ ਹਾਰ ਤੁਸਾਡੀ ਜੇਤ
ਹੁਣ ਮੈਂ ਹਾਰੀ ਆਂ
ਹੁਣ ਮੈਂ ਹਾਰਿਆ ਅਪਣਾ ਆਪ, ਤੁਸਾਡਾ ਇਸ਼ਕ ਅਸਾਡਾ ਖਾਪ
ਤੇਰੇ ਨੇਹੁੰ ਜਾ ਸੂਕਿਆ ਤਾਪ, ਬੁੱਲ੍ਹੂ ਸ਼ਾਹੁ ਕੀ ਲਾਇਆ ਪਾਪ
ਕਾਰੇ ਹਾਰੀ ਆਂ

## B6 PHAGGAN (FEBRUARY–MARCH)

In Phaggan the fields bloom[7] like a girl in her finery who
is adorned with flowers. On every branch there are
flowers and leaves, and it is garlanded with blossoms.

In Phaggan my girlfriends have gone to play Holi,[8] but
torrents of tears flow from my eyes. The days of my
life pass with difficulty. The spears of love transfix
my breast, while Holi is being celebrated.

From the day of pre-eternity,[9] whatever I was to be was
written by the pen of fate, which no one can erase.
Grief and pain were given admittance. Bullha,
let someone go and tell the lord, the one for whom
I weep.

## B7 CHET (MARCH–APRIL)

In Chet the *koil* birds[10] keep cooing and calling in the
garden. Listening to them, I die of grief. When will my
beloved come home?

What can I do now that Chet has come? All the fields are
decked out with blossoms. In the end, he does not
reveal his secret. My defeat is your victory, and now
I am defeated.

Now I have brought about my own defeat. My love for
you is the death of me. I suffer the fever of your love.
Bullha, what sin brought about my defeat?

## ੪੮ ਵਿਸਾਖ

ਬਸਾਖੀ ਦਾ ਦਿਨ ਕਠਨ ਹੈ, ਜੇ ਸੰਗ ਮੀਤ ਨਾ ਹੋ
ਮੈਂ ਕਿਸ ਕੇ ਆਗੇ ਜਾ ਕਹੂੰ, ਇਕ ਮੰਡੀ ਭਾ ਦੋ
ਨਾ ਮਨ ਭਾਵੇ ਸੁੱਖ ਬਸਾਖ, ਗੁੱਛੀਆਂ ਪਈਆਂ ਪੱਕੀ ਦਾਖ
ਲਾਖੀ ਲੈ ਘਰ ਆਇਆ ਲਾਖ, ਤਾਂ ਮੈਂ ਬਾਤ ਨਾ ਸੱਕਾਂ ਆਖ
ਕੌਤਾਂ ਵਾਲੀਆਂ
ਕੌਤਾਂ ਵਾਲੀਆਂ ਡਾਢਾ ਜ਼ੋਰ, ਹੁਣ ਮੈਂ ਝੂਰ ਝੂਰ ਹੋਈ ਆਂ ਮੋਰ
ਕੰਡੇ ਪੁੜੇ ਕਲੇਜੇ ਜ਼ੋਰ, ਬੁੱਲ੍ਹੂ ਸ਼ਾਹੁ ਬਿਨ ਕੋਈ ਨਾ ਹੋਰ
ਜਿਨ ਘਤ ਗਾਲੀ ਆਂ

## ੪੯ ਜੇਠ

ਜੇਠ ਜੇਹੀ ਮੇਰੇ ਅਗਨ ਹੈ, ਜਬ ਕੇ ਬਿਛੜੇ ਮੀਤ
ਸੁਣ ਸੁਣ ਘੁਟ ਘੁਟ ਝੂਰ ਮਰੂੰ, ਜੋ ਤੁਮਰੀ ਯੇਹ ਪਰੀਤ
ਲੂਆਂ ਚੁੱਪਾਂ ਪੈਂਦੀਆਂ ਜੇਠ, ਮਜਲਿਸ ਬਹਿੰਦੀ ਬਾਗ਼ਾ ਹੇਠ
ਤੱਤੀ ਠੰਡੀ ਵੱਗੇ ਪੇਠ, ਦਫ਼ਤਰ ਕੱਢ ਪੁਰਾਣੇ ਸੇਠ
ਮਹੁਰਾ ਖਾਟੀ ਆਂ
ਅਜ ਕਲ ਸੱਦ ਹੋਈ ਅਲਬੱਤਾ, ਹੁਣ ਮੈਂ ਆਹ ਕਲੇਜਾ ਤੱਤਾ
ਨਾ ਘਰ ਕੌਂਤ ਨਾ ਦਾਟਾ ਭੱਤਾ, ਬੁੱਲ੍ਹੂ ਸ਼ਾਹੁ ਬੋਰਾਂ ਸੰਗ ਰੱਤਾ
ਸੀਨੇ ਕਾਨੀਆਂ

## B8  VISAKH (APRIL–MAY)

The day of Vaisakhi[11] is difficult, if the beloved is not
with me. To whom should I go and ask for different
treatment?

There are no joys to please my heart in Visakh, though
bunches of ripe grapes hang on the vine. The bangle
seller has brought his bangles to the house, but I
cannot say anything before the other women. They
have their husbands.[12]

They have their husbands and are full of strength. But now
I grieve like the peacock.[13] My heart is sorely pierced
by thorns. Bullha, I have no one except the beloved,
who has possessed me.

## B9  JETH (MAY–JUNE)

I burn with a fire like the heat of Jeth, since I became
separated from my beloved. Hearing of your
indifference, I anxiously waste away. This is what your
love is like.

Hot winds blow and the sun is fierce in Jeth. The gathering
assembles in the shade of the gardens. Rates have
gone up.[14] The merchants draw up their long-standing
accounts. I must take poison.

I am certainly going to be called for soon. Oh, my heart is
on fire. My bridegroom is not at home, and I do not
have any food to live on. Bullha, the lord is engrossed
with others. Arrows pierce my breast.

## ੪੧੦ ਹਾੜੂ

ਹਾੜੂ ਸੋਹੇ ਮੇਹੇ ਝਟਪਟੇ, ਜੋ ਲੱਗੀ ਪਰੇਮ ਕੀ ਆਗ
ਜਿਸ ਲਾਗੇ ਤਿਸ ਜਲ ਬੁਝੇ, ਜੋਂ ਭੌਂਰ ਜਲਾਵੇ ਭਾਗ
ਹੁਟ ਕੀ ਕਰਾਂ ਜੋ ਆਇਆ ਹਾੜੂ, ਤਨ ਵਿਚ ਇਸ਼ਕ ਤਪਾਇਆ ਭਾੜ
ਤੇਰੇ ਇਸ਼ਕ ਨੇ ਦਿੱਤਾ ਸਾੜ, ਰੋਵਣ ਅੱਖੀਆਂ ਕਰਨ ਪੁਕਾਰ
ਤੇਰੇ ਹਾਵੜੇ
ਹਾੜੂ ਘੱਤਾਂ ਸ਼ਾਮੇ ਅੱਗੇ, ਕਾਸਦ ਲੈ ਕੇ ਪਾਤਰ ਵੱਗੇ
ਕਾਲੇ ਗਏ ਤੇ ਆਏ ਬੱਗੇ, ਬੁੱਲ੍ਹੂ ਸ਼ਾਹੁ ਬਿਨ ਜ਼ਰਾ ਨਾ ਤੱਗੇ
ਸ਼ਾਮੇ ਬਾਹਵੜੇ

## ੪੧੧ ਸਾਵਣ

ਸਾਵਣ ਸੋਹੇ ਮੇਘਲਾ, ਘਟ ਸੋਹੇ ਕਰਤਾਰ
ਠੋਰ ਠੋਰ ਇਨਾਇਤ ਬਸੇ, ਪਪੀਹਾ ਕਰੇ ਪੁਕਾਰ
ਸੋਹਣ ਮਲ੍ਹਾਰਾਂ ਸਾਰੇ ਸਾਵਣ, ਦੂਤੀ ਦੁਖ ਲੱਗੇ ਉਠ ਜਾਵਣ
ਨੀਂਗਰ ਖੇਡਣ ਕੁੜੀਆਂ ਗਾਵਣ, ਮੈਂ ਘਰ ਰੰਗ ਰੰਗੀਲੇ ਆਵਣ
ਆਸਾਂ ਪੁੰਨੀਆਂ
ਮੇਰੀਆਂ ਆਸਾਂ ਰੱਬ ਪੁਚਾਈਆਂ, ਮੈਂ ਤਾਂ ਉਨ ਸੰਗ ਅੱਖੀਆਂ ਲਾਈਆਂ
ਸਈਆਂ ਦੇਣ ਮੁਬਾਰਕ ਆਈਆਂ, ਸ਼ਾਹ ਇਨਾਇਤ ਆਖਾਂ ਸਾਈਆਂ
ਆਸਾਂ ਪੁੰਨੀਆਂ

## B10 HARH (JUNE–JULY)

On fire with love, I enjoy Harh early in the morning.[15]
  Anyone who has experienced love understands its
  burning power, like the moth[16] that destroys its
  allotted life in the flame.

Now that Harh has come, what shall I do? In my body love
  has heated a furnace. My love for you has consumed
  me. My eyes weep and utter supplications as I yearn
  for you.

I make entreaties before the dark lord.[17] Messengers take
  my letters and run. They departed black and have
  returned white.[18] Bullha has no power of endurance
  without the lord. May the dark lord come to my aid.

## B11 SAVAN (JULY–AUGUST)

The clouds look lovely in Savan, the creator looks lovely
  in the heart. "In every place Inayat dwells," calls the
  *papīhā* bird.[19]

The songs of the rainy season[20] sound lovely throughout
  Savan. My enemies suffer pain and depart. The boys
  play and the girls sing. My house is filled with delights.
  My hopes are fulfilled.

The lord has fulfilled my hopes. I have gazed upon him in
  love. My girlfriends have come to congratulate me.
  I say to Shah Inayat, "Lord, my hopes are fulfilled."

## ੪੧੨ ਭਾਦੋਂ

ਭਾਦੋਂ ਭਾਵੇ ਤਬ ਸਖੀ, ਜੋ ਪਲ ਪਲ ਹੋਵੇ ਮਿਲਾਪ

ਜੋ ਘਟ ਦੇਖੂੰ ਖੋਲ ਕੇ, ਘਟ ਘਟ ਦੇ ਵਿਚ ਆਪ

ਆ ਹੁਣ ਭਾਦੋਂ ਭਾਗ ਜਗਾਇਆ, ਸਾਹਿਬ ਕੁਦਰਤ ਸੇਤੀ ਆਇਆ

ਹਰ ਹਰ ਦੇ ਵਿਚ ਆਪ ਸਮਾਇਆ, ਸ਼ਾਹ ਇਨਾਇਤ ਆਪ ਲਖਾਇਆ

ਤਾਂ ਮੈਂ ਲਖਿਆ

ਆਖਰ ਉਮਰੇ ਹੋਈ ਤਸੱਲਾ, ਪਲ ਪਲ ਮੰਗਤ ਨੈਨ ਤਜੱਲਾ

ਜੋ ਕੁਝ ਹੋਸੀ ਕਰਸੀ ਅੱਲ੍ਹਾ, ਬੁੱਲ੍ਹ ਸ਼ਹੁ ਬਿਨ ਕੁਝ ਨਾ ਭੱਲਾ

ਪਰੇਮ ਰਸ ਚਖਿਆ

## B12  BHADON (AUGUST–SEPTEMBER)

Bhadon is pleasing, dear girlfriend, when we are together
all the time. In every heart that I open to look into, it
is he who is there inside.

Come now, Bhadon has made my fortune bright. Through
his divine power, the lord has come. He is contained in
everything. I behold Shah Inayat, when he lets himself
be seen.

At the end of life there was consolation. At every moment
the eyes beg for the sight of his glory. Whatever
happens is determined by God. Bullha, nothing is
good without the lord. I have tasted the delight of
love.

# ਗੀਂਢਾਂ

## ਗ੧

ਕਹੋ ਸੁਰਤੇ ਗੱਲ ਕਾਜ ਦੀ, ਮੈਂ ਗੀਂਢਾਂ ਕੀਤੀਆਂ ਪਾਊਂ
ਸਾਹੇ ਤੇ ਜੰਜ ਆਵਸੀ, ਹੁਣ ਚਾਲੀ ਗੀਂਢ ਘਟਾਊਂ
ਬਾਬਲ ਆਖਿਆ ਆਣ ਕੇ, ਤੈਂ ਸਾਹਵਰਿਆਂ ਘਰ ਜਾਣਾ
ਰੀਤ ਉਥੋਂ ਦੀ ਔਰ ਹੈ, ਮੁੜ ਪੈਰ ਨਾ ਏਥੇ ਪਾਣਾ
ਗੀਂਢ ਪਹਿਲੀ ਨੂੰ ਖੋਲੂ ਕੇ, ਮੈਂ ਬੈਠੀ ਬਰਲਾਵਾਂ
ਉੜਕ ਜਾਵਣ ਜਾਵਣਾ, ਮੈਂ ਦਾਜ ਰੰਗਾਵਾਂ
ਦੇਖੂੰ ਤਰਫ਼ ਬਜ਼ਾਰ ਦੀ, ਸਭ ਰਸਤੇ ਲਾਗੇ
ਪੱਲੇ ਨਹੀਂ ਰੋਕੜੀ, ਸਭ ਮੁਝ ਸੇ ਭਾਗੇ

## ਗ੨

ਦੂਜੀ ਖੋਹਲੂੰ ਕਿਆ ਕਹੂੰ, ਦਿਨ ਥੋੜੇ ਰਹਿੰਦੇ
ਸੂਲ ਸੱਭੇ ਰਲ ਆਂਵਦੇ, ਸੀਨੇ ਵਿਚ ਬਹਿੰਦੇ
ਝਲ ਵਲੱਲੀ ਮੈਂ ਹੋਈ, ਤੰਦ ਕੱਤ ਨਾ ਜਾਣਾਂ
ਜੰਜ ਐਵੇਂ ਰਲ ਆਵਸੀ, ਜਿਉਂ ਚੜ੍ਹਦਾ ਠਾਣਾ

# The Forty Knots

## G1

Tell me about the wedding ceremony, you who know so
　　much; how many knots should I tie? On the appointed
　　day the bridegroom's party will come, so now I will tie
　　forty knots. My father came and told me, "You must
　　go to your in-laws. Things are different there, and you
　　will not set foot here again."
I undo the first knot, and start jabbering: "I will have to
　　go eventually, so I will get my dowry clothes dyed."
　　When I look in the direction of the bazaar, everyone
　　has set out. I have no cash on me, and everyone runs
　　away from me.

## G2

I undo the second knot, and what can I say? Few days
　　remain. Sharp pains gather and settle in my breast.
　　I have lost my wits and do not know how to spin yarn.
　　The bridegroom's party will arrive like the police on
　　a raid.

### ੩੩

ਤੀਜੀ ਖੇਹਲੂੰ ਦੁੱਖ ਸੇ, ਰੋਂਦੇ ਨੈਣ ਨਾ ਹਟਦੇ
ਕਿਸ ਨੂੰ ਪੁੱਛਾਂ ਜਾਇ ਕੇ, ਦਿਨ ਜਾਂਦੇ ਘਟਦੇ
ਗੁਟ ਵਾਲੀਆਂ ਸਭ ਪਿਆਰੀਆਂ, ਮੈਂ ਕੋ ਗੁਟ ਨਾਹੀਂ
ਹੱਥ ਮਲੇ ਮਲ ਸਿਰ ਧਰਾਂ, ਮੈਂ ਰੋਵਾਂ ਢਾਹੀਂ

### ੩੪

ਚੌਥੀ ਖੁੱਲ੍ਹੀ ਕਿਆ ਹੂਆ, ਰਲ ਆਵਣ ਸਈਆਂ
ਦਰਦ ਕਿਸੇ ਨਾ ਕੀਤਿਆ, ਸਭ ਤਜ ਘਰ ਗਈਆਂ
ਵਤਨ ਬੇਗਾਨਾ ਵੇਖਟਾ, ਕੀ ਕਰੀਏ ਮਾਣਾ
ਬਾਬਲ ਪਕੜ ਚਲਾਵਸੀ, ਦਾਈ ਬਿਨ ਜਾਣਾ

### ੩੫

ਪੰਜਵੀਂ ਖੇਹਲੂੰ ਕੁਕ ਕੇ, ਕਰ ਸੋਜ਼ ਪੁਕਾਰਾਂ
ਪਹਿਲੀ ਰਾਤ ਡਰਾਵਣੀ, ਕਿਉਂ ਦਿਲੋਂ ਵਿਸਾਰਾਂ
ਮੁੱਦਤ ਥੋੜੀ ਆ ਰਹੀ, ਕੀਵੇਂ ਦਾਜ ਬਟਾਵਾਂ
ਜਾ ਆਖੇ ਘਰ ਸਾਹਵਰੇ, ਗੰਢ ਲਾਗ ਵਧਾਵਾਂ

## G3

I undo the third knot, and from sorrow my eyes cannot
stop weeping. To whom can I go and ask? The days
keep growing less. The girls with virtues are all loved,
but there is no virtue in me. Wringing my hands and
putting dirt on my head, I weep bitterly.

## G4

When I undid the fourth knot, what happened? My
girlfriends gathered and came. None of them suffered
pain; they all left home and went. We have to behold
a strange country, so why be full of pride? My father
will seize me and send me on my way; I will have to go
without my nanny.

## G5

When I undo the fifth knot, I scream and cry out in
burning pain. The first night is terrifying; how can my
heart forget it? Only a short period is still to come;
how can I get my dowry prepared? Go to the in-laws'
house, and I will increase your wedding fee.[1]

## ਗਿ੬

ਗੀਚ ਛੇਵੀਂ ਮੈਂ ਖੋਲੂ ਕੇ, ਜਗ ਦੇਂਦੀ ਹੋਕਾ
ਘਰ ਪਈ ਮਹਿਮਾਨ ਹਾਂ, ਕੀ ਕਰੀਏ ਲੋਕਾ
ਲੱਗਾ ਫਿਕਰ ਫਰਾਕ ਦਾ, ਕੀ ਕਰੀਏ ਕਾਰਾਂ
ਰੋਵਣ ਅੱਖੀਂ ਮੇਰੀਆਂ, ਜਿਉਂ ਵਗਾਟ ਝਲਾਰਾਂ

## ਗਿ੭

ਸੱਤਵੀਂ ਗੀਚ ਚਾ ਖੋਲੂੰਆਂ, ਮੈਂ ਓਸੇ ਹੀਲੇ
ਰੋ ਰੋ ਹਾਲ ਵੰਜਾਇਆ, ਰੰਗ ਸਾਵੇ ਪੀਲੇ
ਸੂਲ ਅਸਾਂ ਨਾਲ ਖੇਡਦੇ, ਨਹੀਂ ਹੋਸ਼ ਸੰਭਾਲੇ
ਹੁਣ ਦੱਸੋ ਸੰਗ ਸਹੇਲੀਓ, ਕੋਈ ਚਲਸੋ ਨਾਲੇ

## ਗਿ੮

ਅੱਠਵੀਂ ਨੂੰ ਹੱਥ ਡਾਲਿਆ, ਮੈਂ ਹੋਈ ਦੀਵਾਨੀ
ਜੀਵਨ ਮਿਸਲ ਹੁਬਾਬ ਹੈ, ਮਛਲੀ ਬਿਨ ਪਾਟੀ
ਦੁਖ ਦਰਦ ਅਵੱਲੇ ਆਣ ਕੇ, ਹੁਣ ਲਹੂ ਪੀਂਦੇ
ਬਿਰਹੋਂ ਦੀ ਦੁਕਾਨ ਤੇ, ਸਾਡੇ ਘਾੜ ਘੜੀਂਦੇ

## G6

Undoing the sixth knot, I cry out to the world. I am a
guest in this house, oh people, what shall I do? I have
become anxious about separation, but what can I do
about it? My eyes weep like flowing torrents.

## G7

I have undone the seventh knot by that same trick. I weep
and bewail my fate; my face has become blotched.
Sharp pains play with me; I cannot come to my senses.
Now tell me, my girlfriends, will anyone go with me?

## G8

When I laid hold of the eighth knot, I went mad. Life
is like a bubble, or like being a fish out of water.
Unpleasant griefs and pains have now come to drink
my blood. I am being shaped in the workshop of
separation.

## ੧੯

ਨਾਵੀਂ ਨੂੰ ਚਾ ਖੋਲ੍ਹਿਆ, ਦਿਨ ਰਹਿੰਦੇ ਥੋੜ੍ਹੇ
ਮੈਂ ਪੂਣੀ ਕੱਤ ਨਾ ਜਾਤੀਆ, ਅਜੇ ਰਹਿੰਦੇ ਗੋਹੜੇ
ਮੈਂ ਤਰਲੇ ਲੈਂਦੀ ਡਿਗ ਪਈ, ਕੋਈ ਢੋ ਨਾ ਹੋਇਆ
ਗਫ਼ਲਤ ਘਤ ਉਜਾੜਿਆ, ਅੱਗੋਂ ਖੇਡ ਵਿਗੋਇਆ

## ੧੦

ਦਸਵੀਂ ਗੰਢ ਮੈਂ ਖੋਲ੍ਹੂੰ, ਕਿਉਂ ਜੰਮਦੀ ਆਹੀ
ਸਭ ਕਬੀਲਾ ਦੇਸ ਥੀਂ, ਵੀਦੇਸ ਤਰਾਹੀ
ਅੰਬੜ ਘੁੱਟੀ ਦੇਂਦੀਏ, ਜੇ ਜ਼ਹਿਰ ਰਲਾਵੇਂ
ਮੈਂ ਛੁੱਟਦੀ ਏਸ ਅਜ਼ਾਬ ਤੋਂ, ਤੂੰ ਜਿੰਦ ਛੁਡਾਵੇਂ

## ੧੧

ਯਾਰੂ ਗੰਢੀਂ ਖੋਲ੍ਹੀਆਂ, ਮੈਂ ਹਿਜਰੇ ਮਾਰੀ
ਗਾਈਆਂ ਸਈਆਂ ਸਾਹੁਰੇ, ਹੁਣ ਮੇਰੀ ਵਾਰੀ
ਬਾਂਹ ਸਰਹਾਣੇ ਦੇ ਕਦੀ ਅਸੀਂ, ਮੂਲ ਨਾ ਸੌਂਦੇ
ਫੱਟਾਂ ਉੱਤੇ ਲੂਣ ਹੈ, ਫੱਟ ਸਿੰਮਦੇ ਲੈਂਦੇ

## G9

I quickly undid the ninth knot, and few days are left.
  I did not know how to spin the cotton roll; the carded
  cotton is still in balls waiting to be spun. I pleaded and
  fell down, but gained no admittance. Inattention has
  ruined me, and playing about has destroyed me.

## G10

I opened the tenth knot. Why was I born? The whole clan
  has chased me from home, away to foreign parts. Oh
  mother who gave me my first dose,[2] if you had mixed
  it with poison, I should have escaped this torment and
  you would have been rid of all this trouble.

## G11

I have undone eleven knots. I am slain by separation.
  My girlfriends have gone to their in-laws; now it is
  my turn. I am quite unable to relax and sleep properly.
  Salt is rubbed in my wounds, they ooze and erupt.

## ੧੨

ਗੀਂਧ ਖੇਲ੍ਹੀ ਮੈਂ ਬਾਰੁਵੀਂ, ਕੀ ਹੋਗ ਤਮਾਸ਼ਾ
ਜਿਸ ਲਾਗੀ ਤਿਸ ਪੀੜ ਹੈ, ਜਗ ਜਾਣੇ ਹਾਸਾ
ਇਕ ਗਏ ਨਾ ਚਿਤ ਬਾਹੁੜੇ, ਜਿਤ ਚਿਤ ਕੇ ਹਰਦੀ
ਇਹਨੀਂ ਅੱਖੀਂ ਵੇਖਿਆ, ਹੋਇ ਖ਼ਾਕ ਕਬਰ ਦੀ

## ੧੩

ਤੇਰਾਂ ਗੀਂਧਾਂ ਖੇਲ੍ਹੀਆਂ, ਨੈਣ ਲਹੂ ਰੋਂਦੇ
ਹੋਇਆ ਸਾਥ ਉਤਾਵਲਾ, ਧੋਬੀ ਕਪੜੇ ਧੋਂਦੇ
ਸੱਜਣ ਚਾਦਰ ਤਾਣ ਕੇ, ਸੁੱਤਾ ਵਿਚ ਹੁਜਰੇ
ਅਜੇ ਬੀ ਉਹ ਨਾ ਜਾਗਿਆ, ਦਿਨ ਕਿਤਨੇ ਗੁਜ਼ਰੇ

## ੧੪

ਚੌਦਾਂ ਗੀਂਧੀ ਖੇਲ੍ਹੀਆਂ, ਲਹੁ ਪੀਣਾ ਖਾਣਾ
ਜਿਨ ਰਾਹਾਂ ਵਿਚ ਧਾੜਵੀ, ਤਿਨ੍ਹੀਂ ਰਾਹੀਂ ਜਾਣਾ
ਲੱਗੀ ਚੋਟ ਫ਼ਰਾਕ ਦੀ, ਦੇ ਕੌਣ ਦਿਲਾਸਾ
ਸਖ਼ਤ ਮੁਸੀਬਤ ਇਸ਼ਕ ਦੀ, ਰੱਤ ਰਹੀ ਨ ਮਾਸਾ

## G12

I have undone the twelfth knot. Now what a sight there
will be to see. Those who have experienced it know
what pain is; the world thinks it is a joke. Some have
gone and not returned, as God wills.[3] These eyes have
seen that all turn to dust in the grave.

## G13

I have undone thirteen knots. My eyes shed tears of blood.
My companions are impatient. The washermen are
washing the clothes. My beloved is comfortably asleep
in his room. He has still not woken up, although many
days have passed.

## G14

I have undone fourteen knots. My blood is my food and
drink. I must go by roads that are infested with
bandits. I have been smitten by the blow of separation.
Who will give me comfort? The calamity of love is
harsh; I have no blood or flesh left.

## ੩੧੫

ਪੰਦਰਾਂ ਟੁੱਟੇ ਰੋਜ਼ ਨੇ, ਕਰਾਂ ਨਾਅਰੇ ਆਹੀਂ
ਦੱਸਿਆ ਸਭ ਨਜੂਮੀਆਂ, ਏਥੇ ਰਹਿਣਾ ਨਾਹੀਂ
ਪੰਦਰਾਂ ਪੁੰਨੇ ਰੋਜ਼ ਨੇ, ਆਖ਼ਰ ਕਰਦੀ ਆਹੀਂ
ਸ਼ਹਿਰ ਖ਼ਮੋਸ਼ਾ ਜਾਵਟਾ, ਖ਼ਮੋਸ਼ ਹੋ ਜਾਈਂ

## ੩੧੪

ਸੋਲਾਂ ਗੰਢੀਂ ਖੋਲੂੀਆਂ, ਮੈਂ ਹੋਈ ਨਿਮਾਣੀ
ਏਥੇ ਪੇਸ਼ ਕਿਸੇ ਨਾ ਜਾਸੀਆ, ਨਾ ਅੱਗੇ ਜਾਤੀ
ਏਥੇ ਆਵਟ ਕੇਹਾ ਏ ਹੋਇਆ, ਜੋਗੀ ਦਾ ਫੇਰਾ
ਅੱਗੇ ਜਾ ਕੇ ਬਾਰ ਨਾ, ਵਿਚ ਕੱਲਰ ਡੇਰਾ

## ੩੧੨

ਸਤਾਰਾਂ ਗੰਢੀਂ ਖੋਲੂੀਆਂ, ਸੂਲਾਂ ਦੇ ਹਾੜੀ
ਮੋਇਆਂ ਨੂੰ ਦੁਖ ਮਾਰਦਾ, ਫੜ ਜ਼ੁਲਮ ਕਟਾਰੀ
ਤਨ ਹੋਲਾਂ ਸੂਲਾਂ ਵੇੜ੍ਹੀਆਂ, ਰੰਗ ਜਿਉਂ ਫੁਲ ਤੋਰੀ
ਆਏ ਏਸ ਜਹਾਨ ਤੇ, ਇਹੋ ਕੀਤੀ ਚੋਰੀ

## G15

Fifteen days are over. I cry out and sigh. The astrologers
  have all told me that I cannot remain here. Fifteen
  days are completed, and finally I heave deep sighs.
  If you must go to the city of the silent,[4] go in silence.

## G16

I have undone sixteen knots. I have become wretched. No
  one can do anything here, nor will they be able to do
  so in the hereafter. Our coming here is like the passing
  tour of a yogi.[5] Ahead of you there lies no open door;
  your lodging will be in the barren wasteland.

## G17

I have undone seventeen knots. It is the harvest time of
  agonies. Grief grips the dagger of cruelty and slays the
  dead. My body is beset by dread and pain, my color is
  like that of the *torī*[6] flower. I came into this world, and
  this was the robbery that I committed.

## ਗ੧੮

ਖੇਲਾਂ ਗੇਂਧ ਅਠਾਰਵੀਂ, ਦਿਲ ਕਰਕੇ ਰਾਜ਼ੀ
ਇਹ ਚਾਰ ਦਿਨਾਂ ਦੀ ਖੇਡ ਹੈ, ਹੁਜਰੇ ਦੀ ਬਾਜ਼ੀ
ਜਿਨ੍ਹਾਂ ਵਿਚ ਫ਼ਰਾਕ ਹੈ, ਉਹ ਵੈਂਦੇ ਮਰਦੇ
ਨਕਾਰੇ ਵੱਜਣ ਕੂਚ ਦੇ, ਮੈਂ ਸਿਰ ਪਰ ਬਰਦੇ

## ਗ੧੯

ਉੱਨੀ ਗੇਂਧੀਂ ਖੇਲੂਆਂ, ਮੈਂ ਸੂਲ ਪਸਾਰਾ
ਹੁਣ ਇਹ ਦੇਸ ਬਦਾਰਿਆ, ਵੇਖ ਹਾਲ ਹਮਾਰਾ
ਕਿੰਨੀ ਬੈਠੀਂ ਚਾਚੀਆਂ, ਉੱਠ ਕੋਲੋਂ ਗਾਈਆਂ
ਕੋਈ ਦੱਸ ਨਾ ਪਾਉਂਦਾ, ਉਹ ਕੈਂ ਵਲ ਗਾਈਆਂ

## ਗ੨੦

ਵੀਹ ਗੇਂਧੀਂ ਫੇਲ ਖੇਲੂਆਂ, ਹੁਣ ਕਿਤ ਵਲ ਭਾਗੂੰ
ਲੱਗੀ ਚੇਟਕ ਔਰ ਹੈ, ਸੋਊਂ ਨਾ ਜਾਗੂੰ
ਪੰਜ ਮਹਿਮਾਨ ਸਿਰ ਉੱਤੇ, ਸੋ ਪੰਜੇ ਬਾਕੀ
ਜਿਸ ਮੁਸੀਬਤ ਇਹ ਬਟੀ, ਤਿਸ ਬਖ਼ਤ ਫ਼ਰਾਕੀ

## G18

I undo the eighteenth knot, making my heart content. The
game of the chamber of this world is a sport that lasts
only a few days. Those who experience separation
keep dying. The departure drums sound, and the
agents of death are upon me.

## G19

I have undone nineteen knots. Agonies spread within me.
Now this land is destructive. See what a state I am in.
So many cousins have got up and gone away from me.
No one can tell where they have gone.

## G20

I have undone twenty knots. Now where shall I run? I have
been gripped by fresh concern; I am neither asleep nor
awake. Five guests[7] are upon me and five remain. The
trouble I have fallen into is the fate of separation.

## ੨੧

ਇੱਕੀ ਖੋਹਲੂੰ ਕਿਉਂ ਨਹੀਂ, ਮੇਰੇ ਮਗਰ ਪਿਆਦੇ
ਤੇਲ ਚੜ੍ਹਿਆ ਸੇਜ਼ ਦਾ, ਅਸਾਂ ਹੋਰ ਤਕਾਦੇ
ਜੀਵਣ ਜੀਣਾ ਸਾਰ ਕਾ, ਮਾਈਆਂ ਮੂੰਹ ਪਾਏ
ਐਸੀ ਪੁੰਨੀ ਵੇਖ ਕੇ, ਉਦਾਸੀ ਆਏ

## ੨੨

ਬਾਈ ਖੋਹਲੂੰ ਪਹੁੰਚ ਕੇ, ਸਭ ਮੀਰਾਂ ਮਲਕਾਂ
ਉਹਨਾਂ ਡੇਰਾ ਕੂਚ ਹੈ, ਮੈਂ ਖੋਹਲਾਂ ਪਲਕਾਂ
ਅਪਣਾ ਰਹਿਣਾ ਕੀ ਕਰਾਂ, ਕਿਹੜੇ ਬਾਗ਼ ਦੀ ਮੂਲੀ
ਖ਼ਾਲੀ ਜਗ ਵਿਚ ਆਇਕੇ, ਸੁਫ਼ਨੇ ਪਰ ਭੂਲੀ

## ੨੩

ਤੇਈ ਜੋ ਕਹੂੰ ਖੋਲ੍ਹੀਆਂ, ਵਿਚ ਆਪ ਸਮਾਣਾ
ਹੱਥੋਂ ਸੁੱਟਾਂ ਟੋਰ ਕੇ, ਕਿਵੇਂ ਵੇਖ ਪਛਾਣਾਂ
ਉਲਟੀ ਫ਼ਾਹੀ ਪੈ ਗਈ, ਦੂਜਾ ਸਾਥ ਪੁਕਾਰੇ
ਪੁਰਜੇ ਪੁਰਜੇ ਮੈਂ ਹੋਈ, ਦਿਲ ਪਾਰੇ ਪਾਰੇ

## G21

Why should I not undo the twenty-first knot? The
constables pursue me. After being anointed with the
oil of burning passion, I am in further difficulties. My
life is as hard as a piece of iron, placed in my mouth by
the older women.[8] I have seen that my sad destiny is
fulfilled.

## G22

I undo the twenty-second knot, after arriving in a place
where all are lords and kings. But they must all leave
their camp when I open my eyes. What can I do about
staying myself? Which garden's radish am I?[9] I came
empty-handed into the world, and I was deluded by
a dream.

## G23

I undo the twenty-third knot. He is contained within me.
I break my bangles and throw them away. How can I
see and recognize him? An unlucky noose has fallen
on me, and the company cries out. I am in pieces and
my heart is in fragments.

## ੩੨੪

ਚੰਵ੍ਹੀ ਖੇਹਲੂੰ ਖੇਲੁਦੀ, ਚੁੱਕ ਪਵਣ ਨਬੇੜੇ
ਸਹਿਮ ਜਿਨ੍ਹਾਂ ਦੇ ਮਾਰੀਆਂ, ਸੋਈ ਆਏ ਨੇੜੇ
ਤੇਵਰ ਬੇਵਰ ਨਾ ਹੋਇਆ, ਨਾ ਜ਼ੇਵਰ ਗਹਿਣੇ
ਤਾਅਨੇ ਦੇਣੇ ਦੇਵਰਾਂ, ਚੁੱਪ ਕੀਤਿਆਂ ਸਹਿਣੇ

## ੩੨੫

ਮੈਂ ਖੇਲੂੰ ਗੀਂਚ ਪਚੀਸਵੀਂ, ਦੁੱਖਾਂ ਵਲ ਮੇਲਾਂ
ਹੰਝੂਆਂ ਦੇ ਗਲ ਹਾਰ ਨੀ, ਅਸਾਂ ਦਰਦ ਹਮੇਲਾਂ
ਵਟਨਾ ਮਲਿਆ ਸੋਜ਼ ਦਾ, ਤਲਖ਼ ਤੁਰਸ਼ ਸਿਆਪੇ
ਨਾਲ ਦੋਹਾਂ ਦੇ ਚੱਲਣਾ, ਬਣ ਆਇਆ ਜਾਪੇ

## ੩੨੬

ਛੱਬੀ ਗੀਂਢੀ ਇਮਾਮ ਹੈ, ਕਦੀ ਫੇਰ ਨਾ ਪਾਇਆ
ਉਮਰ ਤੇਸ਼ਾ ਪੰਜ ਰੋਜ਼ ਹੈ, ਸੋ ਲੇਖੇ ਆਇਆ
ਪਿਆਲੇ ਆਏ ਮੌਤ ਦੇ, ਇਹ ਸਭ ਨੇ ਪੀਣੇ
ਇਹ ਦੁੱਖ ਅਸਾਡੇ ਨਾਲ ਹੀ, ਸਹਿਜਾਈ ਕੀਨੇ

## G24

I undo the twenty-fourth knot. As I do so, all troubles are
   removed. The one of whom I am mortally afraid has
   drawn near. I have no two- or three-piece outfits,[10]
   no ornaments or jewels. My husband's younger
   brothers[11] will taunt me, and I must suffer their
   taunts.

## G25

As I undo the twenty-fifth knot, I gather griefs. Around
   my neck I wear tears as a garland and pain as a
   necklace. I have rubbed on the cleanser[12] of burning
   pain, and my mourning laments are sour and bitter.
   I must go with the pair;[13] it seems my time has come.

## G26

In the twenty-six knots there is the leading bead,[14]
   which is never turned. Life is a five days' supply,
   which comes as determined by fate. The cups of
   death have come and must be drunk by everyone.
   These sufferings go with us, made to be our close
   companions.

## ਗ੨੧

ਸਤਾਈ ਖੇਲੂ ਸਹੇਲੀਓ, ਸਭ ਜਤਨ ਸਿਧਾਇਆ
ਦੋ ਨੈਣਾਂ ਨੇ ਰੋਦਿਆਂ, ਮੀਂਹ ਸਾਵਣ ਲਾਇਆ
ਇਕ ਇਕ ਸਾਇਤ ਦੁੱਖਦੀ, ਸੌ ਜਤਨ ਗੁਜ਼ਾਰੀ
ਅੱਗੇ ਜਾਣਾ ਦੂਰ ਹੈ, ਸਿਰ ਗਠੜੀ ਭਾਰੀ

## ਗ੨੮

ਅਠਾਈ ਗੀਂਢੀ ਖੇਲੂਆਂ, ਨਹੀਂ ਅਕਲ ਅਸਾਥੇ
ਸਖ਼ਤੀ ਆਈ ਜ਼ੋਰ ਦੀ, ਸਿਰ ਚਸ਼ਮਾਂ ਮਾਥੇ
ਸੁੱਖਾਂ ਤੋਂ ਟੋਟੇ ਆ ਗਏ, ਦੁੱਖਾਂ ਤੋਂ ਲਾਹੇ
ਬੇਚਾਰੀ ਬੇਹਾਲ ਹਾਂ, ਵਿਚ ਸੋਜ਼ ਕੜਾਹੇ

## ਗ੨੯

ਉਨੱਤੀ ਗੀਂਢੀ ਖੇਲੂਆਂ, ਨਹੀਂ ਸਖ਼ਤੀ ਹਟਦੀ
ਲੱਗਾ ਸੀਨੇ ਬਾਣ ਹੈ, ਸਿਰ ਵਾਲਾਂ ਪਟਦੀ
ਇਤ ਵਲ ਫੇਰਾ ਪਾਇਕੇ, ਇਹ ਹਾਸਲ ਪਾਇਆ
ਤਨ ਤਲਵਾਰੀਂ ਤੋੜਿਆ, ਇਕ ਰੂਪ ਉਡਾਇਆ

## G27

I undo the twenty-seventh knot. Oh girlfriends, all my
efforts have gone for nothing. My two eyes have wept
as much as the rains of Savan.[15] Each moment hurts,
in spite of all my efforts. Ahead of me there is a long
way to go, with a heavy bundle on my head.

## G28

Twenty-eight knots are undone. I cannot think what to
do. Harsh difficulties have come as my fate, which is
written on my features. From joys I suffered losses,
from pains I gained profits. I lie helpless and wretched
in the frying pan of burning grief.

## G29

Twenty-nine knots are undone. My harsh fate is not
averted. An arrow has pierced my breast, and I tear
my hair. When he came this way to visit, this is what
he found. My body was cut to pieces by swords; only a
single form was made to fly.[16]

## ੩੦

ਖੇਲ੍ਹੀ ਗੀਂਧ ਮੈਂ ਤੀਸਵੀਂ, ਦੁਖ ਦਰਦ ਰੰਜਾਟੀ
ਕਦੀ ਸਿਰੋਂ ਨਾ ਮੁੱਕਦੀ, ਇਹ ਰਾਮ ਕਹਾਣੀ
ਮੁੜ ਮੁੜ ਫੇਰ ਨਾ ਜੀਵਟਾ, ਤਨ ਛੁਪਦਾ ਲੁਕਦਾ
ਬਿਰੋਂ ਅਜੇ ਖ਼ਿਆਲ ਹੈ, ਇਹ ਸਿਰ ਤੇ ਚੁਕਦਾ

## ੩੧

ਇਕ ਇਕ ਗੀਂਧ ਨੂੰ ਖੋਲ੍ਹਿਆ, ਇਕੱਤੀ ਹੋਈਆਂ
ਮੈਂ ਕਿਸ ਦੀ ਪਾਟੀਹਾਰ ਹਾਂ, ਏਥੇ ਕੇਤੀਆਂ ਰੋਈਆਂ
ਮੈਂ ਘਰ ਵਿਚ ਚਤਰ ਖਿਡਾਰ ਸਾਂ, ਦਾਅ ਪਿਆ ਨਾ ਕਾਰੀ
ਬਾਜ਼ੀ ਖੇਡਾਂ ਜਿੱਤ ਦੀ, ਮੈਂ ਏਥੇ ਹਾਰੀ

## ੩੨

ਬੱਤੀ ਗੀਂਧਾਂ ਖੋਲ੍ਹੀਆਂ, ਜੋ ਖੇਲ੍ਹੀ ਬਟਦੀ
ਅੱਟੀ ਇਕ ਅਟੇਰ ਕੇ, ਫਿਰਾਂ ਤਾਣਾ ਤਟਦੀ
ਤਾਣਾ ਹੋਇਆ ਪੂਰ ਨਾ, ਹੁਣ ਕੀਕਰ ਲਾਹਵਾਂ
ਕਹੁੰ ਘੱਟੂੰ ਨਾ ਭਾਵਰੀ, ਕਿੱਥੋਂ ਲੈਸਾਂ ਲਾਵਾਂ

## G30

As I undid the thirtieth knot, I was troubled by grief and
pain. This endless tale never ceases to trouble my
head. We are not going to live over and over again.
The body is hidden and concealed. Separation is still
the thought that comes to settle in my head.

## G31

I have undone one knot at a time, making it thirty-one.
Whose water carrier am I?[17] There have been so many
girls who have wept here. In my home I was a clever
player, but my throw was not a winner. I played the
game to win, but here I have lost.

## G32

I have undone thirty-two knots, and each one is undone
properly. Having wound a single hank of thread,[18] I
go around stretching out the warp. The warp is not
completed, so now how can I get it off? I hope I do
not lose my breath, so that I can perform my marriage
rounds.[19]

## ੩੩

ਬਹਿ ਪਰਛਾਵੀਂ ਖੇਲੂਆਂ, ਹੁਣ ਹੋਇਆਂ ਤੇਤੀ
ਏਥੇ ਦੇ ਤਿੰਨ ਰੋਜ਼ ਹਾਂ, ਨਿਤ ਸੁਹਰਿਆਂ ਸੇਤੀ
ਰੰਗਟ ਚੜ੍ਹੀ ਰਸੂਲ ਦੀ, ਸਭ ਦਾਜ ਰੰਗਾਵੇ
ਜਿਸ ਦੇ ਮੱਥੇ ਭਾਗ ਹੈ, ਉਹ ਰੰਗ ਘਰ ਜਾਵੇ

## ੩੪

ਚੋਂਤੀ ਗੀਂਧੀਂ ਖੇਲੂਆਂ, ਦਿਨ ਆਏ ਨੇੜੇ
ਮਾਹੀ ਦੇ ਵਲ ਜਾਵਸਾਂ, ਰੋਂ ਕੀਤੀ ਕਿਹੜੇ
ਉੜਕ ਵੇਲਾ ਜਾਣ ਕੇ, ਮੈਂ ਨੇਹੁੰ ਲਗਾਇਆ
ਇਸ ਤਨ ਹੋਣਾ ਖ਼ਾਕ ਸੀ, ਮੈਂ ਜਾ ਉਡਾਇਆ

## ੩੫

ਬੁੱਲੂ ਪੈਂਤੀ ਖੇਲੂਆਂ, ਸ਼ਹੁ ਨੇੜੇ ਆਏ
ਬਦਲੇ ਏਸ ਅਜ਼ਾਬ ਦੇ, ਮਤ ਮੁਖ ਦਿਖਲਾਏ
ਅੱਗੇ ਥੋੜ੍ਹੀ ਪੀੜ ਸੀ, ਨੇਹੁੰ ਕੀਤਾ ਦੀਵਾਨੀ
ਪੀ ਗਲੀ ਅਸਾਡੀ ਆ ਵੜੇ, ਤਾਂ ਹੋਗ ਅਸਾਨੀ

## G33

I sit in the shade and undo the knots; now they come to
thirty-three. I am here for only two or three days, but
I shall be with my in-laws forever. They all dye their
dowry clothes with the dye of the Prophet. Those
whose foreheads are marked with good fortune go the
house of delight.[20]

## G34

I have undone thirty-four knots. The days are nearly done.
I will go toward my beloved, but what good actions
have I performed? I have finally realized the time, and
have practiced love. I wasted this body that was due to
turn to dust.

## G35

Bullha, I have undone thirty-five knots. The lord has
drawn near. In exchange for this torment maybe he
will show his face. I had little pain before, but then
love drove me mad. If the beloved enters my street,
things will be easy.

## ੩੬੬

ਛੱਤੀ ਖੇਹਲੂੰ ਹੱਸ ਕੇ, ਨਾਲ ਅਮਰ ਉਮਾਹੇ
ਸੁੱਖਾਂ ਘਾਟਾ ਡਾਲਿਆ, ਦੁੱਖਾਂ ਤੋਂ ਲਾਹੇ
ਘੁੱਲੀ ਵਾ ਪਰੇਮ ਦੀ, ਸਰਨੇ ਪਰ ਸਰਨੇ
ਟੁੱਟੇ ਕਾਮਟ ਮੀਤ ਨੂੰ, ਅਜੇ ਰਹਿੰਦੇ ਕਰਨੇ

## ੩੬੭

ਸੈਂਤੀ ਗੀਂਢੀ ਖੋਲ੍ਹੀਆਂ, ਮੈਂ ਮਹਿੰਦੀ ਲਾਈ
ਮਲਾਇਮ ਦੇਹੀ ਮੈਂ ਕਰਾਂ, ਮਤ ਗਲੇ ਲਗਾਈ
ਓਹਾ ਘੜੀ ਸੁਲੱਖਟੀ, ਜਾਂ ਮੈਂ ਵਲ ਆਵੇ
ਤਾਂ ਮੈਂ ਗਾਵਾਂ ਸੋਹਿਲੇ, ਜੇ ਮੈਨੂੰ ਰਾਵੇ

## ੩੬੮

ਅਠੱਤੀ ਗੀਂਢੀ ਖੋਲ੍ਹੀਆਂ, ਕੀ ਕਰਨੇ ਲੇਖੇ
ਨਾ ਹੋਵੇ ਕਾਜ ਸੁਹਾਵਣਾ, ਬਿਨ ਤੇਰੇ ਵੇਖੇ
ਤੇਰਾ ਭੱਠ ਸੁਹਾਗ ਹੈ, ਮੈਂ ਰਸ ਕੀ ਕਰਸਾਂ
ਲੈਸਾਂ ਗਲੇ ਲਗਾਇਕੇ, ਪਰ ਮੂਲ ਨਾ ਡਰਸਾਂ

## G36

I undo the thirty-sixth knot, laughing in my delight with
the immortal one. Joys have brought me loss, from
pain I gain profit. The breeze of love has blown, as
days succeed days. It still remains for me to practice
spells and magic on the beloved.

## G37

I have undone thirty-seven knots. I have put on the
henna.[21] I make my body soft, in case he embraces me.
The only auspicious moment is when he comes toward
me. I will sing songs of celebration if he makes love
to me.

## G38

I have undone thirty-eight knots. How can they be
reckoned? The wedding ceremony is disagreeable
unless I see you. Confound your married bliss! How
will I delight in it? I will embrace him, and will not
be at all afraid.

## ਗ੩੯

ਉਨਤਾਲੀ ਗੀਢੀਂ ਖੇਲੁਆਂ, ਸਭ ਸਈਆਂ ਰਲ ਕੇ
ਇਨਾਇਤ ਸੇਜ ਤੇ ਆਵਸੀ, ਹੁਣ ਮੈਂ ਵਲ ਭਲਕੇ
ਚੂੜਾ ਬਾਹੀਂ ਸਿਰ ਧੜੀ, ਹਥ ਸੋਹੇ ਕੰਗਣਾ
ਰੰਗਣ ਚੜ੍ਹੀ ਸ਼ਹੁ ਵਸਲ ਦੀ, ਮੈਂ ਤਨ ਮਨ ਰੰਗਣਾ

## ਗ੪੦

ਕਰ 'ਬਿਸਮਿੱਲ੍ਹਾ' ਖੇਲੁਆਂ, ਮੈਂ ਗੀਢਾਂ ਚਾਲੀ
ਜਿਸ ਅਪਣਾ ਆਪ ਵੰਜਾਇਆ, ਸੋ ਸੁਰਜਨ ਵਾਲੀ
ਜੰਞ ਸੋਹਣੀ ਮੈਂ ਭਾਉਂਦੀ, ਲਟਕੇਂਦਾ ਆਵੇ
ਜਿਸ ਨੂੰ ਇਸ਼ਕ ਹੈ ਲਾਲ ਦਾ, ਸੋ ਲਾਲ ਹੋ ਜਾਵੇ
ਅਕਲ ਫ਼ਿਕਰ ਸਭ ਛੋੜ ਕੇ, ਸ਼ਹੁ ਨਾਲ ਸਿਧਾਈ
ਬਿਨ ਕੰਤੋਂ ਗਲ ਗ਼ੈਰ ਦੀ, ਅਸਾਂ ਯਾਦ ਨਾ ਕਾਈ
ਹੁਣ 'ਇੰਨਾ ਲਿੱਲ੍ਹਾ' ਆਖ ਕੇ, ਤੁਮ ਕਰੋ ਦੁਆਈਂ
ਪੀਆ ਹੀ ਸਭ ਹੋ ਗਿਆ, ਅਬਦੱਲ੍ਹਾ ਨਾਹੀਂ

## G39

I have undone thirty-nine knots, with my girlfriends
    around me. Now Inayat will come to me on the bed in
    the morning. The bangles on my arms, the plait on my
    head, and the bracelet on my wrist all look good. I am
    dyed with the delight[22] of union with my beloved, and
    my whole being is filled with joy.

## G40

Saying *bismillāh,*[23] I have undone forty knots. She who
    loses herself becomes the lord's. Swinging his arms,
    the bridegroom comes, and his beautiful wedding
    party delights me. She who experiences the love
    of the beloved herself becomes the beloved. I have
    abandoned all rational concerns and gone off with the
    lord. Except for my bridegroom, I remember nothing
    else. Now say *To God we belong*[24] and offer your
    prayers. All of me has become the beloved; there is no
    Abdullah.[25]

# ਸੀਹਰਫ਼ੀ

ਲਾਗੀ ਰੇ ਲਾਗੀ ਬਲ ਬਲ ਜਾਵੇ
ਇਸ ਲਾਗੀ ਕੋ ਕੋੱਟ ਬੁਝਾਵੇ


## ਸ੧
ਅਲਫ਼ – ਅੱਲ੍ਹੁ ਜਿਸ ਦਿਲਬਰ ਹੋਵੇ, ਮੂੰਹ ਜ਼ਰਦੀ ਅਖ ਲਹੁ ਭਰ ਰੋਵੇ
ਜੀਵਨ ਆਪਣੇ ਤੋਂ ਹਥ ਧੋਵੇ, ਜਿਸ ਨੂੰ ਬਿਰਹੋਂ ਅੱਗ ਲਗਾਵੇ


## ਸ੨
ਬੇ – ਬਾਲਣ ਮੈਂ ਤੇਰਾ ਹੋਈ, ਇਸ਼ਕ ਨਜ਼ਾਰੇ ਆਣ ਵਗੋਈ
ਰੋਦੇ ਨੈਣ ਨਾ ਲੈਂਦੇ ਢੋਈ, ਲੂਣ ਫੱਟਾਂ ਤੇ ਕੀਕਰ ਪਾਵੇ


## ਸ੩
ਤੇ – ਤੇਰੇ ਸੰਗ ਪਰੀਤ ਲਗਾਈ, ਜੀਉ ਜਾਮੇ ਦੀ ਕੀਤੀ ਸਾਈ
ਮੈਂ ਬਕਰੀ ਤੁਧ ਕੋਲ ਕਸਾਈ, ਕਟ ਕਟ ਮਾਸ ਨਾ ਕਿਉਂਕਰ ਖਾਵੇ


320

# The Thirty Letters

I burn, I burn, I am ablaze with love. Who can put out
the flames in this woman who is on fire?

### S1  ALIF (ا)

She whose beloved is God looks pale and weeps tears
of blood. She who burns with the fire of separation
washes her hands of life.

### S2  BE (ب)

I have become fuel for you to burn. Love has come and
destroyed me with a glimpse of you. My eyes weep but
find no refuge. How can he put salt on my wounds?

### S3  TE (ت)

I have fallen in love with you. I have pledged my soul and
body. I am the goat and you are the butcher next to
me. Why should you not cut me up and eat me?

## ੫੪

ਸੇ – ਸਾਬਤ ਨੇਹੂੰ ਲਾਇਆ ਜੈਂ ਨੂੰ, ਦੂਜਾ ਕੁਕ ਸੁਣਾਵਾਂ ਕੈਂ ਨੂੰ
ਰਾਤ ਅੱਧੀ ਉੱਠ ਥਿਲਦੀ ਨੈਂ ਨੂੰ, ਕੂੰਜਾਂ ਵਾਂਗ ਪਈ ਕੁਰਲਾਵੇ

## ੫੫

ਜੀਮ – ਜਹਾਨੋਂ ਹੋਈ ਨਿਆਰੀ, ਲੱਗਾ ਨੇਹੂੰ ਤਾਂ ਹੋਈ ਬਿਕਾਰੀ
ਨਾਲ ਸਰੋਂ ਦੇ ਬਣੇ ਪਸਾਰੀ, ਦੂਜਾ ਦੇ ਮਿਹਣੇ ਜਗ ਤਾਵੇ

## ੫੬

ਹੇ – ਹੈਰਤ ਵਿਚ ਸ਼ਾਂਤ ਨਾਹੀਂ, ਜ਼ਾਹਰ ਬਾਤਨ ਮਾਰਨ ਵਾਹੀਂ
ਝਾਤ ਘੱਤਣ ਨੂੰ ਲਾਵਣ ਵਾਹੀਂ, ਸੀਨੇ ਸੂਲ ਪਰੇਮ ਦੇ ਪਾਵੇ

## ੫੭

ਖ਼ੇ – ਖ਼ੁਬੀ ਹੁਣ ਉਹ ਨਾ ਰਹੀਆਂ, ਜਬ ਕੀ ਸਾਂਗ ਕਲੇਜੇ ਸਹੀਆਂ
ਆਹੀਂ ਨਾਲ ਪੁਕਾਰਾਂ ਕਹੀਆਂ, ਤਦ ਬਿਨ ਕੌਣ ਜੋ ਆਣ ਬੁਝਾਵੇ

## S4  SE (ث)

Who else should I call out to but the one I love so
steadfastly? I get up in the middle of the night and
go into the river,[1] crying mournfully like the crane.

## S5  JĪM (ج)

I have become separate from the world. Falling in love
made me useless. With a mustard seed I became an
apothecary.[2] Besides, people make me suffer with
their taunts.

## S6  HE (ح)

In my astonishment there is no peace. I utter loud laments
both openly and within. I try my hardest to get a
glimpse of him. The sharp pains of love torment my
breast.

## S7  ḲHE (خ)

My beauty was lost, once my heart was speared by love.
I sigh and cry out. Who but you will come and calm
me down?

## ੩੮

ਦਾਲ – ਦਰੋਂ ਟੁਕ ਦੂਰ ਨਾ ਹੋਵੇ, ਫ਼ਕਰ ਫ਼ਿਰਾਕੋਂ ਬਹੁਤਾ ਰੋਵੇ
ਤਨ ਭੱਠੀ ਦਿਲ ਖਿਲਾ ਧਨੋਵੇ, ਇਸ਼ਕ ਅੱਖਾਂ ਵਿਚ ਮਿਰਚਾਂ ਲਾਵੇ

## ੩੯

ਜ਼ਾਲ – ਝੋਕ ਦੁਨੀਆਂ ਤੇ ਇਤ ਨਾ ਕਰਨਾ, ਖ਼ੌਫ਼ ਹਸ਼ਰ ਦੇ ਥੀਂ ਨਾ ਡਰਨਾ
ਚਲਣਾ ਨਬੀ ਸਾਹਿਬ ਦੀ ਸਰਨਾ, ਉਝਕ ਜਾ ਹਿਸਾਬ ਕਰਾਵੇ

## ੩੧੦

ਰੇ – ਰੋਜ਼ ਹਸ਼ਰ ਕੋਈ ਰਹੇ ਨਾ ਖ਼ਾਲੀ, ਲਵੇ ਹਿਸਾਬ ਦੋ ਜਗ ਦਾ ਵਾਲੀ
ਜ਼ੋਰ ਜ਼ਬਰ ਸਭ ਭੁੱਲਟ ਆਲੀ, ਤਿਸ ਦਿਨ ਹਜ਼ਰਤ ਆਪ ਫੁਡਾਵੇ

## ੩੧੧

ਜ਼ੇ – ਜ਼ੁਹਦ ਕਮਾਈ ਚੰਗੀ ਕਰੀਏ, ਜੇਕਰ ਮਰਨ ਤੋਂ ਅੱਗੇ ਮਰੀਏ
ਫਿਰ ਹੋਏ ਭੀ ਉਸ ਤੋਂ ਡਰੀਏ, ਮਤ ਮੋਇਆਂ ਨੂੰ ਪਕੜ ਮੰਗਾਵੇ

## S8  DĀL (د)

They do not stay far from his door for a moment. The
fakirs weep greatly from separation. The body is an
oven that parches the grains of the heart. Love rubs
chilies in the eyes.[3]

## S9  ZĀL (ذ)

Do not take delight in this world, so that you will not fear
the day of the resurrection. Proceed in the protection
of the Prophet, who will have your final account
drawn up.

## S10  RE (ر)

No one escapes on the day of the resurrection. The lord of
the two worlds reckons up their account. The mighty
are lost in confusion. On that day it is the Prophet who
secures their deliverance.

## S11  ZE (ز)

We can make a successful profit through abstinence, if we
die before our death.[4] But even when we are dead we
should fear him, in case he should arrest and summon
the dead.

325

## ਸ੧੨

ਸੀਨ – ਸਾਈਂ ਬਿਨ ਜਾ ਨਾ ਕੋਈ, ਜਿਤ ਵਲ ਵੇਖਾਂ ਉਹੀ ਉਹੀ
ਹੋਰ ਕਿਤੇ ਵਲ ਮਿਲੇ ਨਾ ਢੋਈ, ਮੁਰਸ਼ਦ ਮੇਰਾ ਪਾਰ ਲੰਘਾਵੇ

## ਸ੧੩

ਸ਼ੀਨ – ਸ਼ਾਹ ਇਨਾਇਤ ਮੁਰਸ਼ਦ ਮੇਰਾ, ਜਿਸ ਨੇ ਕੀਤਾ ਮੈਂ ਵਲ ਫੇਰਾ
ਚੁੱਕ ਗਿਆ ਸਭ ਝਗੜਾ ਝੇੜਾ, ਹੁਣ ਮੈਨੂੰ ਭਰਮਾਵੇ ਤਾਵੇ

## ਸ੧੪

ਸੁਆਦ – ਸਬਰ ਨਾ ਆਵੇ ਮੈਨੂੰ, ਖੁੱਲੀ ਵਸਤ ਬਜ਼ਾਰ
ਕਾਸਦ ਲੈ ਕੇ ਵਿਦਿਆ ਹੋਇਆ, ਜਾ ਵੜਿਆ ਦਰਬਾਰ
ਅੱਗੋਂ ਮਿਲਿਆ ਆ ਕੇ ਉਹਨੂੰ, ਸੋਹਣਾ ਸ਼ੇਰ ਸਵਾਰ
ਰਸਤੇ ਵਿਚ ਅੰਗੁਸ਼ਤਰੀ ਆਹੀ, ਇਹ ਵੀ ਦਿਲ ਭੁਲਾਵੇ

## ਸ੧੫

ਜ਼ੁਆਦ – ਜ਼ਰੂਰੀ ਯਾਦ ਅੱਲ੍ਹ ਦੀ, ਕਰੇ ਸਵਾਲ ਰਸੂਲ
ਨਵੇ ਹਜ਼ਾਰ ਕਲਾਮ ਸੁਟਾਈ, ਪਈ ਦਰਗਾਹ ਕਬੂਲ
ਇਹ ਮਜਾਜ਼ੀ ਜ਼ਾਤ ਹਕੀਕੀ, ਵਾਸਲ ਵਸਲ ਵਸੂਲ
ਫ਼ਾਰਗ਼ ਹੋ ਕੇ ਹਜ਼ਰਤ ਉਥੇ, ਆਵੇ ਖਾਣਾ ਖਾਵੇ

## S12  SĪN (س)

There is no place besides the lord. Wherever I look, there
is just him and no one else. There is no refuge in any
other direction. My guide gets me across.

## S13  SHĪN (ش)

Shah Inayat is my guide, the one whose passage has lain in
my direction. All contention and dispute is finished;
now he deceives and torments me.

## S14  SUĀD (ص)

I am impatient, the goods are laid out in the bazaar. Taking
the messenger[5] with him, he said farewell and went to
enter the court. There he was met by the fair rider on
a tiger. On the way there was a ring, which made his
heart confused.

## S15  ZUĀD (ض)

It is necessary to remember God, whom the Prophet
implored. Ninety thousand[6] words were recited
and accepted in the divine court. This illusory being
was united with the reality of the divine essence.
Becoming free, the holy Prophet came there and ate.

## ੩੧੬

ਤੋਏ – ਤਲਬ ਦੀਦਾਰ ਦੀ ਆਹੀ, ਕੀਤਾ ਕਰਮ ਸੱਤਾਰ
ਜਲਵਾ ਫੇਰ ਇਲਾਹੀ ਦਿੱਤਾ, ਹਜ਼ਰਤ ਨੂੰ ਗ਼ੱਫਾਰ
ਹੱਥ ਨੂਰਾਨੀ ਗ਼ੈਬੋਂ ਆਵੇ, ਮੁੰਦਰੀ ਦਾ ਚਮਕਾਰ
ਬੁੱਲ੍ਹਾ ਖ਼ਲਕ ਮੁਹੰਮਦੀ ਕੀਤੇ, ਤਾਂ ਇਹ ਕੀ ਕਹਾਵੇ

## ੩੧੭

ਜ਼ੋਏ – ਜ਼ਾਹਰ ਮਾਲੂਮ ਨਾ ਕੀਤਾ, ਹੋਇਆ ਦੀਦਾਰ ਭੁਲਾਵੇ
ਰਲ ਕੇ ਸਈਆਂ ਖਾਣਾ ਖਾਧਾ, ਜ਼ੱਰਾ ਅੰਤ ਨਾ ਆਵੇ
ਉਹ ਅੰਗੂਠੀ ਆਪ ਪਛਾਤੀ, ਅਪਨੀ ਆਪ ਜਿਤਾਵੇ
ਬੁੱਲ੍ਹਾ ਹਜ਼ਰਤ ਰੁਖ਼ਸਤ ਹੋ ਕੇ, ਆਪਨੇ ਯਾਰ ਸੁਹਾਵੇ

## ੩੧੮

ਐਨ – ਇਨਾਇਤ ਉਲਫ਼ਤ ਹੋਈ, ਸੁਣੋ ਅਸਹਾਬੋ ਯਾਰੋ
ਜਿਹੜਾ ਜਪ ਨਾ ਕਰਸੀ ਹਜ਼ਰਤ, ਝੂਠਾ ਰਹੇ ਸਰਕਾਰੋਂ
ਫੇਰ ਸ਼ੜ੍ਹਾਇਤ ਅਸਾਂ ਹੈ ਕਰਨੀ, ਸਾਹਿਬ ਦੇ ਦਰਬਾਰੋਂ
ਬੁੱਲ੍ਹਾ ਕਿਬਰ ਨਾ ਕਰ ਦੁਨੀਆਂ ਤੇ, ਇੱਕਾ ਨਜ਼ਰੀਂ ਆਵੇ

## S16  TOE (ط)

He was desirous of a sight of him, and God the pardoner
was gracious. Then God the forgiver granted the holy
Prophet a vision of the divine glory. From the unseen
there appeared a hand full of light, on which a ring
glittered. Bullha, you made the people of Muhammad,
so what should this be called?

## S17  ZOE (ظ)

God was not known in outward form. When he granted a
vision of himself, he caused confusion. The girlfriends
came together and ate the food, of which there was no
end. It was he[7] who recognized the ring himself, and
he who made himself known. Bullha, the holy Prophet
took his leave and pleased his beloved.

## S18  'AIN (ع)

Listen, gentlemen and friends, I enjoy the love of Inayat.[8]
Whoever fails to pray to the holy Prophet will be
rejected as false by the divine court. So we must pray
for his intercession in the court of the lord. Bullha, do
not take pride in the world, which appears just once.

## ੩੧੯

ਗ਼ੈਨ – ਗ਼ੁਲਾਮ ਗ਼ਰੀਬ ਤੁਸਾਡਾ, ਖ਼ੈਰ ਮੰਗੇ ਦਰਬਾਰੋਂ
ਰੋਜ਼ ਹਸ਼ਰ ਦੇ ਖ਼ੌਫ਼ ਸੁਟੀਂਦਾ, ਸੱਦ ਹੋਸੀ ਸਰਕਾਰੋਂ
ਕੁਲ ਖ਼ਲਾਇਕ ਤਲਖ਼ੀ ਅੰਦਰ, ਸੂਰਜ ਦੇ ਚਮਕਾਰੋਂ
ਬੁੱਲ੍ਹੂ ਅਸਾਂ ਵੀ ਉਥੇ ਜਾਣਾ, ਜਿੱਥੇ ਗਿਆ ਨਾ ਭਾਵੇ

## ੩੨੦

ਫ਼ੇ – ਫ਼ਕੀਰਾਂ ਫ਼ਿਕਰ ਜੋ ਕੀਤਾ, ਵਿਚ ਦਰਗਾਰ ਇਲਾਹੀ
ਸ਼ਫ਼ੀਅ ਮੁੰਹਮਦ ਜਾ ਖਲੋਤੇ, ਜਿੱਥੇ ਬੇਪਰਵਾਹੀ
ਨੇੜੇ ਨੇੜੇ ਆ ਹਬੀਬਾ, ਇਹ ਮੁਹੱਬਤ ਚਾਹੀ
ਖ਼ਿਰਕਾ ਪਹਿਨ ਰਸੂਲ ਅੱਲੂ ਦਾ, ਸਿਰ ਤੇ ਤਾਜ ਲਗਾਵੇ

## ੩੨੧

ਕਾਫ਼ – ਕਲਮ ਨਾ ਮਿਟੇ ਰਬਾਨੀ, ਜੋ ਅਸਾਂ ਪਰ ਆਈ
ਜੋ ਕੁਝ ਭਾਗਾ ਅਸਾਡੇ ਆਏ, ਉਹ ਤਾਂ ਮੁੜਦੇ ਨਾਹੀ
ਬਾਝ ਨਸੀਬੋਂ ਦਾਅਵੇ ਕੇੜੇ, ਬੰਨੂ ਕੁਲ ਖ਼ੁਦਾਈ
ਬੁੱਲ੍ਹੂ ਲੋਹ ਮਹਿਫੂਜ਼ ਤੇ ਲਿਖਿਆ, ਉਥੋਂ ਕੌਣ ਮਿਟਾਵੇ

## S19  ĠHAIN (غ)

Your poor slave begs for alms from the court. On the day
of judgment, the sound of terror will be heard, and
the call will be announced from the court. All creation
will be in distress from the glittering light of the sun.
Bullha, we too must go there, although the journey is
not a pleasant one.

## S20  FE (ف)

Fakirs are cared for in the divine court, where Muhammad
the intercessor stands unconcernedly. "Draw near,
draw near, beloved," is what their love desires. He
wears the robe of the Apostle of God, who crowns his
head.

## S21  QĀF (ق)

The divine pen that writes our fate cannot be erased. The
fortune that was granted us cannot be turned back.
Except for fate, what use are the plans that all creation
makes? Bullha, who can erase what is written on the
preserved tablet?[9]

## ਸ੨੨

ਕਾਫ਼ – ਕਲਮ ਨਬੀ ਦੀ ਸੱਚੀ, ਸਿਰ ਨਬੀਆਂ ਦੇ ਸਾਈਂ
ਸੂਰਤ ਪਾਕ ਨਬੀ ਦੀ ਜਿਹਾ, ਚੰਦ ਸੂਰਜ ਭੀ ਨਾਹੀਂ
ਹੀਰੇ ਮੋਤੀ ਲਾਲ ਜਵਾਹਰ, ਪਹੁੰਚੇ ਉੱਥੇ ਨਾਹੀਂ
ਮਜਲਸ ਉਸ ਨਬੀ ਦੀ ਬਹਿ ਕੇ, ਬੁੱਲ੍ਹਾ ਕੌਣ ਕਹਾਵੇ

## ਸ੨੩

ਲਾਮ – 'ਲਾ ਇਲਾਹ' ਦਾ ਜ਼ਿਕਰ ਬਤਾਇਓ, 'ਇੱਲੱਲ੍ਹੁ' ਅਸਬਾਤ
    ਕਰਾਇਓ
'ਮੁਹੰਮਦ ਰਸੂਲੱਲ੍ਹੁ' ਮੇਲ ਕਰਾਇਓ, ਬੁੱਲ੍ਹਾ ਇਹ ਤੋਹੜਾ ਆਦਮ ਨੂੰ
    ਆਵੇ

## ਸ੨੪

ਮੀਮ – ਮੁੰਹਮਦੀ ਜਿਸਮ ਬਟਾਇਓ, ਦਾਖਲ ਵਿਚ ਬਹਿਸ਼ਤ ਕਹਾਇਓ
ਆਪੇ ਮਗਰ ਸ਼ੈਤਾਨ ਪੁਚਾਇਓ, ਓਥੋਂ ਨਿਕਲ ਕੇ ਆਦਮ ਆਵੇ

## S22   KĀF (ک)

True is the word of the Prophet, the lord at the head of
all the prophets. Even the sun and the moon cannot
match the holy appearance of the Prophet. Diamonds,
pearls, rubies, and jewels do not reach that point.
When he sits in the assembly of the Prophet, what
does Bullha amount to?

## S23   LĀM (ل)

You recited the words *There is no god,*[10] and added the
confirmation *but God*. You joined to these the words
*Muhammad is the Apostle of God*. This is the gift that
was given to Adam.[11]

## S24   MĪM (م)

You made Adam's body like Muhammad's. You said he
was to enter paradise. Then it was you who made
Satan come there. He came out of there as Adam.

## ੩੨੫

ਨੂਨ – ਨਿਮਾਣਾ ਹੋ ਮੁਜਰਿਮ ਆਇਆ, ਕੱਢ ਬਹਿਸ਼ਤੋਂ ਜ਼ਿਮੀਂ ਰੁਲਾਇਆ
ਆਦਮ ਹੱਵਾ ਜੁਦਾ ਕਰਾਇਆ, ਅੱਲ੍ਹ ਆਪ ਵਿਛੋੜਾ ਪਾਵੇ

## ੩੨੬

ਵਾ – ਵਾਹ ਵਾਹ ਆਪ ਮੁਹੰਮਦ, ਅਪਣੀ ਆਦਮ ਸ਼ਕਲ ਬਟਾਵੇ
ਆਪੇ ਰੋਜ਼ ਅਜ਼ਲ ਦਾ ਮਾਲਿਕ, ਆਪੇ ਸ਼ਫ਼ੀਆ ਹੋ ਆਵੇ
ਆਪੇ ਰੋਜ਼ ਹਸ਼ਰ ਦਾ ਕਾਜ਼ੀ, ਆਪੇ ਹੁਕਮ ਸੁਣਾਵੇ
ਆਪੇ ਚਾ ਸ਼ਫ਼ਾਇਤ ਕਰਦਾ, ਆਪ ਦੀਦਾਰ ਕਰਾਵੇ

## ੩੨੭

ਹੇ – ਹੌਲੀ ਬੋਲੀਂ ਏਥੇ ਭਾਈ, ਮਤ ਕੋਈ ਸੁਟੇ ਸੁਟਾਵੇ
ਵੱਡਾ ਅਜ਼ਾਬ ਕਬਰ ਦਾ ਦਿੱਸੇ, ਜੇ ਕੋਈ ਚਾ ਛੁਡਾਵੇ
ਪੁਲ ਸਰਾਤ ਦੀ ਔਖੀ ਗਾਟੀ, ਉਹ ਵੀ ਖ਼ੌਫ਼ ਡਰਾਵੇ
ਰਖ ਉਮੈਦ ਫ਼ਜ਼ਲ ਦੀ ਬੁੱਲ੍ਹਿਆ, ਅੱਲ੍ਹ ਆਪ ਬਚਾਵੇ

## S25 NŪN (ن)

Wretchedly he came as a criminal, expelled from paradise
and made to wander the earth. Adam and Eve were
made to separate; it was God who effected their
separation.

## S26 VĀO (و)

How wonderful! It is he who is Muhammad, he who makes
his form Adam, he who is the lord of the first day, he
who comes as the intercessor, he who is the judge of
the last day, he who announces his command, he who
kindly intercedes,[12] he who lets himself be seen.

## S27 HE (ه)

Speak softly here, brother, in case someone hears and
reports you. The torment of the grave seems great,
although someone may grant deliverance. The
passage over the Sirat bridge[13] is difficult; that fear
is overwhelming. Put your hope in divine favor,
Bullha; it is God himself who saves us.

## ੩੨੮

ਲਾਮ – ਲਾਮੂ ਨਾ ਕੋਈ ਦਿੱਸੇ, ਕਿਤ ਵਲ ਕੂਕ ਸੁਟਾਵਾਂ
ਜਿਤ ਵਲ ਵੇਖਾਂ ਨਜ਼ਰ ਨਾ ਆਵੇ, ਕਿਸ ਨੂੰ ਹਾਲ ਸੁਟਾਵਾਂ
ਬਾਝ ਪੀਆ ਨਹੀਂ ਕੋਈ ਹਾਮੀ, ਹੋਰ ਨਹੀਂ ਕੋਈ ਥਾਵਾਂ
ਬੁੱਲ੍ਹਾ ਮਲ ਦਰਵਾਜ਼ਾ ਹਜ਼ਰਤ ਵਾਲਾ, ਓਹੀ ਤੈਂ ਛੁਡਾਵੇ

## ੩੨੯

ਅਲਫ਼ – ਇੱਕਲਾ ਜਾਵੇ ਏਥੋਂ, ਵੇਖਟ ਆਵਟ ਫੇਰ
ਸਾਹਾਂ ਤੇਰਿਆਂ ਦੀ ਗਿਣਤੀ ਏਥੇ, ਆਈ ਹੋਈ ਨੇੜ
ਚਲ ਸ਼ਤਾਬੀ ਚਲ ਫੜ ਬੁੱਲ੍ਹਿਆ, ਮਤ ਲਗ ਜਾਵੇ ਡੇਰ
ਪਕੜੀਂ ਵਾਗ ਰਸੂਲ ਅੱਲਾ ਦੀ, ਕੁਝ ਜਿੱਥੋਂ ਹੱਥ ਆਵੇ

## ੩੩੦

ਜੇ – ਯਾਰੀ ਹੁਟੇ ਮੈਂ ਲਾਈ, ਅਗਲੀ ਉਮਰਾ ਖੇਡ ਵੰਜਾਈ
ਬੁੱਲ੍ਹਾ ਸ਼ਹੁ ਦੀ ਜ਼ਾਤ ਈ ਆਹੀ, ਕਲਮਾ ਪੜ੍ਹਦਿਆਂ ਜਿੰਦ ਲਿਜਾਵੇ

## S28  LĀM- (ل)

I[14] cannot see anyone near me. Where shall I direct my
cries? No one appears, no matter where I look. To
whom shall I describe my state? I have no supporter
besides my beloved, and have no other places to go.
Seize hold of the door of ᵗhe holy Prophet, Bullha,
for he is the one who will grant deliverance.

## S29  -ALIF (ا)

You will depart alone from this world, where many come
to look. The number of your breaths here is nearly
complete. Go quickly, go and enter, Bullha, in case you
are too late. Seize the reins[15] of the Apostle of God,
wherever you get the chance.

## S30  YE (ي)

Now at last I have found love. I played around and wasted
my previous life. Bullha, the divine being takes my
soul as I recite the profession of faith.

# ਦੋਹੜੇ

### ਦ੧

ਇਸ ਕਾ ਮੁਖ ਇਕ ਜੋਤ ਹੈ, ਘੁੰਗਟ ਹੈ ਸੰਸਾਰ
ਘੁੰਗਟ ਮੇਂ ਵੋਹ ਛੁਪ ਗਿਆ, ਮੁਖ ਪਰ ਆਂਚਲ ਡਾਰ

### ਦ੨

ਇਨ ਕੋ ਮੁਖ ਦਿਖਲਾਏ ਹੈ, ਜਿਨ ਸੇ ਇਸ ਕੀ ਪੀਤ
ਇਨ ਕੋ ਹੀ ਮਿਲਤਾ ਹੈ ਵੋਹ, ਜੋ ਇਸ ਕੇ ਹੈਂ ਮੀਤ

### ਦ੩

ਮੂੰਹ ਦਿਖਲਾਵੇ ਔਰ ਛੁਪੇ, ਫਲ ਬਲ ਹੈ ਜਗ ਦੇਸ
ਪਾਸ ਰਹੇ ਔਰ ਨਾ ਮਿਲੇ, ਇਸ ਕੇ ਬਿਸਵੇ ਭੇਸ

### ਦ੪

ਬੁੱਲ੍ਹਾ ਕਸਰ ਨਾਮ ਕਸੂਰ ਹੈ, ਓਥੇ ਮੂੰਹੋਂ ਨਾ ਸਕਟ ਬੋਲ
ਓਥੇ ਸੱਚੇ ਗਰਦਨ ਮਾਰੀਏ, ਓਥੇ ਝੂਠੇ ਕਰਨ ਕਲੋਲ

# *Verses*

### V1

His[1] face is a light, the world is a veil. He is hidden in the
veil, casting its hem over his face.

### V2

He shows his face to those whom he loves. He only comes
to those who are his friends.

### V3

He reveals his face and he hides; the world we live in is
deceptive. He is beside us, but we cannot find him;
he is disguised in everything.

### V4

Bullha, the real name of Kasur is "fault."[2] It is a place
where people cannot speak openly, where the truthful
have their necks severed, and where the false have a
merry time.

## ੮੫

ਬੁੱਲ੍ਹਿਆ ਕਸੂਰ ਬੇਦਸਤੂਰ, ਓਥੇ ਜਾਣਾ ਬਣਿਆ ਜ਼ਰੂਰ
ਨਾ ਕੋਈ ਪੁੰਨ ਨਾ ਦਾਨ ਹੈ, ਨਾ ਕੋਈ ਲਾਗ ਦਸਤੂਰ

## ੮੬

ਬੁੱਲ੍ਹਿਆ ਧਰਮਸਾਲਾ ਢਡਵਾਈ ਰਹਿੰਦੇ, ਠਾਕਰ ਦੁਆਰੇ ਠੱਗ
ਵਿਚ ਮਸੀਤਾਂ ਕੁਸੱਤੀਏ ਰਹਿੰਦੇ, ਆਸ਼ਕ ਰਹਿਣ ਅਲੱਗ

## ੮੭

ਬੁੱਲ੍ਹਿਆ ਵਾਰੇ ਜਾਈਏ ਉਨ੍ਹਾਂ ਤੋਂ, ਜਿਹੜੇ ਗਲੀਂ ਦੇਣ ਪੁਚਾ
ਸੂਈ ਸਲਾਈ ਦਾਨ ਕਰਨ, ਤੇ ਅਹਿਰਣ ਲੈਣ ਛੁਪਾ

## ੮੮

ਬੁੱਲ੍ਹਿਆ ਵਾਰੇ ਜਾਈਏ ਉਨ੍ਹਾਂ ਤੋਂ, ਜਿਹੜੇ ਮਾਰਨ ਗੱਪ ਸ਼ੜੱਪ
ਕੌਡੀ ਲੱਭੀ ਦੇਣ ਚਾ, ਤੇ ਬੁਗਚਾ ਘਉ ਘੱਪ

## V5

Bullha, Kasur is lawless, we go there because we must.
There is no merit or charity there, nor do any
regulations operate.

## V6

Bullha, robbers live in the lodge,[3] and thugs live in the
temple. The impure live in the mosques, but lovers
live their separate lives.

## V7

Bullha,[4] we are sacrificed to those who beguile with their
words. They make a gift of the needle, but hide the
anvil away.

## V8

Bullha, we are sacrificed to those who talk big. If they
find a penny they give it back, but they hang on to
the purse.

## ੮੯

ਨਾ ਖ਼ੁਦਾ ਮਸੀਤੇ ਲਭਦਾ, ਨਾ ਖ਼ੁਦਾ ਵਿਚ ਕਾਅਬੇ
ਨਾ ਖ਼ੁਦਾ ਕੁਰਆਨ ਕਿਤਾਬਾਂ, ਨਾ ਖ਼ੁਦਾ ਨਮਾਜ਼ੇ

## ੮੧੦

ਨਾ ਖ਼ੁਦਾ ਮੈਂ ਤੀਰਥ ਡਿੱਠਾ, ਐਵੇਂ ਪੈਂਡੇ ਝਾਗੇ
ਬੁੱਲ੍ਹੂ ਸ਼ਹੁ ਦਾ ਮੁਰਸ਼ਦ ਮਿਲ ਗਿਆ, ਟੁੱਟੇ ਸੱਭ ਤਗਾਦੇ

## ੮੧੧

ਬੁੱਲ੍ਹਿਆ ਪਰਸੋਂ ਕਾਫ਼ਰ ਥੀ ਗਿਓਂ, ਬੁਤ ਪੂਜਾ ਕੀਤੀ ਕੱਲ
ਅਸੀਂ ਜਾ ਬੈਠੇ ਘਰ ਆਪਟੇ, ਓਥੇ ਕਰਨ ਨਾ ਮਿਲੀਆਂ ਗੱਲ

## ੮੧੨

ਬੁੱਲ੍ਹਿਆ ਹੌਨ ਗ਼ਰੂਰਤ ਸਾੜ ਸੁੱਟ, ਤੇ ਮਾਣ ਖੂਹੇ ਵਿਚ ਪਾ
ਤਨ ਮਨ ਦੀ ਸੁਰਤ ਗਵਾ ਵੇ, ਗੁਰ ਆਪ ਮਿਲੇਗਾ ਆ

## V9

God is not in the mosque, nor is God in the Kaaba. God
is not in the scripture, nor is God found in prayer.

## V10

I[5] did not see God at the holy bathing place, and suffered
the long stages of the journey there for nothing. Once
Bullhe Shah's guide was found, all troubles were
removed.

## V11

Bullha, you became an unbeliever two days ago, and
yesterday you worshipped idols. Actually, we went and
sat in our own house, so no one could say anything.

## V12

Bullha, A is for arrogance.[6] Destroy it, and throw pride
down the well. Lose consciousness of body and mind,
and the guide will let himself be found.

## ੨੧੩

ਬੁੱਲ੍ਹਿਆ ਹਿਜਰਤ ਵਿਚ ਇਸਲਾਮ ਦੇ, ਮੇਰਾ ਨਿਤ ਹੈ ਖ਼ਾਸ ਅਰਾਮ
ਨਿਤ ਨਿਤ ਮਰਾਂ ਤੇ ਨਿਤ ਜੀਵਾਂ, ਮੇਰਾ ਨਿਤ ਨਿਤ ਕੂਚ ਮੁਕਾਮ

## ੨੧੪

ਬੁੱਲ੍ਹਿਆ ਇਸ਼ਕ ਸਜਣ ਦੇ ਆਇਕੇ, ਸਾਨੂੰ ਕੀਤੁਸ ਡੂਮ
ਉਹ ਪ੍ਰਭ ਅਸਾਡਾ ਸਖੀ ਹੈ, ਮੈਂ ਸੇਵਾ ਕਨੂੰ ਸ਼ੂਮ

## ੨੧੫

ਬੁੱਲ੍ਹਿਆ ਆਸ਼ਕ ਹੋਇਓਂ ਰੱਬ ਦਾ, ਮਲਾਮਤ ਹੋਈ ਲਾਖ
ਲੋਗ ਕਾਫ਼ਰ ਕਾਫ਼ਰ ਆਖਦੇ, ਤੂੰ ਆਹੋ ਆਹੋ ਆਖ

## ੨੧੬

ਬੁੱਲ੍ਹਿਆ ਪੈਂਡੇ ਪੜੇ ਪਰੇਮ ਕੇ, ਕਿਆ ਪੈਂਡਾ ਆਵਾਗੌਂ
ਅੰਧੇ ਕੋ ਅੰਧਾ ਮਿਲ ਗਿਆ, ਰਾਹ ਬਤਾਵੇ ਕੌਂ

## V13

Bullha, migrating for the faith[7] is a part of Islam, but
I always enjoy a special rest. I always keep dying and
living, I am always moving and stopping.

## V14

Bullha, my love for the beloved has come and made me a
humble Dum.[8] That lord of mine is generous, but I am
miserly in his service.

## V15

Bullha, you have become a lover of the lord and have
incurred manifold disgrace. When people keep calling
you "Unbeliever, unbeliever," just say "Yes, yes!"

## V16

Bullha, the stages of love's journey[9] lie ahead. What is the
journey of the cycle of coming and going? When the
blind meet the blind, who will lead the way?

## ੲੴੴੴ

ਬੁੱਲ੍ਹਿਆ ਮਨ ਮੰਜੋਲਾ ਮੁੰਜ ਦਾ, ਕਿਤੇ ਗੋਸ਼ੇ ਬਹਿਕੇ ਕੁੱਟ
ਇਹ ਖਜ਼ਾਨਾ ਤੈਨੂੰ ਅਰਸ਼ ਦਾ, ਤੂੰ ਸੰਭਲ ਸੰਭਲ ਲੁੱਟ

## ੲੴ੮

ਬੁੱਲ੍ਹਿਆ ਚੇਰੀ ਮੁਸਲਮਾਨ ਦੀ, ਹਿੰਦੂ ਤੋਂ ਕੁਰਬਾਨ
ਦੋਹਾਂ ਤੋਂ ਪਾਣੀ ਵਾਰ ਪੀ, ਜੋ ਕਰੇ ਭਗਵਾਨ

## ੲੴ੯

ਬੁੱਲ੍ਹਿਆ ਮੁੱਲਾਂ ਅਤੇ ਮਸ਼ਾਲਚੀ, ਦੋਹਾਂ ਇੱਕੋ ਚਿੱਤ
ਲੋਕਾਂ ਕਰਦੇ ਚਾਨਣਾ, ਆਪ ਹਨੇਰੇ ਨਿੱਤ

## ੲ੨੦

ਬੁੱਲ੍ਹਿਆ ਪੀ ਸ਼ਰਾਬ ਤੇ ਖਾ ਕਬਾਬ, ਹੇਠ ਬਾਲ ਹੱਡਾਂ ਦੀ ਅੱਗ
ਚੋਰੀ ਕਰ ਤੇ ਭੰਨ ਘਰ ਰੱਬ ਦਾ, ਓਸ ਠੱਗਾਂ ਦੇ ਠੱਗ ਨੂੰ ਠੱਗ

## V17

Bullha, the mind is a bundle of fiber.[10] Sit in a corner
somewhere and beat it. This is a treasure[11] provided
for you by heaven, so enjoy it carefully.

## V18

Bullha, I am the slave girl of the Muslim, and am sacrificed
to the Hindu. Be devoted to both of them, as the lord
decides.

## V19

Bullha, the mullah and the torch bearer both have the
same intent. They spread light to people, but are
always in the dark[12] themselves.

## V20

Bullha, drink wine and eat kebabs, burning your bones
as the fuel to cook them with. Do a burglary and
break into the house of the lord, to rob that robber of
robbers.

### ੨੨੧

ਬੁੱਲ੍ਹਿਆ ਚਲ ਸੁਨਿਆਰ ਦੇ, ਜਿੱਥੇ ਗਹਿਣੇ ਘੜੀਏ ਲਾਖ
ਸੂਰਤ ਆਪੇ ਆਪਟੀ, ਤੂੰ ਇੱਕੋ ਰੂਪ ਆਖ

### ੨੨੨

ਫਿਰੀ ਰੁੱਤ ਸ਼ਗੂਫ਼ਿਆਂ ਵਾਲੀ, ਚਿੜੀਆਂ ਚੁਗਣ ਨੂੰ ਆਈਆਂ
ਇਕਨਾਂ ਨੂੰ ਜੁੱਰਿਆਂ ਲੈ ਖਾਧਾ, ਇਕਨਾਂ ਫਾਹੀਆਂ ਲਾਈਆਂ
ਇਕਨਾਂ ਨੂੰ ਆਸ ਮੁੜਨ ਦੀ ਆਹੀ, ਇਕ ਸੀਖ ਕਬਾਬ ਚੜ੍ਹਾਈਆਂ
ਬੁੱਲ੍ਹੇ ਸ਼ਾਹ ਕੀ ਵੱਸ ਉਨ੍ਹਾਂ ਦੇ, ਉਹ ਕਿਸਮਤ ਮਾਰ ਫਸਾਈਆਂ

### ੨੨੩

ਬੁੱਲ੍ਹਿਆ ਅੱਛੇ ਦਿਨ ਪਿੱਛੇ ਗਏ, ਜਬ ਹਰ ਸੇ ਕੀਆ ਨਾ ਹੇਤ
ਅਬ ਪਛਤਾਵਾ ਕਿਆ ਕਰੇ, ਜਬ ਚਿੜੀਆਂ ਚੁੱਗ ਗਈਂ ਖੇਤ

### ੨੨੪

ਉਹ ਮੇਰੇ ਅੰਦਰ ਬੋਲਿਆ, ਰੁੜੁ ਪੁੜੁ ਗਏ ਗੁਨਾਹ
ਝਾੜੀ ਲੱਗਾ ਬਾਜਰਾ, ਸ਼ਹਿਤੂਤ ਲੱਗੇ ਫਰਵਾਂਹ

## V21

Bullha, go to the jeweler's, where so many ornaments are
fashioned. Each has its own form, but just say: "They
are all the same silver."[13]

## V22

The season of blossoms has arrived, the birds have come
to peck them. Some birds have been seized and eaten
by hawks, some have been trapped in snares. Some
had hopes of returning, some were mounted on spits
as kebabs. Bullhe Shah, what power lies with those
who are snared and slain by fate?

## V23

Bullha, good times have been left behind, since we did not
practice love for the lord. What use is it to be sorry
now, when the birds have stripped the field?

## V24

He has spoken within me, and my sins have all been swept
away. Millet grows on thorn bushes, and mulberries
grow on pine trees.[14]

## ੮੨੫

ਅੱਲ੍ਹਾ ਤੋਂ ਮੈਂ ਕਰਜ਼ ਬਟਾਇਆ, ਹੱਥੋਂ ਤੂੰ ਮੇਰਾ ਕਰਜ਼ਾਈ
ਉਥੇ ਤਾਂ ਮੇਰੀ ਪਰਵਰਿਸ਼ ਕੀਤੀ, ਜਿਥੇ ਕਿਸੇ ਨੂੰ ਖ਼ਬਰ ਨ ਕਾਈ
ਉਥੋਂ ਤਾਹੀਂ ਆਏ ਏਥੇ, ਜਾਂ ਪਹਿਲੇ ਰੋਜ਼ੀ ਆਈ
ਬੁੱਲ੍ਹੇ ਸ਼ਾਹ ਹੈ ਆਸ਼ਕ, ਜਿਸ ਤਹਿਕੀਕ ਹਕੀਕਤ ਪਾਈ

## ੮੨੬

ਬੁੱਲ੍ਹਿਆ ਕਟਕ ਕੋਂਡੀ ਕਾਮਨੀ, ਤੀਨੋਂ ਕੀ ਤਲਵਾਰ
ਆਏ ਥੇ ਨਾਮ ਜਪਨ ਕੋ, ਔਰ ਵਿਸ਼ੇ ਲੀਤੇ ਮਾਰ

## ੮੨੭

ਭੂਠ ਨਮਾਜ਼ਾਂ ਚਿੱਕੜ ਰੋਜ਼ੇ, ਕਲਮੇ ਤੇ ਫਿਰ ਗਈ ਸਿਆਹੀ
ਬੁੱਲ੍ਹੇ ਸ਼ਾਹ ਸ਼ਹੁ ਅੰਦਰੋਂ ਪਾਇਆ, ਭੁੱਲੀ ਫਿਰੇ ਲੁਕਾਈ

## ੮੨੮

ਬੁੱਲ੍ਹਿਆ ਆਉਂਦਾ ਸਾਜਨ ਵੇਖ ਕੇ, ਜਾਂਦਾ ਮੂਲ ਨਾ ਵੇਖ
ਮਾਰੇ ਦਰਦ ਫ਼ਰਾਕ ਦੇ, ਬਟ ਬੈਠੇ ਬਾਹਮਣ ਸ਼ੇਖ਼

## V25

I took a loan from God, or rather you are my borrower.
There you looked after me, where no one took any
notice of me. From there I then came here, where first
we received sustenance. Bullhe Shah is a lover who has
assuredly discovered the truth.

## V26

Bullha, wheat, wealth, and women—these three are a
sword. People came to meditate on the divine name,
and worldly pleasures destroyed them.

## V27

Into the oven with prayers, into the mud with fasting.
Ink has blotted out the profession of faith. Bullha, I
have found the lord from within myself, while people
wander lost.

## V28

Bullha, watch the beloved coming to you, be sure you do
not watch him go. Because of the pain of separation,
Brahmans and Shaikhs have been driven to settle in
the forest.

## ੮੨੯

ਬੁੱਲ੍ਹ ਸ਼ਾਹ ਉਹ ਕੌਣ ਹੈ, ਉੱਤਮ ਤੇਰਾ ਯਾਰ
ਉਸੇ ਹਾਥ ਕੁਰਆਨ ਹੈ, ਓਸੇ ਗਲ ਜੁੰਨਾਰ

## ੮੩੦

ਬੁੱਲਿਆ ਚਲ ਬਾਵਰਚੀ ਖ਼ਾਨੇ ਯਾਰ ਦੇ, ਜਿਥੇ ਕੋਹਾ ਕਾਹੀ ਹੋ
ਓਥੇ ਮੋਟੇ ਕੱਸਟ ਬਕਰੇ, ਤੂੰ ਲਿੱਸਾ ਮਿਲੇ ਨਾ ਢੋ

## ੮੩੧

ਬੁੱਲ੍ਹੇ ਨੂੰ ਲੋਕੀਂ ਮੱਤੀਂ ਦੇਂਦੇ, ਬੁੱਲ੍ਹਿਆ ਤੂੰ ਜਾ ਬਹੁ ਮਸੀਤੀ
ਵਿਚ ਮਸੀਤਾਂ ਕੀ ਕੁੱਝ ਹੁੰਦਾ, ਜੇ ਦਿਲੋਂ ਨਮਾਜ਼ ਨਾ ਨੀਤੀ
ਬਾਹਰੋਂ ਪਾਕ ਕੀਤੇ ਕੀ ਹੁੰਦਾ, ਜੇ ਅੰਦਰੋਂ ਨਾ ਗਈ ਪਲੀਤੀ
ਬਿਨ ਮੁਰਸ਼ਦ ਕਾਮਲ ਬੁੱਲ੍ਹਿਆ, ਤੇਰੀ ਐਵੇਂ ਗਈ ਇਬਾਦਤ ਕੀਤੀ

## ੮੩੨

ਆਪਣੇ ਤਨ ਦੀ ਖ਼ਬਰ ਨ ਕਾਈ, ਸਾਜਨ ਦੀ ਖ਼ਬਰ ਲਿਆਵੇ ਕੌਣ
ਨਾ ਹੂੰ ਖ਼ਾਕੀ ਨਾ ਹੂੰ ਆਤਸ਼, ਨਾ ਹੂੰ ਪਾਣੀ ਪੌਣ
ਕੁੱਪੇ ਦੇ ਵਿਚ ਰੋੜ ਖੜਕਦੇ, ਮੂਰਖ ਆਖਣ ਬੋਲੇ ਕੌਣ
ਬੁੱਲ੍ਹੂ ਸਾਈਂ ਘਟ ਘਟ ਰੰਵਿਆ, ਜਿਉਂ ਆਟੇ ਵਿਚ ਲੌਣ

352

## V29

Bullha, who is that supreme friend of yours? The Qur'an
is in his hand, and yet he wears the sacred thread.

## V30

Bullha, go to the kitchen of the beloved, where there is
much butchery. Fat goats are slaughtered there, but
you are too skinny to be let in.

## V31

People give Bullha their advice: "Bullha, go and sit in the
mosque." But what happens in mosques, when the
intention to pray is not offered from the heart? What
happens from being pure on the outside, when the
inner pollution has not gone? Bullha, without the
perfect guide, all the worship you perform is useless.

## V32

Can anyone who is unaware of their own body bring news
of the beloved? I am not made of earth,[15] nor am I fire,
nor am I water or air. Pebbles rattle in a jar, and fools
ask who is talking. Bullha, the lord is mixed into every
heart, like salt in flour.

## ੮੩੩

ਅਰਬਾ ਅਨਾਸਰ ਮਹਿਲ ਬਟਾਇਓ, ਵਿਚ ਵੜ ਬੈਠਾ ਆਪੇ
ਆਪੇ ਕੁੜੀਆਂ ਆਪੇ ਨੀਂਗਰ, ਆਪੇ ਬਟਨਾ ਏ ਮਾਪੇ
ਆਪੇ ਮਰੋਂ ਤੇ ਆਪੇ ਜੀਵੇਂ, ਆਪੇ ਕਰੋਂ ਸਿਆਪੇ
ਬੁੱਲ੍ਹਿਆ ਜੋ ਕੁਝ ਕੁਦਰਤ ਰੱਬ ਦੀ, ਆਪੇ ਆਪ ਸਿੰਜਾਪੇ

## ੮੩੪

ਬੁੱਲ੍ਹਿਆ ਰੰਗ ਮਹੱਲੀਂ ਜਾ ਚੜ੍ਹਿਓ, ਲੋਕੀ ਪੁੱਛਣ ਆਖਣ ਖ਼ੈਰ
ਅਸਾਂ ਇਹ ਦੁਨਿਆਂ ਤੋਂ ਵੱਟਿਆ, ਮੂੰਹ ਕਾਲਾ ਨੀਲੇ ਪੈਰ

## ੮੩੫

ਇੱਟ ਖੜਿੱਕੇ ਦੁੱਕੜ ਵੱਜੇ, ਤੱਤਾ ਹੋਵੇ ਚੁੱਲ੍ਹਾ
ਆਉਣ ਫ਼ਕੀਰ ਤੇ ਖਾ ਖਾ ਜਾਵਣ, ਰਾਜ਼ੀ ਹੋਵੇ ਬੁੱਲ੍ਹਾ

## ੮੩੬

ਬੁੱਲ੍ਹਿਆ ਜੈਸੀ ਸੁਰਤ ਐਨ ਹੈ, ਤੈਸੀ ਗ਼ੈਨ ਪਛਾਣ
ਇਕ ਨੁਕਤੇ ਦਾ ਫੇਰ ਹੈ, ਭੁੱਲਾ ਫਿਰੇ ਜਹਾਨ

## V33

You made the four elements your palace, and it was you
who entered and sat there. You are the girls, you are
the boys, and it is you who become their parents. You
are the one who dies and the one who lives, and you
are the one who mourns. Bullha, he is the one who is
recognized in all that the lord has created.

## V34

Bullha, when you went up to the salon,[16] people asked
you how you were. All we got from this world is a
blackened face and feet bruised blue.

## V35

There is a lively scene with the tambourine playing, while
the oven gets hot. The fakirs come and feast before
they go, making Bullha happy.

## V36

Bullha, know the shape of *ghain* is just like that of *'ain*.[17]
The difference lies in a dot. The world wanders lost
in confusion.

## ੲੜੑ

ਬੁੱਲ੍ਹਿਆ ਖਾ ਹਰਾਮ ਤੇ ਪੜ੍ਹ ਸ਼ੁਕਰਾਨਾ, ਕਰ ਤੋਬਾ ਤਰਕ ਸਵਾਬੋਂ
ਛੋੜ ਮਸੀਤ ਤੇ ਪਕੜ ਕਿਨਾਰਾ, ਤੇਰੀ ਛੁਟਸੀ ਜਾਨ ਅਜ਼ਾਬੋਂ
ਉਹ ਹਰਫ਼ ਕਦੇ ਨਾ ਪੜ੍ਹੀਏ ਮਤ, ਰਹਿਸੀ ਜਾਨ ਜਵਾਬੋਂ
ਬੁੱਲ੍ਹੇ ਸ਼ਾਹ ਚਲ ਓਥੇ ਚਲੀਏ, ਜਿੱਥੇ ਮਨੂ ਕਰਨ ਸ਼ਰਾਬੋਂ

## ੲੜ੮

ਬੁੱਲ੍ਹਿਆ ਜੇ ਤੂੰ ਗ਼ਾਜ਼ੀ ਬਣਨਾ ਏਂ, ਲੱਕ ਬੰਨ੍ਹ ਤਲਵਾਰ
ਪਹਿਲੋਂ ਰੰਝੜ ਮਾਰ ਕੇ, ਪਿੱਛੋਂ ਕਾਫ਼ਰ ਮਾਰ

## ੲੜ੯

ਬੁੱਲ੍ਹਿਆ ਹਰ ਮੰਦਰ ਮੋਂ ਆਇਕੇ, ਕਹਿਓ ਲੇਖਾ ਦਿਓ ਬਤਾ
ਪੜ੍ਹੇ ਪੰਡਿਤ ਪਾਂਧੇ ਦੂਰ ਕੀਏ, ਅਹਿਮਕ ਲੀਏ ਬੁਲਾ

## ੲੲ੦

ਵਹਦਤ ਦੇ ਦਰਿਆ ਵਹੋਂਦੇ, ਮੇਰੀ ਵਹਦਤ ਕਿਤ ਵਲ ਧਾਈ
ਮੁਰਸ਼ਦ ਕਾਮਿਲ ਪਾਰ ਲੰਘਾਇਆ, ਬਾਝ ਤੁਲੇ ਸੁਰਨਾਹੀ

356

## V37

Bullha, eat what is forbidden and recite your thanks.
Repent and give up meritorious acts. Leave the
mosque and cling to seclusion. Your soul will escape
torment. Never recite that letter,[18] in case your soul is
unable to answer. Come, Bullha, let us go to the place
where wine is forbidden.

## V38

Bullha, if you want to become a warrior for the faith, gird
your waist with a sword. First kill the Ranghar,[19] then
slay the infidel.

## V39

Bullha,[20] enter God's temple and say: "Explain and tell us
clearly. Why have you sent away learned pandits and
Brahmans and invited fools?"

## V40

The rivers of unity flow; which way does my unity run?
The perfect guide has got me across without a raft
or float.

## ੨੪੧

ਬੁੱਲ੍ਹਿਆ ਸਭ ਮਜਾਜ਼ੀ ਪੌੜੀਆਂ, ਤੂੰ ਹਾਲ ਹਕੀਕਤ ਵੇਖ
ਜੋ ਕੋਈ ਓਥੇ ਪਹੁੰਚਿਆ ਚਾਹੇ, ਭੁੱਲ ਜਾਏ 'ਸਲਾਮ ਅਲੇਕ'

## ੨੪੨

ਬੁੱਲ੍ਹਿਆ ਕਾਜ਼ੀ ਰਾਜ਼ੀ ਰਿਸ਼ਵਤੇ, ਮੁੱਲਾਂ ਰਾਜ਼ੀ ਮੌਤ
ਆਸ਼ਕ ਰਾਜ਼ੀ ਰਾਗ ਤੇ, ਨਾ ਪਰਤੀਤਾਂ ਘਟ ਹੋਤ

## ੨੪੩

ਠਾਕਰਦੁਆਰੇ ਠੱਗ ਬਸੇਂ, ਫਾਹੀ ਦੁਆਰ ਮਸੀਤ
ਹਰਿ ਕੇ ਦੁਆਰੇ ਭਿਖ ਬਸੇਂ, ਹਮਰੀ ਇਹ ਪਰਤੀਤ

## ੨੪੪

ਬੁੱਲ੍ਹੇ ਸ਼ਾਹ ਚਲ ਓਥੇ ਵਸੀਏ, ਜਿਥੇ ਸਾਰੇ ਹੋਵਟ ਅੰਨ੍ਹੇ
ਨਾ ਕੋਈ ਸਾਡੀ ਜ਼ਾਤ ਪਛਾਣੇ, ਨਾ ਕੋਈ ਸਾਨੂੰ ਮੰਨੇ

## V41

Bullha, these steps are all illusory; look toward reality.
   Anyone who wants to get there forgets about *Peace be
   upon you.*[21]

## V42

Bullha, the *qazi* is happy with a bribe,[22] the mullah is
   happy with a death.[23] A lover is happy with music, and
   his faith never grows less.

## V43

Thugs dwell in the temple; there are stranglers at the door
   of the mosque. Fakirs stay by the gate of the lord, this
   is our belief.

## V44

Bullhe Shah, let us go to the place where everyone is
   blind. No one recognizes our caste, nor does anyone
   revere us.

## ੮੪੫

ਬੁੱਲ੍ਹਿਆ ਧਰਮਸਾਲਾ ਵਿਚ ਨਾਹੀਂ, ਜਿਥੇ ਮੋਹਨ ਭੋਗ ਪਵਾਏ
ਵਿਚ ਮਸੀਤਾਂ ਧੱਕੇ ਮਿਲਦੇ, ਮੁੱਲਾਂ ਤਿਉੜੀ ਪਾਏ
ਦੌਲਤਮੰਦਾਂ ਨੇ ਬੂਹਿਆਂ ਉੱਤੇ, ਚੌਬਦਾਰ ਬਿਠਲਾਏ
ਪਕੜ ਦਰਵਾਜ਼ਾ ਰੱਬ ਸੱਚੇ ਦਾ, ਜਿਥੇ ਦੁਖ ਦਿਲ ਦਾ ਮਿਟ ਜਾਏ

## ੮੪੬

ਹੋਰ ਨੇ ਸੱਭੇ ਗਲੜੀਆਂ, ਅੱਲੂ ਅੱਲੂ ਦੀ ਗੱਲ
ਕੁਝ ਰੌਲਾ ਪਾਇਆ ਆਲਮਾਂ, ਕੁਝ ਕਾਗ਼ਜ਼ ਪਾਇਆ ਝੱਲ

## ੮੪੭

ਬੁੱਲ੍ਹਿਆ ਮੈਂ ਮਿੱਟੀ ਘੁਮਿਆਰ ਦੀ, ਗੱਲ ਆਖ ਨਾ ਸਕਦੀ ਏਕ
ਠੱਠਰ ਮੇਰਾ ਕਿਉਂ ਘੜਿਆ, ਮਤ ਜਾਏ ਅਲੇਕ ਸਲੇਕ

## ੮੪੮

ਬੁੱਲ੍ਹਾ ਸ਼ਹੁ ਤੋਂ ਵੱਖ ਨਹੀਂ, ਪਰ ਵੇਖਣ ਵਾਲੀ ਅੱਖ ਨਹੀਂ

## V45

Bullha, he is not in the lodge,[24] where offerings of food are
placed. People get pushed about in mosques, where
the mullah sternly frowns. The rich station guards at
their gates. Cling to the door of the true lord, where
the pain of the heart is removed.

## V46

Everything else is of no account; the only thing is God.
Some of the confusion has been created by religious
scholars, some by paper that has driven people mad.

## V47

Bullha, I am the potter's clay, and I cannot say anything. If
I ask why mine was the shape[25] he made, I fear he will
tell me to shut up.

## V48

Bullha, you are not separate from the lord, but lack the eye
to see this.

## ੮੪੯

ਬੁੱਲ੍ਹਿਆ ਰੱਬ ਕਹੋ ਨਾ ਕਹੋ, ਆਈ ਸੁਰਤੋਂ ਸੁਚਾ ਰਹੋ

## ੮੫੦

ਗਲ ਸਮਝ ਲਈ ਤੇ ਰੌਲਾ ਕੀ, ਇਹ ਰਾਮ ਰਹੀਮ ਤੇ ਮੌਲਾ ਕੀ

## ੮੫੧

ਹਾਜੀ ਲੋਕ ਮੱਕੇ ਨੂੰ ਜਾਂਦੇ, ਅਸਾਂ ਜਾਣਾ ਤਖ਼ਤ ਹਜ਼ਾਰੇ
ਜਿਤ ਵਲ ਯਾਰ ਉਤੇ ਵਲ ਕਾਅਬਾ, ਭਾਵੇ ਫੋਲ ਕਿਤਾਬਾਂ ਚਾਰੇ

## ੮੫੨

ਮੱਕੇ ਗਿਆ ਗਲ ਮੁਕਦੀ ਨਾਹੀਂ, ਜਿਚਰ ਦਿਲੋਂ ਨਾ ਆਪ ਮੁਕਾਈਏ
ਗੰਗਾ ਗਿਆ ਪਾਪ ਨਹੀਂ ਵੜਦੇ, ਭਾਵੇਂ ਸੌ ਸੌ ਗੋਤੇ ਲਾਈਏ
ਗਯਾ ਗਿਆ ਗਲ ਮੁਕਦੀ ਨਾਹੀਂ, ਭਾਵੇਂ ਕਿਤਨੇ ਪਿੰਡ ਭਰਾਈਏ
ਬੁੱਲ੍ਹੂ ਸ਼ਾਹ ਗਲ ਮੁਕਦੀ ਤਾਹੀਂ, ਜਦ ਮੈਨੂੰ ਖਿਝਿਆਂ ਲੁਟਾਈਏ

## V49

Bullha,[26] you may say "Lord" or not, but keep clear of
  mere appearances.

## V50

Now[27] that I have understood, what is all the fuss? What is
  all this "Ram," "Rahim," and "Lord"?

## V51

Hajjis[28] go to Mecca;[29] we are going to Takht Hazara. The
  Kaaba lies wherever the beloved points, however
  much you pore through all four scriptures.[30]

## V52

The[31] matter is not finished by going to Mecca, so long
  as you do not finish off the self from your heart. Sins
  are not shed by going to the Ganges, even though you
  immerse yourself hundreds of times. The matter is
  not finished by going to Gaya,[32] no matter how many
  offerings you make to the dead. Bullhe Shah, the
  matter is finished when the ego is destroyed.

## ੮੫੩

ਜੇ ਮੈਂ ਤੈਨੂੰ ਅੰਦਰ ਢੂੰਡਾਂ, ਤੇ ਫੇਰ ਮੁਕੱਜਦ ਜਾਣਾਂ
ਜੇ ਮੈਂ ਤੈਨੂੰ ਬਾਹਰ ਢੂੰਡਾਂ, ਤੇ ਮੇਰੇ ਅੰਦਰ ਕੌਣ ਸਮਾਣਾ
ਸਭ ਕੁਝ ਤੂੰ ਹੈਂ ਸਭ ਵਿਚ ਤੂੰ ਹੈਂ, ਸਭ ਤੋਂ ਪਾਕ ਪਛਾਣਾ
ਮੈਂ ਵੀ ਤੂੰ ਹੈਂ ਤੂੰ ਵੀ ਮੈਂ ਹੈਂ, ਵਤ ਬੁੱਲ੍ਹਾ ਕੌਣ ਨਿਮਾਣਾ

## ੮੫੪

ਰਾਤੀਂ ਜਾਗੋਂ ਕਰੇ ਇਬਾਦਤ, ਰਾਤੀ ਜਾਗਟ ਕੁੱਤੇ, ਤੈਬੋਂ ਉੱਤੇ
ਭੌਂਕਣ ਬੰਦ ਮੂਲ ਨਾ ਹੁੰਦੇ, ਜਾ ਰੂੜੀ ਤੇ ਸੁੱਤੇ, ਤੈਬੋਂ ਉੱਤੇ
ਖਸਮ ਆਪਣੇ ਦਾ ਦਰ ਨਾ ਛਡਦੇ, ਭਾਵੇਂ ਵੱਜਣ ਜੁੱਤੇ, ਤੈਬੋਂ ਉੱਤੇ
ਬੁੱਲ੍ਹੇ ਸ਼ਾਹ ਕੋਈ ਰਖਤ ਵਿਹਾਜ ਲੈ, ਨਹੀਂ ਤੇ ਬਾਜ਼ੀ ਲੈ ਗਏ ਕੁੱਤੇ,
ਤੈਬੋਂ ਉੱਤੇ

## V53

If[33] I search for you inside, then I think you are confined.
 If I search for you outside, then who is contained
 within me? You are everything, you are in everything,
 you are known to be free from everything. You are me
 and I am you, so who is poor Bullha?

## V54

You[34] remain awake at night and perform your devotions.
 Also awake at night are dogs, better than you. They
 bark and in no way can they be stopped. They go and
 sleep on the dung heap, better than you. They do not
 leave their master's door, even if they get beaten with
 slippers, better than you. Bullhe Shah, buy yourself
 something for the journey, or else the game will be
 won by the dogs, better than you.

# ABBREVIATIONS

## Languages

| | |
|---|---|
| Ar. | Arabic |
| P. | Panjabi |
| Pers. | Persian |
| Skt. | Sanskrit |

## Textual References

| | |
|---|---|
| F | Faqir 1960 |
| J | Jagtar 2008 |
| PS | Puri and Shangari 1986 |
| Q | Qasuri 1896 |
| R | Ruhtaki 1889 |
| S | Sabir 1991 |

## References to Other Poems by Bullhe Shah

| | |
|---|---|
| A | *Aṭhvārā* (The Seven Days) |
| B | *Bārāñ Māh* (The Twelve Months) |
| G | *Gandhāñ* (The Forty Knots) |
| S | *Sīharfī* (The Thirty Letters) |
| V | *Dohṛe* (Verses) |

# NOTES TO THE TEXT

## ੪

٩ The reading *ghoṛe cugaṇ arūṛīāñ utte* S, "horses graze on rubbish heaps," matches better with the following half-verse than *irākīāñ nūñ paī cābak pāuñdī* F J, "the whip falls on fine Arab steeds."

## ੫

٩ Most texts have *rāñjhā yār,* "Ranjha my beloved," but the word *rāñjhā* is superfluous to the meter, and the reference to Hir awaiting the arrival of her beloved hardly requires the mention of his name.

## ੧੬

٩ In this context, *āsā* F (Ar. *'aṣā*), "staff," is a more natural item than *kāsā* Q, "cup."

## ੨੭

٩ This is presumed to be the sense of *khārā* S, literally "wedding seat," suggested as an emendation for the apparently meaningless *qahārā* F.

## ੩੨

٩ The translation "mingle with one another" follows *ik baī de vicc samāo* S, emending *ik banne vicc jā samāo* F J, "go and gather to one side."

## ੩੮

٩ Here *trahi rahioñ* S, "retreated," fits the rhyme and meter better than *gioñ* F J, "went."

੨ S reads *aslā te* with F, but interprets as "at Asal," hence the emendation *āsal ā ke te* J.

## ८०

१ The ingenious emendation *bhae narinjan* S J, "become unsullied," is superior to the popular but clearly corrupt *bahīe tarinjaṇ* F, "let us sit in the spinning party."

## ८१

१ The reading *huṇ ishk asāñ val āiā haiñ* S, "Now, love, you have come to us," establishes the rhyme better than *kiuñ ishk asāñ te āiā e* F, translated by PS as "Why, O love, have you come to me?"

२ Again, the rhyme of *man bhāiā haiñ* S, literally "you have pleased our heart," is better than *main pāiā hai* F, "I have found you."

## ८३

१ Taking *namūnā* F as one word, "model," seems preferable to reading it as two words with the emendation *nā mūnā* S, "nor death."

## ८४

१ The word *jhagaṛ*, "quarrel" does not seem to fit the meter or the sense.

## ८५

१ The problematic expression of *kiā mat kā nām bulāoge* F, perhaps "What will you call this religion?" is doubtfully emended to *mat kāran nām bulāoge* S, interpreted as meaning "Perhaps you will give me at least a nominal invitation?"

२ Here the general sense of "torment" is implied by *shakanje* S, literally "the stocks." The emendation is suggested for the doubtful *shakranjī* F, glossed by J as "irritation."

## ५६

१ The traditional reading *cūcak* F, i.e., "Chuchak the father of Hir," hardly seems possible here. S accordingly suggests *sūcak*, "informer," interpreting the word as referring to the pair of recording angels who appear after death to report on the good and bad deeds performed in life.

## ੬੪

१ The translation follows *pāche vaḍ kī* S. This is offered as an emendation of the problematic *pāchī vaḍh ke* Q F J, "after the poppy heads are cut," which J suggests might be a traditional wedding ritual.

## ੬੬

१ This is the final verse in Q F J. S adds a signature verse from other editions: *shabad salok kī baṇī kiā, kāfī bullhe shāh suṇāī*, "This does not make a *shabad* or a *shalok*, Bullhe Shah has uttered it as a *kāfī*." This has a quite different tone from Bullhe Shah's usual signature verses, and seems more likely to have been created by a performer.

## ੭੨

१ The text of this *kāfī* follows S, which is much superior to the more familiar version printed in R F J and translated in PS, where the refrain begins differently as *nī maiñ suṇiā ishk sharhā kī nātā*, "Oh, now I have heard the relationship between love and law."

## ੭੪

१ The rhyme scheme of this *kāfī* is very irregular, suggesting that the text may have been unreliably transmitted.

## ੮੫

१ "Shadows in a ruined house" (*khole de* F J) are explained as the shifting shadows cast by the changing position of the sun, versus "shadows of a well" (*khūhe de* S), explained as a reference to the revolving wheel that holds the buckets of a Persian well.

## ੮੬

१ The translation "in my body" follows the emendation *deh vic* S, for *dilbar de vic* F J, "that I should dwell in the beloved."

## ੧੦੩

१ S reverses the position of the final half-verses of 103.3 and 103.5. The translation in PS follows their positioning in R Q F J.

## ११८

१ The phrase *sirohī nāl mil gaī sirohī* Q F S, literally "sword blade (of Sirohi) is joined to sword blade," is perhaps an obsolete proverbial expression. Making no sense of it, J questionably emends to *dehī nāl mil gaī dehī*, "body is joined to body."

## १२२

१ The translation is approximate, since the literal sense of the emendation *gur lai ke do sir sāhī* S is hardly more transparent than the evidently corrupt *gur lai ke gur tōṅ sarsāhī* F J.

## १२३

१ The phrase *bīs pacās* F, "twenty or fifty," presumably indicates counting in general. The emendation to *bhes pacās* S J, "fifty guises," hardly makes more sense.

## १३२

१ The emendation *vasnā hāṅ* S, "I flourish," is superior to the traditional reading *dasnā hāṅ* F J, "I tell them," which mechanically repeats the rhyme of 132.2.

## १३३

१ The emendation *guṛh kuṇḍe meṅ* S is explained as "in a deep hole in the ground constructed by yogis for ascetic withdrawal." It is offered as a correction of the apparently corrupt *gorkaṇḍī vic* F J.

## १३७

१ The correct reading is uncertain. The absence of the necessary rhyme word in *jibrāīl pagaṛ liāiā* F J is corrected at the expense of the meter in *jibrāīl pagaṛ liāiā kāran istiqbāl nī* S.

## १८८

१ The emendation *lāl lakhāiā* S, literally "have displayed a ruby," is preferable to the puzzling opposite meaning of *lāl vanjāiā* F J, translated in PS as "have lost a precious jewel."

## ੧੫੭

੧ The translation "has come to me" follows *mil giā* F J. The rhyme is corrected in *mal giā* S, but with the opposite sense of "runs off, disappears."

## ੮੪੨

੧ The text is doubtful, so *nā partīt ghaṭ hot* F, "nor does his faith grow less," is emended on metrical grounds to *partī* S, interpreted as "accounting." PS renders it loosely as "the Melody, whose enjoyment never grows less."

# NOTES TO THE TRANSLATION

## *Lyrics*

### 1

1    This unrhymed half-verse constitutes the refrain of the *kāfī*.

2    The poet is perilously caught in the middle, like Sohni, who leaves her side of the river but without reaching her lover on the far bank. Without access to a spiritual guide, there can be no salvation in this world or the next.

### 2

1    This long poem, with its memorable refrain, is one of Bullhe Shah's most substantial treatments of the *memento mori* theme.

2    The wedding date fixed by her parents for a girl's arranged match marks the inevitable end of her life in her family home. Its rapid approach gives urgency to the reminder that she needs to prepare the clothes that she will take with her as her dowry (*dāj*) when she leaves for her husband's house. The process is frequently used by Bullhe Shah to symbolize the need to build up a store of rightly guided acts before the inevitable approach of death. The theme is developed at length in "The Forty Knots" (G1–G40).

3    The rhyme word *bār* is variously interpreted.

4    The wedding culminates in the ceremony (*muklāvā*) of the bride being taken away from her parents' home to her husband's house, where she will spend the rest of her life.

5    Sikandar, the classical Alexander the Great, is often cited as an example of how death overcomes even the mightiest of rulers.

6    The biblical Joseph, whose beauty and whose birthplace are remembered in the standard epithet "the moon of Canaan" (Pers. *māh-e kan'ān*).

7    See 12.4.

8    See 27.6.

9    This verse uses core imagery from the Persian ghazal. The typical flowers of a Persian garden, like the tulip (Pers. *lāla*), iris (*sosan*), and hyacinth (*sumbul*), and the graceful cypress tree *(sarū*, Pers. *sarv)* flourish in the spring but are withered by the chill wind of autumn (*bād-e khazāñ*).

375

10 The strongly defined center of the narcissus (*nargas*) is regularly compared in the language of the ghazal to the eye of the beloved intoxicated with his own beauty.

11 The piercing cry of the crane, which is believed to express her pain at separation from the flock, is a common image for the suffering of the abandoned lover. Compare 30.3.

12 An original image describing the necessity for good actions in this life as a necessary condition for future salvation.

13 S suggests that the phrase "citadel of knowledge" (*koṭ ilam de*) refers to Bullhe Shah's hometown of Kasur, which was famed for the learning of the local Islamic scholar Maulana Ghulam Murtaza, called "The Master of the Panjab" (*makhdūm-e panjāb*). Rather than study with this great scholar, Bullhe Shah gave his allegiance to Shah Inayat, from whom he received the word (*kalmā*) of his Sufi teaching.

### 3

1 Like other *kāfīs* on Hindu themes, this poem is written in Hindi, the characteristic language of the yogis. Compare 15, 20, 66, 113.

2 The phrase "make the Ganges flow backward" (*ulṭī gangā bahāio*) is an idiom meaning "to do the opposite of the usual," which here refers to the drawing up of psychic energy during the yogic process.

3 The mystic process involved in the yogic reversal of the natural order of things is here described as a process of spinning backward.

4 This reference to the story of the *Rāmāyaṇa* describes a reversal of the arrival of Kumbhakaran to assist his brother Ravan, when his capital of Lanka was under attack by Ram and Lachhman.

5 The "unstruck music" (*anhad nād*) is the mystical sound heard at the climax of the yogic process. Compare 15.2, 47.5, 66.4, 67.3, 117.2, 137.9, 147.2.

6 The "circle of nectar" (*amrit maṇḍal*) is another traditional image for the ecstatic state that is the goal of yoga.

### 4

1 The text of this poem is based on S, which is taken from Mohan Singh Ubirai 1930: 172. Verses 3–8 are omitted in F, and are not translated in PS. The short verses have a single rhyme throughout. The layout of the text follows most editions, which print the verses separately and indicate the recurrence of the refrain after each

verse. But the verses are paired by theme (i.e., 4.2–3, 4.4–5, 4.6–7, 4.8–9), and are so printed in some editions. For other monorhymed *kāfīs* of this same formal type, compare 6, 13, 58, 114.

2 The social turmoil attendant on the internal uprisings of the Sikhs against the authority of the Mughals, which is the unusual subject of this *kāfī,* is interpreted as a manifestation of the mysterious workings of the divine beloved.

3 Literally, "father's elder and younger brothers" (*kiā cāce kiā tāe*), the core kin group of the patrilineal family.

4 Compare 34.4.

## 5

1 See 12.4.

2 The reference is to the famous episode in which Bullhe Shah disguised himself as a dancing girl to regain the affection of Shah Inayat. See 105.7.

## 6

1 This is a tentative interpretation of *bhogaṇ karan adāīñ*.

2 The translation follows S, but the word *jagātar* in the original appears corrupt. Any translation must therefore be guesswork; compare PS, "customs officer."

## 7

1 The verse could be interpreted either as a reference to the condition of man following the fall of Adam or as the poet's statement of bewilderment as to how the disgrace incurred by love is to be resolved.

## 8

1 The sense of the rhyme word *aṇghātāñ* is obscure both here and in 117.1. S implausibly conjectures *ang hātāñ,* "ties are relinquished," while PS translates the verse as "the shaft of *Nam* has struck me a mortal blow."

2 The Indian cuckoo, *Cuculus indicus* (Skt. *kokila*-), regularly cited in poetry for its mournful cry. Compare 49.2, B7.

3 The deerskin is typically associated with yogis, like the skull used as a cup for begging, the long matted hair, and the ashes smeared

on the body.

4    A *mihrab* (Ar. *miḥrāb*) is the niche in the wall of a mosque that marks the Qibla, the direction of the Kaaba toward which those offering prayer must face. But the prayers of lovers are directed toward their beloved, whose face is their *mihrab*.

## 10

1    This is a deliberately familiar way (*ammāñ bābe*, literally, "Mom and Dad") of referring to Adam and Eve, whose original sin in consuming the wheat that God had forbidden them to eat caused their expulsion from paradise and the subsequent troubled history of humanity. The poem is a sardonic reflection on how mankind is collectively held responsible for that first disobedience.

2    In the Islamic tradition, it was wheat that Adam and Eve were forbidden to eat. Compare 55.3, 143.2.

3    The names have no particular significance. The sense is general, that "X enjoys the fruits of a crime, and Y gets arrested for it."

## 11

1    The opening of this short poem makes it an obvious choice as the first *kāfī* in the Persian-script editions F and S. But it is not attested in the earlier editions R and Q.

    The letters of the Arabic alphabet often carry important symbolic values, so *alif* is both the first letter of the Arabic alphabet and the first letter of the word "Allah" (الله). The simple shape of *alif* (ا), A, is identical with the form of the Arabic sign for the number 1 (Ar. *aḥad*), which further underlies its use as a Sufi symbol for the divine unity, as opposed to the second letter, *be* (ب), B, which stands for the world of duality. Compare 22.1, 22.2, 26.2, 26.15, 42.12, 58.4, 92.2, 118.2, 144.3, 150.4.

2    The Arabic letters *'ain* (ع) and *ġhain* (غ) are shaped alike, being distinguished only by the dot written over the latter. They are also symbolically opposed as the initial letters of *'ain*, "essence," versus *ġhair* [*allāh*], "other [than God]." Compare 24.2, 72.7, 78.12, V36.

## 12

1    These words (Ar. *qum bi-idhnī*) are supposed to have been uttered by the mysterious twelfth-century Sufi saint Shams when he

misused his miraculous powers to resuscitate the dead son of the king of Ghazna. For this blasphemous claim to possession of God's power over life and death Shams was sentenced to death by being hanged upside down and flayed alive. Compare 41.3, 95.3, 98.5, 110.3, 143.8.

2   The reference is to Hir, anxiously waiting for Ranjha in the river glades where he comes to graze her father's buffaloes.

3   Yusuf, the biblical Joseph, was put down a well by his jealous brothers, who sold him into slavery in Egypt; there Zulaikha, the biblical Potiphar's wife, saw him in the slave market and was overwhelmed by love for him. Compare 2.14, 5.5, 41.2, 42.15, 75.8, 98.3, 98.4, 110.3, 143.5, 144.3, 154.5, 157.2.

4   The Arabic phrase is from the scriptural verse that records the words of Moses after he had been summoned to Mount Sinai, and God's response to him: [*qāla*] *rabbi arinī* [*anzur ilaika qāla*] *lan tarānī* [*walākini 'nzur ilā 'l-jabali*] (Qur'an 7.143), "[He said] 'Show me (yourself), lord, [that I may look upon you.' He said,] 'You shall not see me [but look at the mountain']." Compare 119.9, 137.10, 143.4, 148.1, 157.4.

### 13

1   The phrase "worldly pleasures" (*lahiv lāab*) recalls *wa-mā 'l-ḥayātu 'l-dunyā illā laʿibun wa-lahwun* (Qur'an 6.32), "What is the life of this world but play and amusement?"

### 14

1   The verse explores the common theme of people's inability to discern the divine reality that underlies surface appearances.

### 15

1   The word "adept" (Ar. *ʿārif*) is a Sufi term, like "fakir" (Ar. *faqīr*). But the *kāfī* also draws on the language of yoga and is written in the characteristic Hindi of the yogis; see 3.

2   See 3.3.

### 16

1   "Turk" was a standard term in medieval India for "Muslim," as opposed to Hindu. Compare 20.6, 40.6, 78.5, 106.5, 131.3.

2 Here the "robbers" (*ṭhag*) are the religious specialists who create the rituals surrounding birth and death and live off the fees they earn from them. Compare V6.

### 17

1 The Arabic phrase is from the verse *ṣummun bukmun 'umyun* [*fa-hum lā yarji'ūna*] (Qur'an 2.18), "Deaf, dumb, and blind, [they will not return]." Compare 70.3, 77.6, also 97.4.

2 See 39.13.

### 18

1 "Real love" (Pers. *'ishq-e ḥaqīqī*) is the mystical love of God as the true reality, which is exalted in Sufism above the human love called "apparent love" (Pers. *'ishq-e majāzī*). Compare 74.1.

2 These Arabic textbooks are classics of the legal syllabus, and are frequently cited as a pair to indicate the formal syllabus of Islamic law. Their full titles are *Kanz al-Daqā'iq* (The treasury of difficult points) by Abdullah ibn Muhammad Nasafi (d. 1310), and *Mukhtasar al-Qudūrī* (The compendium of al-Quduri) by Ahmad ibn Muhammad al-Quduri (d. 1036). Compare 72.8.

### 19

1 The distinction between the mynah and the parrot symbolizes the apparent differences of superficial reality, which are destroyed by the perception of the underlying divine unity.

2 See 121.1.

3 The teachings of love are diametrically opposed to the commandments of formal religion, here exemplified by the Muslim dietary requirement to eat only halal meat, which has been properly slaughtered with the beast being bled after its throat has been cut, while avoiding the flesh of animals that have died a natural death (Pers. *murdār*).

### 20

1 This poem is composed in the kind of Hindi that is associated with its predominantly Hindu theme; see 3.

2 The youngest of the Pandav brothers, famous for his knowledge of astronomy. From the astronomical perspective of Sahadev, the

geographical locations on earth of Lanka and Mecca are identical, proving the meaninglessness of their rival associations with Hindu and Muslim identity.

3   See 16.2.

### 22

1   As often elsewhere, the letter *alif* symbolizes the absolute unity of the divine prior to the multiplicity of creation. See 11.1.

2   The title Hafiz is given to those who have learned the entire Qur'an by heart.

3   The shape of the seed that is left recalls the *alif* (‌ا‌) with which creation began.

### 23

1   The Arabic phrase "Let it be, and it was" comes from the end of the verse [*badī'u 'l-samāwāti wa'l-arḍi wa idhā qaḍā amran fa-innamā yaqūlu lahu*] *kun fa-yakūnu* (Qur'an 2.117), "[The creator of the heavens and earth, and when he decrees a thing he but says to it,] 'Let it be,' and it is." It is frequently used by Bullhe Shah to indicate the act of creation, so here indicates that the lovers were intended for each other from pre-eternity (Pers. *roz-e azal*), even before the moment of creation. Compare 43.5, 54.5, 55.2, 57.2. 65.4, 77.3, 95.4, 122.6.

2   The riverside pastures where Ranjha took the buffaloes to graze, and where Hir used to go and meet him.

3   Bright red (*sūhā*) is the color that symbolizes the joyful state of a bride. The verse describes the happiness of other lovers.

4   See n. 4 on 28.2.

### 24

1   The small dot that distinguishes letters in the Perso-Arabic script symbolizes the concentrated essence of mystical reality. Compare 25.1, 39.8.

2   See 11.3.

3   Sassi was the daughter of the king of Bhambhore in Sindh. She fell in love with Punnun, the son of the chief of the Hot tribe of Baloch, when he was sent to Bhambhore by his father. After he later abandoned her while she lay asleep, she died trying to follow

his tracks in the burning desert of the Maru Thal. Compare 141.1, 143.12, 157.2, B4.

4　See 31.6.

## 25

1　The "whole thing" (*gall*) indicates the divine reality revealed by mystical insight. Compare 64.1, 64.16.

2　See 24.1.

3　The shape of the mark on the forehead that is made by frequent pious prostration in prayer is here compared to that of a *mihrab*. See 8.5.

4　See 45.2.

5　Clothes dyed blue were particularly associated with Muslims in premodern India.

6　The prestige gained from their performance of the hajj, or pilgrimage to Mecca, is exploited by the hajjis on their return in order to increase the offerings of the pious.

## 26

1　See 11.1.

2　Compare V19.

3　A *qazi* is a religious judge, who ranks higher than the humble mullah attached to a local mosque. *Qazis* are regularly castigated for their greed and willingness to take bribes. Compare V42.

4　The term *abjad* is given to the allocation of numerical values to the letters of the Arabic alphabet in the historic order of Hebrew and other older Semitic alphabets. Any given word or phrase may accordingly be represented by a number.

5　The writing of religious formulae to be worn on the body as protective amulets (*tāvīz*) is a recognized skill of Muslim religious specialists.

6　Mullahs are paid a small fee to recite in Arabic when butchers slaughter an animal in the prescribed halal fashion by cutting its throat.

7　A name of Satan, whose arrogant belief in his superior knowledge brought about his downfall. Compare 148.4.

8　The translation "philosopher" is very doubtful, since the rhyme word *junnī* seems to be invented to fit the awkward rhyme with *sunnī*; compare 138.3. S suggests that *junnī* is a distorted form of *yūnānī*, "Greek."

9   By "inspirational knowledge" (Pers. *'ilm-e ladunnī*) is meant the mystical science of Sufism.

10  The two letters *alif* and *mīm* stand for Allah and Muhammad respectively, but the cryptic reference is probably to the mystical identity of Ahad and Ahmad. See n. 4 on 28.2.

## 27

1   Ayub, the biblical Job, is always referred to in Bullhe Shah by the epithet "the patient one" (Ar. *ṣābir*). He was tested by God by having his body filled with worms. Compare 42.15, 110.3, 143.6, 148.3.

2   Zakariya, the biblical Zechariah, took refuge in a hollow tree from pursuit by the soldiers of the Jewish king Herod. He died when the soldiers sawed through the tree while he was still inside it. Compare 41.2, 95.3, 98.5, 110.3, 110.5, 143.7.

3   Yahya, the biblical John the Baptist, was the son of Zakariya. He is here described as one of the many martyrs to the power of love. In Muslim tradition, he was approached by the wife of King Herodian of Damascus to sanction her desire to remarry after the king had divorced her three times. On his refusal to do so, she had him beheaded while he was at prayer, then had his head served up on a china platter. Compare 110.6.

4   The great Sufi saint Mansur al-Hallaj is here described as drinking the wine of mystical awareness, which led to his martyrdom in Baghdad in 919. See 28.7.

5   Sulaiman, the biblical Solomon, was a mighty king who owned a magic ring that gave him power over the jinn and other supernatural beings. They supported the magic throne on which he could fly through the air. Once Sulaiman lost his ring, and was then reduced to poverty and forced to earn his living by stoking a furnace. Compare 2.15, 110.2, 143.6.

## 28

1   This poem is remarkable for its deliberate clustering of Qur'anic and other Arabic phrases, most of which also recur in verses of other *kāfīs*.

2   The vocative invites a general audience to listen to the poet's address to the divine beloved.

3    Some commentators understand the meaning of *har har de vicc* here and in 28.3 to be "As God (Skt. *hari*), you are contained in everything (Pers. *har*)."

4    In the Arabic script, Ahad "the One," i.e., God, is virtually identical with Ahmad, i.e., the prophet Muhammad. Only the letter *mīm* in its very small medial form (*-m-*) marks the difference between *anā aḥad* (انا احد), "I am the One," and *anā aḥmad* (انا احمد), "I am Ahmad, i.e., Muhammad." Compare 23.6, 26.15, 43.4, 43.5, 53.2, 60.2, 77.1, 77.3, 109.1.

5    Similarly, the removal of the initial letter *'ain* from *anā 'arab* (انا عرب), "I am an Arab," results in *anā rabb* (انا رب), "I am the lord." This is another saying inspired by the Sufi belief in the mystical identity between God and the Arab prophet Muhammad, his chosen Apostle (Ar. *rasūl*).

6    The Arabic phrase is from the verse [*fa-ainamā tuwallū*] *fa-thumma wajhu'llāh* (Qur'an 2.115) "[Wherever you turn,] then there is the face of God." Compare 45.4, 102.1, also 117.2.

7    The Arabic word *al-insān*, "man," indicates the essential unity of God and humanity. It is a shorthand reference to the verse [*wa-laqad ḳhalaqnā*] *al-insān* (Qur'an 15.26), "[And we created] man." Compare 42.16.

8    The phrase "a hidden treasure" (Pers. *ganj-e maḳhfī*) alludes to the divine Tradition (Ar. *ḥadīth qudsī*), frequently cited in Sufi literature, in which God explains the reason for creation as the divine desire for self-manifestation: [*kuntu*] *kanzan maḳhfiyyan* [*fa-aḥbabtu an u'rafa fa-ḳhalaqtu 'l-ḳhalqa likai u'rafa*] "[I was] a hidden treasure [and I desired to be known, so I created the creation in order that I might be known]." Compare 57.3, 65.3.

9    The Arabic word *alast*, "am I not?" begins the verse describing the primal covenant between God and mankind: *alastu* [*bi-rabbikum*] *qālū balā shahidnā* (Qur'an 7.172), "Am I not [your lord]? They said, 'Yes, we so testify.'" Compare 45.3, 47.4, 54.4, 65.5, 77.5, 127.6.

10   The Arabic phrase recalls another scriptural description of the divine creation of man, in the verse *fa-nafaḳhtu fīhi* [*min rūḥī*] (Qur'an 15.29), "And I breathed into him [of my spirit]."

11   The phrase "we are nearer" is another scriptural allusion to the immanence of the divine presence in man, from the verse *naḥnu aqrab* [*ilaihi min ḥabli 'l-warīd*] (Qur'an 50.16), "We are nearer [to him than his jugular vein]." Compare 45.4,

70.2, 77.2, 96.2, 138.2, also 64.10.

12    This phrase is from the verse *wa-huwa maʻakum [aina mā kuntum]* (Qurʼan 57.4), "And he is with you [wherever you are]." Compare 91.2, 148.2.

13    This is another scriptural phrase pointing to the divine presence within man, from the passage [*wa-fī ʼl-arḍi āyātun lil-mūqinīn*], *wa-fī anfusikum [a-fa-lā tabṣirūn]* (Qurʼan 51.20–21), "[On the earth are signs for those of assured faith], and in your own selves: [will you not see?]" Compare 70.2.

14    The ecstatic saying "I am God" (Ar. *anā ʼl-ḥaqq*), literally, "I am the (divine) true reality," proclaiming mystical identity with the divine, is famously associated with the great Sufi martyr Mansur al-Hallaj, and led to his execution for blasphemy in Baghdad in 919. Compare 27.5, 41.3, 42.8, 47.3, 55.5, 78.9, 95.3, 96.5, 98.5, 98.8, 109.2, 119.9, 125.4, 140.6, 143.7, 148.3, 156.4.

15    The saying, "There is nothing in my robe [except God]" (Ar. *laisa fī jubbatī*), was uttered by the Sufi saint Shaikh Junaid of Baghdad. Like Mansur's famous *anā ʼl-ḥaqq*, this is another of the well-known ecstatic Sufi sayings (Ar. *shaṭhiyyāt*).

16    The phrase refers to the Arabic description of man as *ashrafuʼl-makhlūqāt*.

17    The Arabic phrase comes from a verse describing God's special favoring of mankind: *wa-laqad karramnā [banī ādam]* (Qurʼan 17.70), "And we have honored [the sons of Adam]." Compare 57.4.

18    The words of the Islamic profession of faith. See 45.2.

## 29

1    This poem is generally considered to be by Bullhe Shah, and is included as such in R, Q, F, and J. Like *kāfī* 63, however, it is excluded from S as the work of Shah Husain. For the notably variant Shah Husain text, see Daudi 1990: 91–92, *kāfī* 148 (trans. Anwar 1966: 25–26), which has the refrain *mitrāṅ dī mijmānī kāran, dil dā lahū chhānīdā*, "To entertain my beloved, my heart's blood is filtered," followed by six verses only partly overlapping with 29.2–3, and with a quite different signature verse starting *kahe Husain faqīr*, "Husain the fakir says." Given the very uncertain early textual history of both poets, this rival attribution can hardly be regarded as definitive, and the poem is therefore included here. Besides *kāfī* 63, other instances of poems also attributed to Shah

Husain include *kāfīs* 130 and 145, which are not excluded by S. Compare the introductory notes on 63, 130, 145.

### 30

1 The bride's last farewell to her girlfriends (*sahelīāṅ*), who must in due course follow her away from their childhood homes, is a poignant metaphor for the inevitable pain of confrontation with death.

2 See 2.18.

3 The "veiler of sins" (Ar. *sattār*) is one the names of Allah.

### 31

1 Unlike the striking catalogue of terms from weaving and spinning in 31.2 (*tāṇī tāṇā peṭā nalīāṅ, pīṭh naṛā chibbāṅ chalīāṅ*), it is hardly possible to translate the names of different kinds of cloth listed in this verse as further examples of the phenomenal diversity that masks the essential unity of all things. But *cauṅsī* and *paiṅsī* are woven from 400 and 500 threads respectively, *khaddar* and *dhotar* are types of coarse cloth, and *malmal* and *khāsā* are varieties of fine muslin.

2 Yogis dress in ochre-dyed garments, whatever the cloth they are made of.

3 Compare V21.

4 Besides the obvious reference to Krishna as the divine cowherd, PS suggests allusions to Jesus as the shepherd and to Muhammad as the driver of camels. There may also be a reference to Ranjha as buffalo herder, but the identity of the donkey-herdsman is obscure.

5 The discrepancy between Bullhe Shah's own high status as a Sayyid and the lower rank of Shah Inayat as an Arain is a prominent theme of the poet's hagiography. See also 24.4, 70.1, 108, 151.4.

### 32

1 The spinning party (*attaṇ*) is where the girls of a village traditionally gathered together to spin. Compare 70.1, B2.

2 The Panjabi idiom *naccaṇ laggī tāṅ ghunghaṭ kāhdā*, literally "She has started dancing, so why the veil?" is used to describe attempts to hang on to respectability when embarking on a questionable course of action.

## 33

1   The lover is as helpless in the hands of the beloved as a fish that has been caught.

2   The reference is to the birth in Mecca of Muhammad, who was appointed by God to be his Apostle.

3   Hir's parents married her off against her will to a man from the Khera tribe, in order to put an end to the disgrace of her relationship with Ranjha. At the end of the wedding ceremony, the Kheras compelled Hir to return with them in a bridal palanquin (*ḍolī*) to her new husband's home. Compare 61.5.

4   The sense is unclear. PS explains as "I have become immortal in Your love and it is only my mind which has been eliminated forever," but this owes more to Radhasoami than to Sufi ideas.

## 34

1   The allusive verses of this *kāfī* appear to refer to a separation of Bullhe Shah from Shah Inayat due to the troubled conditions then prevailing in Panjab.

2   The name of a place in District Kasur.

3   For the wordplay between *kasar*, "fault," and Kasur, compare V4.

4   Literally, "Oh you with a great family" (*vaḍ parvāriā*), i.e., Shah Inayat.

5   The twelfth century of the Hijri era corresponds to the eighteenth century CE (1100 AH = 1688 CE). Compare 4.5 for the allusions to the disturbed state of contemporary Panjabi society.

## 35

1   This *kāfī* is not included in R. All subsequent editions have taken this poem from Q, but some doubts must attach to its authenticity. The language is fairly standard Urdu, and it lacks the usual refrain of a *kāfī*. It is actually a ghazal in the *hazaj* meter of four feet, scanning *mafāʿīlun mafāʿīlun mafāʿīlun mafāʿīlun* (with some irregularities).

## 36

1   The Persian script does not distinguish between *se*, "those," and *sai*, "hundreds," and some editions prefer the latter. The "traders" (*vanjāre*) are the peddlers who supplied the village women with

387

their jewelry, and are here as often elsewhere used to symbolize the saints who bear the uniquely valuable message of all-demanding love for the divine. Compare 70.5, 117.2.

2   Before the introduction of pockets and purses, money was kept tied in the hem of a garment (*kannī*, equivalent to *pallā* 36.6).

### 37

1   The use of spinning as a metaphor for the correct conduct of life is here developed with an abundance of terms referring to different parts of the spinning wheel.

2   A maund (*maṇ*) is a large measure of weight, equivalent to 80 pounds.

### 38

1   The contrast between the orthodox performance of the hajj to Mecca and the lover as pilgrim to the beloved occurs elsewhere. Compare 102.4, 126.9, V51, also 105.6, 128.1–2.

2   The popular Panjabi pronunciation of Ar. *ġhāzī*, "warrior for the faith," as *gājī* rhymes with *hājī*. The contrast between these exemplary Muslims and burglars and thieves symbolizes the simultaneous presence of good and evil in man.

### 39

1   Literally, "wearing an *alfī*," the shroudlike sleeveless garment worn by fakirs, so called because it is straight in shape like the letter *alif.*

2   A seventeen (*satārāñ* F S) is a top throw of the dice in the game of *caupaṛ,* versus the usual idiom in *pauñ bārāñ jāñ paiñde ne* J, "when getting a twelve." Compare 97.4.

3   Wearing the turban at a tilt is the sign of a dandy, like the casual way of wearing slippers.

4   Compare 24.1.

5   The phrase "both heaps" (*doveñ thok*) is better understood with PS as "this world and the world to come," rather than with S as the two words of the formula *lā ilāha*, "there is no God."

6   A Panjabi translation of the Arabic *mūtū qabla an tamūtū.* See 77.7.

7   On the day of judgment, the prophet Muhammad will intercede for those who have followed the commandments of Islam. Compare 17.7, 104.8, 117.4, 119.14, S26.

8    I.e., the announcement of death.

## 40

1    It has often been observed this famous *kāfī* is modeled on Rumi's
     great Persian ghazal beginning *cih tadbīr ai musalmānān kih man
     khud-rā namīdānam, na tarsā nai yahūd-am man na gabr-am nai
     musalmān-am,* "What can I do, oh Muslims, for I do not know
     myself. I am not a Christian nor a Jew, not a Zoroastrian nor a
     Muslim." Compare the thematically similar 106.

2    The Sufi doctrine of "peace toward all" (Pers. *ṣulḥ-e kull*) was
     also adopted in India as a definition of Akbar's policy of religious
     tolerance toward non-Muslims.

3    See 16.2.

## 41

1    When Ibrahim, the biblical Abraham, destroyed the idols belonging
     to his father, Azar, he was sentenced by the evil king Namrud to be
     burned on a pyre, from which he was rescued by God. Compare
     110.2, 143.6.

2    See 27.3

3    See 12.4.

4    A learned Shaikh who became disgraced through his infatuation
     with a beautiful Christian girl, for whose sake he had to put
     on the girdle worn by Christians and to graze pigs. The story
     comes from the *Mantiq ut Tair* by the Persian Sufi poet Attar.
     Compare 110.3.

5    See 12.2.

6    See 28.7.

## 42

1    The *tilak* is the mark drawn on the forehead as a sign of Hindu
     religious affiliation, as opposed to the religious practice and duty
     (*sunnat faraz*) of Islam.

2    The father of the prophet Muhammad.

3    See 77.7.

4    The area near Mathura where Krishna spent his youth as a
     herdsman.

5    The capital of Ravan's kingdom, attacked by Ram.

6    See 28.7.

7    See 11.1.

8    See 133.4.

9    See 12.4.

10   The biblical Jonah, who was swallowed by a large fish. Compare 110.2, 143.4.

11   See 27.2.

12   See n. 7 on 28.3. This verse is included in S, but not in most other editions.

13   The fourteen zones (Ar. *tabaq*) that together make up the entire universe. Compare 77.4, 135.3.

## 43

1    See n. 4 on 28.2.

2    See n. 1 on 23.2.

3    See 117.3.

## 44

1    The refrain expresses the lover's mystical transformation through his experience of the divine self-manifestation, as described in the following verses.

2    Wild geese are symbolically associated with the spiritually aware.

## 45

1    There is a deliberately shocking juxtaposition of the pious Muslim formula "In the name of God" (Ar. *bi'smi'llāh*), which is said before undertaking any action, with the Hindu spring festival of Holi; compare B6. Arabic phrases ending in *'llāh*, "God," recur in the rhymes throughout the poem; compare G40.

2    From the Islamic profession of faith (P. *kalmā*) *lā ilāha illā 'llāh wa muḥammadun rasūlu'llāh*, "There is no god but God, and Muhammad is God's Apostle." Compare 25.3, 28.9, 45.3, 45.7, 119.13, S23.

3    A technical term of Sufism (Ar. *fanā fī 'llāh*), used to describe the obliteration of the self in the divine.

4    See n. 8 on 28.4. The scenario of the first day of creation is here developed with the souls of mankind being conceived as girlfriends (*sakhīāñ*).

5    See 45.2 above, and compare 45.7 below.

6    See n. 11 on 28.6.

7    An allusion to the favorite Sufi saying *man 'arafa nafsahu* [*fa-qad 'arafa rabbahu*], "Whoever has known himself [has known his lord]."

8    See n. 6 on 28.3.

9    The pious Arabic phrase *ṣallā 'llāhu* ['*alaihi*], which is added to any mention of the Prophet, in modern English Islamic usage often abbreviated as (*pbuh*), i.e., "peace be upon him."

10   The Arabic words are from the verses *fa-'dhkurūnī* [*adhkurkum*] *wa-'shkurū lī* [*wa lā takfurūni*] (Qur'an 2.152-3) "Then remember me [and I will remember you]. And be grateful to me [and do not be ungrateful toward me]." Compare 70.4.

11   The Arabic phrase *subḥāna 'llāh* is a common exclamation of praise or wonder.

12   The tube (*pickārī*) used to squirt colored dye at other people during the celebration of Holi.

13   The phrase is understood to signify Islam in the verse *ṣibghatu 'llāhi wa-man aḥsanu min allāhi ṣibghatan* (Qur'an 2.138), "The baptism of God, and who can baptize better than God?"

14   The scriptural phrase *allāhu 'l-ṣamad* (Qur'an 112.2), "God the everlasting one," here daringly indicates the divine presence in man.


### 46

1    The countdown to the day of the wedding is calculated by progressively undoing the knots (*gaṇḍhīṅ*) that have been tied for each day of the waiting period. See G.


### 47

1    The overall sense of the poem is powerfully conveyed, but the precise meaning of some verses is not always entirely clear.

2    See 28.7.

3    See n. 9 on 28.4.

4    The word "unstruck" (*anhad*) is usually applied to the mystical sound heard in the yogic process; see 3.3. Here it appears to have the general sense of "imperceptible, invisible."

### 48

1     An allusion to the story of Sohni, as also in 48.7 below. See n.1 on 81.

### 49

1     All editions follow R in printing *kāfīs* 49 and 50 as separate poems. Their rhymes *-āriā* (49) and *-oliā* (50) may be different, but these two short poems are otherwise so similar that they are probably variants of a single original that diverged in the oral tradition. Compare the similarly paired 130 and 131.

2     This refrain begins with the same words, *kadī ā mil*, as 48.1.

3     See 8.3.

4     This half-verse virtually repeats the refrain 49.1, and appears to be a filler devised to make up the metrical scheme.

### 50

1     See n. 1 on 49.

### 51

1     This remarkable depiction of the strife in contemporary society as a set of disputes between different kinds of snacks and sweets is first recorded in Q. It is absent from R, and its authenticity has sometimes been questioned. It is not translated in PS.

2     "Millionaires" (*lakhpatī*) are perhaps the name of something to eat, since the other verses begin with the names of sweets.

3     The name of the false prophet whose coming will mark the end of the world and whose teachings will destroy true religion and create social chaos.

### 52

1     This exceptionally long *kāfī* on the theme of a girl's need to apply herself to her spinning as an image for the proper conduct of life may be compared with G.

2     See 150.2.

3     I.e., Shah Inayat.

### 53

1     See n. 4 on 23.6.

2    See n. 3 on 151.3.

3    The bodily existence (*khākī*) of human beings creates the illusion of separateness between them. Compare 95.5.

4    The word "Syrian" (*shāmī*), which generates the verse rhyme *-āmī*, is naturally balanced by *rūmī*, here translated as "Turk."

5    The cupbearer (Pers. *sāqī*) who in Persian poetry represents the teacher who dispenses the wine of mystical knowledge. Compare 67.3.

### 54

1    Since God is omnipotent, the fault of sin does not lie with man.

2    The Arabic phrase *lā tataḥarraku*, "You do not move [unless I so command]" is a proclamation to man of divine omnipotence. Although it seems to be understood as scriptural, it does not actually occur in the text of the Qur'an. Compare 77.7.

3    See n. 9 on 28.4. The scriptural quotation reinforces the statements in the preceding verses about the primal compact between God and man, which pre-dates the formal inauguration of Islam.

4    See n. 1 on 23.2.

### 55

1    See n. 1 on 23.2.

2    I.e., in the world created by God in order that he might be loved.

3    See 10.3.

4    The "ignorant one" (*jāhal*) is the prophet Muhammad's arch-enemy, the heathen Abu Jahl. S explains the story: Abu Jahl once hid some stones in his clenched fist and came to ask the Prophet what he had in his hand. Muhammad told him they were stones that would magnify God. Then from his hand could be heard the proclamation "There is no god but God, and Muhammad is his Apostle." Abu Jahl then fled in discomfiture.

5    See 28.7.

6    See 96.5.

7    The *Sikandar-nāma* by the Persian poet Nizami describes how the hero, Sikandar, came disguised as an envoy bringing his message to Nushaba, the queen of Azerbaijan, only for her to recognize who he really was.

8    In Jami's Persian poem *Yūsuf Zulaikhā*, Yusuf comes to Zulaikha in her dreams long before the pair actually meet.

9    The magic stone (*pāras*) that alchemically transforms iron into gold. Compare 146.5.

## 56

1    Pharaoh (Ar. *fir'aun*) was the evil ruler of Egypt who persecuted Moses, and who was eventually drowned in the Nile when he tried to pursue him. Compare 106.2, 143.16.

## 57

1    See n. 1 on 23.2.

2    The phrase "hidden secret" (Pers. *sirr-e makhfi*) is a reference to the mystical reason for creation, i.e., that God might be loved. See 28.4.

3    See n. 17 on 28.9.

4    To indicate the public announcement either of the glory of Adam's special status in creation or else, according to S, of his disgrace when expelled from paradise.

5    A famous pair of lovers in Islamic romance. The Arab princess Laila was loved so passionately by Qais, who came from a rival tribe, that he was driven mad and became known as Majnun ("the madman"). Compare 95.2, 98.4, 101.3, 133.3, 143.10, 150.5, 154.6.

## 58

1    The poem is of the same formal type as *kāfī* 4, with a single rhyme throughout, but since the verses are here clearly grouped as pairs they are numbered accordingly.

2    Stains do not show on the blanket worn by a fakir, which is dyed a dark color.

3    The familiar pairing of *alif* and *be* as the first two letters of the Arabic alphabet is here followed by the third letter, *te,* which begins the word *tilāvat*, "recitation of the Qur'an."

4    Later in the alphabet, the letters *sīn* (س) "S" and *shīn* (ش) "SH" are followed by *suād* (ص) "Ṣ," which begins the words *sādak* (Ar. *ṣādiq*), "sincere," and *sābar* (Ar. *ṣābir*), "patient."

5    The comparison of the ring around the neck of a turtledove with the collar around the neck of a slave is a common conceit of Persian poetry.

6    The words *maiñ maiñ*, literally "me, me," are also an onomatopoeic

representation of the goat's bleating. Compare 112.4.

7  There is a play on the literal meaning, "grace," of the name (*ināit*, Ar. *'ināyat*) of Bullhe Shah's master, Shah Inayat. Compare S18.

## 60

1  This poem is not in R, and is omitted from PS. Most editions derive from Q.

2  See n. 4 on 28.2.

3  Since God is present in the heart, there is no need to direct appeals to him elsewhere.

## 61

1  In this poem, the disguised immanence of the divine is symbolized by the arrival of Ranjha in the dress of a herdsman employed by Hir's father to graze his buffaloes.

2  The alliterative phrase *cākar cāk* emphasizes Ranjha's apparent humble status.

3  I.e., since the act of creation, marking the separation of the creator from his creatures.

4  See 33.4.

## 62

1  This appears to be the sense of the phrase *mārū kehā jhulāṇā*.

## 63

1  This *kāfī*, with its unusually irregular rhyme scheme, is generally considered to be by Bullhe Shah and is included as such in Q, F, and J, although it is absent from R. As with *kāfī* 29, its exclusion from S as the work of Shah Husain cannot be taken as being fully established. For the variant Shah Husain text, see Daudi 1990: 78–79, *kāfī* 125 (trans. Anwar 1966: 71–72), which has the refrain *jhume jhum khel lai manjh vehṛe, japdiāṅ nūṅ har neṛe*.

2  The courtyard represents the body with its nine orifices. The tenth door is the hidden aperture in the skull that is opened at the climax of the yogic process. Compare 136.10.

3  The rampaging mind that resists the practice of spiritual discipline.

### 64

1 See 25.1.
2 This verse and those following describe various Hindu religious rituals, including the marriage ceremonies performed for idols of the gods, as meaningless distractions from reality.
3 I.e., just saying that red is white does not make it so.
4 The great mother goddess.
5 I.e., Chandi's consort, the god Shiv.
6 The proliferation of kinship terms mocks the whole notion of idols being related to one another.
7 A Panjabi translation (*shāh rag thīñ neṛe*) of the familiar Qur'anic phrase *naḥnu aqrab*. See n. 11 on 28.6.
8 The last half-verse, *mujh meñ bhet nā kāī e*, could be understood as the words of either the poet or the divine beloved.
9 "Mothers" (*māīāñ*) is understood by S as "those deluded by illusion (*māiā*)."
10 I.e., it has no authority.
11 Repeating 64.1.

### 65

1 See 28.4.
2 See n. 1 on 23.2.
3 See n. 9 on 28.4.
4 The cousin and son-in-law of the prophet Muhammad, who is particularly revered by Shia Muslims.
5 For the actor (*sāñgī*) who put on the show (*sāñg*), compare 80.3, 144.1.

### 66

1 The poem is addressed to Hindu holy men (*santo*) and describes the beloved as the divine cowherd, Krishna, regularly associated by Bullhe Shah with Hir's beloved, Ranjha, who became first a buffalo herdsman, then a yogi for her sake. In keeping with its theme, the language of the *kāfī* is Hindi; see 3.
2 An idiomatic expression for something unexpectedly wonderful happening.
3 The pastoral tribe among whom Krishna grew up.
4 The mystical realm that lies beyond the ordinary senses. See 3.3.
5 Suggesting the appearance of Ranjha as a yogi.

6    A mark of humble status.

### 67

1    The passage of time was traditionally marked by the beating of a gong. The night and the day were each divided into four watches (*pahir*) of about three hours, which were in turn subdivided into eight units of about twenty-four minutes (*ghaṛī*).

2    Literally, "at every *ghaṛī*."

3    The mechanical beating of the gong is contrasted with the divine sound of the unstruck music (*anhad vājā*) experienced at the climax of mystical union. See 3.3.

4    See 117.3.

5    The distiller (*kalāl*) is the equivalent of the cupbearer, who dispenses the wine that banishes all thoughts of ritual observance. Compare 57.3.

### 68

1    The phrase *bulbul is gulzār dī* is taken from the language of the Persian ghazal, in which the nightingale's song permanently expresses the grief caused by separation from her beloved rose.

### 70

1    These parties (*trinjaṇāñ*) are where the girls of the village gather to spin and to gossip. Compare 32.3.

2    See 31.6.

3    See n. 11 on 28.6.

4    See n. 13 on 28.6.

5    See n. 1 on 17.5.

6    See n. 10 on 45.6.

7    The traveling merchant (*vaṇjārā*) symbolizes the guide who dispenses wisdom. See 36.1.

8    The scriptural verse *yadu'llāhi fauqa aidīhim* (Qur'an 48.10), "The hand of God is over their hands," refers to God's confirmation of the fealty sworn by the Meccan leaders to Muhammad at the conclusion of the treaty of Hudaibiya in 628 CE.

### 71

1    "Reality" (*sacc*, Pers. *haqīqat*) is the third stage on the Sufi path,

reached after the law (*sharī'at*) and the way (*tarīqat*). Compare 78.7, 96.6.

2    The "fourth state" (*cauthā pad,* Skt. *turīyāvasthā-*) is a yogic term that denotes the state of liberation achieved through transcending the three *guṇas* that govern worldly existence. Here it denotes *ma'rifat,* "gnosis," the fourth and highest state on the Sufi path; See 78.7.

3    This seems to be the sense of the phrase *jehā sharhā tarīkat-hāre nūñ,* for which PS offers "After undoing the city of rituals." The same half-verse also occurs in 71.3 above.

### 72

1    The opposition between mystical love (Pers. *'ishq*) and the religious law (*sharī'at*), which is one of the fundamental themes of Persian Sufi poetry, is also the subject of the *kāfī* beginning *ishk sharhā dā jhagrā pai giā,* "A dispute arose between love and law," which is included with translation in Rama Krishna 1938: 65–66, where it is stated to have been obtained from "the late Mīrāsī Maula Bakhsh of Lahore." It has not been included in any of the subsequent standard editions of Bullhe Shah's poetry, unlike the similarly sourced 108, which fulfills a more satisfying hagiographic need.

2    See 11.3.

3    See 18.3.

### 74

1    The rhyme scheme of this *kāfī* is very irregular, suggesting that the text has been unreliably transmitted.

2    "Human love" (Pers. *'ishq-e majāzī*), generally subordinated in Sufi thinking to the higher love of the divine (Pers. *'ishq-e haqīqī*), is here exalted in its own right, as the poet celebrates his love for his human guide Shah Inayat. Compare 18.1.

3    I.e., physical presence is a necessary part of spiritual attraction.

4    The significance of this particular tree (*jindbaṛ*) is uncertain.

5    Compare B3.

### 75

1    The Arabic words *laḥmak laḥmī,* "Your flesh is my flesh," originally spoken by the prophet Muhammad about his beloved son-in-law

Ali, are here taken to indicate the essential unity of God with creation.

2    See 121.1.

3    As elsewhere, an archetypal image of the suffering lover. See 12.4.

4    This is a unique reference in Bullhe Shah's poetry to the great Sufi teacher and poet Jalal ud Din Rumi (d. 1273), whose title derives from his residence in Rum, the modern Anatolia. It invokes his authority as an expert on the divine unity of being in order to settle the apparent dispute of identity between the poet and his beloved.

## 76

1    This *kāfī* is not reckoned as a separate poem in most editions, where it is added on to the end of the Friday verse of the *Aṭhvārā*; see A7. Although linked to that verse in its theme, this poem is, however, rightly classed as a separate *kāfī* in F, where it is numbered as such, but out of the regular alphabetical sequence.

2    There is a wordplay between *pīr*, "Monday," and *pīṛāñ*, "pains."

3    There is another wordplay, between *budh*, "Wednesday," and *budh sudh*, "sense, awareness."

4    The Jat tribe to which Hir belonged.

5    See 117.3.

6    The meaning of the rhyme word *tārotār* is uncertain.

## 77

1    The text of this poem follows S, which is much superior to the truncated and corrupt text of R, F, and J translated in PS.

2    See n. 4 on 23.6, and compare 77.3–4 below.

3    The "pearl of meanings" (Pers. *durr-e ma'ānī*) is variously supposed to refer to the Qur'an or to Sufi teachings.

4    An abbreviated citation of the familiar scriptural phrase *We are nearer.* See n. 11 on 28.6.

5    The "white hand" (Pers. *yad-e baiżā*): when God restored the hand of Moses that had been burned on the orders of Pharaoh, it had been made miraculously brilliant. It is thus a symbol of spiritual powers.

6    See n. 1 on 23.2.

7    See 42.16.

8    See n. 9 on 28.4.

9    From the verse [*inna'llāha 'alā*] *kulli shai'in* [*qadīrun*] (Qur'an

2.20), "[For God has power] over all things."

10 *Yāsīn* (Y S) and *Muzammil* (The wrapped) are the names of chapters 36 and 73 of the Qur'an. Since these two chapters (Ar. *sūra*) contain special reference to Muhammad, the meaning is "for the sake of the Prophet."

11 See n. 1 on 17.5.

12 This popular Sufi saying (Ar. *mūtū qabla an tamūtū*) teaches the need to be dead to the world while still living in it. Compare 39.12, 42.6, S11.

13 See n. 2 on 54.2.

14 From the verse *lan tanālū 'l-birra ḥattā* [*tunfiqū mimmā tuḥibbūna*] (Qur'an 3.92), "You will not attain righteousness until [you give freely of that which you love]."

15 See 137.11.

16 See 105.7.

## 78

1 A reference to the story of Sohni. See n. 1 on 81.

2 The tree *Butea frondosa* sheds its leaves before it fruits. Its buds are black, but open to reveal red petals, here suggesting the contrast between the outward disgrace (*malāmat*) voluntarily assumed by a Sufi and his inner integrity (Pers. *surkhrūī*, literally "red-facedness").

3 The "rival" (*raqīb*) is understood by the commentators to mean the devil, but the sense of the verse is obscure.

4 See 16.2.

5 The *Gulistān* (The rose garden) and the *Bostān* (The orchard) are two collections of stories that form key texts of the Persian literary canon. They were both written by Shaikh Saadi (d. 1292) of Shiraz.

6 I.e., false teachings.

7 The verse describes the four stages on the Sufi path. The law (Ar. *sharī'at*, P. *sharḥā*) is followed by the way (*tarīqat*), then reality (*ḥaqīqat*), and finally gnosis (*ma'rifat*). Compare 71.5.

8 This verse and 78.9 refer to the secret teachings of Sufism.

9 See 28.7.

10 The austerities practiced by the famous Sufi Bayazid Bistami (d. 874) are supposed to have separated his body from his spirit. The text of this verse is very uncertain, and the meaning is doubtful in places.

11    See 11.2.

## 79

1    In this remarkable poem, the lover announces her intention to use all the powers of nature as well as her whole person to create a love spell that will win her beloved to her.

2    A spell is activated by blowing out the words with the breath.

3    The seeds of the wild rue (*harmal*) are burned to banish evil spirits.

## 80

1    See 65.7.

2    Understood by S as the primordial light of Muhammad that preceded the creation of Adam.

## 81

1    In this *kāfī* the poet speaks as the legendary heroine Sohni, who used to come secretly by night to the edge of the river Chenab. She would take with her an earthenware pot as a float to help her make the dangerous crossing to the far bank, where she would meet her beloved, Mahinval. Compare 48.5, 78.1, 83.4, 102.5, 128.4, 137.13, 143.12, 154.6, 155.3, B4, S4.

2    Literally, "I stand flying crows," an idiom indicating the anxiety of trying to communicate with the beloved.

3    The diadem (*mukṭā*) from which a veil is hung over the face and the forehead mark (*tilak*) are both worn by the bridegroom during the wedding ceremony.

## 83

1    I.e., the malign influence of an evil spirit.

2    The verse evokes the fate of Sohni. See n. 1 on 81.

3    Like the turning of ropes into snakes, the display of stars under baskets is a proverbial example of a magic trick, depending upon the illusion of the burning coals tipped during the night from a basket used to carry them looking like stars.

4    I.e., she is so distracted that she cannot distinguish two fruits that are so unlike in appearance.

5    The Indian city is proverbially famous for its fine bamboo.

6    Literally, "I will not put my head on my body again."

## 84

1 The "city of the silent" (*shahir khamoshāṅ dā*) is the land of the dead. Compare 100.3, G15.

## 86

1 This poem is included in Q, S, and J, but omitted from F.

2 There is a wordplay between *cullhā*, "hearth," and the name Bullha.

3 There is another wordplay here, with *khangar*, "a lump of fused bricks." The Ranghars were a tribe of Muslim Rajputs who achieved prominence in eighteenth-century Panjab, and who were proverbial for their arrogance. Compare V38.

## 88

1 Since the refrain is here needed to complete the sense of this verse, it has exceptionally been printed throughout this poem.

## 90

1 The verse attacks the mechanical utterance of the common Arabic phrase *astaġhfiru'llāh*, "I seek God's forgiveness, God forgive me," without having any genuine desire to repent.

## 91

1 See n. 12 on 28.6.

2 Perhaps a general reference to the teaching of Shah Inayat, not necessarily to his written Persian treatises.

## 92

1 The word "dunce" (*kuṭīcal*) is an unusual formation from *kuṭṭṇā*, "to beat," with the sense of "a child who is regularly beaten for poor performance in class."

2 See 11.1.

## 93

1 The "day of pre-eternity" (*roz azal dā*, Pers. *roz-e azal*) represents the period before the beginning of time. Compare B6.

### 94

1 Shah Inayat was affiliated to the Qadiri order of Sufis. Compare 126.9.

### 95

1 Majnun's beloved used to be kept in *purdah*, from which she would steal glances at him. See 57.6.
2 See 12.2.
3 See 28.7.
4 See 27.3.
5 See n. 1 on 23.2.
6 See n. 3 on 151.3. The verse envisages the divine both as creation and as the Prophet for whose sake creation was brought into being.
7 See 53.3.

### 96

1 See n. 11 on 28.6.
2 The meaning here of the word *barātāṅ* is unclear, and the whole verse is somewhat obscure.
3 See 28.7.
4 God was equally present in the martyr Mansur and in the mullahs standing around to witness his execution. Compare 55.5, 109.2.
5 See 71.5.

### 97

1 A cosmetic powder used to tinge the teeth black.
2 Life is compared to a game of *chaupaṛ*, which is similar to ludo. It is played with three four-sided dice, so three ones are the lowest possible throw, while the highest throw is called *pauṅ bārāṅ*, literally "ace and twelve." Compare 39.5.
3 The Panjabi (*gūṅgī ḍorī kamlī*) recalls the Qur'anic phrase *ṣummun bukmun 'umyun*. See n. 1 on 17.5.

### 98

1 As often in Bullhe Shah, the adverb *othe*, "there," denotes the other world of love.
2 When Yusuf was put up for sale in the Egyptian slave market, an old woman offered a hank of yarn for him. See 12.4.

3    Cowrie shells were used as the smallest units of currency.

4    See 12.4.

5    See 57.6.

6    The reference is to Shams. See 12.2.

7    The reference is to Zakariya. See 27.3.

8    The reference is to Mansur. See 28.7.

9    The words that sent Mansur to the gallows. See 28.7.

### 100

1    See 84.5.

2    The traditional text of this verse in F and J seems certainly corrupt, but the emendations and explanations suggested by S both appear forced.

### 101

1    Majnun's mad love for Laila was so great that he longed to become her. See 57.6.

### 102

1    See n. 6 on 28.3.

2    See 38.1.

3    An allusion to the story of Sohni. See n. 1 on 81.

### 104

1    Doubly associated with Krishna and with Ranjha as the preferred musical instrument of herdsmen, the flute is imagined as the vehicle for the transmission of the divine message through the poet's spiritual guide.

2    S explains the rhyme word *māñjhā* as the name given to the custom of dressing the bride in old clothes and confining her to the house for some days before her marriage.

3    The whole verse suggests the further mystical associations of the reed flute in Sufism, as memorably celebrated in the opening verses of Rumi's *Masnavī*.

4    See 3.3.

5    So interpreted by S, but the rhyme word *tāre* normally means "strings."

6    I.e., "live your life in accordance with the tenets of Islam, so that

the Prophet may be your witness on the day of judgment." See 39.13.

### 105

1  This very famous *kāfī* is best known by this second verse of the refrain ending with the syllables *thaīā thaīā,* which are used by teachers of dancing to mark the rhythm of the steps.

2  Symbolizing the gloom created by the master's departure.

3  The Kaaba is the focal point of the pilgrimage, and the Qibla is the direction of Mecca to which those performing the prayer face. Here the sense is that the master points me the direction of himself as the object of my devotion. Compare 38.1, 128.1–2.

4  As bridal colors, these suggest the bliss of being with the beloved. Like the rest of the poem, this verse may be understood as a general expression of lament and rejoicing caused by separation from the beloved and union with him. The most popular understanding of the verse is that it refers to an actual incident in which Bullhe Shah, having fallen out with Shah Inayat, dressed up as a dancing girl and regained his master's favor with his performance. Compare 5.6, 77.10, 126.4, 149.6.

### 106

1  The natural appeal of this *kāfī* across religious and national boundaries has helped it become probably the best known of all Bullhe Shah's lyrics. Compare the thematically similar 40.

2  See 56.6.

3  The four sacred books (*kitābāñ*) of the Semitic tradition, i.e., the Torah (Ar. *tauret*), Psalms (*zabūr*), Gospel (*injīl*), and Qur'an. Compare V51.

4  Compare V32.

5  A city in Rajasthan, which gives the adjective *nagaurī* to rhyme with *lāhaurī* and *pashaurī*.

6  See 16.2.

7  A place in Himachal Pradesh, once a town of some importance, which fits the *kāfī*'s main rhyme *-auṇ*.

8  I.e., Shah Inayat. This profession of the mystical identity between disciple and the master standing directly before him makes an effective conclusion to the poem.

## 107

1    By confusing them with the outward differences between Hir and
     Ranjha, which belie their essential identity.

## 108

1    This unusual *kāfī* is probably overconfidently described in PS as a
     rare instance "where a classic poem depicts a true incident of life."
     It is not included in R, Q, F, or J, and the text printed here is taken
     from S. Its partial first appearance in print seems to have been in
     Rama Krishna 1938: 46–47, where "Mr N. A. Waqar" and "a few
     *kavvālīs*" are cited as sources. Verse 108.4 is substantially identical
     with 31.6. It seems likely that this *kāfī* is a later hagiographic
     elaboration from 31.6 of the familiar theme of the disparity in
     outward status between the Sayyid poet and his revered master
     from the lower-ranking Arain caste. Its genuineness is anyway
     open to question on stylistic grounds, since the dialogue format of
     108.1–3 is otherwise only shared with the spurious *kāfī* beginning
     *ishk sharhā dā jhagṛā pai giā* (Rama Krishna 1938: 65–66), which
     is referred to in n. 1 on 72.
2    Sayyids are all descended from the Prophet through his son-in-law
     Ali, the husband of his daughter Fatima.

## 109

1    See n. 4 on 28.2.
2    See 28.7.
3    See 96.5.

## 110

1    See 41.2.
2    See 27.6.
3    See 42.15.
4    See 12.4.
5    See 27.3.
6    See 27.2
7    See 41.3.
8    The reference is to Shams. See 12.2.
9    Husain, the grandson of the prophet Muhammad and son of Ali, is
     believed to have been attended upon as an infant by the archangel

Gabriel. Revered as Imam by Shia Muslims, he was martyred at the battle of Karbala in the Iraq desert in 680, when leading a small army to challenge the authority of the Caliph Yazid. Compare 137.12, 143.20.

10 Compare 110.3 above for the unusual double reference to a name within a single poem.

11 See 27.4.

12 I.e., a lover of God.

## 112

1 See 58.7.

## 113

1 The Hindu imagery of this poem is typically reinforced by a preponderance of Hindi vocabulary. Compare 3.

2 The phrase *shām sundar* is regularly associated with Krishna. Compare B2, B10.

3 A loose bracelet may turn around and around, but it remains on the wrist.

## 114

1 The structure of this *kāfī* is best understood as a kind of ghazal, with paired verses all having the monorhyme *-ā ke*. Most editions pair the opening refrain with the following line, repeating it at the end to make up the requisite pairing, but the sense seems better served by the grouping adopted here from 114.2 onward. Compare the arrangement of verses in 4.

2 Best understood as the words people say about the poet.

3 Literally "I played *ākā bākā*," a children's game in which figures are made out of mud.

4 Literally, "I perform the *giddhā*," a folk dance in which girls clap and sing.

5 Here to be understood as the lower self (Pers. *nafs-e 'ammāra*) whose subjugation is a principal task of Sufi discipline.

## 117

1 The meaning of the rhyme word *aṅghātāñ* is uncertain both here and in 8.3.

2 See 3.3.

3 See 36.1.

4 The Panjabi phrase *saīñ mukh* evokes the Qur'anic verse "Wherever you look, there is the face of God (Ar. *wajhu'llāh*)"; see n. 6 on 28.3. The mystery of the divine presence in all things is transparent to the Sufi masters.

5 The least elaborate kind of prayer. Compare 43.6, 67.3, 76.7.

6 See 39.13.

7 The rhyme phrase *dast barātāñ* may represent Pers. *dast-burd*, "plunder," but the sense of the half-verse is unclear.


### 118

1 This fragmentary poem is not included in the earliest editions, R and Q.

2 See 11.1.


### 119

1 Verses 119.8 and 119.15 are omitted in F and J.

2 I.e., uttering the refrain "I cannot help saying what comes onto my tongue."

3 I.e., the world.

4 Where Moses came before God. See n. 4 on 12.5.

5 See 28.7.

6 The tension between the poet's mystical vision and the generally abstract expression of this poem is a remarkable feature of this great *kāfī*, which is one of Bullhe Shah's most famous compositions.

7 I.e., *alif*, which symbolizes the divine. See 11.1.

8 In the Islamic profession of faith, with its celebration of Muhammad as the Apostle of God, See 45.2.

9 See 39.13.

10 The narrow bridge that the soul must cross over after death in order to reach paradise, while avoiding falling into the torments of hell. Compare 126.9, S27.

11 I.e., the Islamic profession of faith.


### 120

1 The city that is the seat of royal authority in Panjab (hence called *takhat lahor*) is here celebrated as the home of Shah Inayat.

Compare 121.5, 121.6, 123.2.

2  Ranjha's home, from where he set out to journey to Jhang, where Hir lived.

## 121

1  The folds (*bukkal*) are used as a symbol of intimate closeness. Compare 19.4, 75.7.
2  Typical names of a Hindu and a Muslim.
3  I.e., the divine light entered Shah Inayat. See 120.2.
4  The great saint Abdul Qadir Gilani (d. 1166) of Baghdad, who is revered as the founder of the Qadiri order.

## 122

1  This long poem is unusual in its detailed references to the story of Hir and Ranjha. These are less characteristic of the Sufi lyric than of narrative treatments of the legend like the famous *Hīr* by Varis Shah, and may be insertions by later imitators. The *kāfī* begins with apparently disconnected laments and invocations by Hir (121.2–8) before relating the story of Hir's forced marriage to the Khera (121.9–14). A description of Ranjha's initiation and arrival as a yogi at Hir's marital home (121.15–18) then leads to a final section (122.18–22) that is hardly intelligible without quite close familiarity with the story as narrated by Varis Shah. When Ranjha comes disguised as a yogi to Hir's husband's house, he is at first seized and beaten by Hir's sister-in-law Sahti. Later, however, Sahti, who herself has a secret lover, becomes complicit with the lovers and helps them to elope.
2  Five great saints who are believed collectively to possess special powers. Their miraculous interventions on behalf of Ranjha are a notable feature of Varis Shah's *Hīr*, where the Five Pirs (*panj pīr*) are named as the legendary Khwaja Khizr, Farid Shakarganj of Pakpattan, Baha ud Din Zakariya of Multan, Jalal ud Din Makhdum Jahaniyan of Uch, and Lal Shahbaz Qalandar of Sehwan. Compare 137.17.
3  See n. 1 on 23.2.
4  Hir's father, who employs Ranjha to herd his buffaloes, and who later gets the *qazi* to perform Hir's marriage to the Khera against her will. Compare 122.13.
5  The popular title of Baha ud Din Zakariya of Multan, one of the

Five Pirs. This invitation to visit his tomb in Multan, which is a major center of pilgrimage, strikes a strange note, and the verse may be a later interpolation.

6 I.e., Ranjha, whose wretchedness is contrasted with the proud happiness of the Khera bridegroom.

7 I.e., the Khera bridegroom; compare the phrase "my Pir" in 122.16 to indicate Ranjha.

8 The verse describes the ritual anointing and cleansing of the bridegroom before the marriage ceremony.

9 As a menial employee of Chuchak, Ranjha had to play the drum (*tamak*) during the festivities for Hir's wedding. Compare 137.14.

10 Tilla Jogian high up in the hills of District Jhelum was the headquarters of the order of Kanphat ("split-eared") yogis, who were initiated by having the cartilage of their ears pierced to allow the insertion of a wooden ring.

11 Presumably the name of the yogis' guru Gorakhnath.

12 Gorakhnath, the head of the Kanphat yogis.

13 Sahti gave Ranjha some millet as alms, but at first he angrily rejected this inferior grain.

14 Sahti made it appear that Hir had been bitten by a snake so that Ranjha could be asked to cure her. Compare 156.5.

### 123

1 See 120.2.

2 The rhyme word *cās* suggests a synonym of *jhāt*, "glance."

3 The rhyme word *lās* is taken to be a variant of *lāsh*, "corpse."

### 125

1 His "cup" was filled with the mystical understanding that led him to the famous utterance *I am God*. See 27.5.

2 The prophet Muhammad was given a direct experience of the divine on the night of his ascension to heaven. See 137.11.

3 Perhaps an allusion to Kausar, one of the springs of paradise, but understood by S to mean the use of the whole well rather than the more modest amount of water normally used for ritual ablution (*vuzū*) before prayer.

4 The verse describes the ritual observances of Muslim prayer, beginning with the muezzin's call, as a metaphor for the mystical experience. The preliminary formulation of righteous intent

(*niyyat*) is followed by prostration, which is performed facing the *mihrab*, the niche in the wall of a mosque that marks the direction of the Qibla.

## 126

1    The verse evokes the famous story of Bullhe Shah dressing up as a dancing girl to win Shah Inayat's favor. See 105.7.

2    A legendary pair of lovers from royal Rajput families. Dhola is both the personal name of Sammi's beloved and a word with the general sense of "beloved, darling."

3    See 119.15.

4    See 38.1.

5    See 94.10.

6    The expression here refers to the first night after death.

## 127

1    The attractive bloom of the safflower (*kasumbrā*), *Carthamus tinctorius*, looks like saffron, but it lasts for only a short time. It is regularly used to symbolize the transitory delights of this world.

2    Literally "local headmen" (Pers. *muqaddam*). It is unclear who these four are intended to represent, although PS offers a Radhasoami interpretation, defining them as "mind" (*manas*), "reasoning faculty" (*cit*), "intellect" (*budhi*), and "ego" (*ahankār*).

3    I.e., those who have not been seduced by worldly pleasures.

4    See n. 9 on 28.4.

## 128

1    See 38.1.

2    A loose allusion to the story of Sohni. See n. 1 on 81.

## 129

1    An allusion to the belief that when God was putting the souls into bodies, he promised that he would come with them into the world.

## 130

1    This *kāfī* is a close doublet of the more elaborate 131. Like *kāfī* 29, it is also attributed to Shah Husain. For the variant Shah Husain text,

see Daudi 1990: 56–57, *kāfī* 88 (trans. Anwar 1966: 124), which has the shorter refrain *chūhṛī āñ darbār dī.*

## 131

1 This *kāfī*'s rhyme *-āroñ* is shared with 130, and the refrains of the two poems are virtually identical. It seems likely that they are variants of a single original that have been separately recorded in R from the oral tradition. Compare the similar overlap between 49 and 50.

2 The word is variously spelled, as *taṛbarāṭ* or *tarmarāṭ*, and variously interpreted.

3 As a sweeper girl of the untouchable Chuhra caste, she is reckoned to be neither a Hindu nor a Muslim.

4 Here "twice-born" (*do jarme*) is the familiar designation of Hindus of the higher castes, while "thrice-born" (*trai jarme*) may be intended to refer to Muslims, unless it is meant simply to mock the whole concept of multiple grades of birth.

5 Thanks to the insight I have been given by my teacher, who is both Guru and Pir, all people appear equally worthy of respect.

6 An image for the fruit of great efforts.

## 132

1 Literally "studied a quarter (*pā paṛhiāñ*)," explained by S as "those who have studied [only] a quarter [of one of the thirty sections (*sipārā*) of the Qur'an]." Since "learned scholars (*ālam fāzal*)" are praised in 132.3, the phrase must be taken to indicate those who have hardly learned anything about the teachings of love.

## 133

1 See 57.6.

2 Tegh Bahadur was the ninth Guru of the Sikhs, executed for his faith in Delhi in 1675 by the Mughal emperor Aurangzeb. Compare 42.14.

3 This mention by an eighteenth-century Muslim poet of the distinctive "path" (*panth*) of the Sikhs as distinct from both Muslims and Hindus is very unusual, arousing the suspicion that the verse may be a later interpolation.

4 It is not clear who exactly is meant here.

5    See 137.11.


## 135

1    See 42.16.
2    The "tavern" (*kharābāt*), literally, the ruins where drinkers hang
     out, is a key term in the language of the Persian ghazal. It denotes
     the place where the followers of Sufi teachings gather, as opposed
     to the mosque where the orthodox congregate.


## 136

1    A dumb man may taste the sweetness of raw sugar, but he cannot
     describe it.
2    I.e., nothing of myself is my own, since it has all been made by you.
3    I.e., my eyes have been enslaved by your eyes.
4    That they will lose sight of you.
5    In the language of the Persian ghazal, the "Magian elder" (Pers.
     *pīr-e muġhāñ*) is the master who runs the tavern where the lovers
     drink the wine of love.
6    The devotee is constant in the profession of love, no matter what
     form the divine beloved assumes.
7    See 63.3.


## 137

1    In this verse Hir announces that she will put a yogi's mark (*tilak*)
     on her forehead and become a yogini to accompany Ranjha, who
     had become a yogi in order to win her back after her marriage.
     Compare 122.
2    The home of Hir's tribe, the Sials.
3    Yogis sit in front of a bonfire (*dhūāñ*) and rub its ashes (*bhabūt*) on
     their bodies.
4    The women in Hir's household taunted Ranjha with having become
     a yogi with the purely selfish motive of using his altered appearance
     to win back Hir.
5    See 3.3.
6    Where God spoke with Moses but would not let him see him. See
     n. 4 on 12.5.
7    The Arabic word *'abduh* is used.
8    On the night of his ascension (Ar. *mi'rāj*) to heaven the prophet
     Muhammad was brought into the divine presence, mounted on the

mysterious animal called Buraq, who had been led to him by the archangel Jibrail. According to Sufi understanding, the Prophet's heavenly ascension is an archetypal version of the mystical process. Compare 77.9, 125.4, 133.6, S14.

9    Hasan and Husain were the Prophet's grandsons. It was Husain who suffered the agonies of thirst and died at the battle of Karbala, while his elder brother Hasan met his death through poison. See 110.4, 143.6.

10   See n. 1 on 81.

11   See 122.15.

12   This is a flashback to the time before Ranjha actually became a yogi, when Hir's enforced wedding to the Khera was carried out against her will by the *qazi*, aided by the lies told by her malevolent uncle Kaido.

13   See 122.5.

### 138

1    See n. 11 on 28.6.

2    Literally, "my vessel" (*kunnī*). The word is here apparently chosen to fit the awkward rhyme with *sunnī*; Compare 26.15.

### 139

1    Literally, "100,000," i.e., a large reward.

### 140

1    The higher level of awareness not only removes the distinction between the two banks of the river but also eliminates consciousness of the river itself and the boat used to cross it as separate entities.

2    See 28.7.

### 141

1    The phrase evokes the story of Sassi, who woke up to find herself abandoned by Punnun. See 24.3.

### 143

1    According to Muslim tradition, wheat was the substance that God forbade Adam to eat, on pain of expulsion from paradise. See 10.3.

2    The biblical Noah, whom God instructed to build an ark to escape the flood.

3    According to Qur'an 11.43, the son of Nuh refused his father's invitation to enter the ark and was consequently destroyed with the rest of the unbelievers.

4    See n. 4 on 12.5.

5    The biblical Ishmael. According to Muslim tradition, Ismail was the son whose sacrifice God demanded of his father, Ibrahim.

6    See 42.15.

7    Zulaikha first fell in love with Yusuf when she saw him in a dream. Yusuf was put down a well by his brothers before they sold him into slavery. Later, after Yusuf achieved high rank in Egypt, he summoned his brothers and forgave them. See 12.4.

8    See 27.6.

9    See 41.2.

10   See 27.2.

11   The grandson of the prophet Muhammad and elder brother of Husain, who met his death through poisoning. Compare 137.12.

12   See 28.7.

13   The "monk" (Ar. *rāhib*) here is the early Muslim ascetic Ibrahim ibn Adham (d. c. 782), whose spiritual guide subjected him to numerous tests of his ability not to lose his temper under extreme provocation. The gall bladder is believed to be the seat of anger.

14   See 27.3.

15   An outspoken Sufi who was martyred in Delhi in 1661 on the orders of the Mughal emperor Aurangzeb.

16   See 12.2.

17   Shaikh Sharaf ud Din, a Sufi saint of Panipat best known as Bu Ali Qalandar (d. 1324), whose austerities included a period of twelve years spent immersed in a river.

18   Majnun could not bear to emerge from a well after Laila had bathed in it one day. He received miraculous sustenance during the year he spent there. See 57.6.

19   See 122.15.

20   When the lovers Mirza and Sahiban eloped, they were pursued by Sahiban's brothers, who killed Mirza.

21   See 24.3.

22   See n. 1 on 81.

23   Roda was the lover of the blacksmith's daughter Jalali, with whom

he eloped. When the lovers were captured by the blacksmith's kinsmen, Roda was hacked to pieces.

24 Apparently an allusion to the fierce battles between the Kauravs and Pandavs, named in 143.14.

25 This puzzling reference is apparently to the sufferings of Imam Husain and his forces in the burning heat of the desert at the battle of Karbala, further described in 143.20 below.

26 The rival clans whose epic struggle is the subject of the Sanskrit *Mahābhārata*.

27 The biblical Nimrod. A famous hunter and wicked king of Babylon who persecuted Ibrahim; see 41.2. Namrud believed himself to be the equal of God, but died after being bitten by a mosquito.

28 The biblical Korah, an Egyptian of immense wealth who was hostile to Moses and who was buried with all his treasure after his death.

29 See 55.6.

30 The kingdom of Ravan, which was attacked and destroyed by Ram.

31 Harnakash (Skt. Hiranyaksha) was a king who thought himself the equal of God. He believed that he was invulnerable either outside or inside his magnificent palace, but met his death at the palace gates.

32 The wife of Ram, who was abducted by Ravan, then saved when Hanuman, the ally of Ram, attacked Lanka. S omits this verse, which overlaps with the first half of 143.17.

33 The cow maidens who loved Krishna when he was growing up in Bindraban. As a child, Krishna was famous for stealing the butter he was so fond of. He also destroyed the evil king Kans, who had tried to kill him.

34 Husain, who fought the army of the caliph Yazid at the battle of Karbala. See 110.4.

35 Taken to be an allusion to the Sikhs, whose guerilla horsemen ultimately destroyed the Mughal authority in Panjab.

## 144

1 See 65.7.

2 A standard description of a beautiful person. Compare 12.4, 154.8.

3 Symbolizing the divine unity, the letter *alif* and the numeral 1 (*ahad*) have the same form (‫ا‬) in the Arabic script. See 11.1.

## 145

1   This is one of Bullhe Shah's most famous *kāfīs*. It is nevertheless one of those poems, like *kāfī* 29, that is also attributed to Shah Husain. For the variant Shah Husain text, see Daudi 1990: 80, *kāfī* 127 (trans. Anwar 1966: 4), which has the very similar refrain *māhī māhī kūkdī, maiñ āpe rāñjhaṇ hoī*.

2   The given name of Hir's beloved, usually referred to by his tribal name of Ranjha.

## 146

1   See 55.8.

2   The ocean (*samundar*) is here thought of as containing an infinite supply of fresh water.

3   I.e., Satan.

## 147

1   See 3.3.

2   The *Sharh Wiqāya*, written in Arabic by Ubaidullah Masudi (d. 1349), is a classic textbook of Islamic law.

## 148

1   See n. 4 on 12.5.

2   The words are from the verse [*wa-huwa ma'akum*] *aina mā* [*kuntum*] (Qur'an 57.4), "[And he is with you] wherever [you are]." The verse is usually cited by its first words *He is with you*; see n. 12 on 28.6.

3   See 27.2.

4   See 28.7.

5   Those who prostrate themselves in prayer are actually identical with the God they worship.

6   See 26.13.

## 149

1   The vocative phrase *ve aṛiā*, literally "oh my friend!" used to address a man, is repeated at the end of every line of this poem.

2   I.e., abandon any negative feeling and relax.

3   The *jhumbar* is a round dance performed by women with joined hands. The verse is sometimes taken to be a direct reference to the

story of Bullhe Shah dancing before Shah Inayat in order to win his favor. See 105.7.

## 150

1   To be understood as a reference to God's placing the soul in the body at the time of creation.

2   This represents the actions (Ar. *a'māl*) that are the product of life on earth, and upon which the soul will be judged after death. Compare 52.15.

3   As elsewhere, the first letter *alif* here represents the divine unity, while the three following letters of the alphabet, *be, te,* and *se,* represent the apparent multiplicity of the created world. See 11.1.

4   See 57.6.

## 151

1   The "girdle" (Pers. *zunnār*) is a term regularly used in the Persian ghazal, where it is the mark of Christians and other non-Muslim minorities in the Middle East. It is used here to indicate the Hindu sacred thread.

2   The "idol temple" (Pers. *but-khāna*) is another standard term in the language of the Persian ghazal, here used for a Hindu temple.

3   This is an abbreviated citation of the divine Tradition (Ar. *ḥadīth qudsī*) addressed by God to the prophet Muhammad: *lau lāka lamā khalaqtu 'l-aflāk,* "If it were not for you [I should not have created] the heavens." Compare 53.2, 95.4.

4   Just as Ranjha was despised by Hir's family, so too was Shah Inayat disparaged for being a member of the Arain caste. See 31.6.

## 152

1   The image of the contest (*chinj*) is taken from the practice of putting on shows of wrestling and other sports at shrines on the occasion of their annual festivals. It is here developed to describe what happens to the soul after death.

2   The relentless emissaries of death are compared to tax-collectors' agents.

3   An idiom meaning to abandon pride. Compare 153.5.

4   The verbs "falls" (*girdā*) suggests the fate of the wicked as they unsuccessfully try to cross the narrow Sirat bridge. See 119.15.

5    The phrase *apṇā bhāṇā kardā* is of uncertain meaning. Contrast the translation in PS as "who himself provides an excuse," evidently understanding *bhāṇā* as Pers. *bahāna*.

### 153

1    I.e., your turban, meaning "your pride." See 152.3.

### 154

1    I.e., Shah Inayat.
2    Shirin and Farhad are a famous pair of lovers from Persian romance. Farhad was a sculptor who loved the princess Shirin and was ordered by her to cut a canal through a mountain with his ax in order to bring her water. Compare 157.5.
3    See 12.4.
4    See 57.6.
5    See n. 1 on 81.
6    See 144.3.

### 155

1    An allusion to the story of Sohni. See n. 1 on 81.

### 156

1    I.e., the direction in which the beloved departed.
2    An evocation of the time after Hir's marriage when Ranjha came to her husband's house as a yogi.
3    See 28.7.
4    The idiom *mūñh toñ loī lāhī* literally means "has removed the blanket from his face."
5    Another reference to the story of Hir. See 122.22.

### 157

1    A reference to the story of Sassi, who was abandoned by her beloved, Punnun, while she lay asleep. See 24.3.
2    See 12.4.
3    Shapes (*auñsīāñ*) are drawn on the ground with a rake as a means of foreseeing the future.
4    The biblical "burning bush" on Mount Sinai in which God signaled his presence to Moses is alluded to in the Qur'anic verse *idh rā'a*

*nāran*, "behold, he saw a fire." See n. 4 on 12.5.

5     See 154.4.

## Other Poems
### A  The Seven Days

The literal meaning of the term *aṭhvārā* is "eight-day poem," reckoned as running from Sunday to Sunday. This poem, like others by Muslim authors, is structured so as to climax with Thursday (*jumerāt*) and Friday (*jumhāñ*).

1     Literally, "Whose water carrier am I?" (*maiñ kis dī pāṇīhār*). Compare G31.

2     The text of this verse is uncertain.

3     There is a wordplay on *budh*, "awareness," and *budhvār*, "Wednesday."

4     When someone is possessed by the spirit of Shah Madar, a Sufi saint whose tomb is situated near Kanpur, music is played to make them dance so that the spirit may be exorcised.

5     The verse also forms the refrain of *kāfī* 76, which is a separate poem, although it is treated as a supplementary part of "The Seven Days" in some editions.

### B  The Twelve Months

The genre of the *Bārāñ māh* describes the poet's varying experiences of love through the twelve months of the Indian calendar, which begins halfway through the months of the CE year. Most examples of this genre, which was popular in most North Indian literatures, begin in the spring with Visakh, the first month of the calendar. By beginning halfway through the year in the autumn, Bullhe Shah's poem achieves its climax with the months of the rainy season, traditionally associated with intense feelings. The verses are headed with the Panjabi names of the months, with their CE equivalents supplied in brackets.

1     An epithet of Krishna, poetically used to refer to the beloved. Compare 113.1, B10.

2     Compare 74.3.

3     The tribal name of Sassi's beloved, Punnun, who was taken away

from her by his kinsmen while she slept. See 24.3.

4    A reference to the story of Sohni. See n. 1 on 81.

5    The desert where Sassi died in her desperate search for Punnun. See 24.3.

6    The festival celebrated on the first day of Magh.

7    In the spring month of Phaggan the fields are full of the yellow flowers of the mustard crop.

8    The spring festival in which the participants squirt one another with colored dye. See 45.1.

9    See 93.1.

10   See 8.3.

11   The new year festival celebrated on the first day of the month Visakh.

12   Unlike the woman without her husband, who is not wearing bangles as a mark of her distress.

13   The beautiful peacock is said to be grieved by the sight of its ugly feet.

14   The significance of this half-verse is obscure. The translation follows S, who understands it in the context of the following lines, describing how the need to pay overdue bills compounds the suffering induced by the burning heat of the month Jeth. But J connects the obscure rhyme word *peṭh* with *pīṭh*, "back," and suggests that it means "the wind at one's back."

15   The coolness of the beginning of the day provides a brief relief from the fierce heat of the hot season.

16   In the Persian ghazal the fatal attraction of the moth to the flame of the candle provides a standard image of the destructive power of love.

17   See B2.

18   Perhaps meaning that the messengers departed young and returned only when they were old and white-haired.

19   The common hawk cuckoo, *Hierococcyx varius*.

20   Literally, "songs in Rag Malhar," the musical mode associated with the rains.

### G  The Forty Knots

This poem is simply headed *Gaṇḍhāñ* (The Knots), but it is organized along the same principle of numbered verses common to Bullhe Shah's other longer poems. While they all belong to well-established genres, this poem appears to be unique in its formal conception. Its theme of a girl preparing her dowry during the countdown before her imminent wedding is, however, a common image for the necessary process of preparation for death, found elsewhere in Bullhe Shah's lyrics. Compare 2.3, 46.4.

1   I.e., an increased fee will be paid to the servant who goes to the bride's in-laws if they agree to postpone the date of the wedding.

2   The medicine given to a baby immediately after birth to clear its mouth in preparation for suckling.

3   The precise sense of the phrase *jit cit ke hardī* is uncertain.

4   See 84.5.

5   Yogis keep moving on from place to place.

6   A gourd-producing plant that has yellow flowers. Their color is compared to the pale complexion of the girl in torment.

7   The five evil impulses of ego, pride, anger, lust, and delusion.

8   The preparation of the bride includes anointing with oil and being seated on a stool by the older women of the family.

9   A proverbial expression meaning "I am of no significance."

10  A two-piece outfit (*bevar*) consists of scarf and dress, while a three-piece outfit (*tevar*) comprises scarf, blouse, and trousers.

11  A husband's younger brothers (*devar*): these relatives have a joking relationship with their sister-in-law.

12  This cleanser (*vaṭnā*) is a perfumed compound of meal and oil used as an exfoliant, which is rubbed on the body as a part of the wedding preparations.

13  The phrase *nāl dohāṅ de,* "with the two," is explained by S as denoting the pair of oxen used to draw the bridal cart to her in-laws. Alternatively, the reference may be to the two recording angels who demand from the soul after death an account of the deeds performed in this life.

14  The large bead (*imām*) on a rosary that is held in the hand while the other beads are counted by the fingers.

15  See B11.

16  Apparently meaning the departure of the soul from the body after death.

17  See A3.

18  The quantity is quite insufficient to weave cloth for a complete outfit.

19  The circumambulations of the sacred fire performed by the bridal

couple at a Hindu wedding.

20 The word *rang*, "dye, color," also has the sense of "delight," so *rang ghar* here also suggests "house of color, dyeing house," picking up on *rangaṇ*, "dye," in the preceding verse. Compare G39.

21 Brides are decorated with henna before their wedding.

22 See G33.

23 See 45.1.

24 From the verse *innā lillāhi* [*wa innā ilaihi rāji'ūn*] (Qur'an 2.156), "To God we belong [and to him we return]."

25 The given name of Bullhe Shah.

## S The Thirty Letters

In the long-established acrostic genre of the *Sīharfī*, each verse begins with one of the letters of the Arabic alphabet proper, excluding the extra letters added to write Persian or South Asian languages. This is immediately followed by a word starting with that letter, as in the opening verses of this poem: *alif – allhā* (S1), *be – bālaṇ* (S2), *te – tere* (S3), *se – sābat* (S4). The twenty-eight letters of the Arabic alphabet are made up to thirty by the addition of a second *alif* and *lām* (S28–S29), which together form the distinctive digraph *lām-alif*. Whereas most examples of the genre have a simple succession of verses of identical length, Bullhe Shah's *sīharfī* unusually opens with a refrain, and the verses in their present form vary in length from two lines (S1–S13, S21–S23, S30) to four lines (S14–S20, S24–S29).

1 A reference to the story of Sohni. See n. 1 on 81.

2 Apparently meaning, I thought that dealing in a single grain of mustard was enough to make me an apothecary.

3 To make them water.

4 See 77.7.

5 The later verses of this poem are written in praise of the prophet Muhammad. Here the references are to the heavenly ascension (Ar. *mi'rāj*) of the Prophet, who was guided by the archangel Jibrail; see 137.11. Since Jibrail had been sent by God, he is here called "the messenger" (Ar. *qāṣid*). On his journey, the Prophet is supposed to have been given an advance sight of the ring that was later to be displayed to him on the hand of God; see S16 below.

6 Supposed to be the number of supplications offered by the Prophet to God when he came before him on the occasion of his ascension.

7    The meaning is that God was equally present in the Prophet.

8    Or, if the word *ināit* is not to be understood as a proper name here, "I have been granted grace and favor." Compare 58.8.

9    The "preserved tablet" (Ar. *lauḥ maḥfūẓ*) is believed to contain the divine source text of the Qur'an. Here it is more loosely understood to signify the universal book of fate.

10   The opening of the Islamic profession of faith (Ar. *lā ilāha illā 'llāh wa muḥammadun rasūlu 'llāh*). See 45.2.

11   Adam's fall from paradise was redeemed by God's appointment of Muhammad as his Prophet.

12   See 39.13.

13   See 119.15.

14   This verse is present in F, but is omitted in S and J. The sense fits awkwardly, and it may have been supplied by another hand in order to complete the acrostic sequence.

15   Taking the reins of a visitor's horse is a token of humble service.

## V Verses

No edition attempts a systematic arrangement of these independent verses (*dohṛe*), which were first printed in Q. The traditional ordering of V1–V48 follows F, S, and J. Separate notes below describe the sources of V49–V53, which are additionally included in S, and the classification here of V54, which other editions include as a *kāfī*. As in other collections of short verses of this type, the compressed expression sometimes makes for difficulties of understanding.

1    This *dohṛā* is written in Hindi rather than Panjabi, like the following V2 and V3, with which it forms a group.

2    For the wordplay with *kasar*, "fault," and *kasūr*, "Kasur," compare 34.2. The criticism of the poet's hometown groups this *dohṛā* with the following V5.

3    Besides its common Indian sense of "charitable foundation, especially for the accommodation of pilgrims," the word *dharamsālā* was formerly also used to mean a Sikh temple, for which the modern term is *gurduārā*. Compare V45.

4    This *dohṛā* is closely related in language and theme to the following V8.

5    This *dohṛā* forms a natural pair with the preceding V9, which also begins *nā khudā*, "Not God." The distinctively Hindu "holy

bathing place" *(tīrath)* contrasts with the Muslim locations listed in V9.

6   As often in verses of this type, the poet's signature is superfluous to the meter of the first half-line, *Bullhiā: ġhain ġharūrat sār suṭṭ,* whose proper beginning is with the acrostic *"ġhain* is for *ġharūrat."*

7   Migration *(hijrat)* is sanctioned in Islam by the example of the move by the prophet Muhammad and his early followers from Mecca to Medina in 622 CE, which marks the beginning of the Muslim calendar.

8   A Muslim caste of low-grade musicians and entertainers.

9   The expression is elliptical. The journey of love, which can be accomplished with the aid of a spiritual guide, is contrasted with the mechanical progression of the cycle of birth and death *(āvāgauṇ),* where no such guidance is to be found.

10   Rope is made by beating *munj,* the fiber around the seed of the plant *Saccharum sara.*

11   The divinely bestowed gift of mystical awareness. For it to be enjoyed, the mind must first be disciplined.

12   Compare 26.3.

13   Compare 31.4

14   Meaning that the impossible has come to pass.

15   Compare 106.4.

16   The world is conceived of as the upper-story salon where men gather to watch a dancing girl perform. But disgrace is the only product of such a life.

17   See 11.3.

18   There is a long tradition of using the *dohṛā* for riddling utterances. Here the literal meaning is transparent, but it is open to various interpretations.

19   A tribe proverbial for their arrogance; see 86.4. The word is used here to denote the arrogant self whose subjugation is an essential part of Sufi discipline.

20   PS interprets differently as: "O Bullah, the Lord in His temple asked people to render their accounts. He sent away from Him the pedant and the pedagogue, and beckoned the simpletons to sit by His side."

21   The Muslim greeting *al-salām ʿalaik(um)* is symbolic of the outward observances that must be transcended in the approach to the divine.

425

22 The legendary corruption of *qazis*, who are always open to a bribe when deciding the cases brought before them, is captured in the Persian proverb *qāzī ba-rishvat rāzī*, here translated as *qāzī rāzī rishvate*.

23 Because of the fee he will be given for conducting the funeral.

24 See V6.

25 The expression is very compressed, literally "Why my form was made, perhaps he may go, 'Be quiet!'"

26 Not in F or J, but included in S from modern oral tradition.

27 Not in F or J, but included in S. The verse is of doubtful authenticity, since the play on words between "Ram" as a Hindu name for God and the Muslim "Rahim" (Ar. *raḥīm* "merciful") as an epithet of Allah is a commonplace of premodern north Indian religious poetry not otherwise found in Bullhe Shah.

28 Printed as 38.5-6 in F and J, but also included as this independent *dohṛā* in S from R.

29 See 38.1.

30 See 106.3.

31 Not in F or J, but included in S from R.

32 The standard pairing of Mecca and the Ganges as the respective centers of pilgrimage for Muslims, here extended with the reference to Gaya as an historic place of Hindu (and earlier, Buddhist) pilgrimage in Bihar.

33 Not in F or J, but included in S from modern oral tradition. Again, this item is of doubtful authenticity.

34 This short poem is absent from both R and Q. It is classed as a *kāfī* in most modern editions, but in style and form it is a *dioṛhā*, the extended form of the *dohṛā* that has a repeated extra half-verse, in this case the phrase *taithoñ utte*, translated as "better than you."

# GLOSSARY

ABDULLAH ('Abdullāh) name
of the prophet Muhammad's
father; also the given
name of Bullhe Shah.

ABEL AND CAIN (Ar. Hābīl Qābīl)
the sons of Adam.

ADAM (Ar. Ādam) the first
man, expelled from paradise
for disobedience.

AHAD (Ar. Aḥad) the One, as a
title of God.

AHMAD (Ar. Aḥmad) alternative
name of the prophet
Muhammad.

ALI ('Alī) son-in-law of the
prophet Muhammad, from
whom all Sayyids claim descent.

ARAIN (Arāīñ) the caste of
vegetable gardeners to which
Shah Inayat belonged.

AYUB (Ayūb = Job) prophet whose
endurance earned him the
epithet "the patient" (Ar. ṣābir).

AZAZIL ('Azāzīl) a name of Satan.

BAHAVAL (Bahāval Haq) title
given to the Sufi saint Baha
ud Din Zakariya of Multan.

BAYAZID (Bāyazīd) the early
Sufi saint Abu Yazid Bistami.

BINDRABAN (Skt. Vṛndāvana)
area near Mathura where
Krishna spent his youth as
a herdsman.

BURAQ (Burāq) the mysterious
beast ridden by the Prophet

on the night of his ascension
into heaven.

CHUCHAK (Chūchak) Hir's
father, who engaged Ranjha as
a herdsman.

DHOLA (Ḍholā) name of
Sammi's beloved.

DHIDO (Dhīdo) the given
name of Ranjha.

EVE (Ar. Ḥavvā) the wife of Adam.

FARHAD (Farhād) sculptor who
loved the princess Shirin.

GOPIS (Skt.,P. gopī) the cow
maidens with whom Krishna
played games of love.

GORAKHNATH (Gorakhnāth) the
great yogi Gorakhnath,
from whom Ranjha sought
initiation as a yogi.

HAFIZ (Ar. Ḥāfiẓ) title of
those who have memorized
the Qur'ān by heart.

HANUMAN (Skt.,P. Hanūvant)
the monkey king whose
army helped Ram regain
Sita from Ravan.

HARNAKASH (Skt. Hiraṇyākṣa)
"Golden Eye," king who thought
himself the equal of God.

HASAN grandson of the
prophet Muhammad who
died from poison.

HIR (Hīr) girl of the Sial tribe
who was the lover of Ranjha.

HOT Baloch tribe to which

427

Punnun belonged.

HUSAIN grandson of the prophet Muhammad who was killed at the battle of Karbala.

IBRAHIM (Ar. Ibrāhīm = Abraham) prophet who was condemned by Namrud to be burned on a pyre.

INAYAT (Ar. 'ināyat "favor") Bullhe Shah's spiritual guide Shah Inayat.

ISMAIL (Ismā'īl) son of Ibrahim, commanded by God to be offered as a sacrifice.

JESUS (Ar. 'Īsā) the son of the Virgin Mariam.

JIBRAIL (Jibrāīl = Gabriel) the greatest of the archangels.

JUNAID early Sufi saint of Baghdad.

KAABA (Ar. Ka'ba) the shrine in Mecca that is the goal of the hajj.

KAIDO Hir's uncle who opposed her love for Ranjha.

KANS evil king who persecuted Krishna.

*Kanz* classic textbook of Islamic law.

KASUR (Qasūr) hometown of Bullhe Shah.

KAURAVS AND PANDAVS (P. Kairo Pāṇḍo) the rival clans of the Mahabharatha.

KHERA (Kheṛā) name of the tribe into which Hir was forcibly married.

KRISHNA (P. Kāhn) incarnation of Vishnu, who grew up as a cowherd in Bindraban.

KUMBHAKARAN (Skt. Kumbhakarṇa) brother of Ravan.

LACHHMAN (Skt. Lakṣmaṇa) brother of Rām.

LAILA (Ar. Lailā) Arab princess who was loved to distraction by Majnun.

LANKA the kingdom of Ravan.

MAJNUN (Ar. *majnūn* "madman") name given to the lover of Laila.

MANSUR (Mansūr) the great Sufi saint Mansūr al-Hallāj, who was martyred in Baghdad.

MIRZA (Mirzā) lover of Sahiban, who was killed by her brothers.

MOSES (Ar. Mūsā) prophet who ascended Mount Sinai in a vain attempt to see God.

MUHAMMAD the Prophet of Islam.

NAMRUD (Namrūd = Nimrod) wicked king of Babylon who tried to kill the prophet Ibrāhīm.

NUH (Nūh = Noah) prophet who built the ark to save his family from the flood sent by God.

NUSHABA (Nushābā) queen of Azerbaijan rescued by Sikandar.

PHARAOH (Ar. Fir'aun) arrogant ruler of Egypt who persecuted Moses.

PIR (P. Pīr) Sufi spiritual guide.

PUNNUN (Punnūñ) Baloch prince who was loved by Sassi.

QADIRI (Qādirī) Sufi order with which Shah Inayat and Bullhe Shah were affiliated.

QARUN (Qārūn = Korah)
immensely wealthy opponent
of Moses.

QAZI (Ar. *qāḍī*) judge
qualified in Islamic law.

QIBLA the direction of Mecca,
faced during Muslim prayers.

QUDURI (Qudūrī) classic
textbook of Islamic law.

RAM (Skt. Rāma) Hindu name
of God, the divine hero of the
Ramayana who killed Ravan.

RANJHA (Rāñjhā) the tribal
name of Hir's beloved.

RAVAN (Skt. Rāvaṇa) the ten-
headed demon king of Lanka
who abducted Ram's wife, Sita.

RODA (Roḍā) lover of the
blackmith's daughter Jalali.

SAHADEV the youngest of the
Pandav brothers, famous for
his knowledge of astronomy.

SAHIBAN (Sāhibāñ) girl of the
Sial tribe who was
loved by Mirza.

SAHTI (Sahtī) Hir's sister-in-law.

SAMMI (Sammī) Rajput
princess who loved Dhola.

SANAN (San'ān) learned
Shaikh disgraced by his
love for a Christian girl.

SARMAD outspoken Sufi executed
by the emperor Aurangzeb.

SASSI (Sassī) princess of
Bhambhore who loved Punnun,
and who died following
him into the desert.

SAVAN (Sāvaṇ) the month of the
rainy season corresponding

to July–August.

SHAH (Shāh) honorific title,
placed before names of saints
and after names of Sayyids.

SHAIKH (Shaikh) title given
to Muslim men of learning;
also used by Sufis as the
equivalent of Pir.

SHAMS Sufi saint who was hanged
upside down and flayed alive.

SHARAF Sufi saint of Panipat best
known as Bu Ali Qalandar.

SHIRIN (Shīrīn) Persian princess
who was Farhad's beloved.

SIAL (Siāl) Hir's tribe.

SIKANDAR the great
king Alexander.

SIRAT (Sirāt) the narrow bridge
that leads to paradise.

SITA (Sītā) the wife of Ram.

SOHNI (Sohṇī) potter's daughter
who crossed the river Chenab
to see her beloved Mahinval.

SULAIMAN (Sulaimān= Solomon)
king with magical powers who
was reduced to stoking a furnace.

TAKHT HAZARA (Takht
Hazārā) Ranjha's family home.

TEGH BAHADUR (Tegh
Bahādur) the ninth Sikh
Guru, executed by the
emperor Aurangzeb.

TURK the equivalent of "Muslim,"
as opposed to "Hindu."

YADAVS (Yādavs) the pastoral tribe
with whom Krishna grew up.

YAHYA (Yahyā = John the
Baptist) son of Zakariya.

YAZID (Yazīd) caliph who

was responsible for the
death of Husain.

YUNUS (Yūnus = Jonah) prophet
who was swallowed by a large
fish.

YUSUF (Yūsuf = Joseph) prophet
who was loved by Zulaikha.

ZAKARIYA (Zakariyā = Zechariah)
prophet who was sawn through
by soldiers of Herod.

ZULAIKA (Zulaikhā = "Potiphar's
wife") beautiful wife of the vizier
of Egypt, who loved Yusuf.

# BIBLIOGRAPHY

*Editions and Translations*

Ruhtaki, Anvar Ali. 1889. *Qānūn-e 'ishq.* 2 vols. Lahore: Allah-vale ki Qaumi Dukan.

Qasuri, Prem Singh. 1896. *Kāfīhā-e Hazrat Bullhe Shāh.* Qasur: the editor.

Ubirai, Mohan Singh. 1930. *Bulhe Shāh: 50 Kāfīāñ.* Lahore: University of the Punjab.

Faqir, Faqir Muhammad. 1960. *Kulliyāt-e Bullhe Shāh.* Lahore: Panjabi Adbi Academy.

Ahmad, Nazir. 1976. *Kalām-e Bullhe Shāh.* Lahore: Packages.

Sabir, Muhammad Sharif. 1991. *Bullhe Shāh: Mukammal Kāfiyāñ.* Lahore: Sayyid Ajmal Husain Memorial Society.

Khan, Muhammad Asif. 1992. *Ākhiā Bullhe Shāh ne.* Lahore: Pakistan Panjabi Adabi Board.

Singh, Attarjit and Gurcharan Singh. 2004. *Bullheshāh [jīvan, Dohṛe, Sīharfīāñ te Kāfīāñ].* Delhi: Arsee Publishers.

Jagtar. 2008. *Bullhe Shāh: Jīvan ate racnā.* Chandigarh: Lokgeet Parkashan.

Singh, Atam. 1940. *Songs of Bullah.* Lahore: the translator.

Kuldip, R. K. 1971. *Waris Shah 1730-1790: A Critical Appreciation of the Poet and His Only Heer* [but in fact mostly containing translations of Bullhe Shah]. Calcutta: Intertrade Publications.

Luther, A. Rauf. 1982. *Bullah Shah: Mystic Poet of Punjab.* Lahore: Sheikh Mubarak Ali.

Rafat, Taufiq. 1982. *Bulleh Shah: A Selection Rendered into English Verse.* Lahore: Vanguard.

Puri, J. R. and T. R. Shangari. 1986. *Bulleh Shah: The Love-Intoxicated Iconoclast.* Dera Baba Jaimal Singh: Radhasoami Satsang Beas.

Duggal, Kartar Singh. 1996. *Sain Bulleh Shah: The Mystic Muse.* New Delhi: Abhinav Publications.

Ghaffar, Muzaffar A. 2005. *Masterworks of Punjaabi Sufi Poetry: Bulleh Shaah—Within Reach.* 2 vols. Lahore: Ferozsons.

Smith, Paul. 2012. *Bulleh Shah: Selected Poems.* Campbells Creek, Australia: New Humanity Books.

*Other Sources*

Ahmad, Qazi Moinuddin. 2012. *History of the Shattari Silsilah*. Delhi: Idarah-i-Adabiyat-i-Delli.

Alam, Muzaffar. 1986. *The Crisis of Empire in Mughal North India: Awadh and the Punjab 1707-1748*. New Delhi: Oxford University Press.

Anwar, Ghulam Yaqoob, trans. 1966. *The Paths Unknown (Kafian Shah Husain)*. Lahore: Majlis Shah Hussain.

Bilgrami, Fatima Zehra. 2005. *History of the Qadiri Order in India (16th–18th Century)*. Delhi: Idarah-i Adabiyat-i Delli.

Daudi, Maqbul Anvar, ed. 1990. *Kahiā Shāh Husain neñ*. Lahore: Ferozsons.

Elias, Jamal J., trans. 1998. *Death Before Dying: The Sufi Poems of Sultan Bahu*. Berkeley: University of California Press.

Ernst, Carl W. 1997. *The Shambhala Guide to Sufism*. Boston: Shambhala.

Frembgen, Jürgen Waseem. 2006. *Friends of God: Sufi Saints—Popular Poster Art from Pakistan*. Oxford: Oxford University Press.

Kohli, Surindar Singh. 1987. *Bulhe Shah*. New Delhi: Sahitya Akademi.

Lewis, Franklin D., trans. 2008. *Rumi: Swallowing the Sun*. Oxford: Oneworld.

Losensky, Paul E., and Sunil Sharma, trans. 2011. *In the Bazaar of Love: The Selected Poetry of Amīr Khusrau*. New Delhi: Penguin Books India.

Matringe, Denis. 1992. "Kṛṣṇaite and Nāth Elements in the Poetry of the Eighteenth-Century Panjabi Sūfī Poet Bullhe Śāh." In *Devotional Literature in South Asia*, ed. R. S. McGregor. Cambridge: Cambridge University Press, 190–206.

Nijjar, B. S. 1972. *Panjab Under the Later Mughals (1709–1759)*. Jullundur: New Academic Publishing Company.

Pannke, Peter. 1999. *Troubadoure Allahs: Sufi-Musik im Industal*. München: Frederking & Thaler.

Petievich, Carla. 2007. *When Men Speak as Women: Vocal Masquerade in Indo-Muslim Poetry*. New Delhi: Oxford University Press.

Puri, J. R., and K. S. Khak, trans. 1998. *Sultan Bahu*. Dera Baba Jaimal Singh: Radhasoami Satsang Beas.

Qaiser, Shahzad, trans. 2009. *The Message of Diwan-i-Farid*. Lahore: Suhail Academy.

Quraeshi, Samina. 2005. *Legends of the Indus*. London: Asia Ink.

———. 2009. *A Journey with the Sufis of the Indus*. Cambridge, Mass.: Peabody Museum Press.

Qureshi, Regula Burckhardt. 1986. *Sufi Music of India and Pakistan: Sound, Context and Meaning in Qawwali*. Cambridge: Cambridge University Press.

Rama Krishna, Lajwanti. 1938. *Pañjābī Ṣūfī Poets A.D. 1460–1900*. London: Oxford University Press.

Rinehart, Robin. 1996. "Interpretations of the Poetry of Bullhe Shah." *International Journal of Punjab Studies* 3: 45–63.

———. 1999. "The Portable Bullhe Shah: Biography, Categorization, and Authorship in the Study of Punjabi Sufi Poetry." *Numen* 46: 53–87.

Rizvi, Saiyid Athar Abbas. 1978–83. *A History of Sufism in India*. 2 vols. New Delhi: Munshiram Manoharlal.

Schimmel, Annemarie. 1982. *As Through a Veil: Mystical Poetry in Islam*. New York: Columbia University Press.

Sekhon, Sant Singh. 1993–96. *A History of Panjabi Literature*. 2 vols. Patiala: Punjabi University.

Shackle, Christopher, trans. 1983. *Fifty Poems of Khawaja Farid*. Multan: Bazm-e-Saqafat.

———. 1992. "Transitions and Transformations in Vāris Shāh's *Hīr*." In *The Indian Narrative: Perspectives and Patterns*, ed. C. Shackle and R. Snell. Wiesbaden: Harrassowitz, 241–263.

———. 1993. "Early Vernacular Poetry in the Indus Valley: Its Contexts and Its Character." In *Islam and Indian Regions*, vol. 1, ed. A.-L. Dallapiccola and Stephanie Zingel-Avé Lallemant. Stuttgart: Franz Steiner, 259–289.

———. 1995. "Between Scripture and Romance: The Yūsuf-Zulaikhā Story in Panjabi." *South Asia Research* 15: 153–188.

———. 1999. "Persian Poetry and Qādirī Sufism in Later Mughal India: Ghanīmat Kunjāhī and His Mathnawī-yi Nayrang-i 'Ishq." In *The Heritage of Sufism: 3, Late Classical Persianate Sufism (1501–1750)*, ed. Leonard Lewisohn and David Morgan. Oxford: Oneworld Publications, 435–463.

———. 2011. "Punjabi Sufi Poetry from Farid to Farid." In *Punjab Reconsidered: History, Culture and Practice*, ed. Anshu Malhotra and Farina Mir. New Delhi: Oxford University Press, 3–34.

Singh, Nikky-Guninder Kaur, trans. 2012. *Of Sacred and Secular Desire: An Anthology of Lyrical Writings from the Punjab*. London and New York: I. B. Tauris.

Talib, Gurbachan Singh. 1974. *Baba Sheikh Farid Shakar Ganj*. New Delhi: National Book Trust.

Usborne, C. F. 1982. *Bullah Shah: Sufi, Mystic and Poet of the Punjab.* Lahore: Sheikh Mubarak Ali.

Yusuf Ali, A., trans. 1977. *The Holy Qur-an: Text, Translation and Commentary.* 2 vols. Lahore: Sh. Muhammad Ashraf.

# CONCORDANCE

This concordance is provided for the convenience of readers more familiar with the Persian script, who may wish to check the translations against the standard Pakistani text of the Faqir edition (F). Numbers of *kāfīs* in this book, where they are arranged by first lines in Gurmukhi alphabetical order, are keyed to the corresponding numbers in F, where the poems are arranged in the alphabetical order of the Persian script. The endnotes to 86 and 108 explain that these poems are not included in F.

| MCLI | F | MCLI | F | MCLI | F |
|------|-----|------|-----|------|-----|
| 1 | 7 | 26 | 79 | 51 | 82 |
| 2 | 6 | 27 | 20 | 52 | 87 |
| 3 | 15 | 28 | 75 | 53 | 95 |
| 4 | 14 | 29 | 71 | 54 | 97 |
| 5 | 13 | 30 | 72 | 55 | 90 |
| 6 | 5 | 31 | 70 | 56 | 93 |
| 7 | 4 | 32 | 68 | 57 | 94 |
| 8 | 2 | 33 | 67 | 58 | 98 |
| 9 | 3 | 34 | 69 | 59 | 96 |
| 10 | 16 | 35 | 73 | 60 | 91 |
| 11 | 1 | 36 | 74 | 61 | 88 |
| 12 | 8 | 37 | 151 | 62 | 58 |
| 13 | 17 | 38 | 56 | 63 | 89 |
| 14 | 19 | 39 | 57 | 64 | 100 |
| 15 | 18 | 40 | 153 | 65 | 99 |
| 16 | 21 | 41 | 92 | 66 | 103 |
| 17 | 78 | 42 | 154 | 67 | 104 |
| 18 | 77 | 43 | 152 | 68 | 102 |
| 19 | 76 | 44 | 155 | 69 | 101 |
| 20 | 22 | 45 | 156 | 70 | 55 |
| 21 | 23 | 46 | 81 | 71 | 54 |
| 22 | 11 | 47 | 85 | 72 | 140 |
| 23 | 9 | 48 | 83 | 73 | 51 |
| 24 | 10 | 49 | 86 | 74 | 50 |
| 25 | 12 | 50 | 84 | 75 | 52 |

# CONCORDANCE

| MCLI | F | MCLI | F | MCLI | F |
|------|-----|------|-----|------|-----|
| 76 | 164 | 113 | 112 | 150 | 147 |
| 77 | 53 | 114 | 107 | 151 | 144 |
| 78 | 48 | 115 | 106 | 152 | 145 |
| 79 | 49 | 116 | 109 | 153 | 108 |
| 80 | 60 | 117 | 110 | 154 | 143 |
| 81 | 42 | 118 | 111 | 155 | 149 |
| 82 | 43 | 119 | 113 | 156 | 148 |
| 83 | 44 | 120 | 119 | 157 | 150 |
| 84 | 45 | 121 | 118 | | |
| 85 | 46 | 122 | 115 | | |
| 86 | — | 123 | 116 | | |
| 87 | 47 | 124 | 117 | | |
| 88 | 59 | 125 | 114 | | |
| 89 | 138 | 126 | 127 | | |
| 90 | 137 | 127 | 126 | | |
| 91 | 142 | 128 | 125 | | |
| 92 | 141 | 129 | 132 | | |
| 93 | 139 | 130 | 130 | | |
| 94 | 35 | 131 | 129 | | |
| 95 | 36 | 132 | 131 | | |
| 96 | 37 | 133 | 128 | | |
| 97 | 34 | 134 | 133 | | |
| 98 | 41 | 135 | 135 | | |
| 99 | 38 | 136 | 134 | | |
| 100 | 40 | 137 | 136 | | |
| 101 | 39 | 138 | 122 | | |
| 102 | 80 | 139 | 123 | | |
| 103 | 25 | 140 | 124 | | |
| 104 | 28 | 141 | 120 | | |
| 105 | 29 | 142 | 121 | | |
| 106 | 27 | 143 | 65 | | |
| 107 | 26 | 144 | 61 | | |
| 108 | — | 145 | 62 | | |
| 109 | 109 | 146 | 66 | | |
| 110 | 30 | 147 | 64 | | |
| 111 | 32 | 148 | 105 | | |
| 112 | 31 | 149 | 146 | | |

# INDEX

Abdullah, father of the
  Prophet, 73, 389n42.2
Abdullah, given name of
  Bullhe Shah, vii, 319
Abdul Latif of Bhit, Shah, xiii
Abel, 147
Abu Jahl, 393n55.4
Adam, 17, 71, 77, 101, 105,
  147, 185, 237, 243, 333,
  335, 377n7.1, 378n10.1
*Ādi Granth*, x
Afghanistan, xi
Ahad, God the One, xxi–xxii, 35, 45,
  73, 75, 77, 97, 139, 247, 384n28.4
Ahmad. *See under* Muhammad
Ali ibn Abi Talib, 119, 187,
  398n75.1, 406n108.2
Amir Khusrau, xii
Apostle, the. *See under* Muhammad
Arabia or Arabs, xxii, xxiv, 45, 185
Arabic, xi, xviii, xxi, xxxiii–xxxv;
  letters of the Arabic script,
  378nn11.2,11.3, 381nn22.1,22.3,
  384nn28.4,28.5, 394nn58.3,58.4,
  416n144.3, 418n150.3, 423nS;
  non-Qur'anic Arabic phrases:
  *al-salāmu 'alaik(um)*, 425nV.21;
  *anā aḥad*, 384n28.4; *anā aḥmad*,
  384n28.4; *anā 'arab*, 384n28.5;
  anā 'l-ḥaqq, 385n28.14; *anā*
  *rabb*, 384n28.5; *astaghfiru'llāh*,
  402n90.1; *bi'smi'llāh*, 390n45.1;
  *kanzan makhfiyyan*, 384n28.8; *lā*
  *ilāha illā 'llāhi wa muḥammadun*
  *rasūlu 'llāh*, 390n45.2;

*lā tataḥarraku*, 393n54.2;
  *laḥmak laḥmī*, 398n75.1; *lau*
  *lāka*, 418n151.3; *laisa fī jubbatī*,
  385n28.15; *man 'arafa nafsahu*,
  390n45.7; *mūtū qabl an tamūtū*,
  400n77.12; *qum bi-idhnī*,
  378n12.1; *ṣallā 'llāhu*, 391n45.9;
  *subḥāna 'llāh*, 391n45.11
Arains, viii, xxiii, 51, 187, 386n31.5
Asal, 53
*Aṭhvārā* (The Seven
  Days), xvii, 420nA
Attar, Persian poet, 389n41.4
Ayub, xxiv, 43, 75, 189, 243, 253;
  "the patient one," 383n27.1
Azar, 389n41.1
Azazil. *See under* Satan

Baghdad, xi, 205, 385n28.14
Bahaval Haq, 207
Baloch, 381n24.3
*Bārāñ Māh* (The Twelve
  Months), xvii, xxxi, 420nB
Bareilly, 153
Bayazid Bistami, 143, 400n78.10
Bhambhore, 381n24.3
Bindraban, 73, 416n143.33
*Bostān* (by Shaikh Saadi of
  Shiraz), 143, 400n78.5
Brahmans, 115, 129, 165,
  193, 281, 351, 357
Bullhe Shah: biographical details,
  vii, 187; dancing of, xxiii–xxiv, 11,
  141, 183; as disciple, viii, xiii,
  xvii, xxiii–xiv, xxvii (*see also*

Inayat, Shah); *Dohṛe* of, xviii;
Bullhe Shah *(continued)*
importance or popularity of,
vii, ix, xiv, xix; Indic or Hindu
aspects of poetry of, xxv, xxvii,
xxxii; interpretations of, xiv;
Islamic or Sufi aspects of poetry
of, xx–xxi, xxiv, xxxii; *kāfiāñ* of,
xv–xvii, xix, xxxi–xxxiii; longer
poems of, xvii (see also *Aṭhvārā;
Bārāñ Māh; Gaṇḍhāñ; Sīharfī*);
name of, vii; preservation,
printing, or transmittal of works
of, x, xiii, xv, xviii, xxxi–xxxii;
social critique in poetry of,
xx; style of, ix, xix, xxxiv
Buraq, 413n137.8

Canaan, 5, 375
Chenab River, xxv, 147,
149, 401n81.1
Chishti order, xii–xiv
Chuchak, xxvi, 207, 209, 410n122.9
Chuhra, 412n131.3

Dajjal, 89
Darvesh, Shah Muhammad, vii
Delhi Sultanate, xii
Dhido. *See* Ranjha
Dhola, 217, 411n126.2
*Dohṛe* (Verses), xviii, 424nV

Egypt, xxiv, 11, 19, 189, 263,
379n12.3, 415n143.7
Eve, 17, 71, 185, 335, 378n10.2

Farhad, 263, 267, 419n154.2
Farid, Shaikh, x, xii, xv, 409n122.2
Five Pirs, 409n122.2

Gabriel. *See* Jibrail
*Gaṇḍhāñ* (The Forty
Knots), xvii, 421nG
Ganges, 9, 115, 121, 363,
376n3.2, 426nV.32
ghazis, 61, 388n38.2
God, 13, 23, 25, 39, 69, 139, 245,
291, 319, 321, 335, 343, 351;
Allah, 19, 75; all-powerful or
almighty, 7, 75, 119; Apostle
of (*see under* Muhammad);
becoming or *I am...*, xxiv, 9, 45,
101, 171, 175, 189, 241; blessing
of, 79, 81; creation or creatures
and, xxi, 119, 141; desire to be
loved of, xxi; face or hand of,
45, 79, 127, 177; glory of, 43, 79;
fear or knowledge of, 161, 265;
mercy, forgiveness, or grace
of, xxiii, 51, 119, 161, 207, 209,
235, 329; mosques or temples
and, 343, 357; name of, 109,
265; no God but, 47, 79, 81, 333;
only thing is or Oneness of,
xxi, 361; presence of, xxi–xxii,
193; remembering, 127, 327;
revelation of, xxii, 31; search for
or finding, 119, 281, 343; testing
by, xxiv, 43; unity of or uniting
with, 31, 77; vision of, 9, 43,
193, 329; will of, 49, 107, 301
Gorakhnath, xxvi, 209, 410n122.11
*Gulistān* (by Shaikh Saadi of
Shiraz), 143, 400n78.5
Gurmukhi script, ix–x,
xxxi–xxxiii, xxxv

hajjis, 37, 61, 73, 177, 217,
363, 388n38.2

Hallaj. *See* Mansur al-Hallaj

Hanuman, 247, 416n143.32

Harnakash, 245, 416n143.31

Hasan, 235, 243, 414n137.9

Herod, 383n27.2

Herodian, 383n27.3

Hijri era, 387n34.5

Hindi, xiv; as language of poems on Hindu themes, 376n3.1, 379n15.1, 380n20.1, 396n66.1, 407n113.1

Hindus, ix, xiv–xv, xxiv, 77; Muslims and/or, 69, 205, 227, 347; Turks and/or, xxii, 25, 31, 69, 143, 185, 225, 379n16.1

Hir, xxvi–xxvii, 29, 53, 139, 169, 207, 209, 211, 235, 241, 245, 249, 263, 379n12.2, 381n23.2, 387n33.3, 395n61.1, 409n122.1

*Hīr* (by Varis Shah), vii, xxvi, 409n122.2

Holi, 391n45.12

Hot, 381n24.3

Husain, Imam, 189, 235, 247, 406n110.9, 414n137.9, 416n143.25

Husain, Shah. *See* Shah Husain

Ibrahim, xxiv, 69, 189, 243, 389n41.1

Ibrahim ibn Adham, 415n43.13

Inayat, Shah, 55, 77, 85, 101, 125, 137, 143, 205, 257, 265, 289, 291, 319, 387n34.1; biographical details, viii, xxiii; clinging to, 187, 191; comes (as), 85, 97, 215, 217, 265, 319; dancing for, xxiii–xxiv, 11, 141, 183; delivery or saving by, 41, 161, 219, 271; desire or

love for, xxiii–xxiv, 217, 329; finding or discovery of, 21, 37, 267; guide or guidance by, viii, 271, 327; "lord" epithet for, xvii, xxiii, xxvii, 3, 7, 101, 161, 191, 265, 289; in Qadiri or Shattari order, xiii, 167, 217; separation from or departure of, xxiii, 167; sight of, 15, 215, 259, 291

India, ix–xi

Indus valley, xxv

Iran, xi

Islam, xi–xii, xiv, xxiii–xxiv, 345

Ismail, 243, 415n143.5

Jalali, 415n143.23

Jami, Persian poet, 393n55.8

Jats, xxvi, 399n76.4

Jesus, 243

Jhang, 409.120.2

Jibrail, 189, 235, 413n137.8, 423nS.5

Joseph. *See* Yusuf

Junaid, Shaikh, 45, 385n28.15

Kaaba, 183, 217, 221, 343, 363, 378n8.4, 405n105.3

Kaido, 237, 414n137.12

Kans, 416n143.33

Karbala, 407n110.9, 416n143.34

*Kanz al-Daqā'iq* (by Abdullah ibn Muhammad Nasafi), 29, 380n18.2

Kasur, vii–viii, xxix, xxxii, 53, 339, 341, 376n2.13, 387n34.2

Kauravs, 415n143.24

Kausar, 410n125.3

Kheras, xxvi, 53, 111, 207, 209, 235, 387n33.3

Khwaja Ghulam Farid, xiv–xv

Krishna, xxvii, 73, 121, 151, 181, 199, 247, 386n31.4, 389n42.4, 396n66.1, 404n104.1, 416n143.33, 420nB.1
Kumbhakaran, 376n3.4

Lachman, 376n3.4
Lahore, vii–viii, xiii, xxiii, xxxi, 185, 203, 205, 211, 263
Laila, xxiv, 105, 169, 177, 227, 245, 257, 263, 394n57.5, 404n101.1, 415n143.18
Lanka, 9, 31, 73, 245, 247, 376n3.4, 380n20.2, 416n143.32

Madar, Shah, 275, 420nA.4
*Mahābhārata*, 245, 416n143.26
Mahinval, xxv, 235, 401n81.1
Majnun, xxiv–xxv, 105, 173, 177, 227, 245, 257, 263, 394n57.5, 403n95.1, 404n101.1, 415n143.18
Mansur al-Hallaj, xi, xxiv, 43, 45, 71, 73, 83, 101, 143, 169, 171, 189, 201, 215, 241, 243, 253, 265, 383n27.4, 385n28.14
Mantiq ut Tair (by Attar), 389n41.4
Maru Thal, 381n24.3
Mathura, 389n42.4
Mecca, 29, 31, 53, 61, 73, 177, 217, 363, 380n20.2, 387n33.2, 388n38.1, 405n105.3, 424nV.7, 426nV.32
Medina, 425nV.7
Mian Muhammad Bakhsh, xiv
Mirza, 245, 415n143.20
Moses, xvi, 21, 103, 185, 235, 243, 379n12.4, 394n56.1, 399n77.5, 408n119.4, 419n157.4
Mughals, viii, xi, 247, 377n4.2

Muhammad, vii, xi, xxi, 27, 67, 139, 199, 205, 217, 329, 331, 333, 335, 384n28.5, 388n39.7, 400n77.10, 423nS.5; Ahmad, xxi–xxii, 35, 45, 77, 97, 109, 139, 383n26.10, 384nn28.4,28.5, 387n33.2; the Apostle, xxii, 27, 45, 79, 101, 217, 235, 331, 333, 337, 384n28.5, 387n33.2, 408n119.8; the Arabian, 217; light of or from, 79, 81, 171, 189, 401n80.2; ascension of, 413n137.8; the Prophet, 75, 79, 81, 119, 141, 171, 187, 189, 199, 201, 235, 259, 315, 325, 327, 329, 333, 337, 384n28.4, 403n95.6
*Mukhtasar al-Qudūrī* (by Ahmad ibn Muhammad al-Quduri), 29, 380n18.2
Multan, 207
Murtaza, Hafiz Ghulam, vii
Muslims, viii–ix, xi, xiv, xviii, xxiii, 161; blue clothes of, 382n25.5; Hindus and/or, 69, 205, 227, 347; Shia and Sunni, 41, 69, 237, 396n65.4, 407n110.9

Nadaun, 185
Nagaur, 185
Namrud, 245
Nanak, Guru, x
Nizam ud Din Auliya, xii
Nizami, Persian poet, 393n55.7
Nuh, 243, 414n143.3
Nushaba, 101, 393n55.7

Pakistan, ix
Pandavs, 380n20.2, 416n143.24
Pandoke, vii
Panjab, vii, 53; language or

literature in (*see* Panjabi);
religious milieu, x, xiv;
sociopolitical aspects or
events, viii–ix, xiii–xiv, xx,
xxxi, 387n34.5, 408n120.1
Panjabi: Bullhe Shah's name in
or use of, vii, xix; Gurmukhi
script, ix, xxxi–xxxiii, xxxv; folk
tradition, xiv; literature, poetry,
or poetic genres of, vii–viii, x,
xiv–xv; Persian language and,
xii; Persian script, ix, xxxi–xxxiii,
xxxv; Sikh literature, x; Sufi or
Muslim poetry, vii, x, xiii, xv,
xviii; Urdu or Hindi and, xiv
Persian: language/literature,
xi–xiii, xix; script, ix, xxxi–
xxxii, 387n36.1; Persian
poetic symbols, 375n2.9,
393n53.5, 397n68.1,
400n78.5, 413nn135.2,136.5,
418nn151.1,151.2, 421nB.16
Peshawar, 185
Pharaoh, xvi, 103, 185, 245,
394n56.1, 399n77.5
Pirs, xii, 205, 207, 209, 237
Punnun, xxv, 37, 381n24.3,
414n141.1, 419n157.1, 420nB.3

Qadiri order, xiii–xiv, 167, 217
Qais, 394n57.5
Qarun, 245
Qibla, 378n8.4, 405n105.3,
411n125.4
Qur'an, xi, xxi, xxxiii–xxxiv, 29, 35,
39, 99, 119, 353, 423nS.9; Arabic
phrases from Qur'anic verses:
*aina mā* (57.4), 417n148.2; *alastu
bi-rabbikum, qālū balā shahidnā*
(7.172), 384n28.9; *al-insān*
(15.26), 384n28.7; *allāhu 'l-ṣamad*
(112.2), 391n45.14; *fa'dhkurūnī*
(2.152), 391n45.10; *fa-nafakhtu
fīhi* (15.29), 384n28.10; *fa-
thumma wajhu 'llāh* (2.115),
384n28.6; *huwa ma 'akum* (57.4),
385n28.12; *innā lillāhi* (2.156),
423nG.24; *kulli shai'in* (2.20),
399n77.9; *kun fa-yakūnu* (2.117),
381n23.1; *la 'ibun wa-lahwun*
(6.32), 379n13.1; *lan tanālū
'l-birra* (3.92), 400n77.14; *naḥnu
aqrab* (50.16), 384n28.11; *rabbi
arinī, lan tarānī* (7.143), 379n12.4;
*ṣibghatu 'llāhi* (2.138), 391n45.13;
*ṣummun bukmun 'umyun* (2.18),
380n17.1; *wa-fī anfusikum* (51.21),
385n28.13; *wa-laqad karramnā*
(17.70), 385n28.17; *yadu 'llāhi
fauqa aidihim* (48.10), 397n70.8;
*Yāsīn* and *Muzammil*, 139

Ram, 71, 193, 205, 245, 363,
376n3.4, 416n143.30, 426nV.27
*Rāmāyaṇa*, 9, 245, 247, 376n3.4
Ranghars, 155, 357, 402n86.3
Ranjha, xxvi–xxvii, xxx, 23,
29, 35, 61, 139, 159, 169, 181,
185, 191, 197, 203, 207, 209,
221, 235, 241, 245, 247, 249,
255, 259, 379n12.2, 381n23.2,
386n31.4, 387n33.3, 395n61.2,
396nn66.1,66.5, 409n122.1
Ravan, 376n3.4, 416n143.30
Roda, 245, 415n143.30
Rumi, Jalal ud Din, xi–xii,
389n40.1, 399n75.4, 404n104.3

Saadi, Shaikh, of Shiraz, 400n78.5
Sahadev, 380n20.2
Sahiban, 245, 415n143.20
Sahti, 410n122.14
Sammi, 217, 411n126.2
Sanaan, Shaikh, 69, 189
Sanskrit, xix
Sarmad, 243
Sassi, xxv, 37, 245, 283, 381n24.3,
    414n141.1, 419n157.1, 420nB.3
Satan, 195, 243, 253, 333;
    called Azazil, 41
Sayyids, vii, xxiii, 187,
    386n31.5, 406n108.1
Shah Husain, Sufi poet of Lahore,
    xiii, xv, xxvii, xxxi, 385n29.1,
    395n63.1, 411n130.1, 416n145.1
Shaikhs, x, xii, 39, 71, 193, 227, 351
Shams, 19, 71, 169, 243, 378n12.1
Sharaf ud Din, Shah,
    245, 415n143.17
*Sharh Wiqāya* (by Ubaidullah
    Masudi), 253, 417n147.2
Shattari order, xiii
Shirin, 263, 267, 419n154.2
Shiv, 396n64.5
Sials, xxvi–xxvii, 139, 211,
    233, 249, 413n137.2
*Sīharfī* (The Thirty Letters),
    xviii, xxxi, 423nS
Sikandar, the emperor
    Alexander the Great, 5,
    101, 375n2.5, 393n55.7
*Sikandar-nāma* (by
    Nizami), 393n55.7
Sikhs, viii–x, xiv–xv,
    377n4.2, 412n133.2
Sinai, Mt., 21, 201, 235,
    243, 267, 419n157.4

Sindh, 381n24.3
Sindhi, xiii
Sirat, 203, 217, 335
Sohni, xxv, 235, 245, 263, 401n81.1
Sufis: Islam and, xi, xiv,
    xxi; concepts, 379n15.1,
    390nn45.3,45.7, 398nn72.1,74.2,
    407n114.5; masters, viii, xii,
    xxiii; orders, xi–x (*see also*
    Chishti order; Qadiri order;
    Shattari order); outside South
    Asia, xi; Panjabi, x, xii, xiii;
    poets, x–xiv; poverty of, 167;
    spread in South Asia, xi
Sulaiman, xxiv, 7, 43, 189,
    243, 383n27.5
Sultan Bahu, xiii, xv
Surdas, xv
Syrians, 97

Takht Hazara, xxvi–xxvii, 203,
    207, 221, 241, 249, 363
Tegh Bahadur, 75, 227, 412n133.2
Tilla Jogian, 209, 410n122.10
Turks, xxii, 25, 31, 69,
    97, 143, 185, 225

Uch Gilaniyan, vii
Urdu, xiii–xiv, xxxi, 387n31.1

Varis Shah, vii, xxvi, 409n122.1
Vedas, xvi, xxii, 29, 31,
    119, 143, 165, 185
Vishnu, 117

Yahya, 43, 189, 383n27.3
Yunus, 75, 189, 243
Yusuf, xxiv, 5, 19, 69, 75, 101,
    173, 189, 243, 247, 263,

379n12.3, 415n143.7
*Yūsuf Zulaiḵẖā* (by Jami), 393n55.8

Zakariya, xxiv, 43, 69, 169,
   189, 243, 383n27.2
Zulaikha, xxiv–xxv, 5, 11,
   19, 101, 135, 173, 243, 267,
   379n12.3, 415n143.7

## ABOUT THE BOOK

Murty Classical Library of India volumes are designed by Rathna Ramanathan and Guglielmo Rossi. Informed by the history of the Indic book and drawing inspiration from polyphonic classical music, the series design is based on the idea of "unity in diversity," celebrating the individuality of each language while bringing them together within a cohesive visual identity.

The Panjabi text is set in the Murty Gurmukhi typeface, commissioned by Harvard University Press and designed by John Hudson and Fiona Ross. This original design reintroduces traditional stroke modulation patterns that are apparent in manuscript letterforms and recalls forms found in the *Prayer Book of Rani Jindan* (British Library Panjabi MS D4).

The English text is set in Antwerp, designed by Henrik Kubel from A2-TYPE and chosen for its versatility and balance with the Indic typography. The design is a free-spirited amalgamation and interpretation of the archives of type at the Museum Plantin-Moretus in Antwerp.

All the fonts commissioned for the Murty Classical Library of India will be made available, free of charge, for non-commercial use. For more information about the typography and design of the series, please visit *http://www.hup.harvard.edu/mcli*.

Printed by Gopsons Papers Ltd., Noida.